ROMAN CRETE

Ian Sanders 1949-1977

ROMAN CRETE

AN ARCHAEOLOGICAL SURVEY AND GAZETTEER OF LATE HELLENISTIC, ROMAN AND EARLY BYZANTINE CRETE

I. F. Sanders

British Library Cataloguing in Publication Data

Sanders, I
Roman Crete.-(Classical studies).
1. Crete - Antiquities, Roman
I. Title II. Series
939.1'8 DF261.C8

ISBN 0-85668-150-4

Printed and Published by ARIS & PHILLIPS LTD, Warminster, Wilts, England.

CONTENTS

LIST OF FIGURES AND PLATES

Figures

Plates

ABBREVIATIONS

Journals

AAA	Athens annals of archaeology
ABSA	Annual of the British School at Athens
A. Delt.	'Αρχαιολόγικον Δελτίον
AE year, p.	'Αρχαιολόγικη ἐφήμερις
AE year, no.	L'année épigraphique
AJA	American journal of archaeology
Ann.Sc.At.	Annuario della (regia) scuola archeologica di Atene
AR	Archaeological reports
Arch.Anz.	Archäologischer Anzeiger
BCH	Bulletin de correspondance hellénique
Boll. d'Arte	Bollettino d'Arte
Byz.Zeit.	Byzantinische Zeitschrift
CPh	Classical Philology
DOP	Dumbarton Oaks papers
EEBS	'Επετηρὶς 'Εταιρείας Βυζαντινῶν Σπουδῶν
EEKS	'Επετηρὶς 'Εταιρείας Κρητικῶν Σπουδῶν
Ergon	Το 'Εργον τῆς 'Αρχαιολόγικης 'Εταιρείας
ILN	Illustrated London News
JHS	Journal of Hellenic Studies
JRS	Journal of Roman Studies
Kret.Khron.	Κρήτικα Χρονικὰ
MAAR	Memoirs of the American Academy in Rome
NC	Numismatic Chronicle
PAE	Πρακτικὰ τῆς 'Αρχαιολόγικης 'Εταιρείας
Rend.Linc.	Rendiconte della reale accademia dei Lincei
Rev.Arch.	Revue archéologique
Trans.Penn. Univ.	Transactions of the department of archaeology of the University of Pennsylvania

Works

AC Pendlebury, J.D.S., *The Archaeology of Crete* (London 1939).

Belli ed. Falkener

Falkener, E., 'A Description of some important Theatres and other Remains in Crete, from a MS History of Candia by Onorio Belli in 1586', *Museum of Classical Antiquities,* suppl., (London 1854).

Belli ed. Spanake

Spanake, S., ' Τὸ θέατρο στὴ ρωκαϊκη Κρήτη', *Acts of the 2nd Cretological Congress* II, (Athens 1968), p.142.

BMC Cyr.	Robinson, E.S.G., *Catalogue of the Greek Coins of Cyrenaica* (in the British Museum), (London 1927).
CIL	*Corpus inscriptionum latinarum* I-XVI (Berlin 1863-1975)
Corpus	Pelekanides, S., *Σύνταγμα τῶν παλαιοχριστιανικῶν ψηφιδωτῶν δαπέδων τῆς* 'Ελλάδος I (Thessalonike 1974).
Hayes	Hayes, J.W., *Late Roman Pottery* (London 1972).
IC	Guarducci, M., *Inscriptiones creticae* I-IV (Rome 1939-50).
IGRR	Cagnat, R. *et al.*, (ed.), *Inscriptiones graecae ad res romanas pertinentes* I-IV (1911-27).
ILS	Dessau, H. (ed.), *Inscriptiones latinae selectae* I-III (1863-1916).
Italian guide	Pernier, L. and Banti, L., *Guida degli scavi italiani in Creta* (London 1947).
Le Rider	Le Rider, G., Les monnaies crétoises du Ve au 1er siècle av. J.C., *Etudes crétoises* XV, (Paris 1966).
MAMA	Calder, W. *et al.*, (eds), *Monumenti Asiae Minoris Antiquae* I-VIII (1928-62).
Matz	Matz, F., (ed.), *Forschungen auf Kreta* (Berlin 1951).
Mon.Ant.	Monumenti antichi
Mon. Ven.	Gerola, G., *I monumenti veneti dell'isola Creta* (Venice 1905).
Pashley	Pashley, R., *Travels in Crete* (London 1837).
PIR	Klebs, E. *et al.*, (eds.), *Prosopographia imperii romani* (1897-8).
PIR^2	Groag, E. et al., (eds.), *Prosopographia imperii romani* (1933-70).
Platon	Platon, N., ' *Αἱ ξυλόστεγαι παλαιοχριστιανικαὶ βασιλικαὶ τῆς* Κρήτης ', *Acts of the 9th Congress of Byzantine Studies at Thessalonike,* I (Athens 1955), p.415.
PLRE	Jones, A.H.M., Martindale, J.R. and Morris, J. *The prosopography of the Later Roman Empire* (Cambridge 1971).
PW	Pauly-Wissowa, *Real-encyclopädie der classischen Altertumswissenschaft.*
SIG	Dittenberg, G., (ed.), *Sylloge inscriptionum graecarum* I-IV (1915-21).
Spanake	Spanake, S., *Crete: a guide* (Iraklion 1972).
Spratt	Spratt, T.A.B., *Travels and researches in Crete* (London 1890).
Survey	Hood, M.S.F., *Archaeological survey of the Knossos area* (London 195-?).
Svoronos	Svoronos, J.N., *Numismatique de la Crète ancienne* (Paris 1890).

Pottery after Hayes

ARSW	African red slip ware
E Sig A	Eastern Sigillata A
E Sig B	Eastern Sigillata B
LRC	Late Roman C ware

ACKNOWLEDGEMENTS

In the summer of 1968 when I was between school and university I had the good fortune to be chosen by Professor P. Warren to help on his excavations on the Early Minoan settlement at Fournou Korifi, Myrtos; while I was there, I encountered the neglected remains of the Roman period and the seed which resulted in this book was firmly sown. During my undergraduate days it was kept alive by encouragement from Dr. H. Catling, then at the Ashmolean Museum, and from M.S.F. Hood. These three have continued to provide help and encouragement, and to them I owe a particular debt.

Many thanks are due also to my supervisor at Oxford, Professor S.S. Frere, who was obliged to wade through my illegible drafts, for his constructive criticism and attention to detail. I was enabled to do many months of field work on Crete itself through the cooperation of the Greek Archaeological Service as a whole and Dr. St. Alexiou in particular. I am also grateful to the following for general or special assistance: Drs. S. and H. Brock, Dr. J. Hayes, Mr. and Mrs. D.L. Kennedy, Miss J.M. Reynolds, H. Sackett Esq., Dr. H.L. Turner, Dr. L.V. Watrous, Dr. E. Waywell, M. Vickers Esq., and the authorities of the French and Italian Schools in Athens. It would not have been possible to accomplish the work without the financial assistance of the Department of Education and Science, generously augmented by the Craven Committee, Oxford University (T.W. Greene Scholarship, 1972-74), the British School at Athens (School Studentship 1973-74), and travel grants from the Meyerstein Committee, Oxford University.

Above all else I must thank my wife, without whose constant aid and encouragement this work would have been impossible.

I.F.S.

FOREWORD

Almost without pause since the later centuries of the Bronze Age the island of Crete has lain under the hand of conquerors. Yet through her long history she has been as vigourous in peace as in turbulent conflict. In terms of general prosperity and fair standards of living the most notable combination of peace and conquest was the Roman period, from the capture by Q. Metellus in 69-67 B.C. for some four centuries. Crete and Cyrene became a senatorial province, the capital situated at Gortyna. Building flourished everywhere and so did trading, the island as of old exploiting her central position along the wide sea routes from the west to the eastern Mediterranean. Her status and condition anticipate to an unusual degree the second four centuries of Italian conquest under the Venetians.

Unlike the Venetian age and the Cretan Renaissance of the 17th century and unlike the astonishing achievements of the Minoan Bronze Age, the Roman period has been neglected by scholars, above all on the archaeological side. There are, naturally, exceptions. We think of the early Italian investigations at Gortyna and Lebena, of Margarita Guarducci's four magisterial volumes of *Inscriptiones Creticae*, of Ernst Kirsten's surveys, particularly of the western cities, of R.F. Willetts' analysis of the complexities of religious life in *Cretan Cults and Festivals* (1962), of R.W. Hutchinson's and Michael Gough's notable excavation of the late Antonine Villa Dionysus at the Roman colony of Cnossus and, for the Late Roman and Early Byzantine periods, of the uncovering of fine basilicas and their mosaics, especially by Professors Orlandos at Suia, Platon at Panormos, Kalokyres at Vizari and Frend, again at Cnossus. We recall too that remarkable set of architectural plans of Roman theatres and other public buildings made around 1586 when they had stood to some degree preserved, while now vanished, by the brilliant antiquarian, botanist and physician Onorio Belli, and brought to light by Edward Falkener in 1854. In our own day the numismatics of Roman Crete have received renewed attention after J. Svoronos's great work (1890), notably by Anne Chapman. Precious though these contributions are the need for a thorough field survey of the Roman remains, integrated with a study of their period, had long been felt. How were Crete and her ancient peoples under Roman rule and prosperity? To this need Ian Sanders responded.

His introduction to Cretan archaeology came in 1968 as an undergraduate assistant on the excavation of the Early Bronze Age village of Myrtos. He glimpsed the ruins of some respectable Roman buildings in the modern village and, with a tradition of field archaeology in Britain behind him, became eager to tackle Roman Crete. How nearly one is reminded of Marcus Niebuhr Tod, whose first excavation in Crete was an Early Minoan burial cave near Palaikastro and whose life became devoted to Greek epigraphy. After graduating at Oxford, where he was President of the University Archaeological Society, Ian Sanders chose to make the archaeology of Roman Crete the subject of his doctoral thesis, again at Oxford. Quiet, tenacious, in love with all the topographical problems, he, with his wife Janet, combed the island to make personal examination of his sites, more than four hundred in number. John Pendlebury, who compiled a fine gazetteer of Roman sites, but only three pages of text in *The Archaeology of Crete* (1939), would have approved these hard endeavours. The work being well advanced, Sanders was appointed lecturer in Classical Archaeology at the University of Sheffield. While facing the daunting and heavy task of preparing his first lecture courses he pressed on with his thesis in an exemplary way. With the full support of his wife he brought his labours to fruition in a substantial dissertation, completed a few weeks before its author died from cancer.

The work appears now as a book, one that may be seen as a piece of primary scholarship for Cretan and Roman specialists and as thoroughly comprehensible and interesting for an intelligent, more general audience. In particular Dr Sanders has looked at Roman and Early Byzantine Crete in terms of the patterns of settlement and their changes through time. The gazetteer of sites and the range of plans and photographs, carefully taken by the author, provide now the fundamental archaeological basis for this long period and the ground for the discussion of major topics in each chapter. In these discussions the book takes on a wider, comparative value for all who are interested in the economy, agriculture and religious beliefs of the eastern Mediterranean in the Roman imperial and Early Byzantine periods.

But this was simply a beginning, an introductory study, and would certainly have led on to more detailed investigations of settlement archaeology and land use, integrated within the framework of Cretan and Imperial political history. For one such study there was time, an examination of changing political control in terms of land, and of the formation of estates in the fertile Mesara plain of southern Crete, published in the *Annual of the British School at Athens* 71 (1976).

The fittest memorial to this young scholar's work would be that others take up the challenge of the Roman Cretans. Dr Sanders would have been the first to insist in how many directions, archaeological, artistic, epigraphical and literary, the towns and landscape of the Romanized Cretan stock invite attention and integrating study.

PETER WARREN

To Janet

INTRODUCTION

Considering that Crete is an island of only 150 miles length and a maximum width of about 35 miles, much of which is composed of mountains up to 8,000 feet in height, the amount of work and publication on its Bronze Age must be almost without parallel. Conversely, the history and archaeology of the later periods up to the nineteenth century have suffered an almost total neglect or have been covered only incidentally in works basically devoted to Minoan studies. This book is intended to cover the history and archaeology of the period from the island's conquest by Caecilius Metellus in 69 BC to its fall to the band of heretical Arabs led by Apochaps in AD 827 who were to hold Crete till it was reconquered by Nikephorus Phokas in 961.

The initial date of 69 BC needs no historical justification, but the terminal date might logically have been 1204, when the island was finally lost to the Roman Empire after its purchase by the Venetians. However, not only does the Arab conquest form a real historical break, but more especially the problems both archaeological and historical of the period 961 - 1204 are very different from those of the previous period under Roman rule. Although the political or historical change in 69 BC is clear, archaeologically it is often difficult or nonsensical to date material or sites clearly on one side or the other of this date,so relevant earlier material is included here, but comprehensive cover is only attempted for the Roman period.

This study has two aims. The first is to examine in detail the island as part of the Roman Empire. Crete has practically no 'history' in this period inasmuch as until the 7c nothing regarded as worthy of note by the ancient authors happened, yet the physical remains, although not comparable now to those of Africa or the Near East, show that Crete was prosperous and an integral part of the eastern Mediterranean culture transmitted along the trade routes that pass the island. Although it is obvious that each area of the Empire had its strong local traditions, it is perhaps not too much to claim that Crete forms a typical example of the culture of the Mediterranean area that was the basis of the prosperity and strength of the Empire. The second aim is simply to fill a gap in the island's history in the hope that eventually one will be able to study the development of the island and its inhabitants from its beginnings through to the present day as opposed to the existing state where there are but pinnacles of knowledge and long understudied dark ages.

These latter periods are occasionally illumined by studies of certain areas or topics so that the material known from the Roman period is uneven in depth. On certain subjects, either accidentally or deliberately, there is much better evidence than for others: for example, in the later part of the period the study and excavation of Early Christian basilicas has been undertaken on a considerable scale so that they can be studied in far greater depth than the other structures. Similarly, much of the section on architecture relies on the accident of the interest of Onorio Belli in the late 16c in recording what was then visible. Various areas have also been studied in greater detail than the rest of the island, in particular the cities of Gortyna and Knossos, although at the latter much of the Roman material has been the by-product of excavations basically interested in Minoan levels and so not necessarily undertaken in the most important Roman areas. The result of all this is that the present work is unbalanced; but the fact that so little is known about certain aspects is no reflection at all on their actual importance.

Although this is the first attempt at a comprehensive study of the period, works which include relevant material date back to the 15c with Buondelmonte's fascinating account of his travels around the island in *c.*1415. In the next century Onorio Belli drew most of what was then standing but is now lost, as unfortunately are some of his drawings. The next two centuries were poorer in relevant work but in the 19c, in 1834, the English scholar Robert

Pashley identified most of the major sites and a few years later Captain T.A.B.Spratt RN thoroughly surveyed the island in the course of his duties. Although his classical knowledge was not as profound as Pashley's his description of the remains is better. Towards the end of the century Evans and the Italians Halbherr, Taramelli and Savignoni carried out valuable surveys leading to the excavations of this century. The only major site where there has been deliberate wide scale work on the Roman remains has been Gortyna, where the Italians have been working throughout this century, but unfortunately little has as yet been published in detail. Other surveys were carried out in this century, before World War II by Pendlebury, and since then by Faure and Hood with others. Certain small areas have recently been the subject of very intensive surveys by Watrous and Blackman and Branigan. Much information has also been gathered from the innumerable rescue excavations carried out by the Greek Archaeological Service under the direction of a superb list of Ephors starting with Hazzidakis. Crete has also been fortunate in the fields of numismatics and epigraphy where Svoronos and Guarducci have produced their respective invaluable corpora.

In each part of the book an attempt has been made to bring together all this scattered information with the very small number of references from the ancient authors where relevant. With our present state of knowledge few definite conclusions can as yet be drawn, especially on the more purely archaeological topics. Here far more excavations and surveys are needed specifically aimed at resolving the problems of the later periods and not primarily designed to increase the tremendous amount already known about Minoan Crete.

During the fieldwork for this book it was not possible for various reasons to carry out surveys looking for new sites, but the majority of known sites were visited and a reasonable amount of new material noted. Museum work was again limited: here nearly all the important material was on display and therefore not available for detailed examination, especially all the smaller material in cases. There was comparatively little in the storerooms owing to the lack of interest in this period and the overwhelming mass of earlier material taking up the limited space. However, thanks to the superb Ashmolean Library with its Cretan collection based on Sir Arthur Evans' books I would hope that very little published material has been missed.

CHAPTER 1 : ADMINISTRATION AND ORGANISATION

Historical Introduction: Crete under the Republic

Rome's first intervention in Cretan affairs came in 195 BC when amongst the peace terms offered to Nabis of Sparta was the divestment of his Cretan interests [1]. In the following years there were various attempts by the Romans to mediate in the interminable Cretan wars, starting with Q. Fabius Labeo's abortive mission to bring peace between Cydonia and allied Gortyna and Knossos and to recover the numerous Romans held captive in Crete [2]. It may have been no coincidence that Hannibal was a guest in Gortyna at the time. Over the next hundred years there were other embassies, culminating in Lucullus' visit in 85 BC when he settled Cretan affairs to Rome's, or rather Sulla's, satisfaction [3].

However, a few years later during the third Mithridatic War the Cretans were accused of aiding the King and of piracy [4]; the legitimacy of the charges is impossible to determine. In 71 BC the praetor M. Antonius was sent out to deal with the Cretans but was defeated off Cydonia by Lasthenes. The fetters which the Roman commander had confidently brought out for his Cretan captives were used on his own troops, including his quaestor, while he himself opportunely died and so brought the war to a halt. The next stage was an embassy of thirty Cretans sent to Rome by what Diodorus calls the Boule, almost certainly the Koinon. This embassy effectively persuaded the Senate of their good faith but a pro-Cretan motion was blocked by a tribune, Lentulus Spinther [5]. After the Cretans' departure the Senate agreed that the following terms be put to the Cretans, presumably meaning by this to the Koinon: that they should hand over Lasthenes, all ships with more than four oars, all Roman captives and 4,000 talents. The enormity of this sum can be gauged by the fact that prior to Pompey's conquests all the eastern provinces yielded only 8,500 talents a year [6]. After some debate the Cretans rejected these terms and the war restarted in 69 BC.

Initially the command fell to the consul Q. Hortensius [7], but preferring his legal pursuits he handed over to his colleague Q. Caecilius Metellus. At some point later in this year of 69 Metellus crossed over to Crete with three legions [8] (Fig. 1): the initial action took place in the vicinity of Cydonia and it is probable that the Roman forces crossed over from Gythion [9] and may well have made their base at Kisamos, the port of Polyrrhenia, which seems to have supported Metellus [10] against their neighbour and rival Cydonia. After an initial resistance the Cretan commander Lasthenes abandoned Cydonia to his co-commander Panares and fled back to Knossos, his home city, while Panares surrendered Cydonia to Metellus in return for a guarantee of his own personal safety. Metellus followed up

---

1. H. Van Effenterre, *La Crete et le Monde Grec* (Paris, 1948), p.259f.
   R. F. Willetts, *Aristocratic society in Ancient Crete* (London 1955), p.237f.
2. Livy 37.60. If one can take this passage literally it would imply that there were 4,000 Romans captive at Gortyna alone.
3. Plutarch, *Lucullus* 3.
4. Ancient Sources: Livy, *Ep.* XCVII; Diod. Sic. XL.I; Ps. Ascon. p.176; Dio Fr.11; Florus 3.7. Also F. Foucart, 'Les campagnes de M. Antonius contre les pirates', *Journal des savants* 1906, p.569f.
5. Ancient Sources: Appian, *Sicelica* VI; Velleius Pat. 2.34; Diod. Sic. XL. 1; Livy, *Ep.* XCIX; Dio XXXVI 17-18. Also A. Passerini, 'La Preparazione alla guerra contra Creta nel 70 AC', *Athenaeum* XIV, 1936, p.45.
6. Plutarch, *Pompey* 45.
7. Dio 36.17.
8. Phlegon, *Fr. Gr. Hist.* iib, 257, F12.12.
9. Strabo. X.4.5. for the route.
10. *IC.* II.XXIII. 14, a statue dedicated to Metellus by the city.

this victory with an attack on Knossos which he besieged, burning down Lasthenes' house with all his personal wealth. Lasthenes again fled and it was at this stage of the campaign that the Cretans sent legates to Pompey in order to try to gain surrender on more lenient terms than Metellus' ruthlessness had led them to expect.

Fig 1: Metellus' annual campaigns for the conquest of Crete.

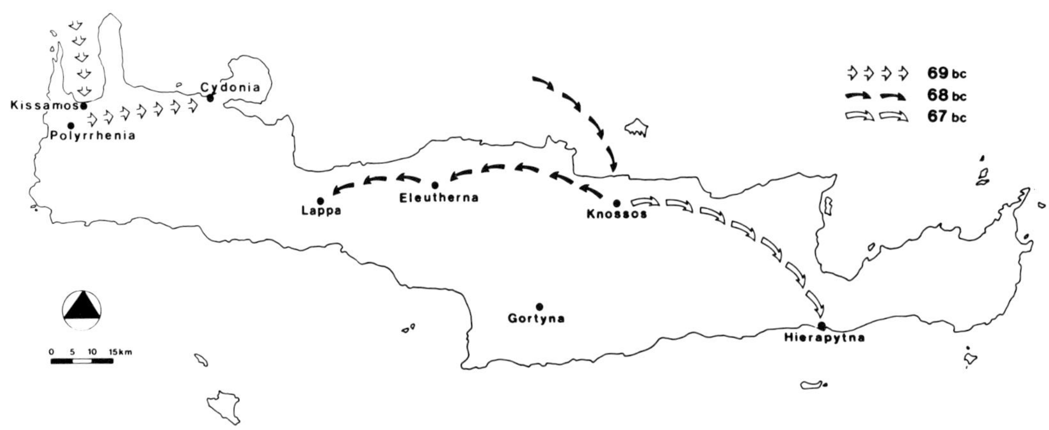

The above account is mainly derived from Appian *Sicelica* VI which now rapidly concludes the war, with Metellus ignoring Pompey's orders and triumphing after Lasthenes' eventual surrender. The relevant passages of Dio for the Cydonia and Knossos episodes are missing but he has more detail about the final stages of the war, all recorded under 67 BC. Dio begins with the despatch of Pompey's legate Octavius to Crete to oppose Metellus. Cornelius Sisenna, governor of Achaea, also crossed over to the island but as yet neither officer actually came to blows with the Senate's official commander in Crete. The account continues with Metellus taking Eleutherna by treachery and by bringing down a brick tower by soaking it in vinegar to make it brittle and then firing it. He then went on to take Lappa, although Octavius was there with Cilician troops whom Metellus put to death on the fall of the city. It would seem likely that these Cilicians were ex-pirates likely to be sympathetic to the Cretans, but nevertheless they had been under a Roman officer.

The order of this campaign makes it likely that Metellus was operating from the east, advancing west back towards Cydonia since Lappa was the natural place to attack first if the advance was in the other direction. If Metellus was advancing from the west towards Knossos the only alternative explanation is that he deliberately attacked Eleutherna first hoping that Octavius would abandon his opposition on the fall of that city. However, another argument against this is that Dio firmly places these sieges after the Cretans had sent envoys to Pompey, which is proved by the presence of Octavius, and Appian is definite that this took place after the fall of Knossos.

With the fall of Lappa and the death of his Cilicians Octavius took an active part against Metellus, using troops which had been brought over by Sisenna, who had now died. Octavius fell back to Hierapytna to join the remaining Cretan forces under Aristion who, after the fall of Cydonia, had taken Hierapytna from Lucius Bassus and had made it his headquarters. However they were forced to retire by sea and the fleet was wrecked, thus causing the final collapse of Cretan resistance. Metellus now organised affairs on the island[11] making Gortyna the capital in return for either its actual aid or its benevolent neutrality while Metellus was crushing its three great rivals. On his return to Rome, Metellus was eventually granted his triumph, although Pompey used a tribune to keep Panares and Lasthenes out of the display. The war had been long and tough, involving three legions and the best part of three years against 24,000 Cretans[12] under two good commanders. Metellus seems to have deserved his cognomen Creticus far more than his predecessor M. Antonius Creticus[13].

Uniquely, in Cretan history there is no evidence of any later rebellion against Roman rule, which is probably to be explained by the normal Roman method of utilising the pre-existing city-state system and only adding a governor to superintend their behaviour. Rather oddly, Metellus or the Senate decided to join Crete with Cyrene to make a

11. Livy, *Ep.* XCIX *'Metellus insulae leges dedit'.*
12. Velleius Paterculus states these two figures (2.34).
13. Sir Ronald Syme's (*Roman Revolution* p.21) 'Creticus usurped a cognomen for petty exploits in a pirate ridden island' is highly unfair.

joint praetorian province [14]. Very little is known about the province until the period of the civil wars, but the governor in 50 BC was Cn. Tremellius Scrofa, an agricultural expert much respected by Varro [15]. Apart from that, a large number of veterans are known to have been settled on the island, for about 20 years later Pompey was able to raise a legion of men from the veterans settled in Macedonia and Crete [16]. It is probable that at least some of these men were amongst the large number of Roman citizens granted Gortynian citizenship in the 1c BC [17]. This is not to deny the possible existence of Italian traders in Crete before the Roman conquest [18] for whom Gortyna with its pro-Roman tradition, not to mention wealth, would have been an automatic choice in which to settle. However, at least one man who was granted Gortynian citizenship had been a soldier and a centurion, Q. Munatidius Maximus [19].

Crete was not greatly involved in the civil war between Caesar and Pompey, although the latter had raised troops there and also obtained supplies of corn and archers[20], and later Caesar, who had used Cretan archers in Gaul[21] employed them in his struggles at Alexandria [22]. The only possible sign of disturbances in Crete itself is a coin hoard[23] from Hierapytna which dates to about 46 BC. However, after Caesar's murder matters became more complicated: one of the moves made to get Brutus and Cassius out of Rome was their curious joint appointment as governors of Crete and Cyrene with Brutus in charge of Crete [24]. This would already seem to recognise the dual nature of the province, albeit in extraordinary circumstances. Not suprisingly, the two liberators were not prepared to be fobbed off with this small and unimportant province but rather took it over as part of their *imperium*, using two quaestors, P. Licinius and Lepidus, to hold it. It would seem that the latter held Crete [25] until Philippi.

Meanwhile Antony was becoming involved in Cretan affairs, 'finding' amongst Caesar's papers a decree freeing Crete after Brutus' governorship. Cicero [26] was quick to point out the inconsistency between the date of the decree and the appointment of Brutus after Caesar's death. After Philippi Crete and Cyrene fell under Antony's control and it is to this period that the governorships of Lollius and Crassus should probably be assigned[27]. This contradicts the 'decree' freeing Crete, but since in 37-6 Antony felt free to grant part of the island to Cleopatra[28], and in 36 Octavian was able to grant land worth 1,200,000 HS to Capua [29], it is clear that in reality Crete was far from free. The grant of the land to Capua in 36 is normally taken to be linked to the founding of the *colonia* at Knossos, but there is no direct evidence for this, and the Greek magistrates at Knossos seem to continue minting coins right down to Actium and immediately after [30]. Furthermore, it would seem generally improbable that Octavian could actually have founded a *colonia* in Crete at this period. One corollary of the redating of the foundation of the *colonia* to after 27BC (see below p.13f) is the rejection of the proposal that the grant to Cleopatra involved the entire island except the *colonia* [31]. It would seem more likely that she was merely given the city of Itanos where there had already been a Ptolemaic garrison [32].

The link to Cleopatra can also be seen on Crassus' coinage [33]where on the dupondius reverse is a crocodile, a symbol of Egypt. Crassus' exact date is uncertain but generally put at 37-6[34], and the crocodile may well have something to do with the acquisitions of Cleopatra in that year. No governors are known beyond this year until after Actium, and it is possible that Antony finally freed Crete (apart from Cleopatra's share) in that year. Antony's decision back in 43 to free Crete may well have something to do with the fact that one of his friends was a certain Cydas,

---

14. The title of the province as Crete and Cyrene is attested passim in *IC*. Robinson's coin group I (*BMC Cyr.* p.ccxi) probably belongs to this early period and would seem to be the only regular joint issue by the province.
15. Cicero, *Ep. Ad. Att.* 6.1.13, for the governorship, otherwise Varro passim.
16. Caesar, *De Bello Civili* III.4.1.
17. *IC.*IV.202 p.279-80, where this is discussed.
18. Cf. *IC.*IV.290 dated to the 1c BC mentioning *'Cives Romani qui Gortynae negiotantur'.*
19. *IC.*IV.220.
20. Note 15 ref. and *BC* IV, 3 (archers) and V.1 (corn).
21. *De Bello Gallico* 11.7 against the Remi.
22. *Bell. Alex.* 1.1.
23. E. J. P. Raven, 'The Hierapytnan coin hoard of Greek and Roman coins', *NC* 5th series XVIII, 1938, p.133.
24. Appian, *BC* III.8. Early Aug. 43.
25. Here I follow M. Grant *From Imperium to Auctoritas* (Oxford 1946) p.35, with Appian *BC* V.2. Ann Chapman, 'Some 1c BC bronze coins of Knossos', *NC* 7th series VIII, 1968, p.13, prefers Lepidus in Cyrene, but the Appian passage is against this and the only illustration of the relevant coin (now lost) is very unclear (Grant Pl. II no. 15).
26. *Phillipics* 2.97.
27. *BMC Cyr.* p.ccii f., groups III, IV. Chapman, *op.cit.* note 25, p.14-15.
28. Dio xlix 32.4-5 ' Κρήτης τινα '.
29. Dio xlix 14. Vell. Pat. 2.81.
30. See p.14.
31. See Grant, *op.cit.* note 25 for this theory and the complex arguments involved.
32. See S. Spyridakis, *Ptolemaic Itanos and Hellenistic Crete* (Berkeley, 1970).
33. *BMC Cyr.* group IV.
34. As ref. note 27.

described by Cicero[35] as 'Cydam Cretensem, portentum insulae, hominem audacissimum et perditissimum'. At approximately this date a Kydas issues provincial cistophoroi as Kretaieon Kretarchas [36] and the same man is known from Gortyna as Kosmos and Kretarchas [37]. Finally a Kydas issues coins at Knossos overstruck on issues of Crassus[38]. It is very tempting to assume that all these men are the same or closely related, and got Antony to free the island for his or their own benefit. Actium swiftly followed all these events and Crete was restored to the fold of the Empire; Augustus, as Octavian became,established Lappa and Cydonia [39] as free cities but Crete as a whole was by 27 BC rejoined in a province with Cyrene [40].

The Province

Under Augustus' scheme Crete and Cyrene became one of the Senatorial provinces governed by a proconsul with praetorian rank who would normally hold office for a single year. Up to Diocletian's reforms some fifty-five individuals are known who held this office although many of them, particularly in the 1c AD, are nonentities known only from this post, often from their coinage, as for instance Augureinus, governor under Caligula. There are, however, a few men who are better known either for their good qualities, such as P. Sulpicius Quirinus, who seems to have been governor in the reign of Augustus [41], or for other reasons, such as Caesius Cordus, who was convicted of extortion in AD 21[42]. Similarly Pedius Blaesus was convicted in 59 on the accusation of the Cyrenaicans as was Antonius Flamma who may have been a Cyrenaican himself. Cestus Proculus was acquitted of a similar charge in AD 56. There were however some other men with distinguished careers, as Cornelius Lupus, governor under Tiberius and cos. suff. AD 42; L. Turpilius Dexter, governor AD 63 and cos. suff. in the 80's; L. Minicius Rufus, governor AD 71/2 and cos. ord. 88; and the most honoured of all Ic governors, G. Antius Iulius A. f. Vol. Quadratus, governor in 84/5, who was possibly of the royal house of Pergamon, a friend of Vespasian, cos. suff. 94, cos. ord. 105 and then proconsul of Asia.

Only fifteen of the second century governors are known but seven of these reached the consulship including two ordinarii, namely the governor in 100, L. Elufrius Severus, who may be the same man as the cos. ord. of 114, and a mid 2c governor Q. Servilius Pudens, who was cos. ord. in 166 and whose marriage to L. Verus' sister may well have aided his career. In the 3c only four governors are known. They include Aglaus who is known from his dedication [43]:

Orbis sui
claris luminibus
Diocletiano et
Maximiano
invictis augustis

Aglaus
proconsule

The title of proconsul proves that he was still governor of the joint province, possibly the last one. Pflaum's suggestion that the province was temporarily split in the early 3c is basically founded on one inscription of the procurator Pomponius Cordus which dates to this period and refers to him as *praeses.* Pflaum argues that this means that he was governor of the province: this is theoretically possible but the title is also used as a general honorific which in context seems more likely[44].

In the period 295-7 Crete was separated from Cyrene and made into a single province under an equestrian praeses in the Diocese of Moesia[45]. Only one governor is known definitely from this period, M. Aurelius Byzes.

---

35. *Phil.* V.13.
36. Svoronos Prov. issues no.1, pl.xxxxii.1.
37. *IC.*IV.250-1 with commentary.
38. Chapman, *op.cit.* note 25, p.21.
39. Dio li.2.
40. A. Pupius Rufus struck coins in 30-27 which seem to be restricted to Cyrenaica (*BMC Cyr.* Group V).
41. See Appendix I for the Governors' Fasti.
42. His accuser was Ancharius Priscus who may have had connections with the colonists at Knossos, cf. *IC.*I.VIII.21, a Nonia Ancharia.
43. *IC.*IV.281.
44. H. G. Pflaum, *Annuaire École des Hautes Études* IVe Section, 1973-4, pp.271-2.
45. Verona List V.11.

Constantine upgraded Crete into a senatorial province under a consularis in the Diocese of Macedonia in the Praefecture of Illyricum[46], an arrangement which was to last into the 7c. Of this long period only four governors are known but interestingly two of them, Flavius Fursidius Aristides, governor *c.*372-6, and Aemilius Quintilius Pyrrhus, may have been Cretans.

From the end of the civil wars in the 1c BC up to the 7c AD Crete enjoyed a unique period of peace, so the governor's role was mainly a judicial one, as opposed to his duties in Cyrene (when it was part of the same province) where he also had problems with Garamantes and Jews. Nevertheless the evidence for the judicial duties of the governor in Crete is poorer than that from Cyrene with its Edicts. There is one rescript from Hadrian to the governor Salvius Carus on the question of whether a tutor had to carry on a case on behalf of a pupil if the latter died[47], and also the account of the trial and execution of the Holy Ten Martyrs at Gortyna in AD 251[48]. In this case the accused came from several cities on the island and seem to have been gathered together at the capital for their trial. If the account can be trusted and if the case was not exceptional this would argue against the usual assize circuit known from other areas. However, the existence in Crete of an assize circuit may be implied by an inscription from Cyrene which deals with the circuit there in the reign of Pius[49]. Although this inscription does not refer specifically to Crete it would seem inherently probable that the judicial organisation was the same in both halves of the province; but we have no certain evidence.

Other aspects of the governor's duty included helping with the reconstruction of important buildings like the Odeion at Gortyna[50]. A more delicate task was to make sure that, at least from the 2c, suitable candidates were appointed or 'elected' to the various posts in the cities[51]. This concern with financial matters and interference in the internal administration of the cities had already been illustrated in the 1c when many[52] of the coins struck by the cities were issued under the authority of the governors[53] Another job that may not have been too easy for the governor was to keep an eye on exiles, for Crete was used for this purpose by at least one Emperor, Tiberius[54].

In all these duties the governor received aid from several sources; firstly, he would bring his own friends, like Asilius Sabinus[55], friend of the governor Occius Flamma. This man seems to have become very popular with the Cretans who offered him the *summum magistratum*, possibly the head of the Provincial Council. Asilius refused it, referring to the fact that Cretan magistrates, like defendants at Rome, wore their hair and beard long, saying that he had had that honour twice and did not want it a third time. This wit was not surprisingly completely lost on the Cretans. On another occasion the Cretans had become infuriated with the other friends of the same governor and besieged them in a temple, demanding that the worst man, called Turdus (the thrush), be sent back to Rome under escort of Asilius. He again displayed his wit by refusing to go back to Rome for such a 'titbit'. Presumably Turdus and the others had become so unpopular by trying to feather their own nests with too great enthusiasm.

Possibly more useful to the governor was the quaestor, of whom seventeen are known up to the end of the 3c. Only three are worth mentioning; Vespasian, who was in Crete in the 30's, P. Septimius Geta, the Emperor Severus' brother, and Q. Fabius Cilo Septiminus Catinius Acilianus Lepidus Fulcinianus who was cos. suff. in 193, cos. ord. in 204 and praefectus urbi. Apart from the quaestors the governor was also aided by legati. These can be divided into two groups; a small number of men sent out in the earlier 1c AD for a specific duty, like Acilius Strabo and Paconius Agrippinus who were both sent out to Cyrene to deal with problems over land, and the regular legates beginning with Pliny's friend Cornutus Tertulus who came out at some date in the 80's. Of the earlier two Paconius is also recorded as *quaestor iterum* and *orothetes* in Crete under Claudius; he is recorded as repairing the roads and *androbamones* in the area around Hierapytna. The meaning of the latter word is uncertain but perhaps denotes a class of minor tracks or built footpaths. At least one of the later legates, Ti. Claudius Priscus Rufinus, is described as *legatus procos. prov. Cretae* alone. This man had been *IIvir quinquennalis* in Capua and given the strong links between that city and Crete it would seem plausible that his duties may have been restricted to Crete.

---

46. *Not. Dig.* Or. 1.75; III.10.
47. Digest 48.16.14.
48. See p.45.
49. See G. P. Burton, 'Proconsuls, Assizes and the Administration of Justice', *JRS* LXV, 1975, p.92f. I am indebted to Miss J. M. Reynolds for a text of, and her opinions on, this inscription.
50. *IC.*IV.331, 100 AD.
51. Digest 50.4.11 to Claudius Titianus, '*si idonei sint*'.
52. See p.13, and note 132.
53. See Svoronos Cydonia no.114, Gortyna no.192, Hierapytna no.45. All issued ' επι Κορν Λυ '.
54. Tacitus *Annals* IV.21. Cassius Severus exiled to Crete in AD 24.
55. Elder Seneca, *Controversiae* 9.4.17-21. On the incident, W. Orth, 'Ein vernachlässigtes Zeugnis zur Geschichte der römischen Provinz Creta et Cyrenae, *Chiron* III, 1973, p.255f.

Of the Emperor's procurators only four are known and the subsequent careers of only two of these, P. Licinius Secundus and Ti. Iulius Alexander, are known. Licinius served in the Judean Wars under another Ti. Iulius Alexander and eventually became a procurator in Syria [56]. Ti. Iulius Alexander's career is more interesting: it is known from an inscription from Ephesus where he was procurator of Asia for Trajan [57]. The inscription shows that his previous post had been the Cretan procuratorship which implies that this post was of centenarian rank: it also suggests that the procuratorship was restricted to Crete alone and not Cyrene:

AUG.PRO[c.imp.ner
VAE.TR[aiani caesa
RIS.AUG[
PROVIN[ciae cre
TAE.ITEM[provinciae
ASIA[e

The reconstruction seems certain and the *item* leaves no room for Cyrene. None of the four Cretan procurators are known from Cyrene and neither of the Cyrene men is known from Crete; this could be merely coincidental but taken with Iulius' career does suggest that, sensibly enough, the Emperor's interests on the island were the full-time concern of one procurator.

The activities of the procurator in Crete are illustrated by inscriptions detailing their work in sorting out land disputes which had been referred back to the Emperor, like the one over the boundaries of Capua's land at Knossos settled by P. Messius Campanus or, earlier, Secundus' dealing with the question of some land sacred to Asklepios at Knossos[58]. In 169 Aelius Apollonius was busy restoring an ornamental crossing at Gortyna: he records the use of marble-like stone for the edges (curb stones) and the replacing of fallen statues of the Emperors [59], all paid for from money from the treasury of Diktynna. An unnamed procurator is also recorded in connection with the levying of *angaria* for the *cursus publicus* at Knossos[60].

Another financial officer recorded from the second or third century is an *advocatus fisci et sacri aerarii*, one Vedius Alcisthenes, who put up a dedication to Asklepios at Lebena[61]. A much less significant person is an imperial freedman, M. Aurelius Euemerus who is recorded as a *tabularius* in the treasury in Crete [62]. In the 4c the only lesser Imperial Officer known is one Serapammon who in 381 issued a decree as *praefectus rei frumentariae* concerning the corn supply for public use[63].

The governor and other officials could also be helped or hindered in their duties by the Provincial Council, the Koinon. This organisation does not seem to have had any real connection to its Hellenistic predecessor of the same name [64] except in its pan-Cretan composition. The main role of the new Council was connected to the imperial cult. The head of the Council was known as the Archiereus (High Priest), and five-yearly games were held called the ἱερὸς ἀγὼν πενταετηρικὸς τοῦ κοινοῦ τῶν Κρητῶν, organised by an official called the Xystarches [65]. These games were not limited to Cretans as is shown by the victories of a Rhodian in several events at the games [66]. Another aspect of the Council's work which initially seems to have maintained a link to the cult was the issuing of coinage [67]. Apart from the cistophoroi issued by Kydas in the late republican period [68] and one silver issue of Tiberius, the provincial series started under Caligula with a cistophorus depicting the Emperor on one side and an elephant-drawn chariot bearing a statue of the deified Augustus on the other [69]. The Council continued to issue coins throughout the first and

---

56. *IC.* I. VIII. 49. *PIR* [2] L242. Neronian.
57. *CIL* III. 7130. Also H. G. Pflaum, *Les carrières procuratoriennes équestres sous le Haut-Empire romain* I, (Paris, 1960), no. 75, p. 170.
58. Secundus as above. Campanus, P. Ducrey, 'Trois nouvelles inscriptions crétoises', *BCH* XCIII, 1969, p. 841.
59. *IC.* IV. 333, 169 AD.
60. W. H. C. Frend, 'The Byzantine Basilica Church at Knossos', *ABSA* LVII, 1962, inscription p. 235.
61. *IC.* I. XVII. 27.
62. *ILS.* 1496.
63. *IC.* IV. 285.
64. On this see M. Van der Mijnsbrugge. *The Cretan Koinon* (New York, 1931). For the Roman Koinon, J. Deininger, *Die Provinzialland-tage der römischen Kaiserzeit* (Berlin, 1965), p. 84-5.
65. *IC.* I. XVIII. 55.
66. *IG.* XII. 1. 77.
67. Svoronos, p. 334ff., pl. xxxii-xxxv.
68. As above footnote p. 334 pl. xxxii. 1.
69. M. Jessop Price, 'Elephants in Crete: New Light on a Cistophorus of Caligula', *Acts of the 3rd Cretological Congress* I (Athens, 1973), p. 279.

second centuries with a single issue under Septimius Severus completing the series[70]. This issue was in silver but the previous ones since Nero had all been in bronze: there appears to have been an attempt to regularise the Cretan denominations in line with those of the imperial mints, with a few coins actual copies of the latter[71]. The Council definitely lasted into the 4c[72] and may have continued into the fifth if the phrase ' *δόγματι νήσου* ' can be taken as the poetic equivalent of the Koinon[73].

At the end of the governor's year the Council was able to display its opinion by denying or voting its thanks: in AD 62 Claudius Timarchus who had boasted that this vote lay solely within his power was condemned to exile by the Senate for this act of contumelia[74]. Although Tacitus does not state whether or not this man had been the Archiereus, it seems very likely that he had, and illustrates the power and wealth of these men. The post was annual[75] but could be held at least twice[76], although it was no cheap honour, as shown by Soarchus who as High Priest in the 1c AD built a new aqueduct for Gortyna[77] or T. Flavius Volumnius who held office for a second year and put on by special imperial permission games of unusual length and magnificence[78]. Their place in society outside Crete is shown by the career of M. Claudius Charmosynos Pratoneikos who had been a student with Cn. Papirius Actius who was quaestor in Crete[79], or by the family of the Flavii Sulpiciani, the most notable of all the Cretans from the late 1c AD to the early 3c[80]. There seems no doubt that the title of the head of the Council was Archiereus although in the period of the civil wars Kydas had called himself Kretarches Kretaieon, but this was an exceptional period and the title may well refer to the old Hellenistic council in any case. Kretarches is also recorded in the mid 4c on an inscription praising the Praeses of Caria at Aphrodisias[81] but the inscription is both obscure and corrupt.

Outside Crete the Council maintained links with various men of position who acted as its patron: the only individual known is from the Augustan period, one M. Nonius Balbus of Herculaneum who had been proconsul of the province[82]. Another possible patron was M. Roscius Lupus Murena[83] who had been quaestor on the island in the 2c. Crete was also represented in Hadrian's Panhellenion although the exact method of representation is uncertain[84] However, quite early in its existence its Archon was a Cretan, Flavius Sulpicianus Dorion[85]. There may also be a reference to this organisation in a dedication from Lyttus[86] and a possible victor in its games from Gortyna[87].

The system of government described above seems to have lasted in its basic essentials up into the 7c, but by the middle of that century Crete's position in the Empire had changed from being securely in the centre to a position right on the frontier with the Arabs. Up to the Arab conquest of North Africa Crete had suffered only very slightly in the upheavals of the 3c onwards; a Gothic raid is recorded in 268[88], a Vandal one in 457[89] and the Slavs attacked the island in 623 and possibly 612[90]. Once the Arabs had established themselves in Africa Crete was under constant threat, although details of actual raids are limited to a major one in 674 when the main Arab fleet wintered on the island and subsequent raids in the 8c[91] before the island finally fell in 827-8.

At some point in this period the governor of Crete became known as the Archon, i.e. the commander of a small province[92]. There is definite evidence for the rank from numerous lead seals inscribed with the title of Imperial

70. As note 67 up to M. Aurelius; the Septimius issue is on display in Chania Museum but not published.
71. See G. K. Jenkins, 'The Cameron Collection of Cretan Coins', *NC* 6th series IX, 1949, p.36f.
72. E.g. *IC.*IV.313f.
73. *IC.*IV.325, 5.
74. Tacitus, *Annals* 15.20.
75. *IC.*IV.275.
76. *IC.*IV.305.
77. *IC.*IV.330. 1c AD.
78. *IC.*IV.305.
79. *IC.*IV.306A.
80. *IC.*IV.275 and Appendix II.
81. *MAMA* VIII.426.
82. *CIL.*X.1430-3.
83. *IC.*IV.297 as suggested by Deininger, *op.cit.* note 62.
84. See J. A. O. Larsen, 'Cyrene and the Panhellenion', *CPh* XLVII, 1952, p.7.
85. See Appendix II and A. E. Raubitschek, 'Greek inscriptions', *Hesperia* XII, 1943, p.73-6, no.22.
86. *IC.*I.XVIII.56.L6. See Larsen *op.cit.* note 8, p.13 n.37, though there seems to be very little evidence for his suggestion that this man is just the Lyttian representative.
87. *IC.*IV.326.
88. *SHA* Claudius Gothicus 12.1 with *Panegyrici Latini* 8 (5) 18.
89. Procopius *De Bell. Val.* III.v.23.
90. For 623, see *Thomas Presbyter of Emesa,* ed. Land, p.116, for 612 see p.181 for the date of the destruction of the Sanatorium Basilica at Knossos.
91. 674 - Theophanes p.354. Other raids, see G. C. Miles, 'Byzantium and the Arabs: Relations in Crete and the Aegean area', *DOP* XVIII, 1964, p.1f.

Fig. 2: Evidence for city organisation in Crete.

City	*Eumenes Treaty 183 BC*	*Coins*		*Kosmoi*		*Hierocles*	*Bishop Lists*
		Hell.	*Roman*	*Hell.*	*Roman*		
Allaria	x	x	-	x	-	-	-
Anopolis	x	x	-	-	-	-	-
Apollonia	x	x	-	x	-	-	x
Aptera	x	x	-	x	x	x	x
Aradena	x	-	-	-	-	x	x
Arcades	x	x	-	x	x	-	? x
Axos	x	x	x	x	x	x	x
Biannos	x	x	-	x	-	x	x
Chersonisos	x	x	-	? x	? x	x	x
Cydonia	-	x	x	x	-	x	x
Dreros	x	x	-	x	-	-	-
Eleutherna	x	x	x	x	x	x	x
Eltynaia	x	x	-	-	-	-	-
Elyros	x	x	-	x	-	x	x
Eranos	x	? x	-	-	-	-	-
Gavdos	-	-	-	x	-	x	x
Gortyna	x	x	x	x	x	x	x
Hierapytna	x	x	x	x	x	x	x
Hyrtakina	x	x	-	x	-	-	-
Inatos	-	-	-	-	-	x	x
Istron	x	-	-	x	-	-	-
Itanos	-	x	-	x	x	-	-
Kantanos	–	–	–	–	–	x	x
Keraia	x	x	-	-	-	-	-
Kisamos	-	-	-	-	x	x	x
Knossos	x	x	x	x	x	x	x
Lappa	x	x	x	x	x	x	x
Lato	x	x	x	x	x	x	x
Lissos	? x	x	-	-	-	x	x
Lyttos	x	x	x	x	x	x	x
Malla	x	x	-	x	-	-	-
Milatos	x	-	-	x	-	-	-
Olus	-	x	-	x	x	x	x
Phaestos	x	x	-	x	-	-	-
Phalasarna	-	x	-	x	-	-	-
Phoenix	-	-	-	-	-	x	x
Polichna	-	x	-	x	-	-	-
Polyrrhenia	x	x	x	x	x	-	-
Praesos	x	x	-	x	-	-	-
Priansos	x	x	-	x	x	-	-
Rhaucos	x	x	-	x	-	-	-
Rithymna	-	x	-	-	-	-	-
Rhizenia	-	-	-	x	-	-	-
Siteia	-	? x	-	-	-	-	x
Sybrita	x	x	-	x	-	x	x
Tarrha	x	x	-	-	-	-	-
Tylissos	-	x	-	x	-	-	-

---

92. See H. Glykatzi-Ahrweiler, 'L'administration militaire de la Crète byzance', *Byzantion* XXXI, 1961, p.217f. V. Laurent, 'Le statut de la Crète Byzance avant et après sa libération du joug Arabe ', *Kret. Khron.* XV-XVI.2, 1961-2, p.382f; G. Zacos and A. Veglery, *Byzantine Lead Seals* (Basel, 1972), Vol.1.2, p.1017. G. Spyridakis, ' *Τὸ θέμα Κρήτης πρὸ τῆς κατακτήσεως τῆς νήσου ὑπὸ τῶν Ἀράβων* ' *EEBS* 1951, p.59.

Spatharios and Archon of Crete. There is also one seal [93] with this title prefixed with Hypatikos; the seal is of one Nikolaos and dated rather insecurely by Laurent to 775-800, or just 8c by Zacos and Veglery. These dates are basically stylistic and if the seal really represents the transition between the old-style consularis of the 4-6c and the later Archon, it would be more satisfactory to assign it to the 7c. However, the major question about Crete's status is whether or not it became a theme before the Arab Conquest. This was first suggested by Xanthoudides[94] on the evidence of one lead seal from Gortyna which mentions Stephen the Strategos and the same title used of Theophanes Lardotyros, the governor in Crete recorded in the Martyrdom of St. Stephen the Younger in 767 [95] . There is also a mention of a strategos of Crete in the Tacticon Uspenskij of 842-856[96] where, however, an Archon of Crete is also mentioned. Laurent rightly points out that Stephen need not have been a Strategos in Crete and that Theophanes' title could just be couched in vague terms, especially since he is called Archon elsewhere in the Life, and also Archisatrap, a title for which there seems to be no good parallel. However, the use of Strategos in the Tacticon Uspenskij ought to imply the existence of a theme, as should the lead seal [97] of John the Timarchos of Crete, dated to the first half of the 9c. On balance, it would seem that Crete remained an archontate through the 8c, but possibly its transformation into a theme had occurred just before the Arab Conquest in 827-8 [98] .

The Cities

In the Iliad Homer calls Crete the land of a hundred cities[99]; the epithet survived in use into the Roman period in Crete itself in a sepulchral poem of a gladiator at Gortyna [100] . Well over a hundred names survive for places in Greek and Roman Crete, but there will be no attempt made here to match up obscure names with even obscurer sites[101]; rather, attention will be concentrated on the poleis of which nearly all are now reasonably definitely attached to actual places. In the Classical and early Hellenistic periods, there seem to have been about 35-40 city states (fig.2-3) of which most survived up to the early 2c BC as is shown by the treaty signed by Eumenes II with 30 individual Cretan states in 183 BC [102] , and there are at least four or five further states known at this date which were not in this alliance for various reasons. During the 2c BC certain of the larger states took over minor ones, the main aggressors being Hierapytna which took over Praesos and Istron; Knossos taking over Tylissos and Rhaucos, and Gortyna taking over Phaestos and Rhizenia.

Fig 3: Independent Hellenistic cities of Crete.

93. Zacos and Veglery, *op.cit.* note 92, 2646.
94. *Byz. Zeit.* XVIII, 1909, p.177.
95. Th. Detorakes Οἱ ἅγιοι τῆς πρώτης Βυζαντινῆς περιοδοῦ τῆς Κρήτης (Athens 1970), p.191.
96. Laurent, *op.cit.* note 92, and J. B. Bury, *The Imperial Administration in the ninth century* (London, 1911), p.14.
97. Zacos and Veglery, *op.cit.* note 92, I.2, 2059 p.1149.
98. On the date of the conquest see G. C. Miles, *op.cit.* note 91, p.10.
99. *Iliad* B 1649.
100. *IC.*IV.373.
101. The most recent survey is by P. Faure, 'La Crète aux cent villes', *Kret. Khron.* XIII, 1959. p.171f. and 'Nouvelles localisations de villes crétoises', *Kret. Khron.* XVII, 1963, p.16f. The case of Korion, now safely located near Melabes (16/15), is a good example of the difficulties involved in this work, see G. Huxley, 'Stephanos of Byzantion *sv* Κόριον'. *Greek, Roman, Byzantine Studies* XI, 1970, p.53.
102. *SIG*^{3} 627.

By the Roman conquest further warfare seems to have reduced the number of states to something over 20 (Fig-4). The exact figure is uncertain and may not have been the same throughout the Roman period. Epigraphically and numismatically there are seventeen states with evidence of magistrates, councils or the like. The evidence is restricted to 1c BC - 4c AD, and mainly only up to the late 2c. Servius, writing in the later 4c, mentions that there were 24 cities in Crete[103], but Hierocles, about a hundred years later, has only 22 cities in his list[104]. However, there are three cities which definitely did have independent status in the earlier period which are not in Hierocles; they are Itanos, Priansos and Polyrrhenia. The latter two may have been replaced by their ports, Inatos and Kisamos respectively, as the political centres for their areas and these two cities are in Hierocles. Itanos, however, which had no obvious replacement, was the local centre and it was undoubtedly flourishing in the later Roman period. The bishop lists[105] do not seem to include more than twelve dioceses at any one time, but it is totally unclear how this figure relates to the secular divisions in the later period at the end of which, if Genesius can be believed[106], there were twenty-nine cities in Crete.

Fig 4: Sites with evidence for city status in the Roman period.

Apart from these cities, the only settlement whose legal status is definitely known is the Kome of Rhytion with Pyrgos[107]. Strabo's classification of Phaestos with Rhytion[108] may be evidence that Phaestos too was a kome and indeed the local settlement pattern may indicate that this site had an administrative role[109]. There must have been other komai, but there is no evidence to identify any others. One possibility is that erstwhile independent states like Phaestos may have survived as local administrative centres with this status.

The evidence for the internal administration of the cities is limited to the earlier period up to the end of the fourth century. The two most important bodies were the councils and the boards of magistrates. Most of the inscriptions mentioning the former body are merely dedications by it, but its administrative and legal role is illustrated by a fragment of the accounts of the Diktynnaion[110] and by a law passed by the council at Hierapytna in AD 125 about the establishment of the sodalitas[111]. The latter inscription includes the title of one of the members as Pregistos of the Boule; it is uncertain whether such a man was just a senior member or an office holder within the council such as Chairman[112]. The magistrates on Crete were known as Kosmoi and, whatever the previous system, there seem to have been four annual appointments in the Roman period[113]. The four included the senior eponymous Protokosmos

---

103. *Ad. Aen.* 3. 1076.
104. Hierocles *Synecdemus* 649.
105. See p.45.
106. II.p.47.
107. *IC.*I.XXIX.1.
108. Strabo 10.4.14.
109. See p.22.
110. See p.39.
111. *IC.*III.III.7.
112. Other pregistoi *IC.*IV.294, *IC.*III.III.52.
113. For the earlier periods, R. F. Willetts, *Aristocratic Society in Ancient Crete* (London, 1955), p.103f. Roman period, four kosmoi, *IC.*I.VII.5 1c BC (Chersonisos). *IC.*IV.293, 1c BC/1c AD. (Gortyna). P. Ducrey and H. van Effenterre, 'Un règlement d'époque romaine sur les bains d'Arcades', *Kret. Khron.* XXV, 1973, p.281-290, ? 2c AD.

but not the secretary of the board. Their duties included the issue of coinage under the Protokosmos' name[114], the supervision of public buildings like the bath house at Arcades[115], and religious duties which were the responsibility of the Kosmos Hieragos[116]. The magistracy could be held more than once[117]. Other junior magistrates known in the Roman period are the Agoranomoi who looked after their namesake and numbered three or four[118]; again the post could be held more than once[119]. Other magistrates known from single examples are the Gynaikonomos at Gortyna[120], Oikonomoi at Arcades who seem to have been created in imitation of aediles[121], and, from fourth century Gortyna[122], the only reference to a Curator or Logistes in Crete, one Kalopodes, Logistes of the Metropolis, i.e. Gortyna. There is no definite evidence for any real assembly in any of the cities and outside Gortyna the Demos is mentioned only in a poetic context at Aptera[123]. At Gortyna the word is used only in the formula 'the people and the Council' or 'magistrates'[124] with the exception of one dedication to the 'people' by Alexander the scribe[125]. The only other reference to a popular gathering is Seneca's account of Sabinus' career at Gortyna, but these meetings need not have been formal assemblies[126].

Several of the cities varied slightly from the norm described above: at Gortyna there was an important segment of the population who were organised separately with their own magistrates. These were Roman citizens who had originally settled there as businessmen *cives romani qui Gortynae negotiantur*[127]. This body was still in existence in 195 when Flavius Titianus and this organisation put up a statue to Severus. From this inscription it would seem that they had their own magistrate, a Decurion, and their own Imperial Cult[128]. Although there seems to have been an above average number of Roman citizens at Lyttus there is no trace of a similar body there[129]. Two other Cretan cities whose status was theoretically different were Cydonia and Lappa, freed by Augustus for their service in the civil wars[130]: the only mark of this privilege was that both cities issued coins longer than any other in Crete, although some issues were minted under the name of the governor[131]. Cydonia minted coins into the 3c, the last being a bronze of Julia Domna, and Lappa minted up to Commodus' reign. Of the other cities who issued coins, six ceased after Caligula when the provincial series began but the *colonia* at Knossos carried on to Nero's reign and there was one Trajanic issue at Gortyna[132].

114. Svoronos passim.
115. Ducrey and van Effenterre, *op.cit.* note 113.
116. *IC.*IV.409, 416, both of 1c BC.
117. *IC.*I.XVIII.55.
118. *IC.*IV.250-4, 302.
119. *IC.*I.XVIII.55.
120. *IC.*IV.252.
121. Ducrey and van Effenterre, *op.cit.* note 113.
122. *IC.*IV.336.
123. *IC.*II.III.44.
124. *IC.*IV.297-300 are examples.
125. *IC.*IV.257.
126. Seneca *Controversiae* 9.4.17, see note 54.
127. *IC.*IV.290-1.
128. *IC.*IV.278.
129. *IC.*I.XVIII passim.
130. See p.6.
131. E.g. Svoronos Cydonia no.113.
132. COINAGE OF CRETE

Axos	Tiberius	1 arg
	Caligula	1 arg
Cnosos	Augustus	18 ae
	Tiberius	8 ae
	Caligula	10 ae
	Claudius	5 ae
		1 arg
	Nero	3 ae
Cydonia	Augustus	15 ae
	Tiberius	4 ae
		8 arg
	Claudius	15 ae
	Nero	3 ae
	Vitellius	1 ae
	Vespasian	2 ae
	Domitian	11 ae
	Trajan	4 ae
	Antoninus Pius	2 ae
	Julia Domna	1 ae
Diktynnaion	Trajan	1 arg
	(probably really a provincial issue)	
Eleutherna	Tiberius	3 arg
Gortyna	Republican	2 arg
	Augustus	1 ae
	Tiberius	1 arg
	Caligula	4 ae
	Trajan	1 ae
Hierapytna	Tiberius	4 arg
	Caligula	3 ae
Lappa	Augustus	2 ae
	Tiberius	1 arg
	Domitian	12 ae
	Hadrian	1 ae
	Commodus?	1 ae
Lato	Caligula	2 ae
Lyttus	Caligula	2 arg
Polyrrhenia	Tiberius	1 arg
	Caligula	1 ae

	Province	*Cities*
Republic	1 arg	2 arg
Augustus	-	35 ae
Tiberius	1 arg	19 arg, 12 ae
Caligula	5 arg and 1 ae	3 arg, 19 ae
Claudius	7 arg and 17 ae	1 arg, 20 ae
Nero	6 arg and 3 ae	6 ae
Vitellius	-	1 ae
Vespasian	9 ae	2 ae
Titus	5 ae	-
Domitian	17 ae	23 ae
Nerva	? 1 ae	-
Trajan	37 ae	1 arg, 5 ae
Hadrian	40 ae	1 ae
Antoninus Pius	14 ae	2 ae
Marcus Aurelius	1 ae	-
L. Verus	1 ae	-
Commodus	-	1 ae
Severus	1 arg	1 ae (Julia Domna)

I have been unable to assess the size of these issues.

It is ironical that the one *colonia* in Crete should be at Knossos, the cradle of the Minoan civilisation. Traditionally the date of its foundation has always been given as 36 BC when Dio[133] records that Octavian granted land at Knossos worth HS 1,200,000[134] to the *colonia* at Capua. However, there is no mention of a *colonia* in Crete at this point and there is actual evidence that this grant of land was a separate matter providing revenue for Capua into the 3c, for in the same passage Dio mentions that Capua still enjoyed this source of wealth in his own day. There is also epigraphic evidence for the treasurer of this money at Capua, one Alexander, *tabularius privati arcarii Cretae*[135]. In addition, this land was the subject of a dispute in the later first century between the *colonia* at Capua and one of the the leading families of the Knossos *colonia* which was eventually settled by a decision of Domitian carried out by his procurator in Crete[136]. Furthermore, it seems unlikely on general historical grounds that Octavian could have settled a *colonia* in 36 BC in an area under Antony's control and indeed Dio qualifies his statement about the land grant with the words ' *ταῦτα μὲν οὖν ὕστερον ἐγένετο* '.

The first mention of the *colonia* is in Strabo[137] but he does not say when it was founded and the only epigraphic evidence about the *lex coloniae* merely mentions the limit of 500 denarii expenditure on games[138]. The only substantial evidence for the foundation date is numismatic, for the series of coins issued by Greek magistrates at Knossos continues past 36 BC and probably after Actium[139]. The dating depends on the stylistic similarity of this series to the coins of the governors of the province, and the absolute dating relies upon two overstrikes of Kydas issues on coins of Crassus and the use of the same obverse die by Kydas and his successor Sauromatas. There is one more Greek magistrate, Aristion, issuing coins after Sauromatas. Crassus' dates as governor are probably *c.*36 BC and so there are three Greek issues after this date at Knossos. The foundation coinage of the *colonia* has normally been identified as a series of issues with unnamed heads on both sides[140]. Grant and Svoronos identified them as Antony and Octavian but Robinson and Chapman prefer Agrippa and Augustus. However, this dispute may be pointless for there are two other issues[141] which bear in one case a plough CC on one side and DD Labyrinth on the other and in the other DD plough AUG and CC Labyrinth. These surely are the real foundation issues and must therefore date after Octavian became Augustus in 27 BC.

The principal reason generally held against such a date is that the *colonia* was not mentioned in the *Res Gestae*, but it has been suggested that this was because it was a civilian, not military, *colonia*. Certainly there is no evidence from the inscriptions for any veterans but on the other hand the title of the colony, *Colonia Iulia Nobilis Cnosos*, is not marked out as a special civilian settlement[143]. Where names can be tied down the colonists do seem to include many south Italians, specifically Campanians[144], and it would seem possible that apart from the gift of land the *colonia* did include Capuans, possibly expelled from their holdings by Octavian's veterans. The link between the *colonia* and that area can also be seen in the *colonia's* dedication to M. Nonius Balbus of Herculaneum, proconsul and patron of Crete[145].

The organisation of the *colonia* seems to have been standard, with Duoviri known epigraphically through the first century and from coin issues to the end of Nero's reign. After the end of the 1c no evidence survives although there seems no reason to doubt the continuing existence of the *colonia* until the site appears to have been abandoned at the end of the 4c. The junior post of Aedile as well as the priesthoods of Augur and of the Imperial Cult are all attested in the career of M. Sonteius Casina[146] who was Duovir as well:

M SONTEIO MF TER CASINAE
SACERDOTI DIVI AUG.QUATER
a] EDILI ET DUUMVIRO COLONIAE
c] NOSIAE AUGURI EIUSDEM
COLONIAE

133. Dio xlix. 14.
134. Vell. Pat. 2.81.
135. *ILS* 6317, Alexander Colol. Tabularius/Privati Arcarii Cretae.
136. Ducrey, *op.cit.* note 58.
137. X.4.9.
138. *IC.* I.VIII.51. Such a limit seems typical for colonies at this time, see R. Duncan Jones, *The Economy of the Roman Empire* (Cambridge, 1974), p.83 n.2 and p.149.
139. Ann Chapman, 'Some 1st century BC bronze coins of Knossos', *NC* 7th series VIII, 1968, p.13. For the Roman Governors, *BMC Cyr.* p.ccxiv.
140. Svoronos Knossos 180-3, p.89-90.
141. Svoronos Knossos 185-6, p.90, pl.viii 6, 7.
142. First by F. Vittinghof *Römische Kolonisation und Bürgerrechtspolitik* (1951), p.131, note 3.
143. On such names, A. N. Sherwin-White, *The Roman Citizenship*^{2}(Oxford, 1973), p.228.
144. *IC.* I.VIII.22, *IC.* IV.295, and IIviri on coins, R. Ashton, 'Some Cnossian Coins of Tiberius', *NC* 7th series XIII, 1973, p.40f.
145. *CIL.* X.1433.
146. *IC.* IV.295.

Other leading families included the Plotii Plebeii who were Duoviri under Augustus[147] and fought the Capuan *colonia* in the later 1c [148] and the Petronii who supplied two Duoviri under Augustus[149].

Overall because of the lack of evidence it is impossible to say how successful Knossos was as a *colonia* and to what extent it was assimilated by the Greeks. All but one of the known Duoviri are obviously of Italian origin, the exception being a certain Cutheron who is known from coins of Claudian date [150]. The legends on these coins are in Latin, as are all the official inscriptions, again with one possible exception [151], but all these date to the first century. In contrast all the private inscriptions are in Greek.

The vitality of city life in Crete is perhaps most clearly seen in the surviving monuments, described below, but there is a certain amount of epigraphic evidence to supplement the physical remains. Apart from statue dedications the largest group of civic inscriptions concerns the games. There were in Crete the five-yearly events organised by the Koinon which could attract contestants at least from the Aegean world; a gladiator Gaius from the Troad is recorded from Gortyna[152] and there is the Rhodian victor already mentioned[153]. Another competitor on the Aegean circuit was the gladiator Polos on whose fragmentary sarcophagus at Gortyna [154] are recorded three victories at Ephesus, one at Tralles, one at Laodicea, one at Aphrodisias and four at Gortyna. The gory games held by Volumnius Sabinus have already been mentioned and it is worth emphasising again their scale, requiring special imperial permission [155]. With the advent of official Christianity gladiatorial shows were banned in 326[156], but chariot races increased in importance, with the Green and Blue factions raising violent and bloody enthusiasm, although the only evidence for factions in Crete is a graffito claiming victory for the Greens and their charioteer John[157].

Other public celebrations included various festivals, both to celebrate Imperial birthdays[158] and other older religious occasions. At Lyttus such festivals included those of Theodaesios and Velchania[159] when in the second or third centuries there were still annual distributions of money from the public funds (the Startoi) and the tribal treasuries. This seems to agree with Dosiadas' description of the Syssitia or public messes at Lyttus, operating on the tithe system. Whether this inscription represents a more general survival or just an Archaic custom linked to these two religious festivals cannot be ascertained. There is no other evidence for these messes surviving into the Roman period and Strabo in his account of them derived from Ephorus states that most of these customs had disappeared by his time [160]. Other clubs did exist in Roman Crete; there are two inscriptions of the late 1c BC dealing with a *collegium* of Priapus at Gortyna [161] and one of 125 from Hierapytna giving the Council's permission for a certain Ago, a woman, to found a *sodalitas,* or dining club[162]. Another important aspect of city life was the public bath house, of which the largest known in Crete was probably the so-called Megali Porta at Gortyna. Recently an inscription was ploughed up at Arcades, modern Ini, detailing the regulations of the boards of Kosmoi and Oikonomoi on the segregation of the bathing hours of the sexes. Such regulations had been brought in by Hadrian in Rome and it is likely that the Cretans were following the trend. The actual hours were not cut in the stone but probably painted on to allow for changes [163].

---

147. Svoronos no.190, 1.
148. Ducrey, *op.cit.* note 58.
149. Svoronos no.188, 192.
150. Svoronos 212-5.
151. *IC.*I.VIII.24.
152. *IC.*IV.374.
153. *IG.*XII.1.77.
154. *IC.*IV.375.
155. See p.9.
156. A. H. M. Jones, *The Later Roman Empire* (Oxford, 1964), p.977.
157. *IC.*IV.513. Also A. Cameron, *Circus Factions* (Oxford, 1976), p.126, 314.
158. *IC.*IV.300, 416, 417. *IC.*I.VII.10.
159. *IC.*I.XVIII.II.
160. X.4.20-22.
161. *IC.*IV.266-7.
162. *IC.*III.III.7.
163. See description in Gazetteer and Ducrey and van Effenterre *op.cit.* note 113.

CHAPTER 2: SETTLEMENT PATTERNS IN ROMAN CRETE

The pattern of cities described in the previous chapter was the result not only of political events but perhaps more importantly it was also dependent on geographic and economic pressures. The resulting pattern of major settlements seems to have been established well before the Roman period, probably already in the Minoan age. Nevertheless there are definite changes in the pattern of minor sites in the period that can help to make up the shortcomings in other historical evidence. Also varying types of settlement patterns can be detected in certain areas, thus producing a partial picture of the landscape of the island in this period.

Such a study is basically dependent on survey work linked to excavation: for Roman Crete neither aspect has been carried out to a satisfactory extent, especially the latter. The detail and dates of each individual site will be found in the Gazetteer: basically it has only been possible to divide the Roman period into two, early and late, with the division at about AD 400, but many sites are not even that closely datable. In each part of the island the Hellenistic sites are also examined in order to set the background for the later period. Ideally the environmental archaeology ought also to have been included but apart from a little work on sea levels and alluviation such evidence has not been recovered. Nevertheless, the physical character of the island as it is now will be summarised by area from east to west to set the sites in their geographic context [1]. All the sites can be located by their number on Fig.64, at the end of the book.

The Siteia/Ierapetra Area

The eastern end of the island beyond the Ierapetran isthmus is basically a high limestone plateau whose north coast is mainly composed of mountains falling almost sheer to the sea. At Siteia there is a small plain with a valley behind that leads across the island down to the south coast along which a narrow coastal plain leads to Ierapetra and beyond. To the east of this valley the terrain is less mountainous until one comes to the east coast with its string of small harbours and their attendant sites.

Only a few Hellenistic sites are known of in this area (as in the rest of Crete), the main ones being Itanos (1/39), Praesos (1/22) and Hieraptyna (2/8), modern Ierapetra. The site of Itanos was undoubtedly chosen because of its strategic position; it served as the main port for trade coming up from Egypt (the Ptolemies maintained a garrison there) and it is also on the route from Asia Minor and Syria. Further down the coast there are sites at Palaiokastro (1/37) with a shrine to Zeus, and Ampelos (1/30), both possible harbours. Inland, Praesos is situated on a hill above the central valley mentioned above, from which its inhabitants could and did control the routes north and south while at the same time the valley itself is fertile and well watered. In addition to these economic advantages, the site being inland and on a hill is reasonably defensible. To the north of Praesos there are several small sites known in the valley, with a possible larger one just before the coast at Piskokephali (1/15) on a little hill at the side of the valley. Then on the north coast is the port of Siteia with the ancient site (1/12) seemingly below the modern town and consequently little known. To the south of Praesos the valley becomes less inviting and no site is known before the coast and the settlement at Makrygialos (1/10), probably ancient Stalis. A Hellenistic inscription mentions the agreement between Stalis and Praesos about fishing for the murex shellfish that yields a purple dye [2]. No further Hellenistic site is known from the area until Hierapytna is reached.

1. Still the basic work on modern Crete is the survey carried out by the Americans for the Rockefeller Foundation and published as *Crete, a Case Study of an Underveloped Area,* by L. G. Allbaugh, (Princeton, 1953). There are also good general introductions to the island in M. S. F. Hood's, *The Minoans* (London, 1971), and R. C. Hutchinson's *Prehistoric Crete* (Harmondsworth 1968). For the question of sea levels see Appendix III.
2. *IC* III. VI. 7.

In the Roman period the main sites stayed constant except that at some point Siteia (1/12) became an autonomous city, probably after Praesos (1/22) was destroyed by Hierapytna in the 2c BC [3]. The site at Praesos continued to be occupied into the Roman period but only on a small scale. Overall the number of known sites in this area trebled in this period, which does however cover a length of time two to three times as long as the Hellenistic age.

On the east coast itself in the early Roman period there was a fairly continuous string of sites: the Samnonium shrine (1/40), then to Itanos (1/39), Palaiokastro (1/37), with the shrine to Dictaean Zeus still in use in the 3c AD [4], past a small site at Karoumes (1/34) to Epano Zakro (1/33) where there was quite a substantial settlement. Further down the coast the site at Ampelos continued with another small site beyond at Pharmakokephalo (1/29).

Off the coast here on Kouphonisi (1/31), the ancient Leuke islands, Spratt [5] saw three giant cisterns more than 200m in length and other considerable remains. On the peak of the island and also at Palaiokastro, large seated statues of marble were found: it has been thought that these statues were of the Ptolemies, but if they are compared to the Porto Raphti statue [6] it seems possible that in fact they are, like the latter, lighthouses or beacons based on a statue of the Oikoumene, and that there was a chain of these guiding lights down this coast for the benefit of the trade route from the East.

On the plateau behind the coast there are a number of small sites including Ziros (1/27) where there is a highland plain. In the late Roman period caves [7] at Vourlidoriza (1/19) and Katsidoni (1/20) were occupied though it is difficult to say whether this indicates a flight to the hills or merely pastoral activity. In the valley from Siteia to the south coast there was an increase in the number of small sites in the early Roman period up to Tourtouli (1/21) with the Piskokephalo group (1/14, 15) seemingly quite rich since a mosaic is reported here, probably indicating a villa or church. Nearly all these sites are between 3 and 5 km distant from each other and although the land is not totally flat nevertheless most of it is cultivable without too much effort. This gives a radius of agricultural land from each village of between 1½ and 2½ km. This figure compares very well with general patterns of rural settlement [8] and if all the sites are contemporary may suggest that the recovered pattern of Roman settlement in this valley is nearly complete. In the later period there are no definite sites in the northern part of the valley which may indicate a shift of population to Siteia, but in the south there are sites at Sklavi (1/23) and Lithines (1/24).

On the south coast no sites are known between Pharmakokephlalo (1/29) and an early one at Pilalemata (1/11). From the latter onwards there is a string of sites, at Makrygialos (1/10) as before, at Koutsouros (1/9) and at Ayia Photia (2/16) which is rather cut off from the others by a range of cliffs. All these sites are 2-3 km away from each other and probably were as dependent on the agricultural land behind them as on the sea with its fish. In the highland between these and those on or near the north coast there are a number of sites of early or uncertain date. It would seem likely that these, like the comparable ones on the plateau to the east, indicate an increasing population with the resultant need to take in more land. The corollary of this is that the absence of sites of the later period, except caves, ought to indicate a drop in or concentration of population.

On the north coast between Siteia and the Ierapetran isthmus there are a number of small sites along the present road, just below the 400m level, again of early or uncertain Roman date, with larger settlements on the coast at Mochlos (1/1) and Tholos (2/18) with Kavousi (2/17) behind. Tholos may have been a port of some importance, given the strange structure (possibly a warehouse as the name suggests) that still stands there. In the late period a dramatic change occurred, with fortifications being built at Leopetro (1/5), Mochlos (1/1) and Pseira (2/19). Tholos seems to continue, as the present chapel stands on the site of a larger earlier building on the same east-west orientation. The date of these defences is hard to establish since none have been excavated, but a date in the mid 7c to 8c would seem most likely, as a reaction to the Arab conquest of the Eastern Empire.

At the north end of the Ierapetran isthmus is the site at Pakhyammos (2/12), probably ancient Minoa, where an interesting Roman building, probably a villa, was excavated in the early years of this century. Along the isthmus,

---

3. Strabo X.479 with *IC.* III.IV.9.
4. *IC.* III.II.2.
5. Spratt I, p.241.
6. See p.51.
7. Most of the caves in Crete have been published by Monsieur P. Faure, whose work has probably biased this type of site distribution.
8. See M. Chisholm, *Rural Settlement and Land Use* (London, 1968), especially Chapter 7, 'The Farmstead and the Village'.

Vasiliki (2/13) of Early Minoan fame also has a small late Roman site complete with Christian basilica, and on the opposite (east) side of the valley, snuggling under the mountains at Monasteraki (2/14), Roman walls have been reported. Further along the valley is Episkopi (2/11) where there is another probable Christian basilica; and at Katachorio (2/10) a group of 1c AD inscriptions [9], mainly dealing with land boundaries, has been found. Possibly this was the boundary of the city lands of Hierapytna (2/8), 7 km to the south. This city seems to have been one of the richest of all those in the island at this period with numerous ornate public buildings that could still be seen in the 16c.

The Eastern Dictaean Massif

The next area to be examined lies to the west of the Ierapetran isthmus and stretches from Milatos on the north coast to the coast below Biennos in the south; in other words, the eastern half of the Dictaean Massif. The settlements lie mainly on the coast or in the highland valleys, often at considerable heights, 600 - 800m. Inevitably, few Hellenistic sites are known; on the Mirabellou gulf Nisi (3/16), possibly ancient Istron; Ayios Nikolaos (3/14), ancient Lato pros Kamara; a temple at Naxos (3/9) and the major city at Olus (3/7), a little to the north. All three settlement sites have good harbours, that of Olus being the best. Inland there are two major sites, both rather inaccessible but with their own farming land immediately below; they are Lato (3/13) (behind Ayios Nikolaos, the other Lato) and Dreros (3/6), inland from Olus. Finally on the north coast Milatos (3/1) which also has a good agricultural plain between it and the mountains.

In the mountain valleys above the south coast smaller sites exist at Olerus (2/7), set on the edge of a fair plain, Malles, ancient Malla (2/2), at the head of the valley of the R. Myrtos and a shrine at Kato Simi (5/9). Further along there are a few small sites before Biannos (5/2) which seems to have controlled most of this highland area. On the coast itself the only definite settlement is at Arvi, ancient Arbion (5/8), but it is likely that the Roman remains at Myrtos (2/4) overlie Hellenistic levels.

In the Roman period more sites, mainly of early date, are known from the coast of the Mirabellou gulf. The site at Nisi (3/16) continued with Priniatikos Pyrgos (3/15) just along the coast and Kalochorio (3/17), a possible early villa, a little way inland. Ayios Nikolaos, ancient Lato pros Kamara (3/14), now replaced Lato (3/13) as the main city in this area. This is one of the clearest examples of increased security leading to desertion of the previous site set on its defensible but inaccessible hill. Lato probably continued on a minor scale and indeed there are a number of other minor sites of Roman date in the mountains round about.

Further north, back on the coast, Olus (3/7) flourished, especially in the later period. Apart from its harbour and land, one reason for its wealth may have been the Cretan whetstone trade which is mentioned in the Digest [10]. Although no place name is given there, Spratt [11] saw whetstone quarries still in use above Olus and mentions older disused ones. At the same place there is a series of fortifications of uncertain but possibly late Roman date. If this is so, the reverse of what happened with the two Latos has occurred, the Roman site now leaving the coast for the hills for the same reason that the Hellenistic or earlier city had been founded there. Similarly, inland at Dreros (3/6) where the Hellenistic city seems to have been deserted in the 1c AD it is possible that the site was reoccupied in the late Roman period. There are also several small, possibly village, sites in the area at Vrachasi (3/2), Dories (3/5) and Skinias (3/4). On the coast Milatos (3/1) seems to have flourished right through the period.

In the highlands above the south coast the settlement at Olerus (2/7) continued but Malles (2/2) seems to have been replaced in the late period by Christos (2/1). Alternatively, this may simply reflect the fact that the site at Malles lies buried below the Mediaeval village whilst Christos has been excavated. Below Malles and Christos, down the valley at Mythi (2/3) is a small early settlement and a late cave. On the mountain slopes to the west there are sites at Kalami (5/10), Kato Simi (5/9) which continued in use into the early period and Amiras (5/7) which could be an early villa and two small late sites are known from Ligaras (5/3) and Khondros (5/1). Biannos (5/2) continued as the main city of the area but very little is known about it archaeologically. On the coast itself there are small towns at Myrtos (2/4) and Arvi (5/8) and possible late fortifications at Keraton (5/4).

The Lassithi Plain

In the middle of the Dicte massif lies the Lassithi plain at an average height of 850m; it is among the richest

9. *IC.*III.III.28-9, 57 and 62.
10. 39.415.
11. Spratt I, p.126.

areas of Crete, being composed of a rich deposit of loam and so, political conditions allowing[12], has always been heavily settled. In the Hellenistic period the main sites were Lagou (4/5), a large settlement controlling the main pass out, and Ayios Constantinos (4/10) on the hill Kephala in the south-east corner of the plain. Other sites included the Tzermiadha cave (4/2) and Karphi (4/1) where a few Hellenistic sherds were found.

In the Roman period the two main sites continued but there were numerous smaller farms or villages all round the plain, spaced at 1-3 km intervals along its edge or on the Kephala to utilise all possible farming land. The famous cave at Psykro (4/15), probably the Dictaean Cave, was at least visited in this period if not actually used as a sanctuary. Usually on the plain it is very difficult to date the sites since the pottery seems to be rather different from the bulk of the Cretan material, nor is concrete used. Nevertheless a little typically late pottery is known from a few sites, mainly on the Kephala.

The North Central Plain

To the north of the Lassithi plain the mountains descend very sharply to the narrow coastal plain which runs from just east of Mallia along past Heraklion. Once past the Dicte/Lassithi mountains this plain extends further inland, rising slowly up to the higher land that stretches across the island to the Mesara. Although it is generally below 400m in height, it can still form a broken, hostile environment, short of water and fertile land except in the valleys and the Pediadhos plain. The area in the centre of the island here is particularly barren and consequently very few sites of any period are known.

In the early Hellenistic period the area was composed of small city states which gradually fell to their more powerful neighbours. However, Chersonisos (6/7) on the coast always seems to have been linked to Lyttos (6/25) which also controlled the Lassithi plain in the mountains behind. On the coast between Chersonisos and Knossos (8/4) the only known site of this period is Amnissos (6/2) with a shrine to Zeus Thenatas; then comes Herakleion (8/1), the port of Knossos. Inland between Lyttos and Knossos there are quite a few small sites in the valleys from Galypha (6/11) and Saba (6/17) to the group centered round Kounavoi/Zagouriana (6/12, 13), ancient Eltynaia and once independent of Knossos. A short way to the west comes Mount Iuktas (8/9), a sacred peak in every period. Then in the direction of the foothills of Ida sites of once independent states are known at Kanli Kastelli, ancient Lycastos (8/10), Ayios Myron, ancient Rhaukos (9/12), with Kroussonas (9/13) above and beyond it and finally, back towards the coast, Tylissos (9/10). Apart from this last site all the other three are situated on difficult hills above their farm land in the valley below.

All these sites continued in occupation into the Roman period but, as before, more rural settlements are known. On the coast there are sites at Mallia itself (6/20), halfway between here and Chersonisos at Vigla or Stalidha (6/19), at Piskopiano (6/8) and at Agriana (6/6), close to Chersonisos. All these sites are early but at Mallia and Piskopiano Christian basilicas have also been found while Chersonisos itself flourished in the late period.

Chersonisos's water was supplied by a long aqueduct coming down out of the Lassithi mountains and the same system supplied Lyttos (6/25), sited on a spur of the mountains ringing the Lassithi plain. The site itself was obviously chosen for defensive reasons while the Pediadhos plain below it afforded the equally vital agricultural land[13] Lyttos is one of the few city sites with known defences; they are of late date, 7/8c AD, and of a similar construction to those on the Acropolis at Gortyna. On the Pediadhos plain there are numerous sites, early and late, probably a mixture of villages, e.g. Kastelli Pediadhos itself (6/26), and farms, e.g. Katalimata (6/29). Lyttos seems to have controlled the Lassithi plain and the main pass to it, up the Avdou valley which has an important site at Avdou with a basilica (6/23).

Between Lyttos and Knossos there is a scatter of sites mainly in the valleys rather than on the fairly arid plateau. One series leads along the Pediadhos plain to the Archanes area via Saba (6/17) and Ayia Paraskeve (6/15). Again as in the Hellenistic period there is the group of sites near Mount Iuktas, Kounavi/Zagouriana (6/12, 13), Komes (6/14), Archanes (8/7) and the sanctuary on Iuktas itself (8/9). All these sites are early. Between Iuktas and the sea lies Knossos with its *colonia*: alone of all the major cities of Roman Crete, Knossos appears to have been deserted by *c.*400 AD, when it is possible that Herakleion (8/1) replaced it as the major centre in the area.

---

12. Spanake I, p.223, for the Venetian ban on occupation here.
13. Polybius 4.54.6 calls Lyttus the most ancient of Cretan cities; the evidence for this statement is unknown, perhaps it refers to some tradition about the Dorian settlement.

West of Knossos the settlement pattern remains farily constant with the previous Hellenistic cities carrying on as small towns. There are new sites at Asites, Ano and Kato (9/14, 15) and at Kastelli Malevyziou (9/11), all on the western road to the Mesara, and on the eastern (main) route there is a basilica at Paliani (8/11). At two of the sites, Kroussonas (9/13) and Kanli Kastelli (8/10), the present archaeological sites are above the modern towns and seem to be mainly pre-Roman or Early Mediaeval. It seems likely that in the Roman period the bulk of the occupation was under the Venetian and modern settlement, i.e. below the citadel site, both periods, Roman and modern, being more concerned with ease of living than defence.

Southwards the area of the high plateau extends up to the Mesara plain.

The Mesara Plain

The plain of the Mesara (Pl.1, Fig.5) covers an area of *c.* 36,000 ha and is watered by the R. Yeropotamos, running east-west, and the R. Anapodaris, running west-east. It is bounded by the Asterousia Mountains, rich in minerals, to the south, the Dicte range to the east and to the north first by a rather desolate plateau and then, beyond the source of the Yeropotamos, by the Ida range. It is the most fertile large area of Crete, forming an alluvial basin with a northern tongue stretching up towards Lyttos.

Fig. 5: Settlement in the Hellenistic and Roman periods on the plain of the Mesara.

On the high plateau to the north of the plain there is a range of once independent sites that by the late Hellenistic period had, with one exception, become part of Gortyna's territory. These sites are Prinias (9/16), ancient Apollonia or Rhizenia; Ayios Thomas (7/2), probably ancient Pannona; the site above Melidochori (7/5) and Pyrathi (7/26), ancient Pyranthos. Beyond these to the east is Ini (7/25), ancient Arcades, which was independent of Gortyna. South of this, controlling the Anapodaris river area, was Priansos at Kastelliana (7/29), below the Venetian fortress on the Kastellos. Its harbour Inatos was on the coast at Tsoutsouros (7/31).

In the Hellenistic period there were few small sites even on the Mesara proper. Rotasi (7/21), ancient Rhytion, seems to have been the main centre for the east end of the plain and again was under Gortynian control[14]. Then a couple of small Hellenistic sites exist on the southern edge of the plain before the pass through the Asterousia Mountains to the sanctuary and harbour at Lebena (10/23). This pass is controlled by the site at Plora/Apesokari (10/15, 16, 17). Then directly opposite lies Gortyna itself (10/10) and a few small sites before Phaestos (11/4) and the shrine at Ayia Triadha (11/3) to Zeus Velchanos are reached. Finally, on the coast there is the harbour at Matala (11/8) and possibly another in the Tymbaki area (11/1).

14. *IC.* I. XXIX. 1.

Pl. 1: View south across the Mesara from the Minoan site at Phaestos.
Pl. 2: View southwards down the Amari valley from the site of Sybrita.

In the Roman period the string of northern sites continued at least for the early part of the period. They seem to have had no dependent minor sites and their distribution – they are all 7-8 km distant, i.e. a radius of 3½ -4 km – means that within their territory all the land, provided it was suitable, was economically worth farming. However, Arcades has a large number of smaller sites to the north with a possible secondary centre at Embaros (6/37). These smaller sites are all quite close to each other, at 2-3 km intervals, which suggests reasonably intensive agriculture on the loamy soil on the edge of the alluvium. Although the dating evidence for these sites puts them in the early Roman period with only Embaros having Hellenistic material, the way they seem to radiate from Afrati (6/36) where a large Geometric site is known may be evidence that the settlement pattern here is much older than the Roman period.

To the south of Arcades the city of Priansos may have moved down from the hill to the large Roman site at Kato Kastelliana (7/30). Here again there are no minor sites known in its probable territory, except possibly at Neochorio (7/28). This area, although watered by the Anapodaris, does not have very good soil, stony with a high lime content, and so can support only a small population. In fact its port Inatos seems to have been more important in the Roman period, flourishing on the trade route running along the south coast of Crete from the Eastern Empire to Rome. All along the south coast here there are small sites, at Stous Agious (7/13), Ayios Ioannis (7/12) and Trypete (10/21), probably basically fishing villages. Beyond these to the west lies the large sanctuary of Asklepios at Lebena (10/23) and 9 km further west Lasea (10/25) of "Fair Havens of St. Paul" fame[15].

Although the Asterousia Mountains behind these sites are nowadays utterly barren with very few villages, it would seem from the density of sites in the now desolate Goulopharango (10/20) and Agiopharango (10/26) gorges that they were more hospitable in the Roman and earlier periods[16]. There are also sites at Antiskari (10/24) and Miamou (10/22) which may be connected with copper or iron ore extraction. There are extant traces of iron workings of uncertain date 2 km east of Lebena.

Before dealing with the Mesara proper, one area still to be considered is the high valley of Zaro that stretches across the south edge of the Ida massif from Ayia Varvara to Kamares. Its height varies from *c.*650m to 350m and it is still well forested, fertile and proverbially wet[17]. At fairly direct intervals of 2½ - 3 km[18] there are sites at Panassos (10/4), Gergeri (10/3) - both late, the latter one of the few sites that can definitely be dated to the 9c AD - then at Nibritos (10/2) where there is a large early building, probably a villa, and finally the largest site in the valley at Zaro (10/1). Here there still exists the *caput aquae* of the aqueduct that goes down to Gortyna more than 10 km to the south, and it seems likely that Zaro may have served as a summer residence for the governor at Gortyna.

The settlement of the Mesara itself divides into roughly three areas: firstly, from the coast to beyond Phaestos, approximately to Moires; then around Gortyna itself; and finally south of the Yeropotamos up to the Anapodaris. The first area is dominated by the site at Phaestos (11/4) which in the Roman period had shifted off the Minoan site on the hill to an area covered by the modern village of Ayios Ioannis. Phaestos seems to act as a focus for a group of sites from Ayia Triadha to the west (11/3), Moires to the east (10/7), the Pobia group (10/12) further to the south and Kamilari (11/5, 6). Many of these sites cannot be closely dated but a settlement pattern does emerge. Phaestos was obviously the main centre in the area and much of the land surrounding it would have been cultivated by its inhabitants. Yet the ring of small sites is quite close (the majority are 2-3 km away) which may suggest that the bulk of their land lay beyond the village [19], away from Phaestos. The alternative interpretation that the village sites were in the centre of their land would seem to reduce Phaestos' immediate territory to a ridiculously small area. If the former interpretation is correct the fact that the minor settlements lie on the edge of Phaestos' land can be explained by the desire of the inhabitants of the small sites to stay as close as possible to their service centre, with social, religious and political reasons likely to be of greater importance than economic ones. Indeed, all this makes it very likely that Phaestos retained some political power after its conquest by Gortyna, probably as a Kome like Rhytion[20].

---

15. Acts 27.8.
16. Sites of the Byzantine B period (961-1204) and the Venetian period are known (*AR* 1971-2, p.23), so perhaps the desolation of the mountains should be attributed to Venetian and/or Turkish deforestation.
17. Spanake I, p.30.
18. These distances are deceptive since they are 'crow flight' measures. When struggling across this valley one map kilometre in muddy conditions took ¾hour.
19. 'Village' is used loosely; only one of these small sites has been excavated, at Ayia Triadha. This seems to have been a large farm of the early period.
20. See p.12.

One problem of this area is the question of the harbour at Matala (11/8): this is one of the traditional harbours of Gortyna [21] but seems rather small for the main harbour. It is tempting to suggest that there was another more important harbour in the Tymbaki area (11/1) despite no mention in any source.

Beyond this area of town and village is the second area, on the north bank of the Yeropotamos, the ancient Lethaeus. Here there are no sites early or late until one reaches Gortyna; and again, beyond the capital, no sites to the east before Asimi (7/16) and to the south before the line of sites on the south edge of the plain. This large gap can be explained: Gortyna itself, covering *c.* 150 ha, obviously had a considerable population of whom many no doubt would have farmed the surrounding territory; conversely, the city must also have served as the major market for much of the produce of the plain as a whole.

To the south of Gortyna, beyond the river, there is a small site at Platanos (10/14) and then just before the mountains begin to rise from the plain the probable site of ancient Pyloros is to be found liberally scattered between Plora and Apesokari (10/15, 16). Behind Apesokari begins the pass across the mountains to Lebena which was probably one of the main reasons for the original siting of Pyloros.

Between Pyloros and Rhytion - Rotasi (7/21), 25 km to the east, there are no known major sites, but at 2-3 km intervals there is a whole string of small sites which unfortunately cannot be securely dated. At many of these the main or only surviving buildings are cisterns, varying in number from one to twelve but of similar construction and size; that is, of fairly good stone-faced concrete, about 10-14m long and 4-6m wide. From these sites with cisterns very little else has been recorded, although exceptionally at Stavghies (7/8) there was a fragment of a column of late style.

The purpose of these cisterns was undoubtedly to conserve the winter and spring rainfall for the irrigation of the crops. Nowadays the sites are all small villages with the inhabitants owning the normal type of Cretan farm, quite small (the average is *c.* 4ha) and comprising several different lots (the average is 13) [23] ; but it would seem probable that in the Roman period they were estate centres. The main evidence for this is the cisterns themselves which represent a large amount of capital investment unlikely to be available to peasants in the Roman period farming their own land. But, except at Stavghies, there is no evidence for any substantial domestic building such as one might expect a rich landowner to possess if he were to live on his own estate.

It would seem, then, quite possible that at least some of these sites were centres for estates with absentee landlords of whom there are three likely categories. Firstly, local dignitaries living in the towns and cities of the plain; secondly, senators or similar wealthy men living elsewhere in the Empire; and thirdly, the city-state or even the Emperor. There is plenty of epigraphic evidence for the first class of owners including numerous Roman citizens from the 1c BC onwards [24] . Of the second group the only known example is Flavius Ursus who Statius tells us owned cornland in Crete and Cyrene[25]. Thirdly, Gortyna had city lands at Pyranthos and Melidochori[26]; although no actual imperial estate is known there is evidence for a *procurator caesaris* from Nero onwards[27].

The area covered by the estates is the watershed between the rivers. It is still mainly rich alluvial but being higher is naturally better drained and must probably constitute the best arable land in Crete, given an adequate water supply. The individual estate probably covered a sort of oblong area of land stretching from the estate centre at the cistern across the plain. The resulting pattern of settlement is very close to modern settlement patterns where the farms have been laid out for maximum efficiency[28].

To the north of Ayia Photia (7/18), the last and largest group of cisterns, there is a group of small sites stretching across the plain to the hills opposite. They all seem to date to the 1-2c AD. Asimi (7/16), Argeion (7/17) and

---

21. Strabo X.4.11, *Stadiasmus Maris Magni* 323.
22. Sites with cisterns, from east to west: Vagiona (7/6), Stavies (7/8), Sternes (7/14), and Ayia Photia (7/18). The suggestion about irrigation was first made by S. Xanthoudides in *A. Delt.* II, 1915, par.24.
23. Figures from Allbaugh, *op.cit.* note 1, p.250.
24. These have normally been taken as traders, e.g. by Hatzfeld in his *Les trafiquants italiens dans L'orient hellénique* (Paris, 1919), p.157. Though obviously true of some, Pomepey raised a half legion of veterans from Crete, (Caesar, *De Bell. Civ.* 3.4.1). There is also from Priansos an inscription of a Tribunus Militum of Leg. XXXI (*IC.*I.XXIV.5) probably a unit of Octavian's.
25. *Silvae* 2.5.67. '*Sive alma fidens messisque negasset Cretaque Cyrene*'.
26. *IC.*I.XXVI.2 and 3.
27. See p.8.
28. Compare Chisholm, *op.cit.* note 8, fig.9d p.139.

Praitoria (7/22) are unusual in actually being situated on the lower lying alluvial as opposed to the majority of the sites which tend to be on the more healthy, better drained edges of the plain, on limestone or loam. It is evident all over the island that the 2c especially was a period of great prosperity and so these rather unpleasant sites may be a reaction to pressure on available land. Finally on the Mesara, there are the sites at Doraki (7/19), Pyrgos (7/20) and Rhytion (7/21). The latter formed a Kome of Gortyna and at Rhytion there was a shrine to Zeus Skyllios that seems to have been honoured by the Romans from Metellus onwards[29].

The Amari and Spili Valleys

Just around the bay from Tymbaki at the western end of the Mesara is the port of Ayia Galini (15/16), ancient Soulia. From here two high, fertile valleys stretch up through the mountains across to the coastal plain behind Rethimnon (14/4). Both the Amari and the Spili valleys have always been densely occupied, especially the former. In the Amari, the eastern of the two, nearly all the sites in the Hellenistic period were towns or cities. Firstly Soulia with a sanctuary to Artemis, then the settlement at Kastri (12/19) on a citadel blocking the southern end of the valley. From this there is a view straight up the valley, past the possible town at Vigla (12/13) to the main site at Thronos (12/4), ancient Sybrita. Close by there are smaller sites at Patsos (12/2), Meronas (12/8) and a cave at Elenes (12/7). Then beyond Thronos there is another Kastri (12/1), blocking the northern end of the valley before the pass over the ridge leading down to the north coast. Just north of this Kastri, however, there is a valley linking the Amari and Spili valleys with an important site on the heights above it, at Onythe Goulediana (14/7), possibly ancient Phalanna. In the Spili valley proper the main site seems to have been at Koxare Ambelo (15/8), another small town, and, high up at the southern end of the valley, Melabes (15/15), ancient Korion.

In the Roman period Soulia and Kastri remained important sites but there is also a group of smaller sites, probably farms or villages, on the valley slopes at Rizikas (12/18), Ardhaktos (12/17) and Apodhoulou (12/16). Also, more in the centre of the valley but again on high ground above its floor and stream, there are two late probable villas at Ayios Ioannis (12/15). Then further up the valley Vigla was replaced by a large town at Vizari (12/12) where an 8c AD church has been excavated. In the valley between Vizari and Thronos (Sybrita) there are several other late villas at Monasteraki (12/11), Skouphia (12/10) and Asomatos (12/9). Similarly on the western side of the valley, a site at Yerakari (12/6) may be a villa and there are several small sites here and at Meronas (12/8) and Elenes (12/7) as before. The major site at Thronos seems to have expanded off its hill in the Roman period, almost certainly remaining as the centre for the valley for the entire period[30] (Pl.2). To the north Kastri was not occupied in this period but there are sites at Mirthios (14/10) in the valley and at the northern end on the pass over to the north coast at Prases (14/6). At Mirthios, however, the side valley to the Spili valley opens up and in this also the number of sites increased in the Roman period with Selli (14/9), Ampelakia (14/8) and Onythe (14/7) which continued in occupation and had a fine 5/6c church.

In the Spili valley the only definitely early site is at Koxare Ambelo (15/8) but other sites of late date are known from Ayia Pelayia (15/9), Preveli (15/10) and on the coast at Ayios Savvas (15/11). All these sites are possibly villas. At the other end of the valley there is another late site at Viglotopi (15/7) where there is a possible basilica below the Mediaeval chapel. Beyond this is the last Roman site in the valley, at Monopari (14/3), of indefinite date and function.

The most obvious change in settlement pattern in the Amari is the great increase in the number of rural sites in the late period. I would class most of these as villas as there are considerable remains of well-built concrete walls, good evidence of substantial buildings and therefore wealthy owners. These sites are not particularly regularly spaced but tend to cluster in groups, one about Ayios Ioannis, the other between Vizari and Sybrita. These villas and the other sites as well tend to be on the higher slopes above the valley bottom, undoubtedly to avoid flooding after the winter and spring rain and snow. Much the same pattern emerges in the Spili valley, although there the sites are more scattered and as the valley is much wider, tend to be situated in the valley itself, though often on slight hills.

The Mylopotamou Valley

Along the north coast between Herakleion (8/1) and Rethimnon (14/4) the land is basically mountainous with the valley of the Mylopotamos bisecting it east-west, with deep side valleys running up into the hills on either side.

---

29. *IC.* I.XXIX.1, 120 AD.
30. There is no evidence to support the view that Vizari replaces Sybrita in the late period as the main centre, as suggested by K. Kalokyres, *Kret. Khron.* XIII, 1959, p.7.

The coast itself is mostly very inhospitable but westwards from the mouth of the Mylopotamos as far as Rethimnon there is a coastal plain stretching inland for a few miles.

As normal, the Hellenistic occupation was basically urban, with a string of coastal sites from Ayia Pelayia (9/1), ancient Dium, Sises (13/14), Bali (13/4), ancient Astale with triple coves forming a good harbour, Panormos (13/3), a large site at Stavromenos (13/1), possibly ancient Allaria, and finally Rethimnon (14/4), ancient Rhithymna. Apart from the last two these sites must always have had to rely on the sea for the bulk of their livelihood. In fact, many of these Hellenistic coastal sites must have doubled as fishing/trading ports and pirate bases. Behind the coast in the Mylopotamou valley there are a few small sites, particularly on the saddle at the eastern end, but the main sites were the cities of Axos (13/16) and Eleutherna (13/5). Both these are off the main valley, the latter in a particularly strong position set on a promontory jutting out into the valley, the only approach being a mere few feet wide (Pl. 3). Beyond Eleutherna is the small site at Amnatos (14/16), probably a small town, whilst opposite on the other side of the main valley is Melidhoni (13/1) with a cave sacred to Hermes Tallaios.

Under Rome all the Hellenistic coastal sites continued at least for the early period. Later Ayia Pelayia (9/1) and Sises (13/14) disappear while Panormos (13/3) seems to have grown in importance if the size of its basilica is an indication of its wealth. In the mountains behind the coast the worship of Hermes continued in the cave at Melidhoni. At the other end of these mountains in the fertile valley of Phodele there is a possible late site (9/2) just a little way inland. The main inland route appears to have been from Tylissos (9/10) up to Axos (13/16) rather than the lower pass taken by the present main road (as opposed to the newly opened motorway) past the small site at Marathos (9/4). The upper route has several sites along it; one at Goniais (9/7), both early and late, and another possibly at Anoyia (13/18) whence one can ascend Mount Ida to the sacred cave (13/20), still used in the 4c AD [31]. At Axos (13/16) the remains include both early and late material but it seems likely that in the late period Eleutherna (13/5) was the more important of the two[32]. In the valley between them there are small sites at Episkopi Aulopotamou (13/13) where there is probably a basilica; at Khoumeri (13/10) where there is a possible village site and at Perama where the site may be a small village (13/9). Eleutherna lies in the hills to the south-west of the latter site, reached by quite a difficult route through deep but fertile valleys, past a probable villa at Plaka Kalis (13/8).

In the hills to the west of Eleutherna there was the small town at Amnatos (14/16) and further down the same valley towards the coast there are small sites in the low hills on either side. To the east there is Pikri (14/15) and Viran Episkopi (13/2) and to the west Arsani (14/14), Pankalokhorio (14/13) and Piyi (14/12) further away. Then on the north coast the large site at Stavromenos (13/1) which must have acted as the centre for most of these sites. Although there are a reasonable number of sites in this area the only physical settlement pattern detectable is that determined by the local geography, each site selecting a suitable position in its valley, normally on a low hill at the side, near to a water supply. Back on the coast west of Stavromenos there is a small late site at Pyrgos (14/11) and 7 km further Rethimnon, Rhithymna (14/4), where little of the Roman site is known.

The Rethimnon and Apokoronou Areas

West of Rethimnon the land rises again but is quite fertile with comparatively dense modern settlement. However, there is no known Hellenistic site before the city of Lappa (14/1) at modern Argyroupolis at the head of the valley of the R. Moursella, which reaches the sea at Dramia (17/16), ancient Hydramia, the port of Lappa. In the mountains behind Lappa there is a small site at Asi Gonia (17/18). Back on the coast at Georgioupolis (17/13) there is what is probably the site of ancient Amphimalla at the mouth of the R. Almyros, and a cave site at Asprosykia (17/14) in the hills behind. No Hellenistic sites are known from the Apokoronou area until one reaches the great fortified city of Aptera (17/2), controlling Souda Bay, with its harbour of Kissamos at modern Kalami or Kalyves (17/1). In the mountainous but fertile land behind Aptera small sites are known from Azoires (17/3) and Skordyliana (18/13), the latter being a possible villa, although it may only have been occupied in the Roman period. In the lower land to the south-east of Aptera, at Stylos (17/4), a Minoan tholos tomb was reused as a possible shrine.

---

31. *IC.* I. XII. 8.
32. No bishop is known from Axos, while Eleutherna is in the Bishops' Lists from the 5c onwards.

Pl. 3: Entrance tower and approach to the site of Eleutherna.
Pl. 4: View of the site at Suia from the east side of the bay.

In the Roman period there is little change known in the area around Lappa although two small sites occur at Zouridhi (14/2). The site of Hydramia has no definite evidence for late Roman occupation but by Lake Kournas (17/17) there is quite a large site of uncertain Roman date, but possibly late. Behind Amphimalla more sites are known: the cave at Asprosykia (17/14) continued in use and there is another cave at Korakia (17/15). In the area north of Amphimalla the land rises to a rather odd plateau, high, very stony and seemingly short of water. Here there are sites at Litsarda (17/11) and, further north on the summit of Drepanokephala (17/10), a small late site. To the west, in the edge of the White Mountains across the valley which runs from Chania through to Aptera, there is a group of small sites in the high valleys; at Melidoni (17/7) a cave and settlement of early date; at Pemonia (17/8) another cave and at Rhamni a probably late site. Further along the mountains the site at Skordyliana (18/13) is definitely of early Roman date and at Kontopoula (18/14), set in a highland plateau, a group of small late sites has been found. Finally, down on the coast Aptera flourished with small sites at Azoires (17/3) (early) and Ta Marmara (17/5) (late). On the coast itself, Kissamos the harbour of Aptera continued, and further eastwards on the coast a fine 6c basilica has been excavated at Almyrida (17/9). In general this entire area is unusual in that there are as many late sites as early, both on the coast and inland.

The North-West Coast

Beyond Aptera, past the end of Souda Bay, lies the second largest area of alluvium in Crete, in the region to the south of Chania, and there is also reasonable land, mainly loam, in the rest of the two coastal plains of Chania and Kastelli Kissamou. There are three large peninsulas jutting out from the coastline, all sparsely occupied in the Roman period. In the Hellenistic period, on the Akrotiri, the easternmost and least inhospitable of the three, the only site is the cave at Khavgiaras (18/20). At the neck of the peninsula lies the site of the city of Cydonia, modern Chania (18/18), probably in this period based on the Kastellos above the harbour. On the coastal plain to the west of Cydonia only two Hellenistic sites are known, one at Stalos (18/6), a small site on a hill above the plain, and another at Platanias (18/4) on the coast itself. South of here in the White Mountains there are sites at Meskla (18/12), deep in the mountains at the head of an exceptionally beautiful valley, and on the heights above Varypetro, Debla (18/11), with a watchtower.

On the ridge separating the coastal plains of Chania and Kastelli Kissamou a Hellenistic pot was found at Gavalomouri (20/20). This ridge extends out into the sea to become the second peninsula, and the shrine of Diktynna (20/29) is to be found at its northern end. Over the ridge, on the Kastelli plain, there is an important site at the citadel of Rocca (20/18) with its port at Nopygia (20/16), ancient Methymna. In the Hellenistic era all this plain, including Kissamos at the western end by the sea, was under the control of Polyrrhenia (20/11), a massive hill site now covered with later defences. Over another ridge of low hills to the west is the west coast and the city site of Phalasarna (20/2) set in its own small plain. Out on the final peninsula to the north lies what is reputed to be the site of the Agneion shrine (20/1).

In the Roman period the occupied caves on the Akrotiri multiply in number from one to five of which one, Lera, is late (18/19) and another, Akhyro, is early (18/21). Apart from these caves there is a large site at Marathi (18/17), ancient Minoa, with substantial buildings on the seashore.

Cydonia (18/18) continued as a flourishing centre right through the Roman period and beyond. The next major site appears to have been below the Venetian fortress at Varypetro (18/9) with evidence of occupation in both early and late periods. Immediately above Varypetro was Debla (18/11) which was used in the 1c BC. Further to the west and deeper in the hills Meskla (18/12) continued to be occupied at least up to the 4c AD. Minor sites include numerous caves, e.g. Ayia Marina (18/5) and Anthropotrypa (18/2), both early, and Kritharos (18/10), late. Small settlement sites are known at Galatas (18/7), Stalos (18/6) and Platanias (18/4), all early, and Modia (18/1) is both early and late. Vrysses (18/3) has been claimed to be ancient Pergamon but the only extant Roman remains are hardly extensive enough to justify calling this site a town or city. From the distribution of sites it seems as if the plain was cultivated in rather different ways (Fig.6). The area immediately about Cydonia was probably cultivated by the inhabitants of the city and the next area, as far as Modia (18/1), by the scattered settlements on the plain, all about 2-4 km away from each other. Between Modia and the separating ridge no Roman sites are known on the Cydonia plain. Given the agricultural potential of the land this seems rather an unlikely situation and it is quite possible that these sites have simply not been found; however, an alternative explanation may be that this land was farmed from sites on the ridge overlooking the plain itself such as Marathokephala (20/26), Skordyliana (20/21) and Episkopi (20/22). At the latter there seems to be the site of a villa of late date. If these sites did farm the plain it seems likely that the latter would be used for arable while cattle and and animals were kept on the ridge[33]. The distances involved are not too great for efficient farming it is 8 km from Marathokephala to Modia and the placing of the farm centre on the dividing line between the two types of land indicates highly efficient farming.

Fig. 6: Settlement on the Chania plain.

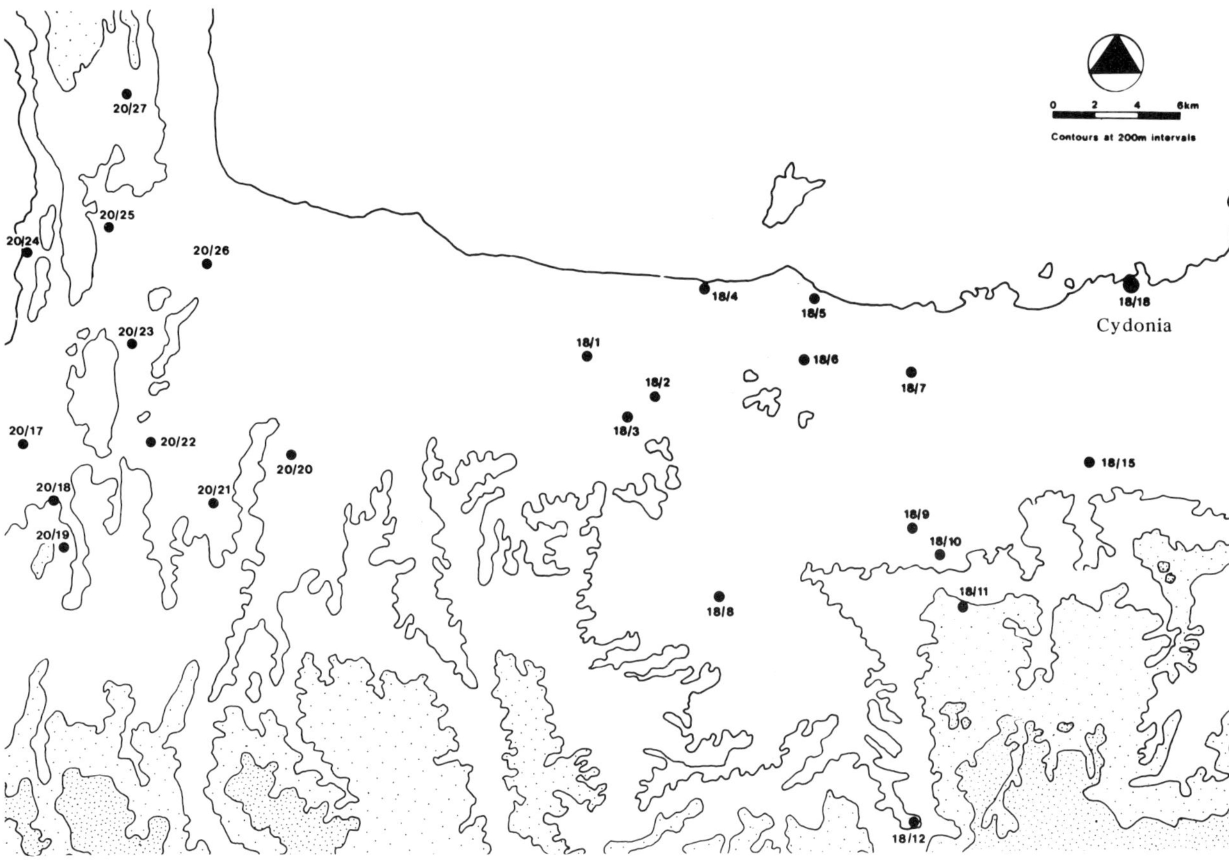

On the Diktynnaion peninsula there is an increase in the number of sites: the Diktynna shrine flourished, there was a possible peak sanctuary on Mount Onykas (20/28) and seemingly a small settlement at Rhodopou (20/27). At the base of the peninsula there is the site of what is possibly a villa at Koleni Kamara (20/25) and further inland on the ridge, the site at Nokhia (20/23)[34]. Finally, on the ridge west of Kamara on the hill Prophitis Ilias, there is a sizable site at Phaleliana (20/24).

On the Kastelli plain Methymna (20/16) and Rhokka (20/18) continued into the Roman period, the latter probably occupied continuously to the present day. Just beyond Rhokka its main cemetery is known at Trialonia (20/19) where Spratt claims to have found the site of the temple of Artemis mentioned by Aelian[35]. Between Rhokka and Methymna there is the site of a farm or village at Phaleliana (20/17) and another settlement, probably an early villa, at Drapania (20/15). At the other end of the bay Kissamos (20/10) flourished: to its south there is a small site at Khorevtiana (20/12) before Polyrrhenia itself (20/11). Possibly the latter declined as Kissamos expanded, but the massive defences may include sections of late Roman date. It is perhaps more relevant to note that the coin series from Kastelli Kisamou (Kissamos) ends in the 7c, exactly when increased insecurity might have induced the population to move back to the hills. Against this it must be noted that at the present it is very difficult to identify 8c material and in general very few coins of

33. *IC.* II. XI. 3 from the Dictynnaion gives a list of rents or debts in terms of cattle, sheep or their products.
34. This site has the interesting characteristic of changing date depending on the specialisation of the archaeologist sherding it. Personally I would claim to have seen sherds likely to be Roman as well as obviously Minoan material. This site illustrates the problems of coarse ware identification on Crete.
35. Spratt II, p. 207-8. Aelian *De Nat. Anim.* 14.20.

this period are known from the island. Beyond Polyrrhenia the Topolia pass over to Chrysokalitissa (20/8) begins, and at Topolia (20/13) a Republican coin of 78 BC has been found, while the cave of Ayia Sophia (20/14) continued in use from the Hellenistic period.

Finally, on the coast to the west of Kastelli Kissamou, Phalasarna may have continued in the early Roman period, while on its plain a group of sites of this date is definitely known; at Kastelliana (20/3) a possible villa, at Mesogeia (20/4) a small settlement and at Patella (20/5) "a large rock cutting", possibly a harbour work[36]. North of the plain the shrine of the Agneion probably also continued into the Roman period: in fact, there may be two sites, one of the Agneion at Ayios Sostis (20/1) and one in the bay opposite Grabousa on the east coast, possibly ancient Korykos[37].

The South-West Coast

The area of Crete remaining to be examined is that of the south coast and its hinterland. Generally, the coast is steep and inhospitable in the extreme, but at intervals there are fertile coastal plains and at the western end, several very hospitable valleys leading up into the mountains. In the Hellenistic period very few small sites are known, but in the valley leading down to Moni Chrysokalitissa there are two small ones at Perivolia (20/6), possibly ancient Inachorion, and at Plokamiana (20/7). On, or rather above, the south coast proper the first site is ancient Pelkis at Kastraki (19/7), then in the valley of the R. Kakodianos the site of the city of Kantanos (19/10) at the present day town of the same name[38]. Then in the valley to the east, Hyrtakina (19/14) above Temenia and at Rhodovani (19/16) the large city of Elyros with its port of Suia (19/17) (Pl.4) at the foot of the valley on the coast. A little to the west of Suia, again on the coast, was the city of Lissos (19/18) with its sanctuary of Asklepios complete with medicinal spring.

Along the coast to the east Tarrha (16/3) at the end of the Samaria Gorge must always have relied on trade for its wealth as its agricultural land is limited in the extreme. Yet further east Loutro (16/5), ancient Phoenix, with its excellent harbour, has a sister city of Aradena (16/4) above on a mountain plain and a similar city at Anopolis (16/6), divided from it by a spectacular gorge. No ancient site of either Hellenistic or Roman date is known from the present centre for this area, Chora Sfakion, but there is a possible site on the plain just to the east at Komitades (16/8) and a similar site of Hellenistic or Roman date has been found at Imbros (16/7) on the edge of the Askyfou plain high in the mountains on the route down to Chora. Curiously, no Hellenistic site is known on the Frankokastelli plain, but to the east on the Sellia-Plakias plain there are two sites; one on the coast, Sellia (15/1), possibly ancient Apollonia, and, on the land above, another Sellia site (15/2). Finally, off the coast well to the south the island of Gavdo has a fair-sized settlement on its north coast (16/12).

In the Roman period the basic settlement pattern remained constant, but with a decided increase in the number of sites on the coastal plains. On the west coast there is a small site at Moni Chrysokalitissa (20/8), while in the valley behind Perivolia continued (20/6), at least for the early part of the period. In the mountain valley to the south-east at Sklavopoula (19/6)[39] there is a considerable settlement of both early and late date, possibly connected with mines for malachite ores (copper) which have been found here.

Just around the south-west corner of Crete, at Elaphonisi, there is a good harbour site at Cape Krio (19/1), ancient Biennos, with a possible basilica. To the east of the Cape there is a fertile plain stretching for 7 8 km to Palaiokhora. On this plain there is an early site at Ayios Yioryios (19/5), but at the latter and also at a second site at Ayios Yoryios (19/4), and at Panayia (19/2) and Archangel Michael (19/3) there are late sites, all 6-7c. At Palaiokhora itself there is no definite ancient site (19/11) but a little way inland on the banks of the R. Vlithias a site does exist. At the head of the valley Kantanos flourished, with definite evidence for Roman mining, and a little below Kantanos (19/10) there is a late site at Plemeniana (19/9).

In the mountains between here and Elyros there are sites, all probably early, at Azogyres (19/13), Hyrtakina (19/14), and Kampanos (19/15). All these are very remote but set in their own fertile valleys, quite

36. Suggested to me by Mrs. Paula Martin.
37. I was not able to visit this area, and it depends on the interpretation of Buondelmonte's account of his visit in *c.* 1415 (ap Cornelius, *Creta Sacra* I, p.87).
38. The claim that Kantanos has moved sites simply originates from an idea of Pashley's (II, p.116-8), for which there is no real evidence.
39. The 'sklav' element in this name as in others on the island probably refers to settlement of such troops after the 10c reconquest rather than 7c settlers.

capable of supporting a reasonable population. Kampanos has the added attraction of iron ore. Elyros (19/16), Suia (19/17) and Lissos (19/18) all flourished in the Roman period, although Suia seems to have been especially prosperous in the late period. Further west along the coast there is a site at Poikilassos (16/1) and Tarrha (16/3) continued as did the Phoenix/Aradena/Anopolis group (16/5, 4, 6). One site that may be Roman is the City of the Greeks, 'Ellenais', above the Samaria Gorge (16/2): this city may be the ultimate in refuge sites. Also in the gorge is the cave of Ayios Nikolaos which contains late Roman material.

Past Chora Sfakion and the two possible Roman or Hellenistic sites at Komitades (16/8) and Imbros (16/7), one comes quite soon to the Frankokastelli plain where in the late period villages are definitely known at Patsianos (16/9), Ayios Evstratios (16/10) complete with church and at Ayios Niketas (16/11) by the Venetian fort there is a church apparently without a village. All these sites date to the 6-7c like the group at the SW corner of the island (sites 19/4, 5 etc.) West of Frankokastelli the Sellia-Plakias plain has sites at Sellia (15/1) on the coast as in the Hellenistic period, with both early and late material; one in the valley above continuing from the Hellenistic period, Sellia (15/2), also both early and late; one site (15/5) which is probably a farm and two others which are similarly late (15/3, 4). Finally, at Plakias on the coast there is yet another late site (15/6).

Although there were obviously agricultural sites in the Roman period in this area of the south coast, on the Frankokastelli plain, in the Sellia area and in the area to the west of Palaiokhora, undoubtedly the most important sites were the big cities on or close to the coast. Some of these have reasonable land nearby, especially those in the valleys like Kantanos and Elyros, but many, like Suia, Lissos, Tarrha and Poikilassos have little or no good agricultural land; all of these must have gained their obvious wealth from the important trade route that ran along the south coast of Crete from Egypt and Syria to Rome.

Conclusions

Although much of the evidence used here has been not as secure as one could wish, it is possible to draw certain conclusions, both in general and on particular aspects, that are probably valid. The general development of the settlement pattern from the Hellenistic period through to the Arab conquest in the 820's AD seems to be standard throughout the island. In the Hellenistic period the urban sites seem to dominate the settlement pattern to a greater extent than in the Roman period. Rural sites do occur but there are very few, if any, definitely Hellenistic 'villa' sites. There may be two reasons for this: first, in a period of almost continual warfare it would obviously have been safer to live in a city, and in addition any invested capital in the form of expensive buildings would be at far less risk inside the city than in the countryside. Secondly, there is a certain amount of evidence that the Doric customs, based on city life, survived until the Roman era[40]. In the early Roman period there seems to have been an expansion in the number of small rural sites, but mostly still of the village or farm type rather than a full-scale villa; a few of the latter are known, e.g. at Koleni Kamara (20/25) in the west, Pachyammos (2/12) on the Ierapetran isthmus and Plaka Kalis (13/8) near Eleutherna. The second century seems to have been the most prosperous and it is perhaps to this century that the system of estates in the Mesara should be assigned.

From the third to the late fifth centuries Crete appears to have been in decline, perhaps accentuated by the series of earthquakes in the 4c[41]. In the late 5c and early 6c the settlement pattern changed in two ways. First a large number of churches appeared, illustrating the effect of the change of religion which apparently was only now making itself really felt. Secondly, in certain areas, particularly the Amari, groups of proper villas appeared, perhaps reflecting increased wealth amongst the local aristocracy. At the same date, or perhaps slightly later, the coastal plains were increasingly settled with groups of villages rather than villas. Finally, the fact that with the Arab conquest of North Africa in the 640's Crete became a frontier of the Empire is also shown by the number of late fortresses and the possible decline of the south coast trading cities.

These chronological conclusions are constricted largely by the lack of well excavated sites, but it is also possible to deduce conclusions from the various types of settlement patterns which developed across the island. All the major sites date to the pre-Roman period and in most cases were chosen for obvious reasons. Often they were originally situated on a hill for defensive purposes but close to their agricultural land and water. In

40. See R. F. Willetts, *Aristocratic Society in Ancient Crete* (London, 1955) passim.
41. Destruction levels of this date are known at Kissamos (20/10), Kantanos (19/10), Knossos (8/4) and Mochlos (1/1).

the Roman period they tended to spill off their hill and extend over the lower land, a process reflecting the increased security of the times and the consequent increase of population. Sometimes indeed,the original hill site appears to have been abandoned, as at Phaestos, or to have become a specialised area of the city, as with the Acropolis at Gortyna and its strange buildings. The ultimate effect of Roman prosperity in two or three cases was the marked decline of the main site inland in favour of its port, as was the case with Polyrrhenia and Kissamos, Knossos and Herakleion, and Priansos and Inatos. Conversely, the greater insecurity of the 7c led to the reuse of the acropoleis although there is very little evidence for any general abandonment of the coasts.

Dependent on the cities were the towns, villages and villas of the island. Without excavation it is very difficult to place many of the smaller sites into their correct category but it is clear that small towns did exist, perhaps most commonly in the central part of the island between Knossos and Gortyna at places like Tylissos, Kroussonas, Ayios Thomas and Melidochori. These sites often seem to exist without smaller settlements nearby and presumably their inhabitants then as now farmed the land roundabout. As with the cities, at several of these towns, for instance Kroussonas and Kanli Kastelli, the major area of Roman occupation appears to have been on lower ground below the acropolis. There are also sites which may have been towns elsewhere on the island which did have smaller dependent settlements; in the Amari and Spili valleys, for example. In the Amari valley Vizari must always have been a secondary centre to Sybrita whilst in the wide Spili valley such places as Melabes and Koxare Ambelo may have been towns or large villages. A similar relationship between sites existed in the plains north of the White Mountains where secondary centres (towns) such as Rhokka, Methymna, Pergamon and Varypetro served a network of small settlements. In the mountainous areas, especially in the White Mountains including the south coast, the terrain imposed a pattern of isolated sites, both towns and cities, with very few dependent settlements.

Amongst the smaller villages and farms scattered over the island little pattern can generally be detected, except a tendency for the individual site to be placed on a convenient hill close to a water supply. However, there are groups of smaller sites that can be seen to be either dependent on a town, like those in the valley behind Siteia or the groups centred round Phaestos or Embaros in the Mesara, or with no obvious major centre, like the villages to be found on the small coastal plains in the SW corner of the island. These include the sites on the Frankokastelli plain where there seems to have been villages with outlying farmsteads scattered haphazardly about. These sites date to the 6-7c and offer an interesting contrast to the villas of the Amari and Spili valleys which seem to be about one or two centuries earlier. The remains at the village sites are all of dry-stone or rubble construction with no obvious central building (except the church at Ayios Evstratios) as compared to the massive concrete walls of the villa sites.

In all the classes of site discussed above the basic factor in both the location of the individual site and its relationship to the others was obviously one of agricultural economy; yet, there are other important reasons for the location of particular sites. Religion seems to have played a decisive role at certain places, such as the sanctuaries of Asklepios at Lebena and Lissos and the numerous cave sanctuaries, often probably dating back to the Minoan period, such as the great caves at Psykhro, Ida and Skoteino. Other attractions included mineral wealth, although the largest centre in the Roman period at Kantanos also has excellent agricultural land in the vicinity. Trade was also important for the existence of coastal sites. In the Hellenistic period such trade included piracy, or perhaps more accurately privateering, and it may be no coincidence that some of the large coastal sites such as Ayia Pelagia or Nisi apparently declined in the early Roman period, perhaps marking their end as pirate bases. More importantly, all along the south coast there were massive cities such as Hierapytna, Inatos and Suia whose wealth was derived principally from the east-west trade carried by ships forced by the prevailing winds to use this route.

CHAPTER 3: THE ECONOMY

The basis of all ancient economies was agriculture, and in the Mediterranean area the staple crops were cereals, especially wheat and barley, the olive and the vine. The evidence for their cultivation in Roman Crete depends on the depiction or survival of the equipment used in their processing and on literary evidence, since traces of the actual crops themselves have not yet been recovered from any of the few relevant excavations.

The evidence for cereal cultivation is very poor: there are only two references to Cretan corn; Caesar mentions Pompey getting corn from Crete for his forces [1] and Statius mentions the cornlands of Crete in a passing reference [2]. A couple of millstones have been found at Gazi (9/5) and at Knossos (8/4) where a set of stones for a donkey mill was reused in a wall above the Unexplored Mansion. There is also what is possibly a representation of such a mill on a tombstone from Armacha (6/30). Other tombstones show mattocks and adzes which would have been in general agricultural use. Olive presses are more common (Pl.5), either as parts found accidentally like the orb from a crusher at Amnatos (14/16) or complete in their building as at Ayia Triadha (11/3). For the vine and its products there is even less evidence: Pliny the Elder praises a Cretan wine called *passum* [3] as a medicinal drink when mixed with poppy seed, and Athenaeus [4] discusses a Cretan cake called Glykinas made of grape-syrup and olive oil.

The evidence for the cultivation of fruit and nuts is derived from the same two sources; Athenaeus mentions Cretan recipes using walnuts, filberts, almonds and sesame while Pliny praises Cretan palms, quince and the extra large Cyprian fig. The latter also mentions several medicinal herbs exported from Crete including anise, 'goat-thorn' and certain seaweeds. Most of the evidence for domestic animals is also literary or epigraphic: the Diktynnaion temple accounts [5] reveal the hire of sheep and cattle and the sale of cheese and wool. Pliny also mentions the use of Cretan seaweed and sponge extract for cloth dying and it is probable that the cloth industry was important. Loomweights are commonly found and there is also one tombstone from Gras (1/8) that may show a distaff and spindle. Bees were also kept, for Pliny praises them for their productivity both in terms of actual honey and the comb as well. Their wax he rates as second best to the Pontus variety.

There is also one bone report to supplement this secondary evidence; the report reveals cattle, pigs and goats all present at Knossos [6] as well as dogs, hare and deer. These animals prove the existence of hunting and indeed the Cretan hunting dog was, and is, famous for its strength and agility [7]. Fishing was also practised [8] and at Siteia (1/12), Mochlos (1/1) and Chersonisos (6/7) fish tanks have been found, linked by channels to the sea [9].

The organisation of agriculture in Roman Crete is obscure; there is very little direct evidence about land tenure and even when it is possible to detect coherent settlement patterns [10] the information is of little or no use in ascertaining the legal status of the landholders. Throughout the entire period there are obviously flourishing urban sites, vill-

---

1. Caesar, *De Bello Civili* V.I.
2. *Silvae* II.6.66-7.
3. *NH*.14.81. Other refs. to Crete passim. Pliny in this chapter always means the Elder.
4. Deipnosophistae XIV.645. Other refs. passim.
5. *IC*.II.XI.3.
6. M. Jarman and J. N. Coldstream, *Knossos, The Sanctuary of Demeter, BSA* Suppl. Vol.8 (London, 1973), p.177.
7. Aelian, *De Nat. Anim.* III.2.
8. *Ibid.* VII.300.
9. *ABSA* LIII-LIV, 1958-9, p.264, on these and fish tanks in general.
10. See chapter 2.

ages or farms and even a few villas. Often there are comparatively few sites near the larger settlements and this may indicate that the surrounding land was farmed by the townsfolk. In other areas farms and villages indicate the continuing existence of a peasantry of uncertain status, but there are a number of tombstones with reliefs from such sites indicating that certain of these people had a degree of wealth; possibly this is evidence for freeholders as opposed to farmers of tenant status. At the opposite end of the scale, the only evidence for *latifundia* are the postulated estates covering the central area of the Mesara plain. There are other substantial rural sites, particularly in the later period, e.g. in the Amari valley, but the composition of the presumed estates of these villas is not known.

Whether or not the Emperor had land in Crete is not known but his procurator was active by the mid 1c AD, settling land disputes[11], and this may be an indication that there were Imperial estates in his jurisdiction. Other 'foreign' landowners included the *colonia* of Capua, granted land worth HS 1,200,000 by Octavian in 36 BC[12]. Inevitably, later on a boundary dispute broke out between Capua and an inhabitant of the *colonia* at Knossos, Cn. Plotius Plebeius, which was settled by the procurator on behalf of Domitian in AD 84[13]. Another foreign landowner was Flavius Ursus whose lands in Crete Statius records[14]. However, the bulk of Cretan land was no doubt owned by the islanders themselves, either as individuals or corporately by the cities or shrines[15]. Boundary inscriptions of public lands are known from the territory of Arcades[16] and Hierapytna[17]. Further west there are inscriptions[18] from the area of Pyranthos concerning the restoration of public lands of Gortyna squatted on by private persons. This clearance was carried out by the proconsul L. Turpilius Dexter on the authority of Nero and the Senate in AD 63. In earlier periods these public lands must have been vital in maintaining the public messes, the Syssitia or Andreia, that were the basis for the social organisation of the cities[19]. By the later Hellenistic period these messes seem to have disappeared and the public lands probably lost their importance and drifted into private hands until the Roman conquest brought new pressures in the form of imperial taxation. Some of the land must have been owned by the smaller landowners or peasants, often holding parcels of lands in various places in the general area of the settlement like the modern peasant farmer. There are two inscriptions listing such plots[20] but unfortunately both records are fragmentary and neither the amount of land nor the number of plots can be made out. The proportions of land held by all these different organisations or individuals cannot be ascertained.

By comparison with agriculture the various industries known from Roman Crete were probably of little importance and produced nearly entirely for local demand. The island is comparatively rich in minerals and ores[21] but the only ones known to have been exploited in this period were copper and possibly gold in the west of the island, where mines are known at Kantanos (19/10), Kampanos (19/15) and Sklavopoula (19/6): only the first seems to have been of any size. There are no particularly fine stones on the island but it is obvious that there must have been numerous local quarries to supply local demand. The only specialised quarries were not for building material but for whetstones: these were exported, for the Digest[22] contains strict instructions about periods when vessels carrying whetstones were allowed to sail. This entry does not mention the site of the quarries but the existence of whetstone quarries below Mount Oxa (3/9) above the excellent port of Olus (3/7) from which whetstones were still being shipped in the last century[23] makes it virtually certain that it is with these quarries that the regulations were concerned.

In the same area today there are still salt pans: Pliny mentions this method of salt production as being used on Crete[24] although as yet there are no such pans known from the island that can be shown to be of Roman date. Another industry that is even more elusive but must also have been of great importance was the production of timber. Both Vitruvius[25] and Pliny[26] praise Cretan cedar and cypress and from these sources it does seem that there was an export trade in these commodities. Another local result of building was a new demand for tiles or bricks to

---

11. E.g. *IC.* I. VIII. 49.
12. Dio xlix.4. Vell. Pat. 2.81.
13. *BCH* XCIII, 1969, p.846.
14. *Op. cit.* note 2.
15. See p.39 for the latter.
16. *IC.* I. V. II, 44-5.
17. *IC.* III. III. 62-3.
18. *IC.* I. XXVI. 2.
19. See R. F. Willetts, *Aristocratic Society in Ancient Crete* (London, 1955), p.252. Strabo X.4-16.
20. *IC.* IV. 337-8.
21. P. Faure, *Rev. Arch.* 1966, p.45-78.
22. *Dig.* 39.4.15. Pliny also mentions Cretan whetstones as of the highest quality - *NH.* 36.164.
23. Spratt I, p.122.
24. Pliny *NH.* 31.81.
25. Vitruvius II. 9. 13-14.
26. *NH.* 16.197.

face concrete: there are very few stamped tiles known but from Zaro (10/1), Gortyna (10/10) and Lebena (10/23) there are tiles from the same factory, of Lucius Felix[27], and there are further tiles, stamped MAP from Gortyna[28]. Their distribution should imply a site somewhere on the Mesara, presumably resulting from the need for the product at the capital. Evidence for the related pottery industry is scarce with only three known Roman kilns, at Platanos (10/14), Knossos (8/4) and Kalochorio (3/17): only the latter has actually been excavated and unfortunately could not be closely dated; it seems to have been part of a larger complex producing the common rilled cooking pots.

Lamps were made locally and some may even have been exported, for there is a specific type of 1c AD date found in the Knossos area[29] which has also been found at Sidi Krebish, Benghazi[30]. Terracotta figurines are common and two moulds of Augustan date, one of Heracles and the lion and the other of an actor, were found above the Unexplored Mansion, Knossos[31]. In the same excavations glass waste and mould fragments were found and other sites, notably in the area of modern Kantanos (19/10) have produced glass slag[32]. Other small localised industries are best illustrated by the excavations at Knossos where unfinished bone objects, iron slag etc. show a predictable range of activity.

Because of this comparative lack of manufacturing and exporting industry it is very difficult to form a true picture of the trade of Roman Crete. It is obvious that apart from the whetstones, timber and a few lamps the bulk of Cretan exports were agricultural, notably herbs and spices. There is only one reference to corn being exported and that was under the exceptional circumstances of the Civil Wars.

Manufactured imports are easier to identify; the commonest class of material is fine pottery which was imported from all over the Mediterranean, although the most important factories were probably to the east. In the 1c BC the most important ware was Eastern Sigillata A ('Pergamene Ware') and to a lesser extent Eastern Sigillata B, but towards the end of the century and up to the mid 1c AD Arretine Ware also took a large part of the market[33]. In the 2c Çandarli Ware dominated the market and continued to do so until replaced by Late Roman C and African Red Slip Ware in the 4-5c. Of these two LRC seems to have taken most of the Cretan market, in particular with the bowl Form 3 which is the commonest identifiable form on all sites of the later period. Other lesss important wares include, in the early period, thin-walled Italian wares such as Aco beakers, a little Gaulish Samian, Pompeian Red Ware, Koan Ware and Cypriot Sigillata. In the later period there is less variety but the later Cypriot wares are found, especially at Itanos.

Although glass was manufactured in Crete, much was imported from the great eastern factories and only a little from the west. Some Italian amphorae are also known but the bulk of these vessels and therefore their contents come from the Aegean, with Koan, Knidian and Rhodian common. Off Matala (11/8) a wreck with a cargo of the latter vessels has been found. Later, ribbed amphorae are common but their source is unknown. Locally produced lamps were supplemented by others imported from Italy, Africa and Ionia, the latter being apparently the most important source. Several stamped examples of Gamos and Preimos are known[34].

Another very obvious import was marble. Sometimes it was brought in as finished articles, as for instance statues like the numerous Hadrians probably made in Attica, sometimes in part-worked form. There are a number of sarcophagi, either Attic or Asiatic, and one Italian example in Luna marble[35] (Pl.8-10). This is the most easterly one of its type known and must have been extremely expensive. Like the commoner Attic and Asiatic examples it is not quite finished, as one end is quite rough and the other nearly completed. Similarly, many of the decorated architectural fragments are in Proconnesian marble and were probably completed on site, although there is no definite evidence for this. Numerous marble columns are scattered over the sites, coming from quarries in Euboea (pink and white columns at the Villa Dionysus, Knossos), specifically Carystus (Gortyna), and the Proconnesian area: there

---

27. *IC.* I.XXXI.10, XVII.58-9, *IC.* IV.526-7.
28. *IC.* IV.531.
29. Discussed, K. Wardle, 'Two Notes from Knossos', *ABSA* LXVII, 1972, p.274.
30. Information from P. M. Kenrick. J. Riley also informs me that there may be amphorae from Crete here.
31. *AR.* 1972-3, p.68.
32. Displayed in the Chania Museum. For Hellenistic glass manufacture in the area see G. Weinberg, 'Glass Manufacture in Ancient Crete', *Journal of Glass Studies* I, 1959, p.11.
33. The best available reports are those on the recent work at Knossos, note 31, and J. Hayes, 'Four Early Roman groups from Knossos', *ABSA* LXVI, 1971, p.249-276. Other evidence collated from my field work.
34. E.g. *IC.* I.XII.6, *IC.* I.VIII.42, *IC.* IV.540.
35. The section on marble and the identification of the Euboean example owes much to discussion with J. Ward-Perkins and his Shuffrey Memorial Lectures, Lincoln College, 1976. See also chapters on Architecture and Art.

are also many in both the red and grey Egyptian granites. All these imports point to a busy traffic between Crete and the Greek mainland and perhaps even more so across to Asia Minor, but the most important sea route of the early Empire, between Egypt and Italy, ran past the southern coast of the island, via the southern coast of Asia Minor. This was the route taken by St. Paul and, more importantly for trade, by the corn fleet, one of whose ships, the Isopharia, was driven in to Phoenix where its steersman put up a dedication[36]. This corn route and its attendant trade brought great wealth to the cities of the south coast as is best shown by the city on the now desolate Kouphonisi Islands (1/31) and such cities as Suia (19/17). Even when the Egyptian corn fleet was switched to Constantinople, the use of this route for east-west trade seems to have continued, for those cities which must have derived their wealth from trade continued to flourish at least into the 7c.

In the Roman period as today Crete's main wealth must have been derived from agriculture which produced not only for its own consumption but also for export. Much of its other needs could also be supplied from the island's own resources, but fine manufactured goods seem to have been imported to a large degree from the nearest available sources; these often lay somewhere along the Asia Minor coast. Perhaps the most important effect of trade was on the southern coast cities, some of which must have relied on it for their wealth, if not their existence.

Pl. 5: Olive press at Olus.

36. Acts 2.7. and *IC.* II.XX.7.

CHAPTER 4: RELIGION

Pagan

Although there are no temples that survive in Crete above their foundations, the importance of the gods and goddesses is shown by the number of dedications and literary references to them: since this evidence has been recently thoroughly discussed[1] it will not be necessary to repeat the detail here, but rather examine the general results and the archaeological evidence which, with the exception of cave and peak sanctuaries [2], has not been adequately dealt with.

There is evidence for the worship of all the principal inhabitants of Mount Olympos, the most popular members by number of dedications being Zeus (18), Asklepios (18), Artemis (11), Hermes (6) and Kore/Persephone (5). This popularity rating is not purely accidental as the two goddesses and Zeus have strong Cretan connections. According to the myths Zeus was born on Crete and several of the inscriptions call him Zeus Cretagenes; on others he has the epithet of his birthplace, Diktaios; and there are also dedications to the guardians of his infancy, the Kouretes, including of course the famous hymn. Also, to the disgust of general educated opinion in the ancient world, the Cretans insisted that the island also contained the tomb of Zeus at Mount Iuktas (8/9). This Zeus is obviously not quite the same as the mainland father figure but rather a syncretism of him and another earlier, presumably Minoan, deity who may have been less important than his female counterpart.

This goddess also survived into the Roman period in various guises: Zeus' classical wife was probably less important in this respect than figures such as Artemis, Diktynna and Britomartis. The latter is definitely a Cretan goddess and Diktynna may be also. Other popular goddesses in Crete who were strongly linked to Nature were Demeter and Kore, but perhaps the most honoured of all was Eileithyia, goddess of childbirth, who was commonly worshipped in caves, as at Inatos (7/31) and most famously at Amnissos (6/2).

This evidence shows that as in the rest of the Greek world, the worship of the traditional deities continued in their temples and caves. In Crete there were perhaps slightly more indigenous divinities than normal, but it is hard to judge the degree of continuity from pre-Greek, Minoan, religion. Diktynna may have Minoan origins but is also known known outside the island [3]: her counterpart Britomartis has a Minoan name meaning 'sweet maiden'[4]. Other possible traces of Minoan cults may be seen in words used on a 2c AD sacrificial inscription[5] such as 'siakuka' and 'parelain': these words are not used simply for historical interest, for their prices are quoted in contempary denarii. Unfortunately it is not known which deity is involved.

The only foreign cult of any importance was that of Isis and Serapis; this was introduced into Crete as into the rest of the Greek world in the Hellenistic period [6]. Its spread was closely linked to Ptolemaic influence, so it is not surprising to find dedications to Isis in her guise as Fortuna Primigenia at Itanos (1/39) which once had a Ptolemaic

---

1. R. F. Willetts, *Cretan Cults and Festivals* (London, 1962). F. Dunand, *Le culte d'Isis dans le bassin oriental de la Méditerranée* II (Leiden, 1973). W. Hornbostel, *Sarapis* (Leiden, 1973). G. J. F. Kater-Sibbes, *A Preliminary Catalogue of Sarapis Monuments* (Leiden, 1973). G. J. F. Kater-Sibbes and M. Vermaseren, *Apis* II (Leiden, 1975).
2. P. Faure, *Fonctions des cavernes crétoises* (Paris, 1964).
3. Willetts, *op.cit.* n.1, p.184-5.
4. *Ibid.* p.179 - Hesychius.
5. *IC.* I.V.23.
6. Dunand, *op.cit.* n.1, p.73f.

Egyptian garrison [7], and at Gortyna (10/10) where two early dedications were made by mercenaries [8], at least one of whom served the Ptolemies. Inscriptions from the ports of Chersonisos [9] (6/7) and Olus [10] (3/7) illustrate the main method of cultural transmission in the peaceful days of the Empire: via trade. In this period temples are known at Gortyna [11], Poikilassos[12] (16/1) and Amnissos[13] (6/2); dedications at Lasea[14] (10/25), Soulia[15] (15/16) and Phoenix [16] (16/5); other finds from Hierapytna [17] (2/8) and Lappa[18] (14/1); a head of Serapis and a figurine of Serapis enthroned from the Idaean Cave [19] (13/20). The bulk of these places are ports, most of them on the southern coast, lying along the trade route from Egypt and the east to Rome. The importance of this trade in the diffusion of the cult is most clearly illustrated by the inscription from Phoenix:

IOVI SOLI OPTIMO MAXIMO
SARAPIDI ET OMNIBUS DIIS ET
IMPERATORI CAESARI NERVAE
TRAIANO AUG GERMANICO DACICO N
EPICTETUS LIBERTUS TABELLARIUS
CURAM AGENTE OPERIS DIONYSIO SOSTRA
TI FILIO ALEXANDRINO GUBERNATORE
NAVIS PARASEMO ISOPHARIA T CL THEONIS

This dedication was set up by the helmsman, an Alexandrian, of a ship called the Isopharia to Jupiter Sol Serapis as well as to the other gods and Trajan: it is most likely that this was one of the cornships calling, or rather driven, into one of the ports on the southern coast of Crete[21]. The syntheism displayed in the inscription is common and there are other associations of Serapis and Zeus/Jupiter from Crete, for example at Amnissos and Lebena [22]. The latter inscription also connects Asklepios with the other two. There is also one instance of Isis being linked to another goddess, Artemis [23].

From the surviving evidence it seems that Serapis was a more popular divinity in Crete than his consort Isis, though he appears often not by himself but together with Zeus whose iconography, especially as Zeus Cretagenes, is very similar to that of Serapis. This comparative lack of enthusiasm for Isis may perhaps be explained by the existence in Crete of its own strong traditions of a Mother Goddess who was not sufficiently close to Isis to effect a syncretism, as occured with her half-Greek husband.

Of other foreign cults, there are possible traces of Gnosticism for a few gems and plaques[24] and the suggestion of a cult of Cybele, if the identification of a head from Chersonisos as one of her eunuch priests can be accepted [25].

These foreign cults offering hope of an existence beyond death answered a religious need: it may be doubted whether the imperial cult was as much a religious phenomenon as a political one. No temple that can definitely be identified as of the imperial cult has yet been found but there is sufficient epigraphic, numismatic and literary evidence to demonstrate its existence. Possibly the earliest reference is a fragmentary inscription from Gortyna[26]; all that survives is . . . .] ET AUG[. . . . but it is recorded that a statue of a female with mural crown was found at the

7. *IC.*III.IV.14. Also S. Spyridakis, *Ptolemaic Itanos and Hellenistic Crete* (Berkeley, 1970), p.99f.
8. *IC.*IV.243-4.
9. *IC.*I.VII.3.
10. *IC.*I.XXII.II.
11. See p.73.
12. *IC.*II.XXI.1.
13. See p.144.
14. *IC.*I.XV.2.
15. *IC.*II.XXV.4.
16. *IC.*II.XX.7.
17. See p.47.
18. Hornbostel, *op.cit.* n.1, p.241.
19. Kater-Sibbes, Catalogue, *op.cit.* n.1, p.58, no.343.
20. Cf. Seneca, *Ep.* 77.1 for this use of Tabellarius.
21. The best parallels for the form of the dedication to Jupiter Sarapis come from Jerusalem with a dedication by the III Cyrenaica - the old Alexandrian garrison - to IOM Sarapis (Trajanic). From Italy there is a dedication of 127 to Jupiter Sol Sarapis. L. Vidman, *Sylloge Inscriptionum religionis Isiacae et Serapideae,* nos.362, 523.
22. *IC.*I.XVII.27.
23. *IC.*II.XXV.4.
24. *IC.*I.V.3 (a gem), *IC.*I.XII.8 (plaque).
25. See p.50.
26. *IC.*IV.270.

same spot. It would seem very likely that this was a statue of Roma whose joint cult with Augustus was common in his own lifetime. Once he was safely dead and deified games were established in his divine honour[27]; coins were minted with his head radiate by most of the cities of Crete that were issuing coins under Tiberius and the first issues of the Provincial Council dating to the reign of Caligula showed Augustus radiate on the obverse. This issue with its seven stars also seems to have linked Zeus Cretagenes, the father figure of the island, with Augustus, father of the Empire[28]. The issues of Cydonia showing the radiate Augustus have on the reverse a hexastyle temple which may represent the actual shrine [29]. The cult rapidly became well established and early in Tiberius' reign [30] the Cretans were claiming the right of asylum for Augustus' image. The latest evidence for his cult is a mention of a *sacerdos* of the divine Augustus in 195 [31].

Tiberius was not deified but there is a dedication to his *numen et providentia* on the occasion of Seianus' downfall [32] : from the *colonia* at Knossos there are references [33] to the deified Claudius and a tombstone of a man who was *aedituus, flamen divi Vespasiani, duovir* and finally *patronus* of the *colonia.* This career illustrates the prestige and cost of these priesthoods and so their limitation to the highest of the local aristocracy. Vespasian's eldest son Titus was posthumously venerated at Lyttus [34] though Domitian failed to become an immortal because of a decision of the senators whose mortality he had so often proved. Trajan's cult is commemorated at Gortyna[35] but there is also a dedication to his *fortuna*, put up in his lifetime by the city of Arcades [36]. Of the succeeding Emperors there are records of the celebration of the birthdays of Antoninus Pius, Faustina [37] and Marcus Aurelius [38], and dedications to Lucius Verus [39] and Septimius Severus [40] as θεῖος, probably during their lifetimes.

Of the actual organisation of the cult comparatively little is known: the main cult was based on the Provincial Council, the Koinon, which had an annually appointed Archiereus at its head. Only five of these men are known, dating from the first to the third centuries [41]. The site of the principal temple at Gortyna, the capital, is not known but was probably either near that of Pythian Apollo (from which area came the evidence for the cult of Rome and Augustus) or in the Agora (from which came several of the relevant inscriptions and the group of imperial heads[42]). The latter do however include imperial personages who were not deified, such as Caligula. The last of the inscriptions from this place seems to indicate that the Roman citizens at Gortyna were organised into their own body which had a separate cult of the Emperor. The only other city that definitely had its own cult centre was the *colonia* at Knossos: there are two inscriptions, one mentioning a Sonteius Casina who was *sacerdos div. Aug. quater*[43], the other of a man who had been *flamen div. Vespasiani* [44].

The career of the last man clearly shows how these priesthoods fitted into their public careers and there are other recorded Cretan careers including priesthoods other than those of the imperial cults which were also held as part of the *cursus honorum*[45]. There are a few inscriptions which may record genuine professional priests; these include a certain Panares, priest of Zeus and Hera of Olympos, Phoibe, priestess of an unknown god[47] and possibly Tryphera, priestess of Artemis[48]. Although a single individual, possibly not even full-time, would have sufficed for a small country shrine like Kato Simi (5/9), some of the temples had extensive lands and property needing full-time

27. *IG.* XII.i.77, 13 (Rhodes).
28. M. J. Price, 'Elephants in Crete?: New Light on a Cistophorus of Caligula', *Acts of the 3rd Cretological Congress* I, p.279 (Athens, 1973).
29. Svoronos II, pl.X, no.17, 18 etc.
30. Tacitus, *Annales,* III.63, AD 22.
31. *IC.* IV.278.
32. *IC.* IV.272.
33. *IC.* I.VIII.49, 54.
34. *IC.* I.XVIII.15.
35. *IC.* IV.278.
36. *IC.* I.V.9.
37. *IC.* I.VII.10.
38. *IC.* IV.300.
39. *IC.* IV.277.
40. *IC.* IV.279.
41. *IC.* IV.275, 305, 306A, 330. *IC.* III.IX.10.
42. *IC.* IV.269 . . . to sacrum, 272 Numen et Providentia Tiberii, 278 dedication to Severus in 195 by the priests of the Imperial Cult. See p.48 for the heads.
43. *IC.* IV.295.
44. *IC.* I.VIII.54.
45. *IC.* I.VIII.58. Lucanus, an aedituus. *IC.* IV.443. Pontifex son of a M. Antonius.
46. *IC.* II.XXV.3, 1c BC.
47. *IC.* III.III.45, 2c AD.
48. *A. Delt.* XXII.3, 1967, p.488.

staff. Evidence for sacred lands comes from an inscription from Knossos which refers to five *iugera* of land [49] which Aesculapius seems to have had difficulty retaining, and probably a similar situation occasioned the inscription from the temple of Zeus Skyllios at Rhytion[50] of AD 120, when Hadrian settled a matter which had caused trouble since the conquest.

However, the best evidence for the wealth of a deity is associated with Diktynna. First there are five 2c inscriptions from Gortyna [51], Viran Episkopi [52] (13/2) and the area of the Diktynnaion itself[53] (20/29) which all record the use of the sacred wealth for public works carried out by the imperial procurator or the governor. It is not clear whether all the money came from the one great shrine or whether there were subsidiary shrines with their own treasuries [54], but it is obvious that the extent of the wealth was considerable and that by the 2c it was controlled by the imperial authorities. This wealth must have had two principal sources; offerings made to the goddess, and revenue derived from its land and possessions. It is very fortunate that an inscription of 6 BC survives, detailing part of the temple accounts [55]. At this date the revenues were not part of the provincial finances, for all the accounts were to be written down only in the books held by the Council at Polyrrhenia and at the shrine itself; there is no indication in the fragment that the provincial authorities had any power at all at this date over Diktynna's wealth. The accounts list the hiring out of slaves, including craftsmen like Onasiphorus the potter, and also of animals. The men to whom these were leased included Roman citizens, likely to be men of some standing, possible Italians like Publius Sergius, and others possibly of Cretan origin like G. Volumnius Diogenes. The accounts also list the sale of wool and cheese and the purchase of wine and oil for the temple attendants, the Neokoroi. Between this list and the evidence of the 2c there is also the story of Apollonius of Tyana's visit here in the mid 1c[56] when he was locked up as a suspected robber on the grounds that the ferocious dogs guarding the treasure had not barked at him!

The only other shrine of comparable size was that of Asklepios at Lebena, but apart from one inscription [57] of 3-4c date put up by Vedius Alkisthenes the *advocatus fisci et sacrii aerarii* nothing is known of its secular administration. However, the surviving buildings do include a treasury and what are probably guest accomodation for the sick and/or devout, who even came across from Africa according to the account in Apollonius' *Life* [58].

The remaining temples fall into roughly three classes. First there were those in the cities and towns acting as the religious centres for their communities such as the temple of Pythian Apollo at Gortyna (10/10) or that of Athena Polias at Itanos (1/39). Many of these temples were basically Archaic buildings, sometimes rebuilt or extended in the Hellenistic period, again such as that of Pythian Apollo, but often still in their simple original form like the Acropolis temple at Gortyna[59] or those at Palaiokastro (1/37), Dreros (3/6), Praesos (1/22) and Prinias (9/16). There are also a number of late Hellenistic temples such as the temple of Pan at Hyrtakina (19/14) or that of Asklepios at Lissos (19/18). The number of new Roman temples is small when compared to the building activity in other sectors but includes the second temple at Mavropapas, Gortyna, of 2-3c date, the temple of Artemis at Soulia (15/16) of the 1-2c and the new Serapeia at Gortyna and Poikilassos (16/1). It is however noticeable that there are very few known temples of Classical date or of the conventional Greek form of pronaos, cella and opisthodomos; of the latter there are only the temple of Hellenistic or Roman date at Axos (13/16), and (probably) the Diktynnaion.

The second group consists of a number of small shrines in the countryside. The most important of these is the one to Hermes and Aphrodite at Kato Simi (5/9) which really does seem to have been in continual use from the Minoan period to the 3c AD. There are other small shrines known, to Pan at Pateraki (3/11) and to Artemis at Kamilari (11/5) and at Afrati (6/36). These are all of Hellenistic date, a period when there seems to have been a revival in religious activity which did not in all cases last into the Roman period: for instance, the shrine to Zeus Velchanos at Ayia Triadha (11/3) seems to have been abandoned by the time of the Roman conquest. The basic function of these shrines was as small rural religious centres but at least the one to Ares and Aphrodite at Ellinika (3/9) seems to have been deliberately built on the border between Olus and Lato. This leads to the third class of temple, where there is

---

49. *IC.* I. VIII. 49.
50. *IC.* I. XXIX. 1.
51. *IC.* IV. 333, 334.
52. *AE* 1962, 129.
53. *IC.* II. XI. 5, 6.
54. See p.162 for the possible temple at Viran Episkopi.
55. *IC.* II. XI. 3.
56. Philostratus, *Life of Apollonius* VIII. 30.
57. *IC.* I. XVII. 27.
58. *Op. cit.* note 56, IV. 34.
59. This temple may have had a sub-Minoan predecessor, for there are buildings of this date below it.

a decided 'practical' function of the shrine besides its religious aspect. The most important of these are the coastal temples which also served as navigation points; these include the Diktynnaion (20/29), Athena's sanctuary at the Samnonium Point (1/40) and possibly the (putative) temple to Britomartis on the Kastri at Chersonisos (6/7). The *Stadiasmus Maris Magni* mentions the first two as distinguishing marks, and also the temple to Apollo at Agneion (20/1) which has not yet been found. Whether some of these sites were deliberately chosen to aid navigation or became important navigation points simply because of their physical prominence is impossible to decide.

The final class of places of worship is not a building at all but the cave. Crete is justifiably renowned for its religious grottoes and there can be no doubt of their importance, although there has been a tendency to identify ritual caves on very slender evidence. Nevertheless the sanctity in the Roman period of caves such as Psykhro (4/16), Amnissos (6/2), Patsos (12/12) (to Hermes), Melidoni (13/11) and the Idaean Cave (13/20) cannot be doubted. Amongst these natural religious sites must be placed the only peak sanctuary definitely in use in the Roman period, namely the Tomb of Zeus on Mount Iuktas (8/9).

Although archaeology has not revealed any great sanctuaries to awe the eye of the present day beholder, there can be no doubt of the importance of the various cults in the early Roman period in Crete. The epigraphic evidence shows the normal range of divinities but, with the exception of Isis and Serapis, there is a decided preference for Cretan deities. This conservatism is also reflected in the architecture, as so many date back to the Archaic period and two possibly into the Minoan. Continuity of worship in the caves is very difficult to prove without material of a definitely religious character from every period: such places would always have attracted attention even if their previous religious connotations were not known.

Burial Customs

No definite evidence survives from Roman Crete for any practice except inhumation in tombs of three basic types[60]. The commonest and obviously by far the cheapest was the cist or slab grave, simply made up of a stone-lined and stone-covered pit. Such graves are common from all over the island right through the Hellenistic and Roman periods, particularly in the later, Christian, period. Normally these graves were for individuals only but more elaborate ones are known from Gortyna, consisting of up to six graves contained within stone and tile walls forming four parallel compartments with a further unit at right angles at each end. This particular example was dated by its grave goods to the early 3c: a similar but probably later tomb is known from Pobia (10/12).

The other simple and equally ubiquitous type of burial was the tile grave where tiles instead of stones were the material used to build the same type of grave. These too were normally used for individuals, but again like the slab graves, Gortyna has produced a tomb with six compartments which now forms the crypt of the church of the Ayioi Deka. These multiple tombs were presumably family graves but are unusual and not found outside the Mesara; yet even here the chamber tomb was commoner in this role, as it was over the rest of the island. Unlike the previous types these tombs do not seem to have continued in use once Christianity had become established, by the end of the 4c. One possible factor here might have been their expense as compared to the others, but the change of religion must have been the decisive point. The finest group of chamber tombs are those at Matala (11/8) (Fig.7) where there are very large numbers cut into the soft rock of the cliffs around the site. There are three types of chamber tomb, all with arcosolia, again of three basic types. The basic tomb types are first, plain rectangular chambers with arcosolia on all sides except that with the entrance; secondly, a type with an ante-room with arcosolia on either side and a third in the rear wall of the second chamber; thirdly, a type with side chambers to the ante-room which therefore has no room for arcosolia. The number of arcosolia per tomb does vary slightly from the norm described above, but they are all cut into the rock of the wall and are either rectangular, semicircular, or semicircular with 'head' and 'feet' rests: all may have further small niches cut into their walls.

These types of chamber tomb are found all over the island, although again slight variations are known from Gortyna where three tombs exist built of tile and stone with vaulted roofs, not cut into rock but below ground. The niches here have been taken as evidence for possible cremations and in one of the examples where the niches were not in the arcosolia but by the door a clay jar which could have been a cinerary urn was found [61] (Fig.8). Possibly this was the tomb of one of the numerous Italian immigrants known to have been settled at Gortyna from the 1c BC.

---

60. See the Gazetteer entry for detailed references, by site.
61. Taramelli, *AJA* VI, 1902, p.162.

Fig. 7: Matala: three standard types of rock-cut chamber tomb.

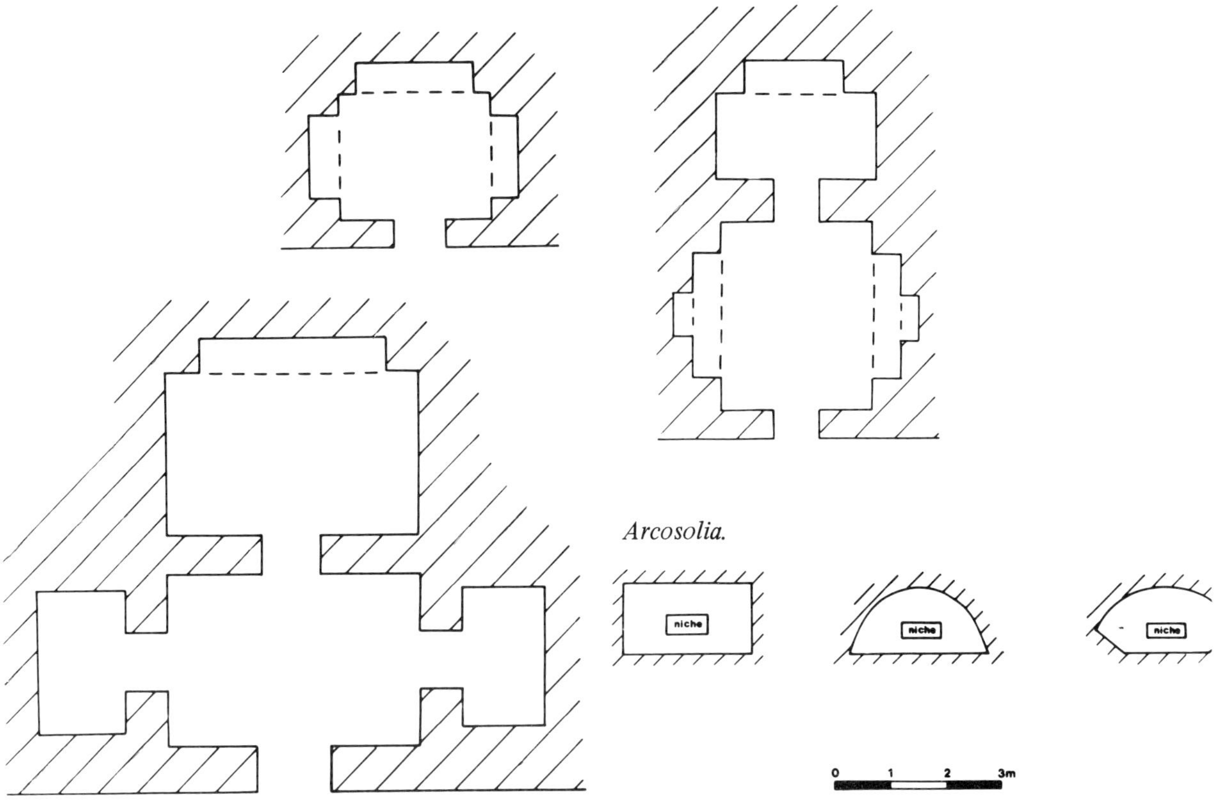

Other niches in arcosolia have also been found in tombs with definite inhumations as at Knossos and are most likely to have been for lamps or figurines. No trace of a wooden coffin has yet been found but sarcophagi were used, although as yet none have been found definitely in their original tomb [62] .

Other variants of the chamber tomb include a stuccoed one from Asi Gonia (17/18) of which unfortunately no other details are known, and the so-called Hypogaea from Cydonia (18/18) (Fig.9). These are basically parallel chambers set on either side of an elevated passageway approached by a long dromos. The type obviously resembles the multiple tomb that ultimately developed into the catacombs of Italy, but the Cretan examples more closely

Fig.8: Gortyna: underground built chamber tomb.

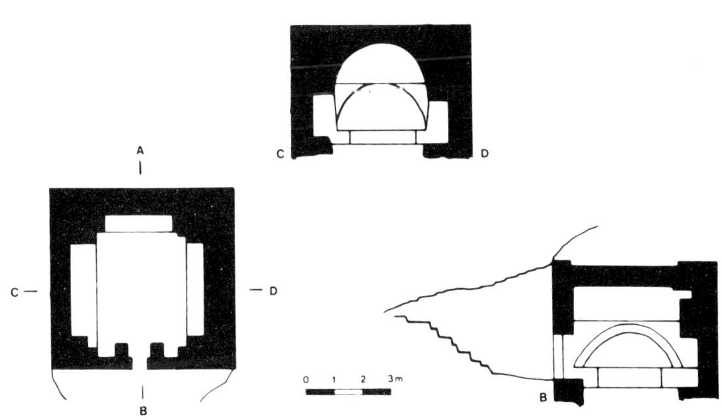

After Taramelli.

62. See p.90 for the sarcophagi.

resemble the hypogaea from the Eastern Empire, e.g. at Palmyra [63]. However these are far more complex and it may be better to view these examples as a local variant of the chamber tomb rather like the multiple chamber tombs of Hellenistic Melos[64]. The 1c BC date of the Cretan examples is also comparable.

Fig. 9: Cydonia: smaller hypogeion.

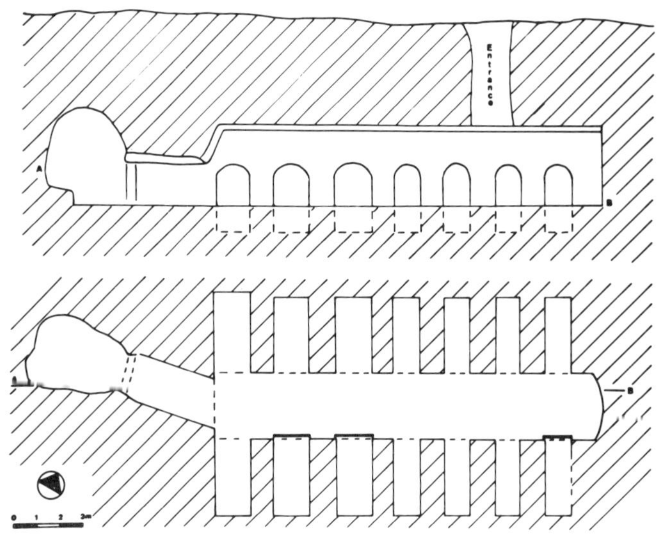

Section.

Plan.

One type of tomb that seems to have a very distinct distribution is the freestanding mausoleum constructed of stone or concrete; as yet these are known only from Knossos [65], dating to the 4-5c. This may be a false distribution caused by the extensive excavation of the cemeteries at Knossos. However, the other type of freestanding tomb found in Crete seems to have a genuinely limited provenance along the south coast, with examples known from Lasea (10/25), Suia (19/17) and most importantly at Lissos (19/18). The tombs are barrel-vaulted, constructed of rubble masonry with the interior surface covered with thick plaster: most of them stand on built platforms and are about 2 x 3 x 2m high with a narrow doorway and arcosolia built into the three other walls. At Lissos these tombs cover the slopes of the western side of the site, forming an impressive necropolis which has never been excavated or even adequately surveyed (Pl.6, Fig. 10). This type of tomb resembles tombs from Cilicia[66], although the Cretan examples are of the simpler type and the arcosolia are built into the wall and not out into the room as at Anemurium. However the arrangement of the tombs on their terraces at Lissos is similar to the necropolis at Anemurium. In its turn this has been compared to the Isola Sacra cemetery at Ostia where there are similar tombs. However, given their frequency in Cilicia they would seem to be a local type and it would therefore be logical to assume that their presence on the southern coast of Crete, in the trade ports, should indicate Cilicians in Crete. The problem with this theory is the lack of foreign names on the tombstones from these sites and the ubiquity of the tomb type, for instance at Lissos, an undoubtedly Cretan city. Until proper survey and excavation has been carried out it is not possible to decide how these Cretan tombs really relate to the others.

Of the tombstones known from Roman Crete, most are simple dedications to the dead person by the husband, wife or children. A few are more ambitious, with poems about the dead and their fate, such as the tribute to Mattia of Cydonia [67]. Others were more concerned about violation of the tomb and had the appropriate curses invoking the aid of the underworld divinities carved on their tombstone [68]. An informative class of tombstone is that where

---

63. J. M. C. Toynbee, *Death and Burial in the Roman World* (London, 1971), p.223f.
64. L. Ross, *Reisen auf den griechischen Inseln des ägäischen Meeres* III (Stuttgart, 1845), p.10.
65. W. H. C. Frend, 'Excavations of the Basilica Church at Knossos', *ABSA* LVII, 1962, p.209-10. J. N. Coldstream, *The Sanctuary of Demeter at Knossos* (London, 1973) p.17.
66. E. Alföldi-Rosenbaum, *The Necropolis of Anemurium* (Ankara, 1971), p.89.
67. *IC*. II.X.20.
68. *IC*. I.XVIII.64. *IC*. II.XVI.28. This is a lead *defixio* mentioning Pluto, Demeter, Persephone and the Furies.

objects associated with the dead person were carved on the stone; these tend to be standardised, a woman having a basket, mirror and comb, and a man agricultural implements such as a pruning hook, mattock or axe[69]. On one tombstone a double axe appears[70] which may be coincidence or might be symbolic. From the entire Roman period there are only 31 tombstones (for 34 individuals) that mention the age, varying from 1 to 65[71].

Fig. 10. Lissos: built vaulted tomb.

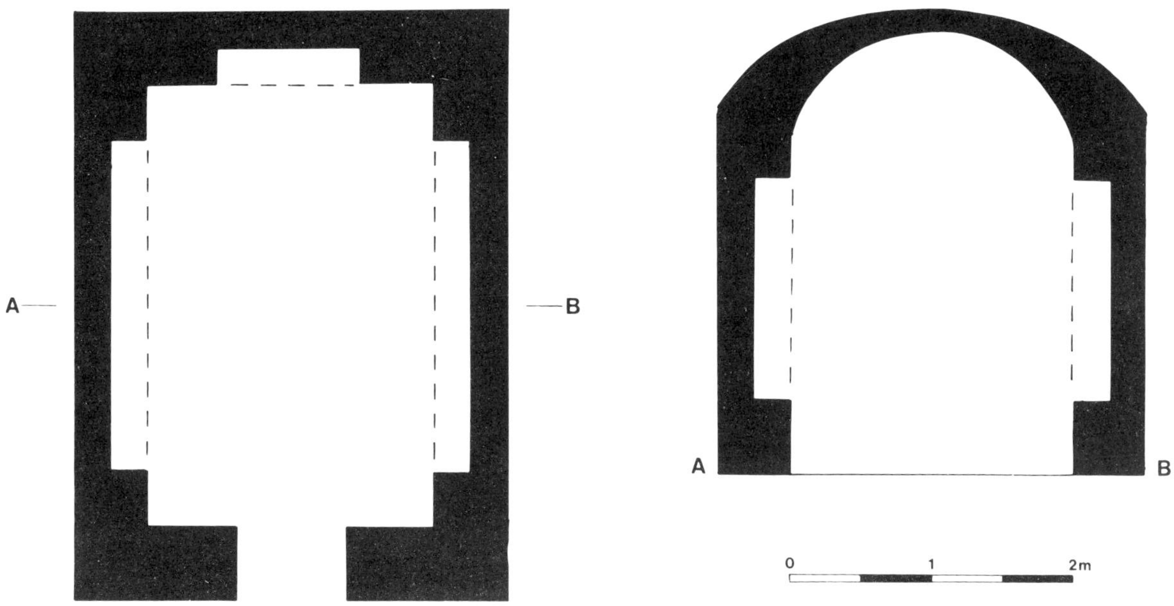

Judaism and Christianity

The existence of Jews in Crete in the Roman period is testified by a small number of inscriptions[72] and some literary references. The inscriptions range in date from the 1c BC to the 5c AD and are all tombstones. One of these[73] includes the only evidence for the organisation of the faith, the dead person, Sophia of Gortyna, being an Elder and leader of the synagogue at Kissamos. The literary references depict a peaceful, rich community, if somewhat gullible: they gave money to an impostor from Sidon who was pretending to be Alexander, son of Herod, in the time of Augustus[74]. In AD 431 they were fooled again when somebody claiming to be Moses walked over a cliff leading many of them to their death[75] and not dry shod to the promised land. Josephus' third wife was a Cretan[76] and at the same period there was no trouble from the Jews in Crete, nor later when Jews in Cyrene revolted in 115.

Certain Cretan Jews were in Jerusalem at Pentecost and were converted to Christianity[77]; these formed the basis for the church in Crete. This was initially organised by Paul who left Titus there as its first bishop[78]. The next evidence for the community comes about a hundred years later in the letter of Dionysus of Corinth recorded by

---

69. E.g. *IC.* I.V.15, *IC.* I.XVIII.66 (Females), *IC.* I.V.13 (Male).
70. *IC.* II.XXIX.5.
71. These figures give the following life expectancies:

At Birth		5 years		15 years		25 years	
M	21	M	23	M	30	M	53
F	18	F	29	F	32	F	41

I would place no reliability on these results because of the minute sample and the general weakness of the method.

72. A. C. Bandy, *The Greek Christian Inscriptions of Crete* (Athens, 1970), Appendix p.140, and *IC.* IV.211 and possibly *IC.* II.XIII.8.
73. Bandy, *op.cit.* n.72, B3.
74. Josephus, *Ant. Jud.* 17.327.
75. Socrates Ecclesiasticus 38. Retailed in the Anglo-Saxon Chronicle for the year!
76. *Vita Josephi* 5.427.
77. Acts 2.11.
78. Letter to Titus. Also T. Detorakes *Οἱ ἅγιοι τῆς πρώτης Βυζαντινῆς περιόδου τῆς Κρήτης* (Athens 1970), p.191.

Pl. 6: Built vaulted tombs at Lissos.
Pl. 7: Tomb in Basilica A, Chersonisos.

Eusebius [79] written to Philip of Gortyna and Pinytus of Knossos. In the letter the phrase is used *τῇ ἐκκλησίᾳ δὲ τῇ παροικούσῃ* Γόρτυναν *ἅμα ταῖς λοιπαῖς κατὰ* Κρήτην *παροικίαις* which shows the pre-eminence of Gortyna, but whether *παροικιαις* should be interpreted as just other Christian communities or more formally as other dioceses is uncertain. Obviously there was at least one other bishop, Pinytus, but if there were more one might have expected them to be named. Physical evidence for Pinytus' congregation has been found, as the cemetery below the Sanatorium basilica at Knossos starts to include what are probably Christian graves at this date [80].

The next evidence for Christianity is the martyrdom of the Ten at Gortyna at the Place of the Threshing Floor on 23rd December 250 for their refusal to worship any other god. The ten beheaded were 5 Gortynians, a Knossiot, a man from Lebena, one from Panormos, one Cydonian and one from Herakleion. The main point of interest is this evidence for the wide spread of Christianity in the island by the mid 3c [81] . The next known martyr is Cyrillus, Bishop of Gortyna and Archbishop of Crete, who was beheaded on 9th July 304[82]: in the same period (although the exact year is unknown) there were the more dubious martyrdoms of Theophilus and his companions (31st March) and the Twelve Soldiers of Crete (12th August)[83].

With the establishment of Christianity as the recognised religion of the Empire the evidence becomes somewhat more reliable. Cretan bishops appeared at the Council of Sardis in 343; they were three in number and came from Hierapytna, Cydonia and Kissamos[84]. These definitely do not include all the bishops since St. Myron was Bishop first of Knossos and then of Gortyna at this period according to his *Lives*, which seem reliable, except perhaps about the unfortunate dragon [85] . There were seven Cretan bishops at the Council of 451; four sees known of before are not among this list, but one, of Apollonia, is only known of here. From the later lists, particularly the Tacticon 1555 A of the early 8c, it seems that the Cretan bishops or their dioceses eventually numbered 12, including the Metropolis of Gortyna with its Archbishop. The 12 were Gortyna, Hierapytna, Chersonisos, Siteia, Arcades, Knossos, Sybrita, Eleutherna, Lappa, Cydonia, Kissamos and Kantanos, thus fairly covering the island with its 70+ churches and probably 24 poleis.

In the late 7c, with St. Andrew of Crete the island had its only really important figure in the early church. After him came the martyrs of the iconoclastic period and at the same time the removal of Crete from the See of Rome to that of Constantinople by Leo's politically motivated reorganisation in 732-3[86]. There is no definite proof, but it would seem likely that Crete had always previously been under the Papal Vicar at Thessalonike[87]. With the Arab conquest Christianity was crushed on the island, but not before it had produced its final martyr of this period in Cyrillus, Bishop of Gortyna [88].

Of the lower orders of the clergy some individuals are recorded on tombstones. Of the lowest order, or readers, there are three examples [89] including Ioannes who was also a *chartularius,* presumably of the church; of the second order, of Psaltes, there is only one example and of the third, under-deacon, two instances; there are also one deacon and two elders known. There is in addition evidence for monasticism with a tombstone of a monk from Gortyna[90], a possible Abbot [91] and mention of a monastery on a tombstone from Lappa [92] .

The majority of the burials from this period seem to have been of the simple cist type, often in association with a church, as for instance at Arvi (5/8) and at Ayia Sophia, Knossos (8/4). However, there were rich commemorative tombs inside the churches, as at Chersonisos basilicas A and B (6/7) (Pl.7). There were also cemeteries some distance from known churches, such as the osteotheke with 36 secondary interments found at the Fortetsa turn at Knossos[93]. The tombstones normally bear a cross and tend to have more information than pagan tombstones about the age of the deceased and date of death, given by the day, month and indiction year.

79. *Hist. Ecc.* IV.21. Detorakes *op.cit.* note 78, p.46, 50.
80. Frend, *op.cit.* note 65. From the report it does not seem really possible to prove that these graves are Christian.
81. Detorakes, *op.cit.* note 79, p.53.
82. *Ibid.* p.95.
83. *Ibid.* p.124, 130.
84. G.I. Konidares, ' *Αἱ ἐπισκοπαὶ τῆς* Κρήτης *μέχρι καὶ τοῦ ι' αἰῶνος* ', *Kret. Khron.* VII, 1953, pp.462-478.
85. Detorakes, *op.cit.* note 78, p.133. Spanake I, p.84.
86. *Cambridge Mediaeval Hsitory* IV.1, p.71.
87. *cf. IC.*IV.481. The tombstone of Aristeas who had been a reader and lessor of the Church at Thessalonike. See Bandy, *op.cit.* note 72, p.66, on this inscription, which may be of 10c date, although dated by letter form by Guardicci to 6c.
88. Cedrenus II, p.94.
89. See Bandy, *op.cit.* note 72, p.22.
90. *IC.*IV.486.
91. *IC.*IV.478.
92. *IC.*II.XVI.16.
93. *AR* 1973-4, p.35f.

Pl. 8: Attic sarcophagus from Hierapytna (copyright British Museum).
Pl. 9: Medusa head from an Asiatic sarcophagus in the church of the Panayia, Lissos.
Pl. 10: Italian sarcophagus of Luna marble from Arvi (copyright Fitzwilliam Museum).

CHAPTER 5: ART

This chapter does not aim to produce a comprehensive study of art in and of Roman Crete, partly because some aspects have already been well treated in existing works [1] and partly because of the difficulty of dealing with museum material, often unpublished but on display. However it is possible to illuminate provincial life by brief examination of groups of material such as sarcophagi, statuary and mosaics.

Sarcophagi

A reasonable number of sarcophagi are known from the island, mostly dating from the 2c or 3c and mainly imported. However, the earliest known example of Roman date may well be of local manufacture; this is the Polybos sarcophagus [2], probably from Knossos. It is of white marble and depicts in rather poor low relief a flute player, a man possibly a pedagogue, reading a scroll to a skeleton, probably the personification of death, who stands by a table with offerings below which is a basket that has been identified as a 'kiste' of the Eleusinian Mysteries; beyond this again is a youth, possibly the dead Polybos. The date of the piece is likely to be the 1c AD.

The remaining sarcophagi are all of 2-3c date and consist of 12 Attic examples, 2 Asiatic, 1 Italian and some local pieces. The Attic ones are all listed by Giuliano [3] with the largest group from Gortyna (5), the next from Hierapytna (Pl.8) (2, a lid outside the museum is probably a third not in Giuliano) and other examples from Arvi (just a lid), Mallia and Chersonisos (a lid again). All fit into the established categories with the legends of Achilles, Meleager and Bellerophon all depicted. One interesting aspect of this group is that both the Hierapytnan examples and the Mallia one had been reused for fresh burials, at Mallia in the 4c and at an unknown date at Hierapytna. The Chersonisos lid had also been reused, as the altar base for the basilica on the Kastri (Bas.B). The two Asiatic sarcophagi come from Hierapytna and Lissos: the first is possibly the most interesting from Crete although unfortunately it is in fragments; in form it is a typical columnar example, probably of the so-called Pamphylian or Phrygian type, with scenes from the cult of Isis and Serapis [4]. This is a unique sarcophagus, presumably carved for an initiate of the cult although it is thought that the scenes depicted do not actually reveal an initiation. The other Asiatic piece only survives as one fragment of the gabled lid, built into the basilica of the Panayia at Lissos [5]. All that can be seen is a Medusa head from one end (Pl.9) and relief decoration on a piece of the ridge very similar to architectural decoration on fragments from Gortyna [6] of the late 2c. The one Italian sarcophagus is from Arvi (Pl.10): it is of Luna marble and dates to the Hadrianic or early Antonine period [7]. In splendid if somewhat overpowering detail it shows Dionysus' triumphal re-

---

1. C. C. Vermeule, *Roman Imperial Art in Greece and Asia Minor* (Harvard, 1968). A. Giuliano, *Il commercio dei sarcofagi attici* (Rome, 1962). Ferrari's equivalent work on Asiatic sarcophagi does not include the Cretan examples.
2. *IC.*I.XI.2. Platon, *Guide to Heraklion Museum* (Athens, 1968), p.125-6. In the same room (XX) of the Museum there is an earlier Hellenistic sarcophagus made up of a lower half of two tile boxes with a protuberance at one end and three upper half tile boxes; *Kret. Khron.* XXV, 1973, p.475.
3. *Op.cit.* note 1, numbers 310-18, 338-40. For the Mallia example, H. van Effenterre, 'Le sarcophage attique de Mallia', *BCH* C, 1976, p.525.
4. G. J. F. Kater-Sibbes, *A Preliminary Catalogue of Sarapis Monuments* (Leiden, 1973), p.58, no.342. G. Mendel, *Musées Imperiaux Ottomans: Catalogue des Sculptures* (Constantinople 1912), I no.40, p.135f.
5. Personal observations.
6. See p.66.
7. L. Budde and R. Nicholls, *A Catalogue of the Greek and Roman Sculpture in the Fitzwilliam Museum, Cambridge* (Cambridge, 1964), p.98 no.161. R. Turcan, *Les sarcophages romains à représentations dionysiaques* (Paris, 1966), p.140.

return from the east. In complete contrast the local limestone sarcophagi include three at Gortyna with bucrania (swag) decoration; two of these are of quite good workmanship but the third is very stiff and poor [8].

Given the proximity of Crete to Attica it is not surprising that most of the imported sarcophagi are of the Attic school. Considering the lack of excavation their number, 12, compares favourably with groups from other provinces - Asia 16, Lycia 10, Italy and Sicily 30 [9] - and the Achilles sarcophagus from Hierapytna, Giuliano no.316, is of a very high class of workmanship. It is obvious from the small number of Asiatic sarcophagi that this school found it hard to break into the Cretan market even though the Asiatic style dominated in architectural work. It is probably not just a coincidence that the two examples of the style from Crete come from sites on the main trade route from the east. The same factor applies to the Italian sarcophagus from Arvi which is the finest of all the Cretan pieces. Finally, there is evidence for local products, none of which are very elaborate, although it is likely that they were far more numerous than their expensive imported competitors.

Imperial Sculpture

It is perhaps ironic of Roman studies in Crete that one of its finest monuments, the Knossos cuirassed statue of Hadrian (Pl.11), which has Roma not the usual Athena on his breast, stands in the garden of the Villa Ariadne of Sir Arthur Evans, whose work did so much to distract archaeologists in Crete from any period later than the Minoan. However, it is the imperial sculpture that has been the most comprehensively studied of any aspect of Roman Crete, in the work of C.C.Vermeule [10], so my aim here is to gather together the examples from Crete in order to place them in the context of the island within the Empire.

From the period between the conquest in 69-7 BC and Augustus no statue survives but there is a dedication by the city of Polyrrhenia to Metellus [11] as its saviour and benefactor and there are two issues of the Gortynian mint [12] which carry the elephant head of the Metelli. Similarly no statues or heads that are definitely of Augustus survive but there are dedications to him and later references to his cult [13]. One attempt has been made to identify a head normally attributed to Caligula as his, but the reason given ("too noble a head and too sweet an expression for Caligula") cannot regrettably be accepted as evidence [14].

However, from the reign of Tiberius onward there is a succession of both busts and statues right up to period of the end of the Tetrarchy. Of the Julio-Claudians there are two busts of Tiberius, including one from a group from the Agora area at Gortyna which also includes busts of Livia, Germanicus and the head of Caligula mentioned above. Possibly from this same group is the only portrait of Octavia found in the eastern Empire, now in the National Museum in Athens, as Vermeule considers it to have "the same dry tentative quality of the Livia from Gortyna" [15].

No statues of the Flavian dynasty survive but again there are dedications, this time to Titus and Domitian [16], and a reference to the cult of the divine Vespasian [17]. However, with the 2c comes a great burst of activity particularly at Lyttus where there are numerous statue bases or dedications to Trajan, Plotina, Marciana, Hadrian and Paulina, but only one actual piece of sculpture, a head of Trajan. Two heads of Plotina come from Crete but their find spots are unknown, although it is quite likely that either or both could have come from Lyttus. It would seem anyway that Plotina was unusually popular in Crete for only one other head is known from the rest of the eastern Empire. In contrast statues of her protégé Hadrian are common from all over the eastern Empire; nevertheless Crete has more than the average number of heads and cuirassed statues of him. Knossos and Kissamos each have one and there are two each from Gortyna, Hierapytna [18] and the Diktynnaion with a further head from an unknown site in the Louvre. There is no proof that he ever visited the island, but it was on his route in 123 on the way from Africa to Asia [19].

---

8. In the museum at Gortyna. Giuliano, *op.cit.* p.19. Personal observations.
9. Numbers from Giuliano, *op.cit.* note 1.
10. Passim in *op.cit.* note 1, especially p.441-4.
11. *IC.*II.XXIII.14.
12. Svoronos, Gortyna nos. 190., 191.
13. See p.37f.
14. L. Mariani, 'Some Roman Busts', *AJA* I, 1897, p.266.
15. Vermeule, *op.cit.* note 1, p.173. The group was first published in Mariani, *op.cit.* note 14.
16. *IC.*I.XVII.15, 16.
17. *IC.*I.VIII.54.
18. The famous Istanbul statue (Mendel, *op.cit.* note 4, no.585) and an unpublished fragment in the Museum.
19. B. W. Henderson, *The Life and Principate of Hadrian* (London, 1923) p.289.

Pl. 11: Cuirassed Hadrian from Knossos.
Pl. 12: Pyramidal fish mosaic at Chersonisos.

After Hadrian the amount of extant statuary falls off sharply, with one rather rough Antoninus Pius from the amphitheatre at Gortyna, and a posthumous Hadrian of Pius' reign from the Diktynnaion (included in the numbers above). For the rest of the 2c and up to the time of Diocletian there is only one imperial head, that of Septimius Severus from Gortyna, but there are a reasonable number of statue bases dedicated to Marcus Aurelius, Lucius Verus, Septimius Severus and Caracalla. There is one head in Heraklion Museum (no.230) that could be Marcus Aurelius and and the female (no.334) from Chersonisos has been claimed to be Julia Domna. From the period of the Tetrarchy there are two heads from Gortyna, one of Maximianus Herculeus and one of Constantius I as Caesar: the latter head has been recut from a Julio-Claudian piece that may have been of Augustus. There are various later dedications including a veritable portrait gallery of the imperial administration put up by Oecumenius when as governor he rebuilt the Palace at Gortyna in the 380's.

Enough has survived to illustrate the importance and the physical presence of the Emperors and their families in the cities of Crete. Many of the statues are of a high standard but it is uncertain where most of them were made. The Hadrians came from the centre producing these works, probably in Attica; most of the rest also seem to be Greek in origin although sometimes based on Roman prototypes, like the Tiberius from the Gortynian Agora. Whether others could have been made in Crete itself is debatable, but given the obvious market there seems to be no reason why some at least should not have been locally made.

Other Sculpture

To complement this range of imperial sculpture there was clearly a greater amount of other work and this can be roughly divided into four classes. First there is sculpture depicting actual local inhabitants, for private or public display, but with the exception of some funeral reliefs there are very few names and statues that can be matched together. Of the public statues there are several heads in Heraklion Museum which could have come from such work and there is sufficient epigraphic evidence to prove the existence of such memorials, e.g. the Flavii Sulpiciani dedications from Hierapytna [20]. The Trajanic bust recently scooped out of Knossos [21] is perhaps more likely to be a private bust coming from the rich house where it was discovered. There is one bronze statue that deserves mention in this group; this is the young boy from Hierapytna which seems to be related in style to the late Hellenistic Tralles boy [22].

The second class comprises sculpture connected with religion: there is one problem here, that out of context it is very difficult to decide whether a particular piece of work, such as the Neronian Aphrodite of Lappa [23], should be regarded as a religious or purely artistic piece. Several statues have been found on the sites of temples but most of them are pre-Roman, often Hellenistic, like the Pan from Hyrtakina or the Pythian Apollo. One group, however, which dates from the Roman period and includes some of the finest of this class in Crete are the statues and busts connected with the cult of Isis and Serapis. The most impressive of these pieces is the group of Isis, Serapis, Cerberus and Hermes Anubis, probably dating to the Antonine period, that came from their temple at Gortyna [24]. This Serapis is of the early hairstyle 'Anatolentypus' as compared to the head from Lappa of the later 'Fransentypus' of, in this case, Severan date. The class of religious sculpture may also include statues of priests or dedicants like the Antonine Asklepiad from Gortyna [25] described in the words "the expression of the face is serious, in fact somewhat stupid". There is also a bust from Chersonisos which may be of a eunuch priest of Cybele [26].

The third group is of purely decorative work: the subject matter is varied but is often mythological, like the rather heavy Niobe group [27], probably Antonine in date, from Inatos, or the 1c BC Europa and a very placid-looking bull from the Larger Theatre at Gortyna [28], a city which also used this group as a badge on its coinage.

---

20. *IC.* III.III.20, 21.
21. G. Waywell, 'A Portrait Bust from Knossos,' *ABSA* LXVIII, 1973, p.295.
22. *Kret. Khron.* XII, 1958, p.481. Tralles boy, see M. Robertson, *A History of Greek Art* (London, 1976), p.524.
23. D. Papastamos and K. Staehler. ' Ἄγαλμα Ἀφροδίτης ρωμαϊκῶν αὐτοκρατορικῶν χρόνων ', *Kret. Khron.* XXIV, 1972, p.93-106.
24. See p.130 for the temple. Kater-Sibbes, *op.cit.* note 4, p.57 no.340, and W. Hornbostel, *Sarapis* (Leiden, 1973), p.189 for the statues. The terminology used here is from the latter work.
25. Mariani, *op.cit.* note 14, p.279.
26. *Ibid.* p.274.
27. Sp. Marinatos, ' Οἱ Νιοβίδαι τῆς Ἰνάτου ', *AE* 1934, p.1ff.
28. See p.63, and A. M. Smith, *Catalogue of Greek Sculpture in the British Museum* III (London, 1904), no.1535, p.8.

In complete contrast the final class is that of functional sculpture: there are two more than life-sized seated statues in Parian marble known from high points above the coast at Palaikastro and Leuke Island and it seems quite likely that, like the Porto Raphti statue, these were Oikoumene statues serving as beacons at night [29].

This brief summary has shown the range of statues that were visible in Roman Crete, mainly erected in the early period. As with the imperial works it is not clear how much was local work and how much was imported or made locally by foreign craftsmen. Three pieces are signed, one by Zeno of Aphrodisias [30], the second by Eisidotos of Athens [31] and the third by Athenaios of Paros [32]. From Paros also comes the Timotheus clan who dedicated a statue to Artemis at Arcades [33], signing themselves as sculptors: the latter were obviously working in Crete but whether the former pieces were imported or also made on the island by foreign sculptors is not clear. In either case an active influence from Athens, the Islands and Asia Minor in Crete is clearly shown, but it is very likely that, as in the Hellenistic period [34], there were also Cretan sculptors working to fulfill local demand.

Mosaics

Comparatively few mosaics other than those from Christian basilicas are known from Crete but such as there are form a pleasing group, varying in quality and date. There is no published corpus of this material so the following list attempts to describe and discuss all the mosaics from the island.

Chersonisos (6/7) On the sea front within the harbour is a low pyramidal fountain *c.* 0.75 x 2.50m square whose four sides were once adorned by polychrome mosaics (Pl.12). The water would have flowed mainly down the steps dividing the mosaic sides but a thin trickle would have run over the mosaics themselves, keeping the colours bright. Only one side is sufficiently well preserved to make out the design. There is a surround of a wide brown band, a narrow black stripe, then a band of white step pyramid on a brown background, another black band, a white band and a final black band. This encloses a sea scene where against a blue-grey sea numerous fish, squid, a goose and a duck observe a fishing boat with a rower in the stern and a man hauling in a large octopus in the bows. At the base of the mosaic a man wearing a blue hat gaffs an eel while a squid appears to be climbing up his back. This part of the mosaic illustrates the primitive perspective used in the composition; obviously the fisherman at the bottom of the mosaic is meant to be on a rock or the shore while the boat and fish higher up the panel are further out to sea. One failure of this scheme is that although the boat is shown correctly, i.e. only down to the water line, the rather incongruous goose and duck are shown standing on the water. Although there is no direct parallel for the form of the mosaic the scenes and their use in the context of a fountain are quite common: there is a good group of such works from Utica of the second and third centuries.[35]

Knossos (8/4): the Villa Dionysus The finest mosaics from the island are the group that give this villa its name (Pl.13); the figured pavements are of an extremely high quality, equal to contemporary work anywhere in the Empire. The largest mosaic, in the 8.5m sq. oecus, has a border of a wave scroll, then a band of triangles on a dark background and finally a guilloche about a central square. Set within this is an octagon with a central circle and eight panels; the inner circle, the edge of the octagon and the connecting 'spokes' are all a single guilloche. In the four corners of the main square not occupied by the octagon are figures, perhaps the seasons, standing within leaves. In the eight panels are heads of the followers of Dionysus with a bust of the god himself in the centre. The mosaic is of polychrome tesserae with the figures given depth and expression by the skilful use of many colours. In the first of the western rooms of the north range (Pl.14) another set of attendants are found in hexagons within a circle framing the god, this time depicted as a wild youth: all the figures are busts and all except for the god himself carry thyrsoi. The containing circle is itself set within a square and the resulting corners are filled with cocks and peacocks, and the whole is surrounded by a band of linked swastikas and a final outer scroll. The next room is split in two with a northern band of peltae and then a central half-bust of Dionysus in a

---

29. See p.17 for the Cretan sites and C. C. Vermeule, 'The colossus of Porto Rafti, a Roman female personification', *Hesperia* XLV.1, 1976, p.67.
30. *IC.*I.XVIII.60. Signed on a seated figure from Lyttus.
31. *IC.*IV.344. *Ergon* 1970, p.190. Standing female.
32. *IC.*IV.343. A fragment of a very odd statue showing a little boy next to a large foot.
33. *IC.*I.V.6.
34. See L. Beschi, 'Antichità Cretesi a Venezia', *Ann. Sc. At.* L-LI (new series 34-5), 1972-3, p.479.
35. See gazetteer for the site at Chersonisos; the mosaics have never been really published. Utica, *Corpus des Mosaiques de Tunisie* (Tunis, 1973). Maison de la Casque at Utica, p.27 no.28, pl.IX, also no.51, p.47.

Pl. 13: Mosaic bust of Dionysus from the north range, Villa Dionysus, Knossos.
Pl. 14: Dionysus and attendants, mosaic in the westernmost room of the north range, Villa Dionysus, Knossos.

guilloche circle intermeshing with semicircles and tangents in a 'vault' pattern. The parts of the circles contain flowers and birds. The final mosaic on this side is a plain circle or shield of concentric rows of triangles. On the south side of the villa opposite the last mosaic is another similar but with putti in the corners and a damaged central emblem, probably a Medusa head. The final complex mosaic of the villa, in the fore-room of the shrine, to the west of the putti room, is bordered in the same way as the second Dionysus mosaic but with an extra guilloche. There are three parts to the main mosaic; at either end there are single rows of 'perspective blocks' looking like box-tiles; between these and separated by a guilloche is a mat of an intricate design of interlocked circles resulting in a pattern of Maltese crosses and squares. In the centre of this there is a small emblema of a dove drinking from a bowl. The shrine itself has a simple tessellated floor.

The villa was constructed in the Hadrianic period[36] and the mosaics must therefore be of this date. No exact parallels are known to me for the Dionysus pavements but their basic geometrical arrangement can be paralleled from mosaics of a similar date, for instance the hexagon in a circle is used in a mosaic of 133 in Rome[37], the shield with putti in a Hadrianic-Antonine mosaic in Corinth[38]. However, the most outstanding feature of the group is the technical and artistic excellence of the work, comparable to the best from Rome, Antioch or Africa.

Knossos: Apollinaris Mosaic This was found in the northern half of the city but unfortunately its context was not recorded. The mosaic border is composed of an inhabited scroll, with nearly triangular leaves, and a wave scroll, forming the square for an octagonal design with eight panels containing Tritons which radiate out from a central octagon framing Poseidon in his chariot drawn by Hippocamps. The latter design is in blue and brown tesserae while the rest of the mosaic is in black and white. The lozenges and triangles left by the octagon within the overall square are filled with geometric patterns. Below the Poseidon is the signature ' Ἀπολλίναρις ἐποίει'. The inhabited scroll and the design of the mosaic date it to the early 2c although the popularity of the sea creatures can be traced back into the 1c[39].

Knossos: Four Seasons Mosaic A mosaic depicting this scene was found by Halbherr at the end of the 19c; no other details are recorded by him but this may be the mosaic shown in the Knossos Survey at KN 68 - "semi-circular mosaic". The theme is very common; probably the nearest other examples physically are from the House of Jason Magnus at Cyrene and from Ay. Taxiarchis near Argos[40].

Knossos: Theodosius Mosaic In the centre of the city a mosaic was cleared and drawn[41]: it is a geometric panel bordered by a scroll, the basic pattern executed in red and blue against a cream background, very similar to the mosaic in Room XI of the Odeion at Gortyna. The likely *terminus ante quem* for the Knossos pavement is the reign of Theodosius, given by a coin of that period found on the mosaic, but the Gortyna pavement is probably of late 2c/early 3c date.

Gortyna (10/10): Odeion The only adequately recorded mosaics from Gortyna are from the Odeion[42]; even here very little survived and nothing is now visible. In the Odeion proper there was a fragment of mosaic west of the *pulpitum* in the passage by the entrance: the design is in two panels of black and white tesserae; one is of compass-drawn circles with central equal-armed crosses but of the other only a fragment of scroll survives. Outside the entrance in the portico a small fragment of a diamond border still existed. It is likely that these mosaics date to the Trajanic reconstruction of the Odeion.

The largest fragment comes from Room XI of the range east of the main building; these rooms are secondary to the main structure and have a possible *terminus ante quem* of the early 4c given by a coin of Constantine II from the floor of another room here. The mosaic sealed a layer containing a coin of the 1c BC. The design consists of a scroll in black and white containing two polychrome panels, the first with a design very like that of

---

36. See p.69.
37. *MAAR* XIII, 1936, p.130, pl.26.2.
38. S. E. Ramsden, *Roman Mosaics in Greece, the Mainland and the Ionian Islands,* Ph.D., 1971, submitted to the Institute of Archaeology London, p.591 (only incidental mention of Crete).
39. Ramsden, *op.cit.* note 38, for a brief description of the mosaic and *MAAR* VIII, 1930, p.121, on the sea creatures.
40. F. Halbherr, *The Antiquary* XXVIII, 1893, p.111. P. Mingazzini, *L'Insula di Giasone Magno a Cirene* (Rome, 1966), tav. XXX. G. Åkerstrom-Hougen, *The Calendar and Hunting Mosaics of the Villa of the Falconer in Argos* (Stockholm, 1974).
41. *Knossos Daybook,* 21st January 1950, p.10 (kept at the Taverna there).
42. See pp.65ff for the building: mosaics p.42, 49, 67 of the report.

the Theodosius pavement from Knossos and the second made up of peltae and four-petalled crosses: a small fragment of the guilloche border of an emblema survives in the centre of the second panel. Within the limits of Trajan to the early 4c, the date of the mosaic may be fixed with some certainty between 150 and 250 when its design is compared with the late 2c mosaics from the Odeion of Herodes Atticus[43], and the Tablinum mosaic from the House of Dionysus at Nea Paphos in Cyprus[44] which is dated to the second half of the 3c.

Sybrita (12/4) The mosaic from the main square of Thronos will be discussed in relation to the basilica here[45]. A further mosaic was discovered by the Russian fleet at Ta Marmara[46]; this was re-excavated by the Germans and shown to be of red, blue and white peltae, possibly 3-4c in date.

Vizari (12/12) South-east of the basilica a probable bath house was located[47] containing a small fragment of a black and white mosaic in a room measuring 3.35 x 5m with a niche in its south wall. The mosaic consisted of a jagged scroll about a wide band of white edged by narrow black lines with a small double row of black squares in the centre; within this surround was a small portion of the main design. This consisted of a circle set within the square of the edge. Nothing survived within the circle but in the space between it and the edge of the square were three objects, identified as a helmet flanked by two greaves. The overall shield design in black and white is very similar to the mosaics at Kastelli Kissamou and the scroll is similar to the ones at Nea Paphos mentioned above; both these examples date to the 3c so it is very likely that this one from Vizari is of the same date.

Lappa (14/1) The mosaics found here in 1918, or rather a part of them, are now in Rethimnon Museum[48]; their normal attribution to a basilica seems somewhat unlikely as within a border of swastika/Greek key pattern and wavy scroll they depict vigorous hunting scenes. These include hunters and hounds attacking a boar and others a deer, possible fallow. From the poor illustrations available the mosaic would seem to be one of the many hunting mosaics dating to the 4-6c.

Cydonia (18/18): Poseidon and Amymone Mosaic A mosaic showing two scenes from this myth came from a house in what must have been the outskirts of Cydonia. Within a twisted rope border in blue and red Amymone is being attacked by a Satyr on the left and comforted by Poseidon on the right. At each corner of the border there are masks set in circles; above the border there is a panel of four-petalled crosses with little straight crosses between them which is interrupted on the right by an emblema of two opposed fighting cocks. The mosaic measures 1.65 x 2.50m, set in a room 5.10 x 4.20m and is aligned to be viewed from the side opposite the entrance; possibly there were further panels like the crosses filling the rest of the floor.

This mosaic has recently been dated to the late 2c/early 3c[49] on the basis of various African parallels and some associated material. However the style of the mosaic is much closer to one from the Roman Villa at Corinth dated to the Hadrianic or Antonine period[50], where the rope border is identical, as is the setting of a polychrome scene (of a shepherd boy) against a plain background. In general it would seem preferable to accept this close stylistic parallel to mere parallels of the same or similar common mythological representation. From the same house in Cydonia there was a further plain mosaic[51] and in the same general area other mosaics were found of which there are no further details available[52].

Cydonia: Cathedral Square Part of a bath house was excavated here revealing two rooms with mosaics: the first shows a Triton outlined in black against white blowing a conch; the second has a vine scroll set in a long panel. Another fragment of the second mosaic has the letters ΛΑ superimposed on a pair of sandals. This is probably a welcoming sign λοῦσαι ἀσφαλῶς or may be a prophylactic against the evil eye[53].

---

43. Ramsden, *op.cit.* note 38, p.145.
44. K. Nikolaos, 'Excavations at Nea Paphos: the House of Dionysos', *Report of the Department of Antiquities, Cyprus* 1967, p.100f.
45. See p.114.
46. Matz p.145, 149, pl.119.4.
47. *Kret.Khron.* XIII, 1959, p.33.
48. *A.Delt.* IV, 1918, par.31. Pelekanides, *Σύνταγμα τῶν παλαιοχριστιανικῶν ψηφιδωτῶν δαπέδων τῆς* Ἑλλάδος I (Thessaloniki 1974), p.118, no.99, pl.90b, 91.
49. Original publication, V. Theophanides, *AE* 1945-7, p.37. Now, F. Berti, 'Poseidon ed Amymone. Un mosaico romano di Chania', *Ann. Sc. At.* L-LI (new series 34-5), 1972-3, p.451.
50. Ramsden, *op.cit.* n.38, p.591.
51. *Kret. Khron.* XIII, 1959, p.392.
52. *A. Delt.* XXI.2, 1966, p.428.
53. *A. Delt.* XXV.2.2, 1970, p.417. The feet, Ramsden, *op. cit.* n.38, p.354, and J. Russell, 'Mosaic Inscriptions from the Palaestra at Anemurium', *Anatolian Studies* XXIV, 1974, p.95f. A very similar Triton mosaic has recentlybeen found at the Isthmian Sanctuary in a bath house dated to the 1c AD, *ILN* October 1976, p.91.

Lissos (19/18) The temple of Asklepios [54] contains a black and white mosaic with coloured emblemata covering part of the floor, measuring 6.9 x 5.5m (Pl.40). Within a fine scroll are panels of varying geometric designs, 5 on the short sides (north and south) and 6 on the long. The corner designs consist of white floral crosses set against a black square with rosettes in the corners; next on the long sides a star on a white lozenge against a black lozenge with L shapes in the corners; the central two panels have been destroyed. On the short sides the surviving three panels on the north are (from E to W) a circle made up of black and white diamonds, a large panel of interlaced petal crosses, and a complex of 10 linked black and white boxes with brown circles in the centres of the resulting white lozenges. Within this framework of panels is a large black and white maze including 5 emblemata. The central one was totally destroyed by the pit dug here when the temple was destroyed and very little survives of the two corner ones on the west side; these seem to have been white creatures on a black setting. The two on the east side show polychrome birds on a blue background; one is a quail. Between this panel and the northern geometric ones was a long *tabula ansata* now almost totally destroyed. The mosaic is of very good workmanship and probably dates to the 1c AD: a head of Tiberius with its dedication was found in the temple and it is tempting to associate this with the refurbishing of the 4-3c BC structure by the addition of a new mosaic floor.

Kissamos (20/10) Two of the rooms of a house discovered during the construction of the National Highway through the northern part of the town contained mosaic floors [55] . The first, measuring 7.60 x 6.80m (RoomA), was composed of two central panels surrounded by a Greek key pattern round one panel and a scroll round the other: both were damaged. The first was a guilloche circle or shield set in a square with interior triangular and oblong panels separated by further guilloche. These minor panels contained a bird sitting on a twig or stylised shoot and the corner between the circle and the square contained plain kantharoi. The centre was lost but enough tesserae were found to show that, unlike the rest of the mosaic, it had been polychrome. The second panel was badly destroyed and only one fragment survived showing a dog and goat in black and white outline. Beyond this main mosaic there were further panels of either black and white squares or plain areas of tesserae.

The second mosaic, 7.50 x 3.70m (Room B), was basically a panel of 9 squares surrounded again by more geometric panels, either split squares with smaller squares in their centres or areas with small diamonds or triangles outlined in black on white, rather similar to part of the border of the Vizari mosaic. The central border panels were also of geometric designs; the central ones on each side are the same, a white lozenge with black swastika design set on a black square with white cornucopiae in the corners; the corner panels were either circles with six-pointed stars made up of diamonds with further central patterns or eight pointed stars filling the whole panel. The central panel was an octagon set in a square which contained a polychrome scene of a centaur fighting a lion. Both mosaics were orientated north-south.

The house containing these mosaics was dated to the second half of the 3c which is quite acceptable for the design and style of the mosaics although some of the geometric patterns are known earlier; for instance, the lozenges from Room B are very similar to those used in the mosaics of the Odeion of Herodes Atticus of late 2c date [56] .

Lebena (10/23) This mosaic (Pl.15), dating to the 4-3c BC, is not strictly within the limits of this thesis but is included for completeness of the group [57]. On the panel, measuring *c.* 3 x 1m, is shown a sea-horse, depicted in white pebbles with black detail and a red mane all on a dark background surrounded by a scroll of black waves on white. The east end of the mosaic, beyond this scroll, contains two very delicate palmettes, again white on a dark ground.

These mosaics illustrate a reasonable level of wealth and workmanship in producing the pavements of the first to fourth centuries; in subsequent centuries it appears that the art of the mosaicist was largely directed towards the adornment of churches, although there can be no doubt that there are many more secular mosaics of this period waiting to be discovered, apart from the Lappa example and one leaf of a scroll in a pig sty at Suia (19/17)! All the pavements from the earlier period are competent pieces of work and the Villa Dionysus mosaics are very fine indeed. Because of the very small number known it is impossible to detect any schools of mosaicists within the island and equally difficult to discern any particular area influencing the styles used in Crete. In general the continuing use of polychrome fits Crete into the common eastern tradition with perhaps more connections to the Aegean, Asia Minor and Syria than to Africa.

54. See p.84.
55. See gazetteer. *A. Delt.* XXIII.2.2, 1968, p.416-7.
56. Ramsden, *op.cit.* n.38, p.145.
57. See p.80 ff for the temple.

Conclusions

This brief survey of some of the major monuments of art in Roman Crete has revealed both the necessary wealth and the inclination among its richer classes during the first three centuries AD to adorn their private houses and public buildings to a standard comparable with the wealthiest cities of the eastern Empire. The same men also could and did import or commission statuary and very fine sarcophagi. The most frequent statues must have been those of imperial personages, whose stone effigies affirmed to the Cretans the link between Crete and the Emperor. Most of these statues and many of the others seem to have been imported from Greece or Asia Minor or made by sculptors from those parts, and it is quite possible that some of the finest mosaics were also laid by foreign craftsmen, but there was probably sufficient demand to encourage local schools of sculptors and mosaicists even though as yet there is not enough evidence to identify these. Overall, the art of Roman Crete, like so much else from the island in the period, seems to fit very well into the general framework of the eastern Empire, unexceptional but with a few pleasant surprises such as the Villa Dionysus mosaics, the Arvi sarcophagus and the nine superb Hadrians.

Pl. 15: 4-3c BC pebble mosaic of a sea-horse in the Treasury at Lebena.

CHAPTER 6 : ARCHITECTURE

Apart from the remains at Gortyna there is very little Roman architecture still visible in Crete and even less has been excavated and published. However, in the 16c much more was visible and fortunately it was recorded by the polymath Onorio Belli whose work has mostly survived[1] . It is very difficult to ascertain how accurate Belli's plans are because, of the nine that survive from his work, only three can be compared with the actual visible or excavated structures and all three are far more ruinous now than they were in the 16c. It would seem unlikely that the buildings were as complete as Belli drew them[2]so a degree of reconstruction is to be expected. However, the general dimensions seem to be correct where they can be checked, at the theatres of Gortyna and Chersonisos. More recent surveys and excavation have revealed various monuments other than those recorded by Belli: the most important of these are the sanctuaries at the Diktynnaion and at Lebena (where ironically the part recorded by Belli seems to have been missed by the later work).

The buildings to be dealt with in this chapter are, or were when recorded, reasonably complete; the other more fragmentary structures are described under their site entry in the Gazetteer. The various miscellaneous buildings will be described in this chapter after the group of theatres and related structures. In addition to the theatres with known plans there are others from the Kouphonisi (ancient Leuke) Islands (1/31), Inatos (7/31), Knossos (8/4), Aptera (17/2), Cydonia (18/18), Lissos (19/18) and Kissamos (20/10). Amphitheatres also existed at Hierapytna (2/8), Chersonisos (6/7) and Kissamos (20/10): an inscription from Knossos (8/4) mentioning *ludi* is presumably evidence for some form of amphitheatre there [3].

Theatres

Hierapytna (2/8): Smaller Theatre (Pl.16) The site of the smaller of the two theatres[4] here was near the eastern edge of the ancient city, near the church of Timios Stavros. Part of it can still be seen in the form of the remnants of the concrete core of a wall 4.50 - 5.00m in height.

The theatre was entered through a colonnaded portico *c.*90 x 45m and then via the *postscenium* up to the single-tiered *cavea* with seats 0.60m wide. There also appear to have been stairs leading directly up to the *cavea* from the rear exterior. This was decorated with an arcade with 15 *fauces* leading into the theatre. The *cavea* itself had a diameter of *c.*48m and the orchestra 27m.

Belli does not show the actual stage on his plan of the theatre here (nor on any of the others) but he shows the *scaenae frons* which is about 40m long and was carried round the *parodoi* to meet the *cavea.* The facade itself consists of six small rectangular exedrae, with flanking columns, on either side of a large central rectangular exedra. This in its turn has a small rectangular niche at each side and two semicircular ones flanking a central rectangular niche. There are four doors to the stage from the *postscenium*, two on each side of the central exedra[5]. The facade is carried round to the *cavea* with two more rectangular exedrae set on either side of the *parodos* door.

1. The main edition is that of E. Falkener (London, 1854), who redrew and restored the plans: his introduction includes a full account of Belli's career. More recently S. Spanake has published the text with the original plans in the *Acts of the 2nd Cretological Congress* (Athens, 1968), Vol 2, p.142. He also has short notes on the sites.
2. Belli does seem to have 'excavated' to some extent, e.g. at the Smaller Theatre at Hierapytna; Belli ed. Falkener p.12.
3. *IC.*I.VIII.51.
4. Belli ed. Falkener p.12-13, ed. Spanake p.153, pl.K,Spratt 1, p.262.
5. Falkener shows a central fifth door through this but on the original this is not shown.

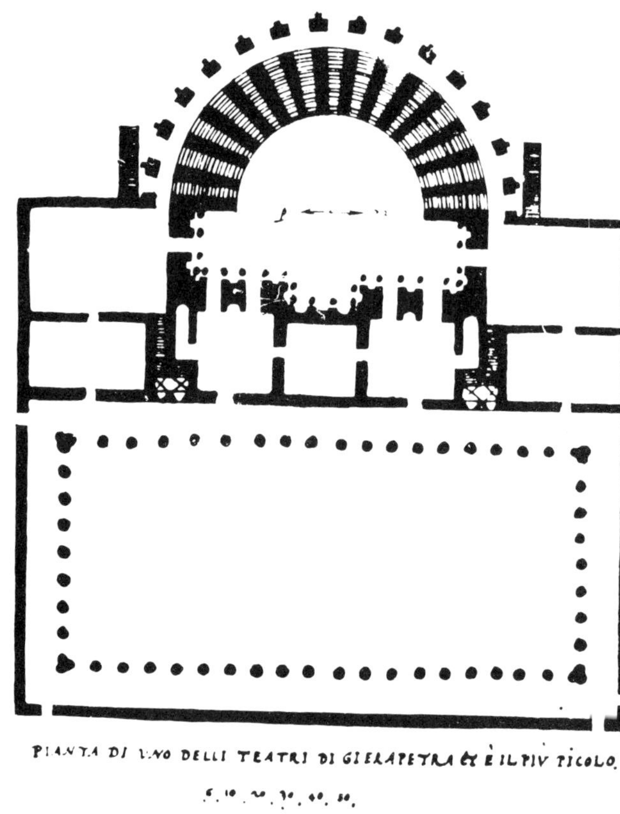

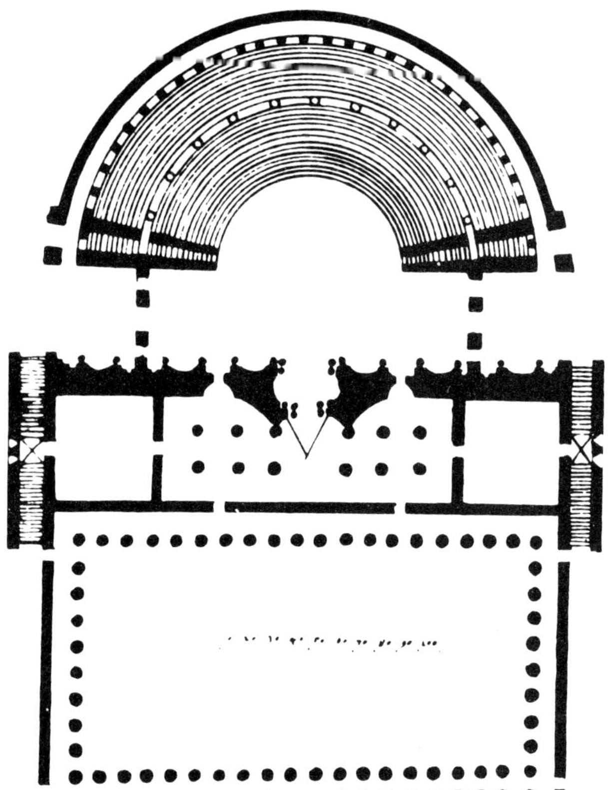

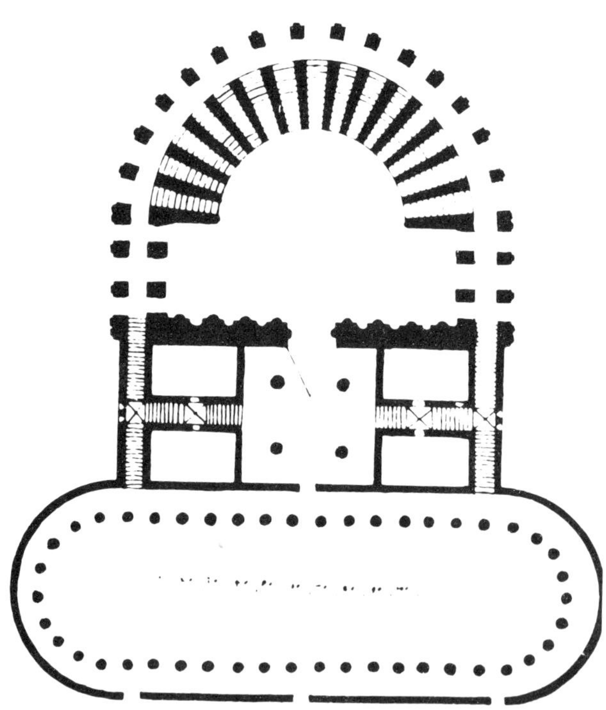

Pl. 16: Belli's plan of the Smaller Theatre at Hierapytna.
Pl. 17: Belli's plan of the Larger Theatre at Hierapytna.
Pl. 18: Belli's plan of the theatre at Chersonisos.

Belli records two orders of columns from the facade, both Ionic of white marble, the lower *c.*3.50m high and *c.*0.43m diameter and the upper 3.15m high and 0.34m diameter. He also excavated the front of the *scene* where he found statues of 'stucco' which fell into powder when he tried to remove them: as he remarks that the columns had been mainly destroyed by fire it seems quite likely that the statues had originally been of marble but had been reduced to calcium oxide by the heat.

Amongst the ruins of the theatre several damaged inscriptions were found[6]. These are probably dedications by the city of statues of local dignitaries. The dedication to L. Flavius Sulpicianus must date to the end of the 2c[7] and thus gives a *terminus ante quem* for the theatre. Given its construction in concrete, which in Crete does not seem to be widely used before the late 1c AD, the theatre ought therefore to date from some point in the 2c.

Hierapytna (2/8): Larger Theatre (Pl.17) The larger theatre[8] was at the other side of the city quite close to the sea, on the left of the modern road to Viannos. Even less remains of this theatre owing to destruction caused by World War II coastal defence works. Before this staircases and vaulting could be made out but all that survives now are portions of the concrete core; it is greatly to be regretted that nobody appears to have photographed the monument before the war.

The portico of this theatre was about the same length as that of the smaller one, *c.*90m, but deeper, *c.*52m, with a colonnade with a double row of columns on the outer side. The *postscenium*, consisting of a large hall flanked by two rooms, unlike that at the smaller theatre does not give direct access to the *cavea* from the portico but via external staircases going up, presumably, to the level of the bridges over the *parodoi.*

The cavea itself, *c.*88.50m external diameter and 32m internal, is in two tiers separated by an *ambulacrum* where there were mountings for sounding jars or *echeia.* The *ambulacrum* above the seating does not appear to have had a gallery. Belli claims that the theatre was partially excavated out of a mountain, which given the flat coastal plain is hard to understand if the site has been correctly identified. Whatever he does mean here this claim may explain the odd buttresses only shown at the ends of the *cavea.* Falkener reconstructs these as staircases but, if this theatre was built into a hill, it may be that these are arcades leading into the *fauces* extending the slope of the hill. This would certainly seem to have been the case in the larger theatre at Gortyna.

Again no stage is marked, but the *scaenae frons* is unusual in that it extends the entire width of the building through the *parodoi.* The part of the facade here is made up of a shallow curved exedra flanked by smaller rectangular ones. Within the stage area proper, 55m long, the sequence is a small rectangular exedra; then a shallow curved one with columns; a rectangular exedra for a stage door and then another curved one flanking the elaborate main door in the centre. At each side of the porch here, on both faces, are groups of three columns with a shallow curved exedra between them inside the porch. The porch leads into, or out of, the long central hall of the *postscenium,* 48m x 18m. Within the hall are two rows of six columns on the axis of side doors which lead into flanking chambers that are linked to the external staircases[9].

Although Belli is not entirely clear on this point, it would seem that there were three orders of columns, one of each style. The *scene* was of white marble and 'red marked' stone. It seems to have been from this theatre that the headless statue now adorning the fountain in Kornaros Square in Heraklion came in 1552[10].

Chersonisos (6/7) (Pl.18, 19). Just before the modern settlement of Limani Chersonisou is reached coming from Heraklion, a track leaves the road to the left (north) and at a short distance from the main road runs right through the stage area of the theatre[11] here. The main element of the theatre now surviving is what must be the supporting wall of the *cavea*; this is of concrete, 0.75m thick and up to 3.0m high. The internal diameter of this wall is 33.25m. Beyond the wall are the fourteen bases of the exterior arcade of the building; these are 2.0m minimum width and 2.20m deep, linked to the wall by tile-faced concrete ribs; the distance between the piers

---

6. *IC.*III.III.21-5. It is not clear from which theatre the statue of Larcius Cydicles came.
7. See Appendix II on this family.
8. Belli ed. Falkener p.13, ed. Spanake p.162-3, pl. KE, Spratt 1, p.261. Falkener's plan of the *scaenae frons* differs in many details from the original.
9. There appears to be a confusion in levels as this staircase ought to be at a higher level than the rooms behind the stage.
10. Falkener, 'Antiquities of Candia I', *Museum of Classical Antiquities* II, (London, 1860), p.276.
11. Belli ed. Falkener p.16, ed. Spanake p.162, pl. KΔ, Spratt I, p.107. *Mon. Ant.* VI, 1895, p.240. Personal observation.

Pl. 19: Rear wall and piers of the cavea of the theatre at Chersonisos.
Pl. 20: Belli's plan of the theatre at Lyttos.

and the wall is 8.0m. However, at the ends of the *cavea* there is a difference in design with a massive 2.0m thick wall between the first wall and the piers; the resulting gap of 2.50m was later blocked rather crudely with large stones concreted together. Quite what this second wall means is unclear but Belli's plan also shows a thickening here and a double pier. It may be that this strengthening is connected to the *parodoi* and the lateral thrust from the *cavea*. Traces of the *parodoi* may survive in the two walls in front of the *cavea*, the first, 5.0m in front, is 0.90m wide and the second, 3.50m further out, is 1.25m in width. There is no trace of the *postscenium* although there is much cut stone in the area. However, since the site has never been excavated further details must be derived from Belli's plan.

The portico shown by Belli is unique: it has rounded ends which make it look like a stadium and is 83m long and 30m deep, with a colonnade. Although there is an entrance into the *postscenium* and so to the stage, the main entrances into the theatre proper are the staircases that lead into the *parodoi* and so to the single-tiered *cavea*, external diameter 46m, internal 27m. The exterior of its outer wall is composed of the customary arcade which in this case also stretches right round past the *parodoi*. There are in total fourteen arches round the *cavea* and three more for each *parodos*. The *scaenae frons*, 43m long, is quite simple with one central door and a simple facade of small semicircular niches and engaged half-columns. The central door leads into the hall of the *postscenium*, 18m square, which has four centrally grouped columns. From here staircases lead up to side-chambers and continue to join the stairs from the *postscenium*.

Lyttus (6/25) (Pl.20) The site of the theatre [12] here is not certainly located: Mariani and Taramelli placed it on the north side of the hill, but the south slopes provide an equally good position far better sheltered with a better view over the plain. Belli apologises for the state of his plan of the *scene* here, saying it was in ruins and impossible to plan. This gives some additional weight to his other plans as here he was definitely unwilling to reconstruct beyond his evidence. The fact that he mentions enormous blocks may be evidence that here the theatre structure, where it was not cut out of the hillside, was of stone rather than concrete.

This theatre is the largest in Crete, with a *cavea* diameter of 55m internally, 167m externally. It is arranged in four tiers with a colonnade at the top, within the final wall and what looks like a further double colonnade beyond this. Belli claims that the cells for three rows of bronze sounding vessels were still visible. This fits very neatly with Vitruvius's instructions for the use of these vessels [13] but it is always possible that Belli was influenced by this passage in his interpretation of what he saw. Before the *parodoi* there appears to be some sort of narrow passage. It is uncertain whether this is just the final portion of the *cavea* supported by substructures as at Hierapytna or an actual entrance. Of the *scaenae frons*, 76m long, all that Belli could make out was that it had three doors, the central one set in the middle of a large but shallow curved exedra.

Belli found several inscriptions in the theatre [14] but unlike those from Hierapytna they are all sepulchral and therefore cannot be in their original position. Lyttus is one of the rare sites in Crete with a defensive circuit of late Roman date and it seems possible that the theatre was incorporated into it and extraneous material used in the conversion.

Gortyna (10/10): Smaller Theatre (Pl.21) This theatre [15], which is situated next to the temple of Pythian Apollo, is now the best preserved of all the theatres of Roman Crete. Taramelli carried out an extensive survey of the *cavea* area in *c.*1900 and Colini carried out a small scale excavation in the 1930's: it seems clear that the monument had deteriorated severely in the intervening period, partly at the hands of the local peasantry. No details about the stage area and the portico have been recorded since Belli.

According to Belli the portico, 76m x 36m, has an external colonnade, 88m x 45m, as well as the more normal internal one. From the portico there are doors to the *postscenium* and so through to the theatre proper. An alternative way in seems to have been via staircases alongside the *postscenium* which presumably led into the *cavea* over the *parodoi*. The *cavea* has a perimeter of 102m with an external wall 1.30m wide; it is constructed of brick-faced concrete but also uses the local stone, the blocks linked together with bronze clamps [16]. The exterior wall is composed of the usual arcade, stretching round to the *scene*. At the apex of the *cavea* there was a wider

---

12. Belli ed. Falkener p.18, ed. Spanake p.158, pl. ΚΓ, *Mon. Ant.* VI, 1895, p.10. Personal observation.
13. V.5.5.3.
14. *IC.* I.XVIII.63, 88, 154 etc.
15. Belli ed. Falkener p.21, ed. Spanake p.156, pl. ΚΑ, Taramelli, *AJA* VI, 1902, p.112f. Colini *Boll. d'Arte* XXX, 1936, p.547f.
16. Taramelli, *op.cit.* note 15, p.117 Fig.8.

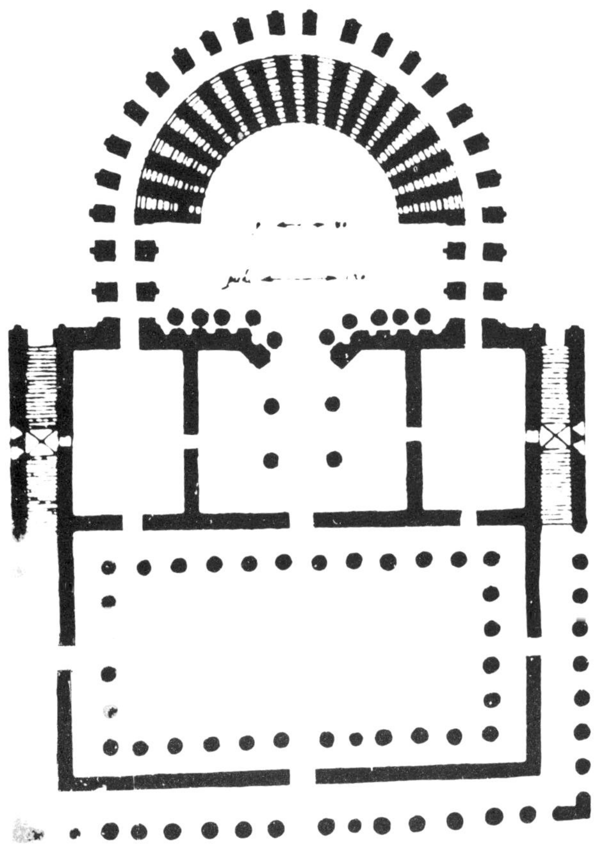

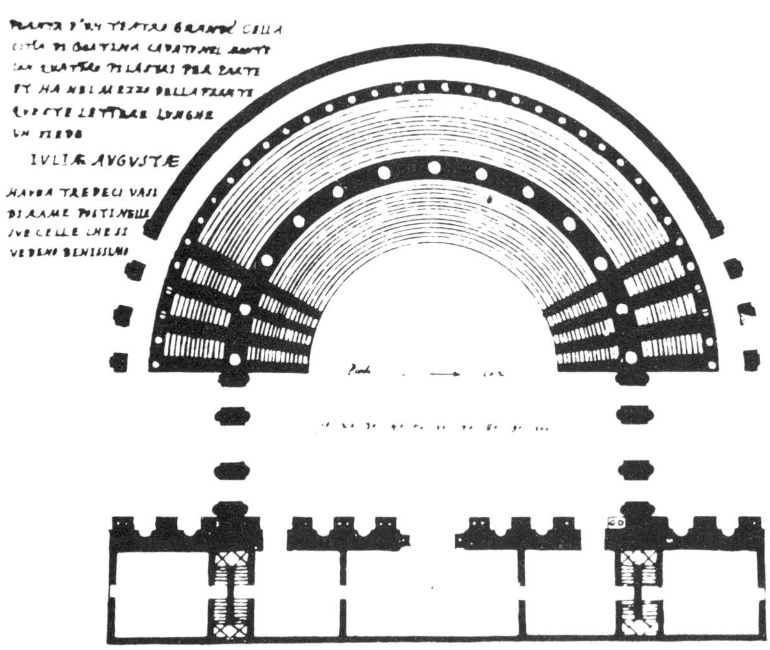

Pl. 21: Belli's plan of the Smaller Theatre at Gortyna.
Pl. 22: Belli's plan of the Larger Theatre at Gortyna.

entrance flanked by a double buttress instead of the single ones which flanked the other ten archways, 2.60m wide, around each side of the *cavea* itself. The latter was 31.40m in diameter internally, *c.*50m externally, with two tiers of seats separated by an *ambulacrum* 3m broad with another at the top of the seats 2.50m wide. All this was supported on vaults of the substructure which was also divided in two, the *fauces* carrying through the first band to the corridor from which the *vomitoria* led up to the central *ambulacrum* above. The facing in this lower corridor was of stone with the mason marks ME and

The *scaenae frons*, 50m long, is quite simple with four small rectangular exedrae with free-standing columns in front of them on each side of the central door. At the door the facade is bent in with a further single exedra and column. The door leads into the main hall of the *postscenium,* 30m x 27m, with its four columns grouped about the axis of its doors. These columns, like those in the rest of the theatre, were of the Doric order in black and white marble. In the portico the columns were made of granite. Marble was also used to inlay the walls of the theatre.

Gortyna (10/10) : Larger Theatre (Pl.22) This theatre [17] is cut into the slopes of the acropolis on the other side of the Lethaeus from the Odeion and Forum. No portico is recorded by Belli and the proximity of the river makes the existence of one unlikely although the river was here canalised in a culvert which could have carried some light structure.

The *cavea*, 140m perimeter and *c.*40m internal diameter and 88m external, has a channel behind it cut into the rock, probably both for winter drainage and also to serve as an entranceway into the upper tier of the *cavea* through five gaps in the 2.2m thick outer wall. The two ends of the *cavea* are not cut from the rock but supported on vaulted substructures of concrete which have the normal arcaded exterior. Within the outer wall ran a colonnaded *ambulacrum,* 2.0m wide, above the upper tier of seats and a wider walk, 3.60m, divided this tier from the one below. This lower tier was larger, probably with 18 rows of seats as against 11 in the upper. Most of this structure still survives though in a very battered and overgrown state; where the natural rock is not used it is constructed of concrete with brick facing and at the bottom of the aggregate large column drums have been reused to form a stable base.

The stage building is 120m long and the *scaenae frons* takes up only 70m of this. It is only recorded by Belli and had disappeared by the 19c. He shows the facade continuing through the *parodoi* with the same pattern as in the stage area, rectangular exedrae with a curved niche at the back. Each exedra is separated by a pair of columns on a base from its neighbour. There are three doors into the *postscenium,* the central ones having flanking columns. According to Belli the *scaenae frons* was composed of five orders of columns, the height (presumably of the lowest ones) being 5.4m and the diameter 0.53m. They were of white marble of the Ionic order [18]. Also built into the *scaenae frons* was an inscription to Iulia Augusta [19] which Belli thought had been reused there. Definitely not in its original position was a 1c BC sculpture acquired by Spratt from this theatre; it shows the Rape of Europa by a very benign-looking bull and can now be found in the British Museum [20].

Gortyna (10/10) : Amphitheatre On the south-east edge of the city are the remains of the amphitheatre [21] constructed of massive brick-faced concrete walls. It has never been properly excavated. Belli planned it but unfortunately his plan has been lost; Maffei says he showed it as just like the Colossuem at Rome. The outer wall was made up of 56 arches in two orders with a possible portico round the top. There were four entrances on the axes and in the interior two tiers of seats. A little clearance has been done, revealing the internal dimensions as 66m north-south, 50m east-west.

On the west side, 3m out from the outer face of the main wall, a wall had been constructed to give a straight facade flanked by two towers that held internal staircases. There also seems to have been a main stairway leading up to this facade at the point where there was a large niche containing a statue . The head of this is in Heraklion Museum (no.73) and is claimed as Antoninus Pius. The remainder is still on the site by the west facade

---

17. Belli ed. Falkener p.21, ed. Spanake p.156, pl. KB, Taramelli, *op.cit.* note 15, p.108f., fig.4. Spratt II, p.29.
18. Five orders seem excessive for the *scaenae frons,* especially if the height of even the tallest columns was 5.4m.
19. *IC.*IV.273. It is uncertain which of the many imperial Iuliae it is.
20. A. M. Smith, *Catalogue of Greek Sculpture in the British Museum* III, (London, 1904), no.1535, p.8.
21. A. Maiuri, *Ausonia* VI, 1911, p.7. G. Bendinelli, *Ausonia* VI, 1911, p.29. Belli ed. Falkener p.22-3. F. Maffei, *A compleat history of the ancient amphitheatre,* trans. A. Gordon (London n.d.) p.82. *IC.*IV.Praef. p.12. Pococke, *A description of the east and some other countries* (London, 1745), II, 252.

Pl. 23: *Fragment of limestone architrave from the amphitheatre at Gortyna.*
Pl. 24: *Odeion at Gortyna.*

and consists of a large togate seated figure. If it is the Emperor it would seem likely that he was responsible for the construction of the amphitheatre; it is known[22] that he did carry out some work somewhere in the city. However the imperial nature of the statue has been held in doubt[23] and a certain High Priest of the Cretan Koinon, Volumnius Sabinus, has been suggested as an alternative. This man held games by imperial permission [24] at some date probably in the 3c. It seems impossible to decide which of these two claimants, if either, the statue represents. The statue itself is probably of the Aphrodisian School for it can be compared to a very similar work from Lyttus signed by Zeno of Aphrodisias[25]. Another statue from this amphitheatre is now in the British Museum [26] and shows a draped female standing on a nude prostrate boy; to the right is a Gryphon, to the left a serpent. The woman is normally held to be Nemesis.

Fragments of the amphitheatre architrave have survived and are of considerable interest (Pl.23). They are all very finely carved in local limestone and between the ovolo-edged modillions are various reliefs including a Medusa head, a lion, a dove, a ram's head and an eagle with a serpent. One fragment decorated with plants, flowers and bucrania is curved and must therefore come from an arch. The closest parallels [27] all come from Asia Minor, in particular the reliefs from the *scaenae frons* at Aspendos dated to the Antonine period. The ovolo edge to the modillions is a further sign of influence from Asia Minor [28]. Other parallels from this area include material from Sagalassos and Termessos, also dating to the 2c AD.

Gortyna (10/10) : *Odeion* (Pl.24, Fig.11) On the other side of the Lethaeus from the Larger Theatre is the site of the Odeion [29] which contains the only well-known monument of post-Minoan Crete, the Law Code of Gortyna. This inscription, which probably dates to the mid 5c BC, is incorporated into a building that as it now survives must date to AD 100; presumably this is the last of a series on the site from one of which the Code originally came [30].

Fig.11. Gortyna: plan of the Odeion.

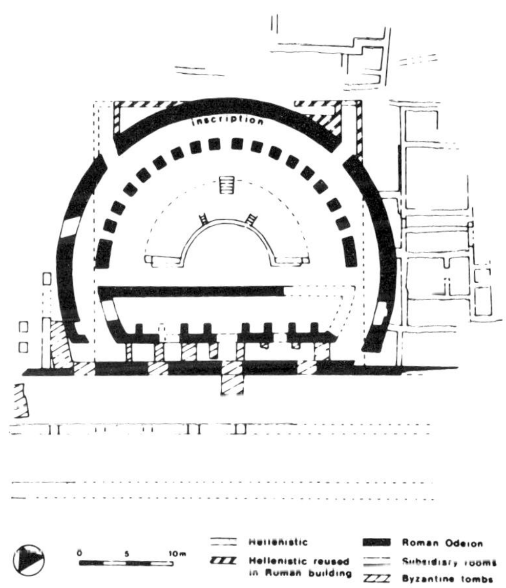

Of the earlier buildings the first to survive to any appreciable extent is Pernier's Period 4: the predecessors to this are only represented by various scraps of architectural mouldings etc. The Period 4 building is of regular

22. *IC.* IV.373.
23. *IC.* IV. Praef. p.12. C. C. Vermeule, *Roman Imperial Art in Greece and Asia Minor* (Harvard, 1968), p.275, leaves the question open but claims that, if the emperor, it is 'a crude portrait with a square face, topping a local work'.
24. *IC.* IV.373.
25. *IC.* I.XVIII.60 (fig.6, p.25 in *Ausonia* VI, 1911).
26. Smith, *op.cit.* note 20, no.794.
27. Listed by Bendinelli, *op.cit.* note 21.
28. M. Lyttelton, *Baroque Architecture in Classical Antiquity* (London, 1974), p.264.
29. L. Pernier, *Ann. Sc. At.* VIII-IX, 1925-6, p.1. *IC.* IV. Praef. p.8-9 with the commentary on the Code no.72. The latest edition of the Code is that of R. F. Willetts, *The Law Code of Gortyn* (Berlin, 1967), but this adds nothing to the archaeology.
30. Theoretically the inscription could have been moved some distance but in practice this seems unlikely. Also the Forum or Agora is where one would expect such a Code to be.

ashlar masonry in alternating thin and thick courses. It survives on the north side beyond the wall of the Code and within this wall on the west side. Its south wall apparently coincided with the later south wall of the *postscenium:* from these walls it seems to have been a building 28m square. To the south there are traces of other walls that might have been part of a portico. The date of this building must be 4-2c BC from the style of the construction and also from various sculptures associated with it. Its purpose is uncertain but the interior of the walls was rough and given the later Odeion and the Code it is quite likely that this was a bouleuterion with a *cavea* within the walls, not impossibly containing the Code in a different position [31] . Amongst the pottery Pernier published from this phase [32] is a stamp *in planta pedis* of the Arretine potter P. Clodius Proculus which is evidence for the continuation of this building into the Augustan period.

It was probably in this same period when Gortyna seems to have been rebuilt as the new capital that the building was remodelled. The main evidence for this is that the blocks of the inscription carry letters of 1c BC form presumably to indicate their order when it was moved, and also that the blocks rest on smaller ones of a different style from the Hellenistic walls. These were reused in the main entrances in the north side leading into the *ambulacrum, c.*29m in diameter and 2.58m wide, which contained the Code and, with its inner wall of 18 arches, helped to support the *cavea.* The walls were of concrete with a stone facing approximating to *opus quadratum.* From the *ambulacrum* the *cavea* and the orchestra could be reached either via the *parodoi* or through three *vomitoria* reached through the inner arcade of the *ambulacrum.* This gallery continued past the *pulpitum* or stage to the *postscenium,* 21.50 x 2.50m. The *opus quadratum* work probably dates to the original Augustan building but much of the structure as it is now visible, including the arcade, is in brick-faced concrete which probably dates to AD 100 when the Odeion was rebuilt, apparently on the same plan as before [33] .

The *cavea* is divided into 3 wedges or *cunei* at the base by the staircases from the orchestra; but there is a second series of four *cunei* divided by the *vomitoria.* The marble seats, 0.70m wide, are supported by concrete on stone vaulting at the rear that originally must have joined the wall of the *ambulacrum.* The orchestra is *c.* 8.50m in internal diameter and is floored with white and blue marble. The *pulpitum* is 3.00m wide with three doors flanked by square niches that probably contained statues of which several fragments were found in the excavation. The *postscenium* was floored with geometric mosaics that only survived at the west end [34] . To the south and west a portico was partially excavated; the western one had another fragmentary mosaic but was much narrower than the 5.00m of the southern portico.

The later history of the Odeion is not too clear: within the building there is a third century AD dedication [35] reused as a step from the east *parodos* up to the *pulpitum* and in the same area a small fountain has a drain inserted around the *ambulacrum.* East of the Odeion there is a range of rooms of uncertain date and function which are definitely secondary to the Odeion. One floor seals a late Hellenistic coin but the other coins from on top of the floors are of the 4c AD, thus dating at least the final period of their use. The mosaic in the largest of the rooms is probably of late 2c or early 3c date [36]. South of this room others appear to have been added on, possibly as a bath range, rather crowding in the east side of the Odeion.

This development of the east side, the changes within the building mentioned above and also the fact that the marble floors were patched with tiles may well indicate a change or series of changes in the use of the Odeion. The date of these is really unknown, but the coins in the east range and the reuse of the dedication makes the late 3c or early 4c quite likely. A parallel for the change of use of an Odeion at about this time is found at the very similar building at Corinth [37] : this was originally built in the last third of the 1c AD, embellished in the later 2c and converted slightly earlier than the Gortyna example, *c.*225, into an arena.

---

31. Macdonald, *Political Meeting Places of the Greeks* (Baltimore, 1943), p.189f., seems over cautious in his analysis of these early phases. If this building was a bouleuterion it would have been similar to those at Miletus or Priene.
32. p.31. This potter is Oxe-Comfort no.454.
33. *IC.*IV.331 Imp. Caesar Divi Nervae f.
Traianus Aug. Germ. p.m. t.pot.
IIII p.p. cos.III civitati Gortyniorum
Odeum ruina conlapsum restituit
curante L. Elufrio Severo pro cos.
34. No longer visible. See p.53.
35. *IC.*IV.257.
36. See p.53.
37. J. O. Broneer, *Corinth* X (Harvard, 1932).

Finally at the Odeion, most of the building appears to have been abandoned except the area of the *postscenium*. Here the original walls were reinforced with small buttresses inside against the north wall and the apertures in the south wall were blocked up. In addition a new wall was built at the west end on top of the mosaic shutting off this end. In the west and south porticoes tombs were built, made of rough stones. These tombs were built on the earlier floors but seem to have been dug down onto them, indicating that at the date of their construction this area of the Odeion had been ruinous for some time. Pernier suggested that these tombs were associated with the cathedral of St.Titus of *c.* AD 600 a short distance to the south. This seems very likely but the only dating evidence for the tombs is a fragment of a late 5c/early 6c capital [38] and a much earlier – 4/5c – belt fitting of the zoomorphic type with two dolphins holding the bar for the pin [39].

Other Structures

Knossos (8/4): Basilica (Pl.25) The only public building apart from the theatre known from the *colonia* is the basilica[40], situated in the SE quarter of the city, just a short distance south of the theatre. All that can be seen nowadays are a few fragments of its barrel-vaults just east of the main road, before the entrance to the Villa Ariadne on the opposite side. As with the theatres the main source for this building is Belli's plan and limited trial trenches dug in 1937.

The basilica basically consisted of a long hall ending in an apse with an elaborate fore-building flanked by peristyle courtyards. The apse was *c.* 12m long with massive buttresses at its apex and sides. The hall itself was composed of a central nave with 24 barrel-vaulted arches opening into it on each side and double piers beyond the arches. The total width from outer pier to pier was 32 m and the length of the hall *c.* 105m[41] ; while the central nave was only 12m wide. It would seem most likely that the plan as drawn by Belli shows the substructures supporting the triple-aisled hall itself above. Belli shows the arches as being of all the same width but Pococke[42] distinguished a difference between the north and south sides; in fact he must have been a bit muddled since the long sides of the hall are orientated nearly north-south. He claimed the width of the north arches as 6feet (*c.* 2m) and the south as 18 (*c.* 5.5m). These measurements can only be checked on the west side – Pococke's north probably – where the two surviving vaults are of 4m and 9m width! The walls of the vaults survive to the springing point of the arch and are 2m high above present ground level. They are constructed of coarse cement with no surviving facing although a tile levelling course can be seen in one of the walls.

The fore-building of the basilica was an oblong group of rooms, 64m x 27m, entered through a porch, 30m x 9m, with eight free-standing columns between the side walls which seem to end in piers with three engaged half-columns. On either side of the group of rooms are peristyle courtyards with 12 columns, perhaps grouped round a fountain [43] . The actual building is divided in two down its long axis and each half is further divided with a small room at each end of the central long room. In the outer of the two groups of rooms the main room is further divided into three. Originally there must have been staircases up to the higher hall from this building.

Because of the extremely limited nature of the 1937 work and the even more cursory report, Belli's plan is really our only evidence for the building overall. It is normally identified as the Basilica of the *colonia* and this would seem to be reasonable. The best evidence for this structure having a central vaulted hall is the existence on the plan of the massive buttresses around the apse. What is shown by Belli between the apse and the fore-building must be the substructures carrying the aisles above; possibly the lack of any outside walls on the plan is quite accurate for the piers and vaults would have made excellent shops opening out from the Basilica. The 12m span between the vaults is not too great for a floor either of timber or carried by some type of vault.

The only parallels for the basic design of the building is the Basilica at Aspendos [44] which is almost identical as far as the main hall is concerned; it is 105.48m x 26.90m and the nave is 11.15m wide However, its fore-

---

38. Pernier, *op.cit.* note 29, p.61, fig.56.
39. Pernier, *op.cit.* note 29, p.60, fig. 54. An identical buckle has been found at Anemurium in the recent excavations (Dr. J. Williams, Lecture at Oxford, 1973).
40. Belli ed. Falkener p.24, ed. Spanake p.150, pl. KZ, M.S.F. Hood, 'Archaeological Survey of the Knossos area', (London, n.d.) no.64 for ref. to R. Radford's unpublished excavations of 1937. Personal observation.
41. This measurement is greater than that given in the Radford report, but it is admitted in the report that the southern end was not clear and the other dimensions given agree with those from Belli, from where the 105m is taken.
42. Pococke, *op.cit.* note 21, p.255.
43. There is no evidence for such fountains, but given the design of the courtyard it seems quite likely that they existed.
44. G. Niemann and E. Petersen, *Städte Pamphyliens und Pisidiens* I (Wien, 1890), p.87, fig.76, pl.xvii.

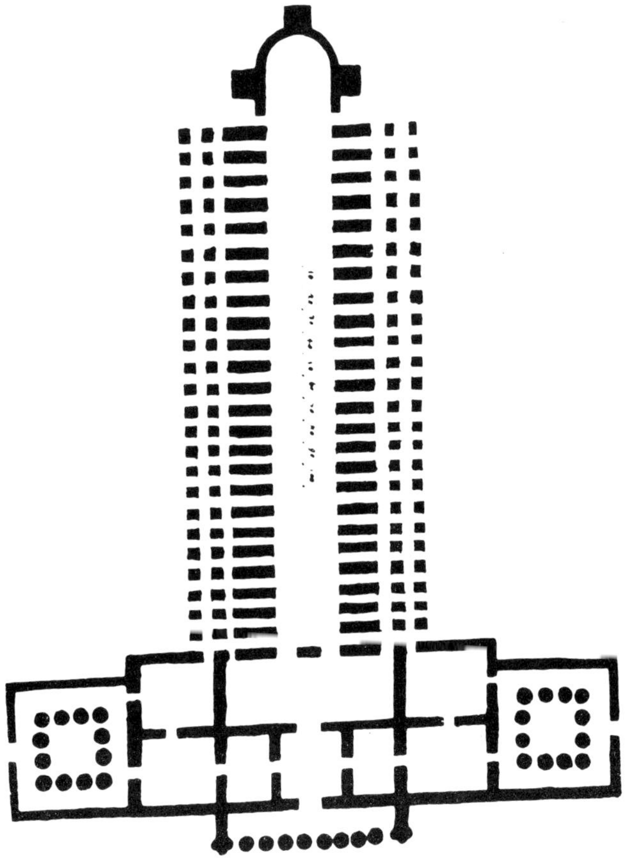

Pl. 25: Belli's plan of the basilica at Knossos.
Pl. 26: Peristyle of the Villa Dionysus, Knossos.
Pl. 27: Capital from the doorway to the oecus of the Villa Dionysus, Knossos.

building is simpler and the entire structure is in stone and therefore lacks the complex concrete substructures. This building dates probably to the 2c AD. The dating of the Knossos Basilica is uncertain; the 1937 excavations claimed a 2/3c date but the report gives no reasons. Possibly the true date may be given by an inscription found in the area in 1887[45]. It is a dedication either by Claudius in January of 43 or by Nerva in late 97 to the *colonia;* unfortunately quite what the Emperor gave has been lost but it might have been this new building. If this was the case the style of construction would make it more likely that the Emperor involved was Nerva than Claudius. The occasion of Domitian's judgement between Capua and the *colonia* in AD 84[46] may perhaps have afforded the opportunity for the *colonia* to ask for their new 'town hall'. Architecturally the design of the forehall is indeed reminiscent of parts of the Domus Flavia in Rome[47].

Knossos: Villa Dionysus (Pl.26, Fig.12) Opposite the Basilica is the site of this villa[48] with its splendid mosaics[49] of the god which have given the house its name. The mosaics are laid in a series of rooms set about a central peristyle courtyard with Doric columns which once had slight stucco fluting. The peristyle measures 10m E-W and 9m N-S with 6 columns on each long side, 5 on the east and 4 on the west. On this side there is also a brick nymphaeum with a small central exedra facing the main room or *oecus* through the gap left by the missing column. There seems to have been a balustrade between the columns round the rest of the courtyard, interrupted only by a small well at the SW corner.

Fig.12. Knossos: plan of the Villa Dionysus.

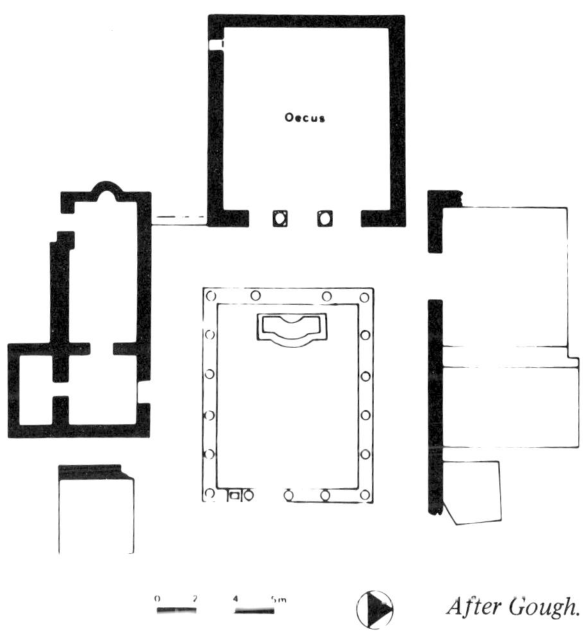

After Gough.

The *oecus*, 8.50m square, with its mosaic covering the entire floor, has in its doorway two Corinthian columns of pink marble 3.50m high on bases 0.26m high. The capitals, 0.52m high, are good examples of the early 2c type found on the coast of Asia Minor at Ephesus and Pergamon[50](Pl.27). The walls of the room had marble inlay and on the south side were pierced by two windows looking out onto a narrow passage. The north range is composed of three rooms, two with mosaics of the Dionysiac cult and the other with a plain geometric one. The south range includes what seems to be a shrine with a brick niche in its end wall and a geometric mosaic floor. There had originally been a window here also, looking towards the south, but in the 3c this was blocked off by another house. From the porch of this room there may have been a stair up to a gallery or second storey.

---

45. *IC.*I.VIII.50.
46. P. Ducrey, 'Trois nouvelles inscriptions crétoises', *BCH* XCIII, 1969, p.841.
47. W. Macdonald, *Architecture of the Roman Empire* (Yale, 1965), p.140.
48. *JHS* LV, 1935, p.164; *AR* 1957, p.24; *AR* 1958, p.22, *AR* 1960-1, p.29-30, *AR* 1971-2, p.22. *Survey* no.67. Personal observation.
49. See p.51.
50. W. D. Heilmeyer, *Korinthische Normalkapitelle* (Heidelberg, 1970), pl.25, 28.

The date of the villa's construction must be the early 2c from the style of the capitals, mosaics and pottery. The most important find from the site was a statue of Hadrian now to be seen in the front garden of the Villa Ariadne[51] and this would also fit the suggested date. However, the life of the building seems to have been very short as the pottery from its destruction dates to 160-180[52] : this would explain the blocking of the window in the south range in the 3c when the building was presumably in ruins. The purpose of this typical Mediterranean peristyle house seems to have been linked to the cult of Dionysus, as witnessed by the mosaics of the god and his entourage, and wall plaster fragments showing women and satyrs, not to mention the large number of amphorae and erotic lamps recovered from the building.

Kato Asites (9/14) (Fig.13) On the SW edge of this village stands a trilobate bath house surviving up to roof height[53] . It is constructed of rough ashlar-faced concrete with tile levelling courses. The entrance was by a doorway, now blocked, in its west wall which led into a rectangular chamber, 5.80m x 10.30m, floored with a red, blue and white marble geometric mosaic with a guilloche border and white marble quarter-round moulding around the edges. Three apsidal-ended baths opened out of this chamber, each bath 3.70m x 2.50m and at least 1.65m deep. The best preserved bath is on the east side where the lining of *opus signinum* can be clearly seen, as well as the three steps leading down into the bath and the narrow bench at 1.20m depth. The eastern wall of the building had windows on either side of the bath but one of these was later converted into a doorway, presumably when the original western doorway was blocked. The date of its construction is unknown but is probably earlier rather than later in the Roman period: later still it was reused as a church dedicated to St. Catherine. The closest parallel in Crete is the 5c martyrion at Gortyna[54] while outside the island the type of building seems to be commoner in Italy and Africa than in Greece and the east[55].

Fig.13. Kato Asites: plan of the bath house.

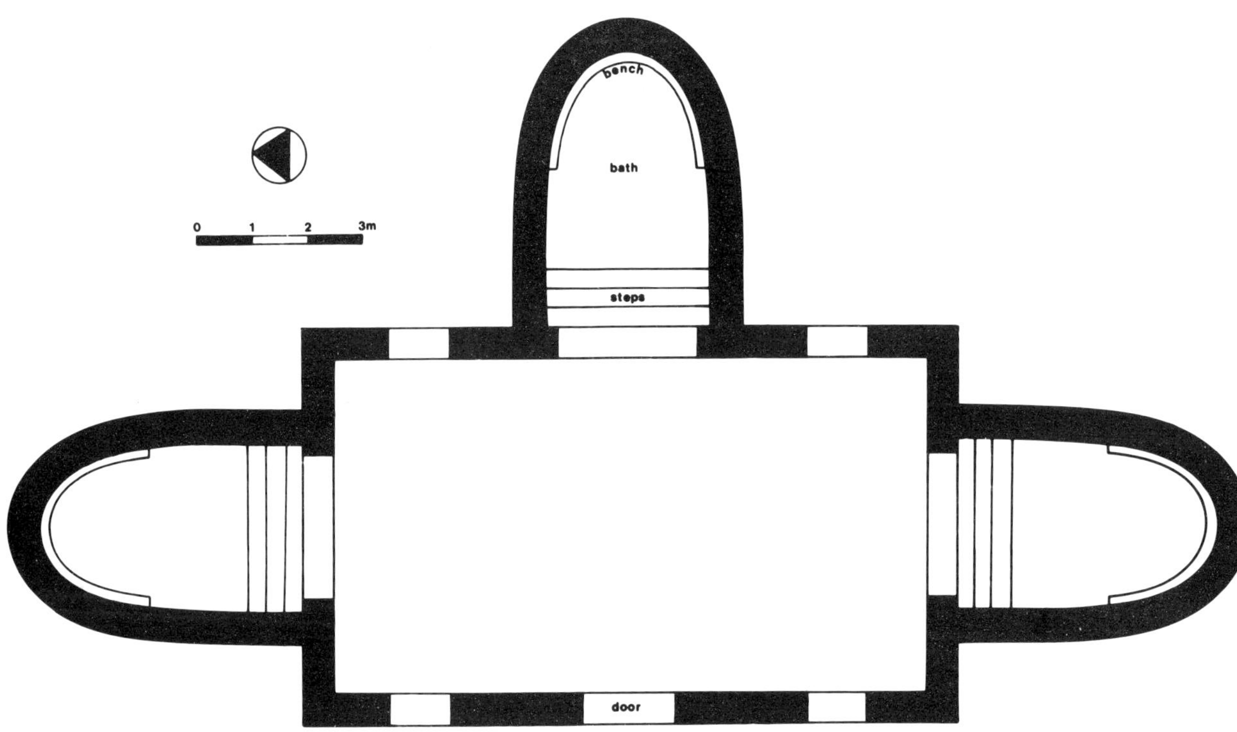

Gortyna (10/10): The Circus On the edge of the city, south of the amphitheatre, is the site of the circus[56]: very little can be seen as the entire area is now under arable cultivation. Very limited work has shown it to have been about 374m long and a maximum of 68m wide, narrowing to 51.50m at the *carceres* at the northern

---

51. C. C. Vermeule, 'Hellenistic and Roman cuirassed statues', *Berytus* XIII.1, 1959, no.185.
52. Information from letter of 18/3/74 from Dr. John Hayes.
53. *Mon. Ven.* II, p.245. *A. Delt.* XIX.2, 1964, p.444. Personal observation.
54. See p.113. Another possible conversion of a bath house to church occurs at the site of Ligortynos (7/27).
55. Dealt with in E. H. Freshfield, *Cellae Trichorae* (London, 1913).
56. A. M. Colini, *Boll. d'Arte,* XXIX, 1935-6, p.364. Personal observation. Belli ed Falkener p.23 adds no real information.

end. No trace of the gates themselves was found but at the centre of each long side various fragments of columns and statuary were recovered. The latter were confined to the east side and probably marked the position of the governor's box. The west side differed from the eastern in that it was not straight but kinked in to give a clear start from the *carceres.* Only two fragments of the *spina* were found; at 219 and 277m along the track. The entire structure was built of stone-faced concrete with the piers of the substructure 1.95m apart.

There is no evidence for the date of its construction but a date in the 2c is not improbable, given the type of building and the general development of the city in this century. It was used at least into the 6c when an inscription proclaiming support for the Greens was put up [57]. The circus at Gortyna is slightly smaller than the suggested standard size of 400m [58] if the dimensions given, derived without proper excavation, are correct.

Gortyna: The Acropolis (Fig.14) The extent of occupation on the Acropolis at any period is still largely unknown but from the excavations carried out by the Italian School on the Temple/Basilica site and the Altar on the east slopes, it would seem that there was little activity in the early Roman period. On the temple site some 1c AD work is probable, but the Altar appears to have gone out of use in the Hellenistic period [59].

Fig. 14. Gortyna: plan of the Acropolis area.

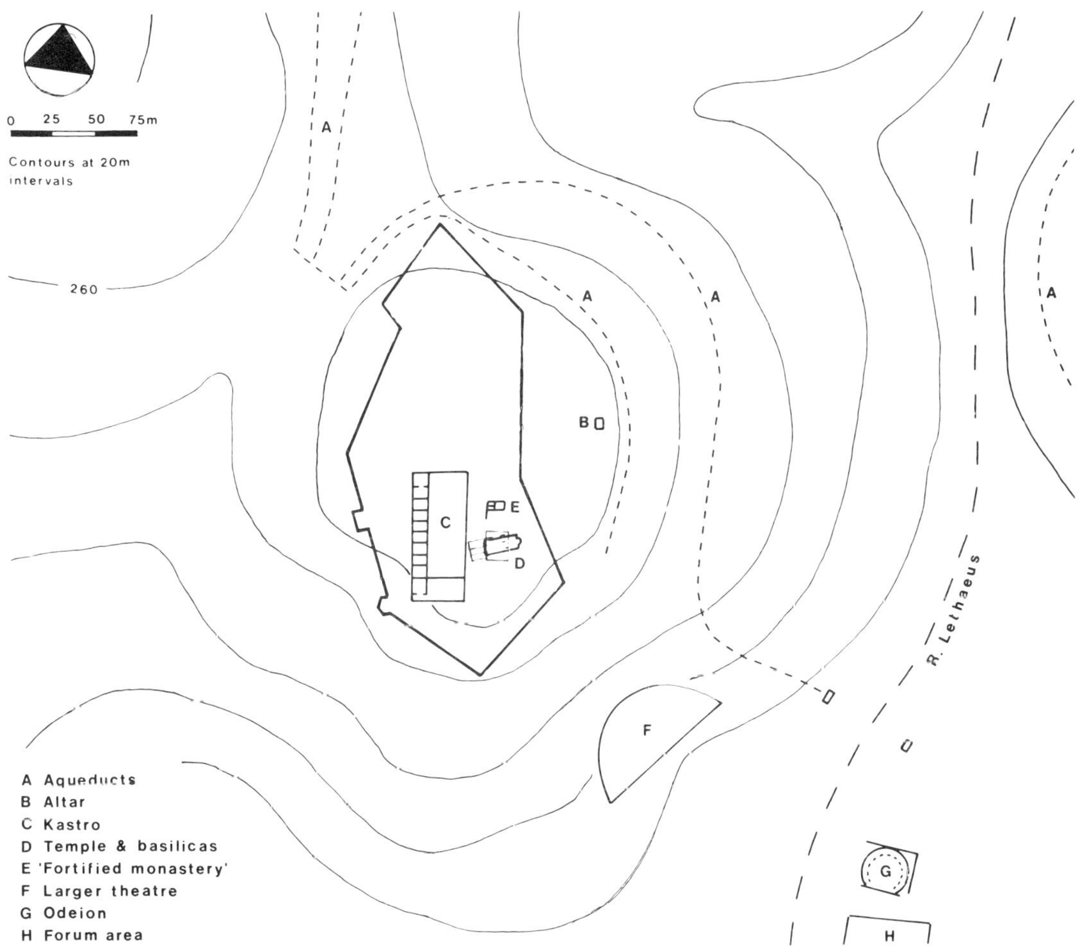

It was probably in the 6c AD that the temple site was reused as a church [60], just a short distance away from the vast construction known as the Castrum or 'To Kastro' [61]. This has never been excavated and was only roughly planned by Taramelli. The main part of the building is a rectangular hall, 59m x 24.50 x 8m high, with

---

57. *IC.*IV.513.
58. M. Vickers, 'The Hippodrome at Thessaloniki', *JRS* LXII, 1972, p.29.
59. G. Rizza and V. Scrinari, *Il Sanctuario sull'Acropoli di Gortina* (Rome, 1968), part I, ch.2, Part II, ch.4.
60. See p.109.
61. A. Taramelli, *AJA* VI, 1902, p.101f. Spratt II, p.31. Personal observation.

Pl. 28: Western wall of the main hall of the Kastro, Acropolis of Gortyna.
Pl. 29: Joint between the wall of the main hall and an outer chamber of the Kastro, Acropolis of Gortyna.
Pl. 30: External facing and core of the defensive wall of the Acropolis of Gortyna.

smaller chambers on its west and south sides. These are at a higher level than the main hall which is sunk 5-6m into the rock. This main portion of the building is of splendid brick-faced concrete (Pl.28), 1.50m thick, while the outer chambers are of stone-faced concrete with tile levelling courses. These side chambers are obviously of secondary construction though well keyed into the original wall (Pl.29).

The date and function of the original hall are unknown; it respects the temple site although this could be a coincidence and the church seems to be later, having various walls apparently joining it to the Kastro. From the nature of its construction it is unlikely to be earlier than *c.* AD 100. Both Spratt and Taramelli thought it had been vaulted but it is no longer possible to verify or disprove this. Its size and position make it almost certain to have been an official building but beyond this it is hard to see what it could have been: it has no obvious military function and although it could have been a cistern, there is no trace of lining and the aqueduct runs well below the top of the hill. When the church had been built it might have been used by the church authorities but it seems rather too large and well built a building to be subordinate to such a small and scrubby basilica.

The outer chambers, of a later date, number nine on the west side, measuring 9.50m x 5-6m with walls standing up to 4m high. The two northern ones are intercommunicating but all the rest simply have doors, 1.50m wide, to the exterior. On the south side there are two rooms, one 11m x 9.50m, the other 11m x 5.50m, with an entrance 3.50m in width. This end is now totally in ruins. The side chambers are built in a very similar way to the great wall surrounding the acropolis and may indicate that by this date at any rate, the whole building had acquired a military function.

This defensive wall (Pl.30), *c.* 500m in circumference, is of concrete with good stone facing and occasional tiles used as levelling or in relieving arches. It is a minimum of 2m width, set on a slightly wider foundation and survives up to 6m in height. It is irregular in plan, following the contours of the hill, and has extra bastions at certain weaker points, especially the SW corner where there is a massive polygonal bastion with internal tile relieving arches or what is left of an internal vaulted chamber. Taramelli claimed that there was a secondary fore-work on the SE corner but this is no longer visible. No gate can be made out at any point on the circuit. The date of this wall, and therefore of the interior building, can be assigned with reasonable accuracy to the 7-8c. The evidence for this consists of a lead seal of one Antiochus, *cubicularius* and *chartularius,* found in the construction trench of the wall in the north trench of the Italian excavations in the Altar area[62]. Stylistically this is dated to the 7c which links in to coins of Heraclius found associated with a late building in the Altar area. Given the undoubtedly military nature of these works it would seem reasonable to connect their construction to the disturbances of the 7c in the form of either the Slavic raids early in the century or the Arab conquest later on.

Gortyna: The Temple of Isis and Serapis (Fig.15) Although the cult of these Egyptian divinities is known from several other sites on the island[63], the only temple known is that at Gortyna. The basic temple[64], constructed of stone, is a very simple *cella,* wider than it is long at 8.70m x 8.10m, with an entrance on the west side and a tripartite podium opposite it against the east wall. The floor of the room was of red tiles. The podium is 1.50m deep and 0.90m high; the central part is 2.55m long and the two side portions 1.80m. On the podium stood the statues of the gods, with Serapis in the centre flanked by Isis on one side and probably Hermes Anubis on the other. At the south end of the podium are three small steps on which the ritual vessels probably stood.

3.80m in front of the *cella* is a stylobate stretching 13.50m NS across the front of the entire temple. In her plan Salditt-Trapmann only shows this with four bases just in front of the actual *cella,* but Oliverio's photograph[65] clearly shows it continuing right across the building with one column base at its far south end. The columns are of grey granite and are 3.60m tall, tapering from 0.54 to 0.43m on bases 0.64m square. They are of the Ionic order and originally numbered six.

---

62. *Op.cit.* n.59, p.116-9, find no.19. The seal is no.747 in G. Zacos and A. Veglery, *Byzantine Lead Seals* (Basel, 1972), I.1, p.556.
63. See p.37.
64. G. Oliverio. *Ann. Sc. At.* I, 1914, p.376; II, 1916, p.309. *Italian Guide* p.23. Personal observation. R. Salditt-Trappmann, *Tempel der ägyptischen Götter in Griechenland und an der Westküste Kleinasiens* (Leiden, 1970), ch.6, p.54.
65. *Ann. Sc. At.* II, Fig.3, p.311.
66. *IC.* IV.249.

Pl. 31: Crypt of the temple of Isis and Serapis, Gortyna.
Pl. 32: Nymphaeum by the Praetorium, Gortyna.

Fig.15. Gortyna: plan of the temple of Isis and Serapis.

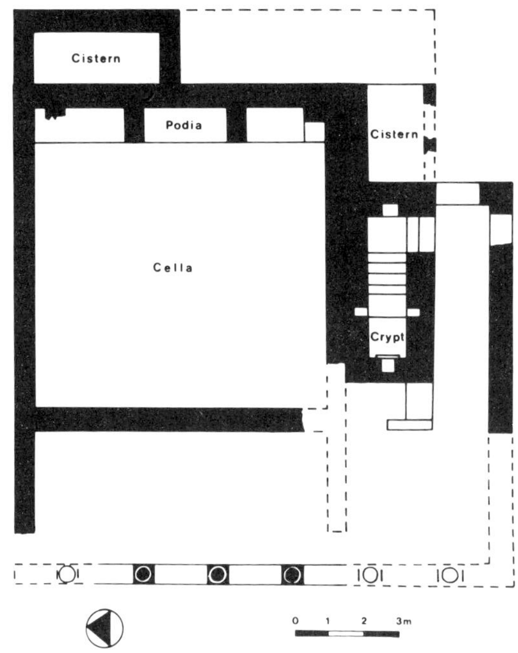

South of the main room is a group of rooms comprising a narrow hall, a crypt and a possible cistern. The hall is one the south side of the complex and was entered either from the pronaos or through a door in its east wall. Right in the SE corner of this hall is a large niche in the wall, 0.30m above the floor. Between this hall and the *cella* is the crypt (Pl.31); this is entered from the hall by a flight of two steps down to a platform, then four more steps at right angles to the first flight down to a wider step and so down to the floor, 1.15m square at 2.20m depth. In the walls of the crypt there are four rounded niches; one in the east wall at the top of the second flight of stairs, one on either side of the final wide step and the largest one in the west wall above the final floor. The three bottom niches almost certainly held small statues of the gods. The crypt would have been the place of initiation where the worshipper symbolically drowned to be reborn in the 'waters of the Nile', fed from a group of cisterns to the east of the crypt. One cistern was directly behind the crypt with a further large tank, 3.70m x 1.50m, behind the main *cella*.

The date of the temple is given by the dedication by Flavia Philyra [66] of 1/2c AD where she describes how, with her children, she rebuilt the temple from its foundations. This proves the existence of an earlier temple and inscriptions of the 2c BC reused in the present building [67] must have come from this Hellenistic shrine.

Gortyna: Nymphaea About 90m north of the probable bath complex are the remains of a rectangular nymphaeum (Fig.16), 17m x 6m, partially excavated and published by P. Perali [68] . The building is of quite good rubble cement with a tile facing. The walls on the three sides of the actual basin, which is 12.40 x 2.80 x 0.42m deep, are all decorated with half-round niches and tile pilasters, ten in the rear wall and four on each side wall. Free-standing columns 2.88m high were found at the rear corners but there were probably also others along the facade. The main feed came through the central niche into the central basin and thence into smaller marble basins set along the front of the nymphaeum. At some date after its initial construction the open basin was converted into a vaulted cistern.

The nymphaeum by the praetorium is very similar to the one just described (Pl.32, Fig.17): it is about the same length, 17m, but slightly wider at 8m and its basin is larger at 11.50 x 4.50 x 1.00m deep [69] . The walls are decorated in exactly the same manner with the same number of niches and pilasters. Only one column base was found but several Ionic capitals, very similar to those from the nearby Mavropapas site [70] , were uncovered.

---

67. *IC.*IV.243-8, 290.
68. Perali, *Ann. Sc. At.* I, 1914, p.149.
69. A. Maiuri, *Ann. Sc. At.* I, 1914, p.119.
70. See p.109, dated 2/3c.

This nymphaeum was also converted into a covered cistern with a barrel vault *c.*3.00m high. At the same time the front was rebuilt and cut-down sarcophagi used as basins. Possibly associated with this are four columns erected in front of the nymphaeum with dedications to M. Heraclius and his family[71]. Alternatively these columns may be later and the conversion rather connected to the late 4c rebuilding of the Praetorium where very similar brickwork was used.

Fig.16. Gortyna: plan of the Nymphaeum near the baths.

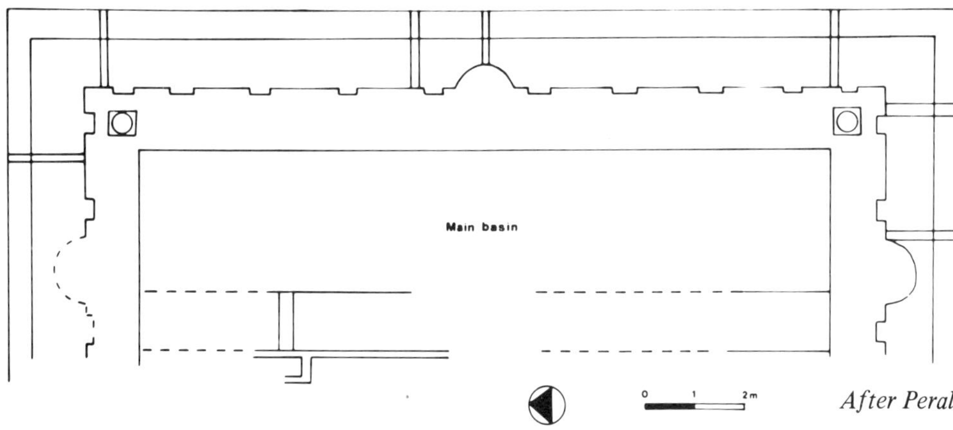

After Perali.

Both nymphaea are obviously built in the same method and style and so are likely to be close in date if not actually contemporary. Their rectangular form compares closely to the 2c AD nymphaea of Asia Minor [72] and differs from the curved nymphaeum of Herodes Atticus at Olympia on the mainland [73] . Here again as with the theatres, the strongest architectural connections seem to be with the coast of Asia Minor.

Fig.17. Gortyna: plan of the Nymphaeum near the Praetorium.

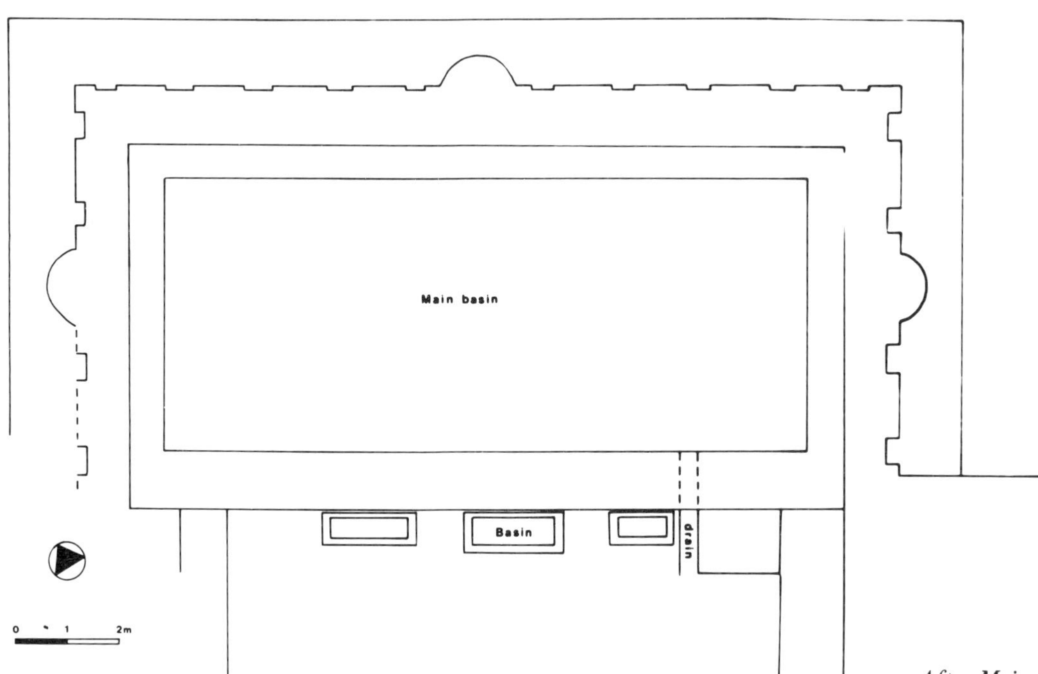

After Maiuri

71. *IC.*IV.512.
72. Lyttelton, *op.cit.* note 28, p.265.
73. *Ibid.* p.278, fig.47.

Pl. 33: Temple of Pythian Apollo, Gortyna.
Pl. 34: Northwest end of the Praetorium complex, Gortyna, from the north side.

Pl. 35: Capitals from the 2c phase of the Praetorium, Gortyna.
Pl. 36: Architectural fragments from the 2c phase of the Praetorium, Gortyna.

Gortyna: The Temple of Pythian Apollo (Pl.33, Fig.33) In the centre of the city is the site of the greatest of its temples [74], probably dating back to the 7c BC in origin and continuing as the religious centre of the city until it was replaced by the cathedral of St. Titus *c.*600 AD. Apart from the conversion of the building into a church [75] little of the structure is of Roman date. The original simple *cella,* 16.30m x 14.45m, probably dates back to the 7c BC with the interesting feature of a rectangular bothros, 1.62 x 1.01 x 2.10m deep, just inside the doorway to the right. In the 3/2c BC a more elaborate pronaos, 16.80m x 6.08m, was added. The actual date may be 183 BC when the treaty between the city and Eumenes of Pergamon was concluded and engraved on one of the four pilasters on the front of the temple [76]. These pilasters were flanked by half-engaged Doric columns, 1.00m in diameter, making the Hellenistic temple pseudo-prostyle hexastyle. Various architectural fragments of similar date were found, including a fine lion head *sima* and an acroterion. In front of the temple is a small prothysis, 1.43m square, which originally had a column 0.875m high set on it. Beyond this is a stepped monumental altar, 4.62 x 3.73 x 1.09m high [77]. The prothysis included concrete which must indicate repairs of Roman date. Just NE of the temple is a small Heröon made of orthostats surrounding a chamber 2.70m x 1.40m in which cinerary remains were found. This is also Hellenistic, *c.*2c BC as dated by its dedicatory inscription [78].

Gortyna: The Praetorium (Pl.34, Fig.18) The Palace of the governor has been excavated at various times since 1912 but as yet little has been published of this large and complex structure [79]. It is clear that there are at least two major phases, one dating to the 2c AD and the other to the 4c, and there is probably a third, possibly Augustan, phase. Little of this earliest building has yet been found but there is definitely Augustan material in a layer above a Hellenistic structure of unknown function [80].

Fig.18. Gortyna: plan of the Praetorium.

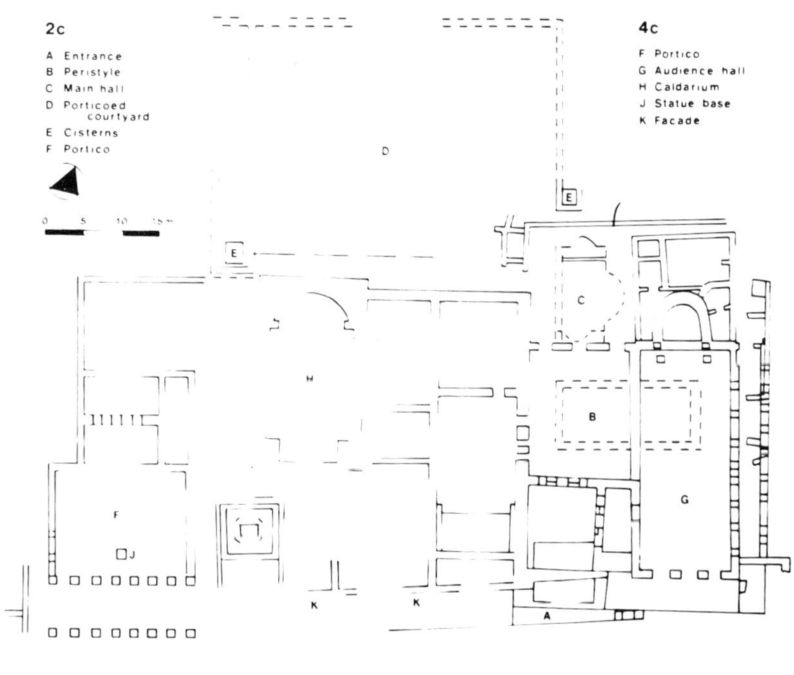

After Colini.

The 2c AD palace underlies the entire later building and is consequently much destroyed. It must have covered at least 10,000 square metres, and possibly more, extending off to the SE. Not enough has survived to reconstruct the plan but it is clear that the official part of the building was below and south of the later basilica. The original entrance seems to have been opposite the nymphaeum, which was probably built at the same date as the palace. From the entrance one passed through a peristyle with cisterns feeding a bath suite to its east into

74. F. Halbherr, *Mon. Ant.* I, 1889, p.1. Savignoni, *Mon. Ant.* XVIII, 1907, p.177. *IC.*IV.Praef. p.5.
75. See p.108.
76. *IC.*IV.179-186.
77. Of the group 71 Stepped Monumental Altars in C. G. Yavis, *Greek Altars* (St. Louis, 1949). The altar is rather small for this group but no.9 from Delos is comparable.
78. *IC.*IV.259.
79. *Ann. Sc. At.* I, 1914, p.377; II, 1916, p.306; XXXI new series II, 1969-70, p.349. A. M. Colini, *Kret. Khron.* XXV, 1973, p.469-70. Personal observation. Personal communication from Dr. D. Levi.
80. *Ann. Sc. At.* XXXI-II, 1969-70, p.449: Arretine in layer.

what was probably the main hall. This was aligned E-W and had a triple-apsed end. The hall seems to have formed the north side of a porticoed courtyard which stretched *c.*30m N-S and 35m E-W. At the two west ends of the porticos, cisterns were found, no doubt to supply fountains or baths in the complex.

South-east of this portico was another, reused in the 4c palace but originally 2c. It is possible that its northern side was rebuilt in the later period but on the other three sides the columns are slender, fluted marble ones which contrast with the gigantic monolithic granite columns of the double row on the northern side. The architectural fragments cluttering up the courtyard are of finely carved white marble with capitals of both the Ionic and the Corinthian orders. The latter (Pl.35) closely resemble ones from the Villa Dionysus at Knossos and from Asia Minor those from the Temple of Hadrian at Ephesus and the Temple in the Traianeum at Pergamon. There are also some slightly squatter capitals that resemble those from the Asklepeion at Pergamon [81] . The fragments of the architrave (Pl.36), bearing an imperial dedication to a nameless Emperor, are extremely similar to those from the upper order of the *scaenae frons* of the theatre at Aspendos [82] . From these parallels it would seem most likely that the palace should be dated to early-middle 2c and again shows the strong influence of Asia Minor in the architectural decoration of this period in Crete.

In 381-3 the governor of Crete, Oecumenius Dositheus Asclepiodotus, rebuilt the palace, which had probably suffered from the earthquake of 375[83], and loyally placed statues of the three Emperors, Gratian, Valentian and Theodosius, by the new entrance[84]. The area redeveloped seems to have been the north side of the building, which was rearranged so that the major reception area was now in the NW corner where a large audience hall, 27m x 12m, was built. In this hall there were numerous statues of contemporary imperial officers whose dedicatory bases have survived although the statues themselves have not [85] . This hall was built of stone-faced concrete with tile levelling courses as distinct from the bulk of this phase which was of tile-faced concrete, including the large fragment of wall separating the public and private areas to the south. This still stands *c.*8m high and over 1m thick and included a 7m wide archway that could still be seen in the 18c by Tournefort and Pococke. F. Barozzi [86] drew the arch in 1577, showing it with Ionic pilasters on either side; then two Ionic columns in front with four statues on bases on either side. Unfortunately this drawing cannot be accurate unless the perspective is totally wrong and the bases that seem to be at right angles to the wall are in fact parallel to it. Also, the wall between the hall and its statues and the high wall is not shown at all. It may not have been visible, and the two free-standing columns might mark a doorway in it.

East of this wall lay the bath suite which had a large apsidal-ended caldarium, 20m x 10m, with the stoke-holes in the south wall. Beyond this is a range of rooms as yet uncleared, linking in to the north with the 2c portico with its new north wing of the mammoth columns *c.*7m high that seem to form part of the whole north facade of the new palace. Within the courtyard of the portico is a statue-base 1.85m^2 that is aligned onto the new colonnade and so is presumably of the same date. Various other rooms are known including "late lavatories" just north of the caldarium. It is not known what lies south and east of the area excavated, but the nymphaeum on the northern side continued in use as did the courtyards to the west where there were two square fountains which probably date back to the 2c palace.

The life of the palace continued through the late Roman period, probably into the Arab era, after which it seems to have become a monastery with the basilica cut up into cells and the area south of it made into storage rooms [87].

Lebena (10/23) (Figs. 19,59) The great sanctuary of Asklepios here was partially excavated by the Italian School at the beginning of the century but apart from very brief accounts has never been properly published [88] . The sanctuary is on a bay of the coast, open to the south but sheltered by capes on its east and west sides; the actual shrine is grouped about the spring whose reputed medicinal qualities led to the founding of the site.

---

81. Heilmeyer, *op.cit.* note 50, Taf. 25.2 (Ephesos, temple of Hadrian), Taf. 27.1 (Pergamon, Traianeum), Taf. 28. 3-4 (Asclepeion).
82. Lyttleton, *op.cit.* note 28, p.264, pl.185.
83. Zosimus *Hist. Nov.* IV.18.
84. *IC.*IV.284, a, b.
85. *IC.*IV.313-22.
86. R. Ricci, *Mon. Ant.* II, 1890, p.317f. This article collects all the references to the wall in previous works.
87. *Boll. D'Arte* XXX, 1936-7, p.548 fig.3. *IC.*IV.468 for the inscribed lid found in the stores. Guarducci's date of 6c is far too early when compared to the context of the vessels and their form.
88. *IC.*I.XVII passim. *Rend. Linc.* X, 1901, p.300f. F. Halbherr and G. Porro, 'Il tesoro dell'Asclepios di Lebena', *Studi Romani* II, 1914, p.373. *Italian Guide* p.67f. Belli ed Falkener p.20, ed. Spanake pl.Kξ. Personal observation.

Fig.19. Lebena: plan of the sanctuary area.

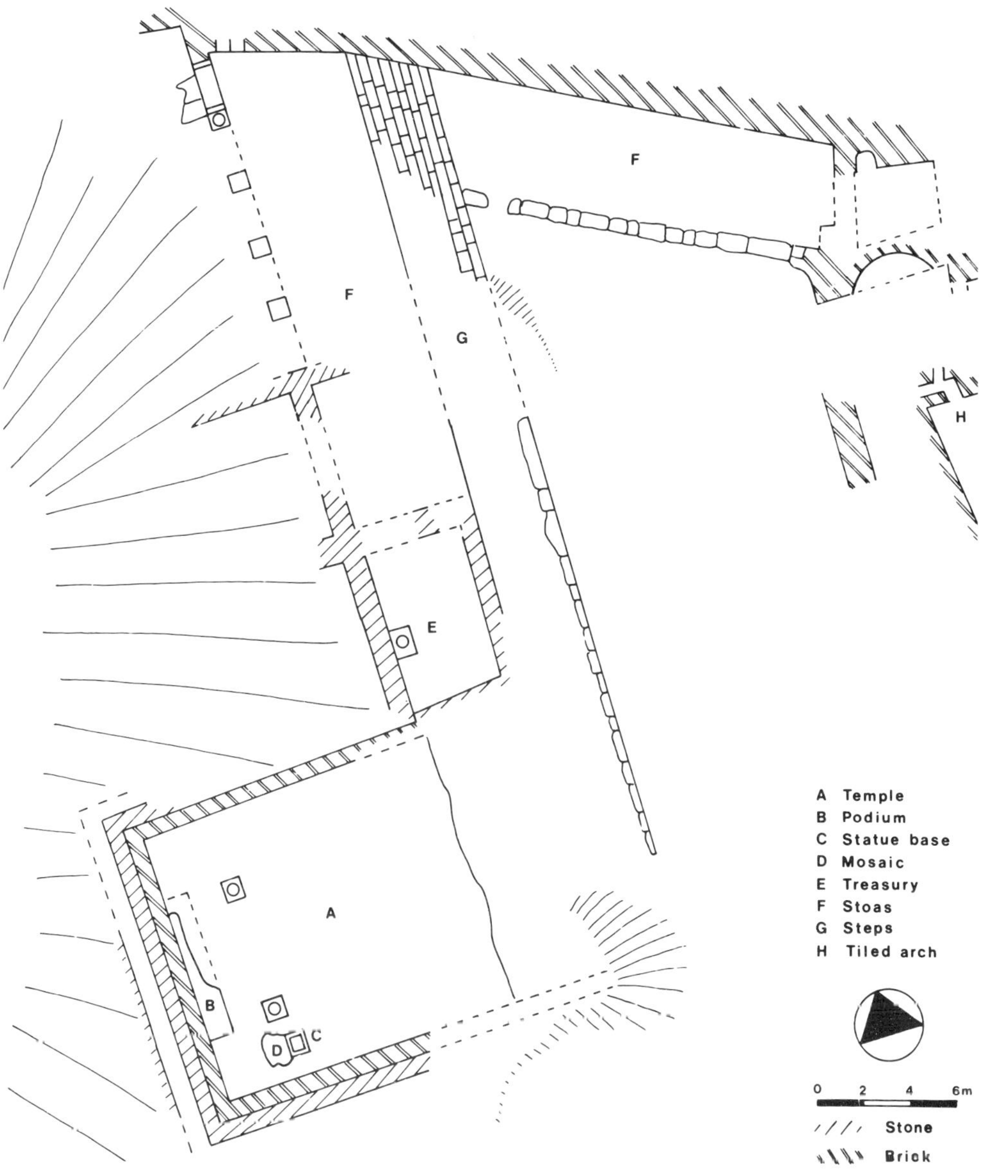

The part of the sanctuary excavated by the Italians is basically of early Hellenistic date, modified or restored in the late Hellenistic period and in the 2-3c AD. The temple itself is very simple; a *cella* 12m x 13m with a podium at its west end (the inner end), 6.00 x 1.35 x 0.65m high, for the statue of the god, like the temple of Asklepios at Lissos. The temple was originally built of stone but in the Roman restoration it was rebuilt with a lining of brick. The walls still stand 3.50m high. In front of the podium two granite columns stand, 4.70m high above the Roman mosaic floor, now only surviving in a patch by the more southerly of the columns, behind the statue-base erected by Xenion in the 2/3c [89]. The mosaic is in blue and white tesserae set in geometric patterns. In the temple Belli discovered a panel showing a large serpent, no doubt the one that originally 'found' the site [90].

To the north of the temple, at right angles to it, is a stoa, 27m x 5m, and to the east a flight of partially preserved marble stairs leading up to the stoa and temple which seem to have been raised on an artificial terrace. The northern part of the stoa was colonnaded but the southern 6.50m of it is taken up by the treasury. In the early Hellenistic phase a very fine pebble mosaic of a sea-horse had been laid [91]; it probably dates to the 4th or

89. *IC.* I. XVII. 25.
90. *Ibid.* no. 10.
91. See p.55.

Pl. 37: Arch of the spring at Lebena.
Pl. 38: Belli's plan of the temple at Lebena.
Pl. 39: Belli's plan of the building at Lappa.

early 3c BC (Pl.15). In the 2c BC the horse's tail was amputated by the sinking of a circular hole, 0.58m in diameter and 1.50m deep. This had a stone plug with locking lugs. In front of this, through the body of the unfortunate creature, another hole, 0.91m square, had been cut more crudely to a depth of 1.90m. This room is identified as a treasury by the inscription from it [92] which must date from the 2/1c BC from the letter forms. On the stones of the circular hole there are further well-cut letters, all alpha, presumably for Asklepios.

At an acute angle to the northern end of the stoa is another portico, 18m x 5.10m, of stone but ending in a curved exedra of concrete faced with stone and tile. In front (south) of this more work in similar material including a tiled arch where the excavators found an actual spring of the therapeutic waters (Pl.37) was uncovered. It seems very likely that this is part of the vast complex planned by Belli but not yet excavated. Additional evidence for the position of this great temple in front of the earlier sanctuary is the existence in this area of large walls up to 1.50m wide made of concrete sticking out of the large mound that now covers the area.

The building planned by Belli (Pl.38) was entered through a large fore-hall *c.*90m x 30m with sixteen columns in two rows. The interior face of the walls had a facade of engaged half-columns and alternating rectangular and curved exedrae, very similar to the *scaenae frons* of a theatre. The main door into the hall was in the long side opposite the entrance into the temple proper. The latter was a building 55m square, with a central rotunda *c.*28m in diameter, surrounded by ambulatories divided into three rooms per side with a small circular room in each corner. Each of these round rooms had four niches. The central room on each side (except the one connecting the fore-hall and temple) led to a larger semicircular apse extruding beyond the line of the wall and in each apse there were a further three exedrae. Similarly, the central rotunda had a slightly more than semicircular exedra in each corner, masked by two columns. In the centre of the rotunda Belli drew two circles with a dot in the middle: perhaps this may represent the main fountain of the spring of Asklepios.

The excavated remains in tile-and stone-faced concrete are possibly part of either one of the round rooms in a corner or else one of the apses in the centre of a wall. The orientation of the building must also remain obscure for it is not known whether the fore-hall was on the east or the south side. Either could be fitted into the surviving plan and remains.

Other buildings of the same type of construction lie to the west: a long structure, *c.*110m x 10m, is divided up into rooms which also had a facade of engaged half-columns and ended at the west end with a round room 12m in diameter. South of this is another building 20m x 32m. Both of these were probably for the numerous pilgrims.

The shrine as a whole is obviously of the same class as the mid 2c Asklepeion at Pergamon [93] but it was far more complex in its internal plan and bears a greater resemblance to buildings such as the Baths of Caracalla in Rome or on a smaller scale Antioch Bath House C [94]. The design of the external apses resembles that of Herodes Atticus' nymphaeum at Olympia of the mid 2c. The facade of the fore-hall is like the *scaenae frons* of the theatres in Crete which seem to date from the 2c.

Lappa (14/1) (Pl.39) Just to the west below the main site on the hill the remains of the building planned by Belli 400 years before are still standing up to 3.50m in height [95]. All that now survives are two tile-faced concrete piers about 2m square and 6m apart, demonstrating how much has been destroyed since the last century when Pashley drew the monument which then still had complete arches and at least 6 piers. Attached to one of the surviving piers are two cisterns in series, 4m wide and of an unknown length; just above the building are a number of springs and there can be little doubt that this was a bath house and not a temple as Belli calls it.

The building is oval, 82m x 36m, dominated by a rotunda of 18m internal diameter with 13 exedrae, 3.3m in width. The latter was entered from an oval porch with 6 columns and 6 steps in front of them. On either side of the rotunda are large oval rooms with exedrae in their corners: a small but similarly shaped room although with no exedrae lay at the apex of the rotunda. All these rooms are set in a rectangle 45m x 36m; the remaining open space within this was taken up by various square rooms. According to Belli's plan none of these side rooms, square or oval, could be entered from the central rotunda but only by narrow entrances on either side of the

---

92. *IC*.I.XVII.5.
93. A. Boethius and J. B. Ward-Perkins, *Etruscan and Roman Architecture* (Harmondsworth, 1970), p.394 fig.148.
94. *Ibid.* p.444, fig.164.
95. Pashley I, p.83. Belli ed. Falkener, p.25, ed. Spanake, pl. KH, p.150. Spratt II, p.117. Personal observation.

The design of this bath house fits into the series of buildings that culminated in the great imperial bath houses of Rome from Caracalla to Constantine. However, in detail the plan is most closely paralleled by the so-called Temple of Minerva Medica in the Licinian Gardens in Rome, dating to the early 4c[96].

Lissos (19/18) (Pl.40, Fig.20) The temple of Asklepios here [97] is a small Hellenistic building of the Doric order, 9.90 m x 6.0m in dimensions and built of ashlar blocks in pseudo-isodomic style, except for the eastern wall. The latter acts as a terrace up against the steep hillside here and is of much rougher masonry, which might either be earlier or may reflect the need for additional strength to withstand the thrust from the hillside. The temple is entered through a central door in the south wall up two steps 0.50m wide; most of the floor is taken up with a fine mosaic[98] which however is not original but of 1c AD date; material from below it dated to the 4/3c BC and possibly formed part of the original floor. The mosaic is 6.50m in length and is surrounded by a slightly raised bench 0.40m wide. Between the mosaic and the podium at the north end of the temple there is a band of stone slabs 1.20m deep. The central part of the podium where the statue would have stood is 2.45m wide, 1.30m deep and 0.90m high; between this and the west wall is a curious series of steps leading up to a bench with a hole in it either for the libations or perhaps for the sacred snake of the god.

There was a small forecourt to the south of the temple and a stoa to the west from where a flight of steps 1.50m wide and 0.40m deep ran down next to the outflow of the sacred spring. The temple appears to have been destroyed by fanatical Christians who defaced the walls with their symbols: a pit was dug either by the Christians or by devotees of the god through the mosaic to dump about 20 fragmentary statues of youths, Hygieia and a headless Asklepios. A head, minus body, of Tiberius was also found together with a dedication to him[99]: it would seem likely that these could be associated with the refurbishment of the temple by the addition of its mosaic floor. The type of temple is obviously very similar to the one at Lebena of approximately the same date.

Diktynnaion (20/29) The temple of Diktynna and its associated buildings was excavated in July 1942 and subsequently published[100] but unfortunately the site had been almost totally robbed out. The temple terrace measured 55m x 50m and was surrounded on three sides by stoas, probably with Doric columns, enclosing the paved court and the temple. On the south side the columns sat on square bases joined to the wall but on the east side they were raised up on stub walls protruding from the main back wall. The north side was totally destroyed. On the west side was a series of four large cisterns (Pl.41), 20.10m x 11.75m with water tanks 2.70m deep; these tanks could have held 240 cu.m. while the entire cisterns had a capacity of 384 cu.m.

The temple itself was built of limestone but with marble paving; all that could be made out of the plan was that it was prostyle and probably pseudo-peripteral. The east front had Ionic columns in blue marble while the rest had white Corinthian columns. The latter seem to have been similar to those from the Villa Dionysus, if their reconstruction from the fragments is correct[101]. From within the temple *cella* came the fragmentary base Pococke first described (Pl.42); as Spratt remarked, it would seem to show the hind legs of an animal rather than Pan as Pococke suggested. Given the association of the goddess with the Cretan agrimi [102] it would seem most likely that the base originally showed one of these. There is also another base, this time decorated with a bunch of grapes.

North of the temple there seems to have been a stepped altar, 5.30m square, of white marble; to the NW there was a circular area, 4m in diameter, where there was no paving which the excavator suggested might have been the site of a round building, possibly a treasury although it seems rather small for this. It was from here that the statue of Diktynna found in 1913 came[103].

---

96. Boethius and Ward-Perkins, *op.cit.* note 93, p.509 fig.194.
97. *A. Delt.* XVI, 1960, p.273. *Kret. Khron.* XI, 1957, p.337; XII, 1958, p.465; XIII, 1959, p.376; XIV, 1960, p.516. Personal observation.
98. See p.55.
99. *BCH* LXXXIV, 1960, p.854.
100. G. Welter and U. Jantzen ap Matz, p.106f and Taf. 1-2, 76-104. Personal observation.
101. *Ibid.* Taf.80.
102. *IC.* II.XI. Praef. Taf. 86 for the base.
103. Chania Museum No.79.

Pl. 40: Temple of Asklepios at Lissos.

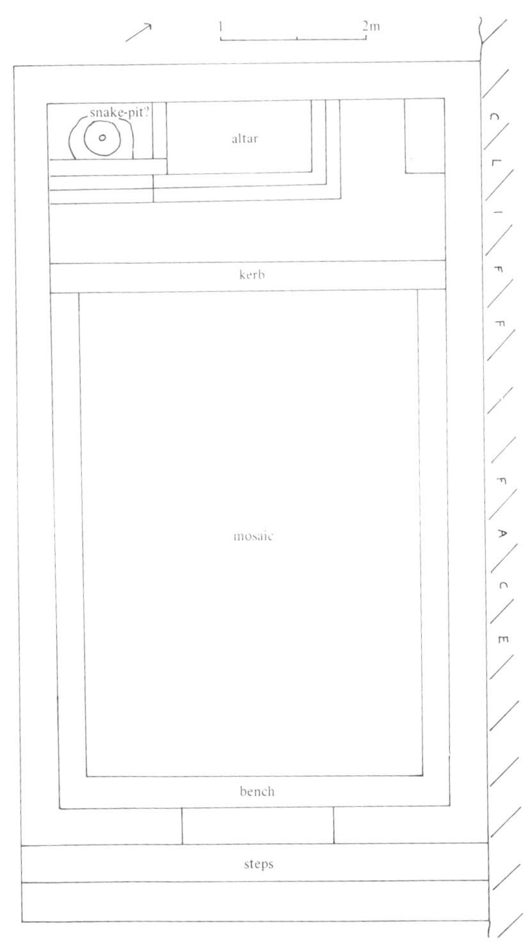

Fig. 20. Lissos: plan of the temple of Asklepios.

Pl. 41: Cisterns immediately south of the temple of the Diktynnaion.
Pl. 42: Pococke's base at the Diktynnaion.

The date of the main temple is probably early 2c AD from the style of the architectural fragments. Hadrian is usually given the credit for its construction because of his known activity in the area [104] but it is perhaps more likely that it was under Trajan that the temple was at least begun. The evidence for this is a series of coins associating the Emperor and the goddess issued by the Provincial Council and possibly by the temple authorities as well[105]. However, there was certainly an earlier temple on the site, as indicated by fragments to the west of the Roman temple marking the site of a Doric predecessor and there is also the story of the death of Apollonius of Tyana here in the 1c AD [106].

Conclusions

But for the interest of an obscure 16c Venetian doctor the architecture of Roman Crete outside Gortyna would be a very limited subject indeed. Although it is difficult to be sure how accurate his plans are, when they can be checked, as at Gortyna and Chersonisos, it seems that even if Belli may have reconstructed some details overall they can be trusted. His remarks at Lyttus and his excavations at Hierapytna reinforce this impression.

The theatres can be considered as a group first. With the exception of that at Lyttus, they are all of a similar type with very deep *postscenia* and elaborate porticoes. The larger theatre at Gortyna is closer to the normal plan of a Roman theatre which has a much narrower *postscenium* but this might have been because of its position by the Lethaeus. From Belli's plans the smaller theatre at Gortyna, the larger at Hierapytna and the one at Chersonisos all have similar arrangements in the *postscenia,* especially the elaborate columned halls.

None of the *scaenae frontes* are particularly elaborate, except the central portion in both theatres at Hierapytna. In general the design of the facade does not relate to those in Africa and the west which usually have three large curved exedrae. The closest parallels seem to come from Asia Minor, in the theatres at Ephesus [107] (AD 66) and Aizanoi[108] (second quarter 2c) and from Athens in the *scaenae frons* of the Odeion of Herodes Atticus[109] (late 2c). The dates of these parallels from the late 1c to the late 2c fit the probable dates of all the Cretan examples with the exception of Lyttus. At this site, from what can be made out from Belli's plan, there seems to be one large curved exedra in the centre. Such a facade would seem more likely to belong to the early-mid 1c AD when compared, for example, to the final form of the *scaenae frons* of the Larger Theatre at Pompeii[110].

An early date for the Lyttus theatre is also likely from the materials used in its construction: Belli stresses the fact that it was difficult to make out the plan because of the "enormous blocks which lay about". At all the other theatres brick-faced concrete was the basic material with stone only used for some facing. This use of stone for facing in the smaller theatre at Gortyna may be evidence that this building is earlier rather than later in the date-range for the theatres. Concrete, faced with rough *opus quadratum,* had been used in the Augustan Odeion so the material was known in Crete in the 1c AD. However, the use of bricks or tiles as facing on present evidence cannot be dated earlier than AD 100 when it appears in the Trajanic reconstruction of the Odeion. This date provides an approximate *terminus post quem* for all the brick-faced buildings of the island. The evidence from the smaller theatre at Hierapytna seems to provide an equally rough *terminus ante quem* of *c.* 200 for the stylistically similar theatres. These dates would also fit the probably Antonine date of the amphitheatre.

Indeed, one of the interesting points about Cretan architecture in the period is the comparatively large number of amphitheatres for a Greek province. This interest in a very Roman pursuit is paralleled by the lack of evidence for early theatres. There is only one definitely pre-Roman example, at Aptera (17/2); some of the others such as the larger theatre at Gortyna may well have been converted from Greek theatres but there is no material evidence for this apart from a 1c BC inscription [111] honouring actors, but even these were actually Romans, not Greeks.

This surge of activity in building Roman type theatres contrasts interestingly with the comparatively small number of temples of Roman date. The most important one is that of Diktynna, and there are also the Temple of Isis and the one at Mavropapas, both at Gortyna. Generally, however, the Cretans preferred to use their old, often

---

104. *IC.* II.XI.6.
105. Council of Crete coin no. Svoronos 63 (ae 32). Diktynnaion coin no. Svoronos 4 (arg 24). On this coin Trajan has the title Parthicus, indicating a date after AD 115.
106. Philostratus *Life of Apollonius* viii.30.
107. D. de Bernardi Ferrero, *Teatri Classici in Asia Minore* III, (Rome, 1970), Tav. VIII, p.161f.
108. *Ibid.* Tav. XXXVI, p.177f.
109. J. Travlos, *Pictorial Dictionary of Ancient Athens* (London, 1971), p.378, fig.492.
110. M. Bieber, *A History of the Greek and Roman Theater* (Princeton, 1961), p.172-3, fig.608.
111. *IC.* IV.222-3.

basically Archaic, temples. One other new temple was that at Lebena: this building shows a remarkable grasp of the combination of rectangular and circular design, as do also the bath houses at Lappa and at Preveli (15/10). At Lebena there is also the contrast between the strictly linear but very ornate fore-hall and the domed main shrine which immediately recalls the design of the Pantheon.

It would seem unlikely that the architect of these buildings was a Cretan: the two possible areas which could have supplied such a man are Rome itself, the best parallel for the Lappa bath house being the Minerva Medica 'temple' in the Licinian Gardens, or one of the great Ionian centres such as Ephesus or Miletus. The latter area has much to recommend it; other buildings such as the nymphaea at Gortyna are best paralleled from Asia Minor as are the *scaenae frontes* of the theatres. The architectural fragments from all the buildings are also closely linked to those from this area and it is highly likely that the relevant marbles were shipped out in roughed out form from the centres such as Proconnesos. Other evidence for this trade comes in the form of columns which are often in lengths of Roman feet [112]. However, not all architectural decorative work was imported for there are pieces in the same style in local stone, such as the architectural fragments from the amphitheatre at Gortyna. Whether such a piece was carved by a local man trained by an Ionian craftsman or the latter working on local material it is impossible to say. The only evidence for such men comes in the field of sculpture where it is known that Aphrodisians and Parians were working in Crete[113].

Overall, the architecture of Roman Crete very much reflects the position of the island in the Empire. There are a few native Cretan facets, such as the majority of the temples, but these, though of great significance socially, pale into insignificance architecturally when compared with the theatres. Generally, these reflect both east and west; west in the material of their construction and east in their design, although some at least were built in Roman feet (the portico of the smaller theatre at Hierapytna measures 300 x 150 Roman feet). Other buildings reflecting western influence are the amphitheatres although again the only one really known has architectural fragments of Ionian style. Buildings like those at Lebena and Lappa owe their existence to the tradition started in Rome and Italy but by the date of their construction it is difficult to tell how widespread such designs using concrete were. To conclude, like much of the rest of the Empire this great activity in building was over by the early 3c and until the great programme of church construction in the late 5c few buildings were erected. Again, whether this really represents financial exhaustion or simply the fact that there was no need for any more public buildings is a question applicable to the whole Empire, not just to Crete.

---

112. All this on the marble trade owes much to J. B. Ward-Perkins' Shuffrey Memorial Lectures, Oxford 1976, and discussion with him. Examples of columns are: Villa Dionysos 12 R.ft., Lebena 16 R.ft., Suia 7 R.ft., Ay. Galini 14 R.ft., Gortyna, (larger theatre) 18 R.ft.

113. See p.51.

CHAPTER 7: CHRISTIAN BASILICAS

This class of monument is better known than any other from the Roman period on the island, owing to the interest and activity of Greek 'Byzantine' archaeologists [1]. At least 68 churches are known or suspected and most of them are of the simple Aegean type with narthex, three aisles and single apse, often floored with mosaics and built of mortared rubble. Although there are one or two which may be earlier than the mid 5c and a few that may be after Justinian, the great majority would seem to date from the period 450-550. Unfortunately this dating is almost entirely derived from stylistic judgements and so is far from certain. Only one basilica, that at the Sanatorium site at Knossos, can be dated more securely from stratigraphical excavation, and unfortunately this site seems rather unlike the other Cretan basilicas.

The following catalogue is set out by eparchy from east to west and by site number within the eparchy.

Siteia (1/2) On the quay side of the modern town, at Timios Stavros, part of a large basilica was exposed by wave action. The south pastophorion and apse were revealed as well as part of a marble eucharist table. The rest of the church is below modern housing [2]. A Corinthian capital of Kautzsch [3] Leierkapitelle type in Heraklion Museum probably comes from this site and dates from the late 5c/early 6c.

Itanos (1/39): Basilica A (Fig.21) On the SW side of the main acropolis of the city lies the site of the first of two excavated but practically unpublished basilicas of Itanos[4]. It is basically of the standard three aisled plan but with a triple chancel and a peculiar central aisle. It seems that the church was built on top of, or converted from, an earlier temple, probably dedicated to Athena Polias[5].

Fig.21. Itanos: Basilica A.

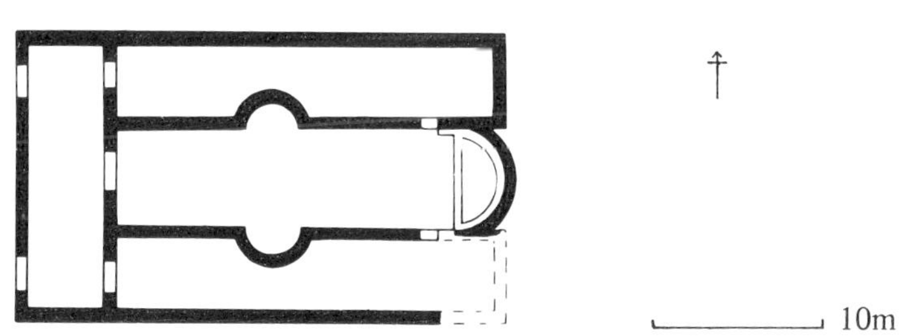

1. The main excavators have been A. K. Orlandos and K. D. Kalokyres, with numerous reports in *PAE, Ergon* and *Kret. Khron.* N. Platon has compiled a list of the 36 basilicas known to him in 1953 in ' Αἱ ξυλόστεγαι παλαιοχριστιανικαὶ βασιλικαὶ τῆς Κρήτης ', *Acts of the 9th Congress of Byzantine Studies at Thessalonike* I, (Athens, 1955), p.415. This work is referred to as Platon with the church number in this chapter. The mosaics are included in the Corpus *Σύνταγμα τῶν παλαιοχριστιανικῶν ψηφιδωτῶν δαπέδων τῆς* 'Ελλάδος I, compiled by S. Pelekanides with P. Atzaka (Thessaloniki, 1974), referred to as 'Corpus' in this chapter.
2. *Kret. Khron.* VIII, 1954, p.511; *PAE* 1954, p.364. Platon no.35.
3. R. Kautzsch, *Kapitellstudien* (Berlin, 1936).
4. Excavations by the French School are briefly reported in *BCH* LXXV, 1951, p.193f., and C. Tiré and H. van Effenterre, *Guide des fouilles françaises en Crète* (Paris, 1966) p.93-4. Also Platon no.16. The details and measurements given here are from field-work undertaken for the thesis.
5. *IC.* III.IV. Praef. p.75-6.

The basilica is *c.*26.60m long by 15.50m wide, constructed of reused stone with stone slab floors. The narthex, 4m deep, was entered by two doors, one at each end of the 'west' wall, and from the narthex doors with marble thresholds led into each aisle. Both side aisles are 3.60m wide and extend to the end of the apse. The central aisle is 4.80m wide and separated from the side aisles by walls or stylobates that are still over 1m high. These walls are pierced by narrow doors just in front of the apse and are also interrupted by small semicircular apses 3m in diameter placed 7m from the west end of the aisle. The east end of the aisle finishes in a raised apse having a diameter the full width of the aisle. Within the apse is a synthronon 0.40m wide.

Several incomplete columns of grey-white marble survive as do some pessiscoi reused in the walls of the central aisle, but the only architectural fragment of any merit is an ornamented door- or window-block. This is decorated with circles enclosing flowers or stars of 8 or 10 equal and unequal rays or petals. One circle differs and surrounds a Greek cross flanked by *α* and *ω* (Pl.43).

The design of the east end of the church resembles those in Cilicia or Syria rather than the Aegean region. The closest parallel seems in fact to come from Syria rather than Cilicia; it is the basilica at Kerratin[6]. The other unusual feature of this church is the design of the central aisle with its opposed mini apses. However, the fact that pessiscoi are used in this area rebuilt into the walls suggests that the apses and the high walls are secondary to the main church. If this is the case, it might be that the central aisle was rebuilt as a small church or chapel, possibly with a central dome springing off the apses, to serve the now deserted village of Eremoupoli. Because of the present state of the building and the lack of any report, it is impossible to prove this or the alternative possibility that the central aisle simply had these niches in its walls. No firm date can be given to this church but the basilica at Kerratin is dated to 480-520 and the style of the architectural fragment is similar to ones from the basilica at Panormos (13/3) which seems to be farily securely dated to the early 6c.

Itanos B (Fig.22) The second church[7] is on the slopes of the hill across the valley to the south of the main acropolis. Even worse preserved than the first one, it is a standard basilica constructed in very rough reused stone, 23.50m x 14.30m, excluding the apse. The narthex is still partially buried in the hillside and no entrance door could be seen, but as at the other basilica it is 4m deep. Each aisle has a door from the narthex but the central door at 3.2m is nearly three times the width of the side doors at 1.2m each. The side aisles are both 3.6m wide and both have small doors in their east wall. The central aisle is 6.4m wide with stylobates 0.55m wide. The apse is slightly unusual, being of horse-shoe shape, 3.80m in base diameter and 3.30m internal length with a synthronon of three benches. At the SW corner of the church a partially excavated baptistery survives. It is not quite square in shape, divided in two internally by a wall on the same alignment as the east wall of the narthex. Nothing of the resulting western half can be made out, but in the eastern half the southern part of the floor is lower, composed of a square of granite slabs.

Fig.22. Itanos: Basilica B.

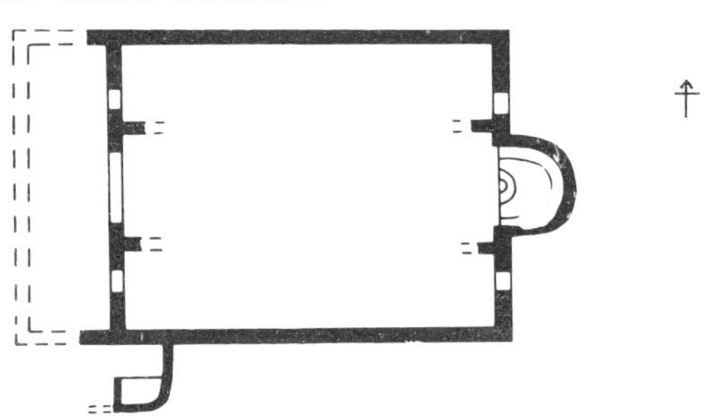

Fig.23. Itanos: Basilica C.

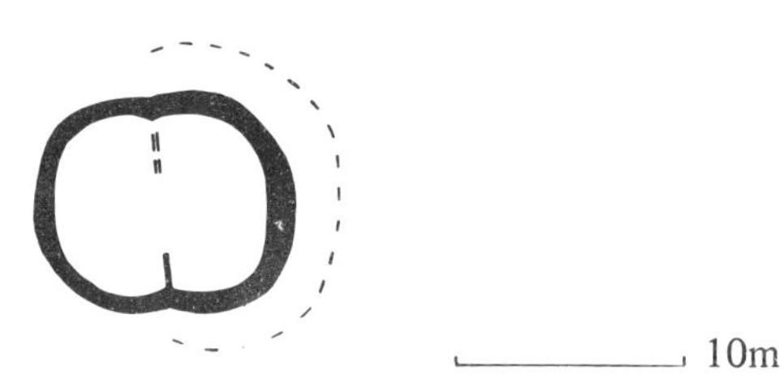

Itanos C (Fig.23) Just to the east of Basilica B a curious building[8] is perched on a ledge of the hill. It comprises a double apse with the remains of a wall dividing it at the join. The maximum height is *c.*0.50m. The internal diameter along the long axis is 9.0m and at the 'waist' the building is 7.0m wide. In the eastern half the wall is 0.70m wide, while the western wall is 1.0m wide. 2.0m beyond and mirroring the west wall is a further line of individual large stones. The construction was similar to, if a bit better than, the church. Within the 'building' two pessiscoi stood, and it seems possible that this is a further baptistery.

---

6. J. Lassus, *Les sanctuaries chrétiens de Syrie* (Paris, 1947), p.36, fig.115. Also R. Krautheimer, *Early Christian and Byzantine Architecture* (Harmondsworth, 1975), p.161.
7. As for note 4, Itanos A. Platon no.17.
8. Personal observation. *BCH* LXXV, 1951, p.193.

Episkopi Ierapetra (2/11) A large number of ecclesiastical architectural fragments have been found here, but most seem to have been lost. Those published by Gerola [9] include fragments with stylised foliage which seem to have been of late Roman date, but others appear to be later, post Arab. In the mediaeval church now standing in the village there is a reused spiral column, while the building of the new church in the square opposite produced 12 columns up to 4m high. Of these columns three were in a pink-grey marble and the rest of granite; one was fluted, the rest plain. There was also one column base in the square and a smaller one outside the church. All this would seem to indicate the existence, probably on the same site as the new church, of an early basilica, which may well have been rebuilt or replaced by another church when the village became the episcopal seat after the 10c reconquest. If this was the case it would account for the two styles of fragments and the differing columns.

Vasiliki (2/13) A small basilica is reported from this site but no other details are given [10].

Tholos (2/18) Three metres from the NE corner of the chapel of the Panayia a grave was found containing fragments of 'red ware of probable Roman or Byzantine date' [11]. Given the existence of this grave and also the fact that the church is obviously built on the same alignment as an earlier building[12], it seems quite likely that there is a basilica below the later chapel.

Olus (3/7) (Fig.24) The basilica [13] here is situated just beyond the channel that now divides Spinalonga from the mainland, cutting the city of Olus in two. The basilica is of standard form, 34.90m long and 17.50m wide excluding the apse, constructed of quite good small blocks of local stone with mosaics in the nave and apparently in the narthex.

Fig.24. Olus: Basilica.

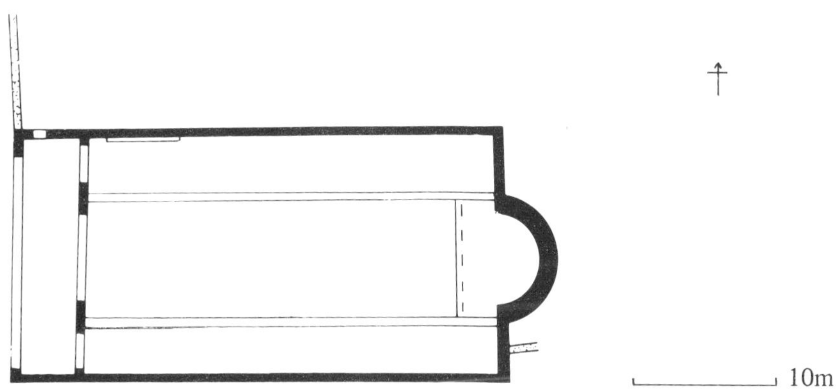

The narthex is somewhat irregularly shaped with the wall dividing it from the rest of the church at an angle oblique to the other walls, resulting in the depth of the narthex increasing from 3.7m at the south to 3.9m at the north wall. The excavator claimed that the floor was originally a mosaic which had been completely destroyed. The west wall of the church seems to have been totally destroyed so that the only known entrance into the narthex is a small door in the north wall. At this corner of the church a wall of unknown date and purpose abuts it.

From the narthex doors lead into each aisle: the two side aisles are separated from the centre by stylobates. The north aisle is 4.12m wide, the south 3.47m and the main central aisle 7.52m. Both side aisles are floored with rough stone slabs and in the north aisle there were some crude graves. The nave was partially covered with a mosaic but this only extends 12.50m from the west wall and 6.0m from the north stylobate. The chancel or bema protrudes 2.50m in front of the apse which is 6.12m in diameter with a synthronon. Also, at the east end, a short length of wall joins the east wall of the south aisle. A short distance to the SW of the church there was another building with what may be small cisterns built into its west wall; its function is unknown [14].

---

9. *Mon. Ven.* II, p.90 fig.51-2. Platon no.15. Personal observation.
10. *Kret. Khron.* XXV, 1973, p.460. *Ergon* 1972, p.113.
11. *AJA* V, 1901, p.155.
12. Personal observation.
13. A. K. Orlandos, *PAE* 1955, p.336 and 1960, p.308. Tiré and van Effenterre, *op.cit.* note 4, p.88. It was the French Navy who first cleared the mosaic in 1898. Platon no.14. Corpus no.96, p.115, pl.86-9. Personal observation.
14. No longer visible.

The mosaic in the nave (Pl.44) is probably the oddest in Crete; it is composed of a large number of black and white panels of varying geometric or natural designs, the latter being peacocks or dolphins [15]. Two of the panels contain the names of donors [16] (Helidorus, Theodolos and Antaxios); each man dedicated one semissis. Although there is a rough overall design in that most of the panels are somehow logically placed in relationship to each other and there is a border of a tendril design, it is rather tempting to suggest that the mosaic was laid down over a period of time as the money became available.

Not only the mosaic but also the capitals are peculiar [17]; most are of a type belonging to the early or imperial Corinthian style and are 0.48m high. These could date to the 4c by comparison with similar ones illustrated by Kautzsch [18]. These capitals are of a grey marble. Of the other capitals one (Pl.45) is much larger than the others as well as being almost square in section. It seems to be related to the other Corinthian capitals in the way the helices are treated but the acanthus leaves are so stylised as to become scrolls rather than foliage. This capital is 0.78m high and cut in the top is an oval depression 0.25m deep (Pl.46). The remaining capital, 0.60m high, is different again, still Corinthian but of a round 'basket' type with its decoration in fairly low relief (Pl.47) and may be much earlier, reused in the church. Both these odd capitals are in local limestone. Other architectural fragments include a lekane stand with a fragment of the lekane, a moulding with a single row of acanthus leaves and slabs with crosses on them [19]. Column fragments included some spiral ones, in grey marble, others unfluted in pink or white marble.

It has been suggested that the site represents two churches, the first quite small if, as seems probable, the area of the nave is marked by the mosaic, the cut-out portion at its east end being for the Sacred Gate through to the bema. It is also possible that the odd angle of the east wall of the narthex might be explained by the earlier church. If the first group of capitals came from the first church, their 4c date would match that assigned to the mosaic by a study of the form of the letters of its inscriptions. The date of the second (present) church is uncertain.

Kolokythia (3/8) (Fig.25) On the other side of Spinalonga, opposite the island of Kolokythia, are the remains of a small but interesting basilica. It is situated at the southern end of a small settlement right down by the sea which has destroyed much of its east side, which in this case constitutes a side aisle since the building is aligned along the coast approximately north-south [20].

Fig.25. Kolokythia: Basilica.

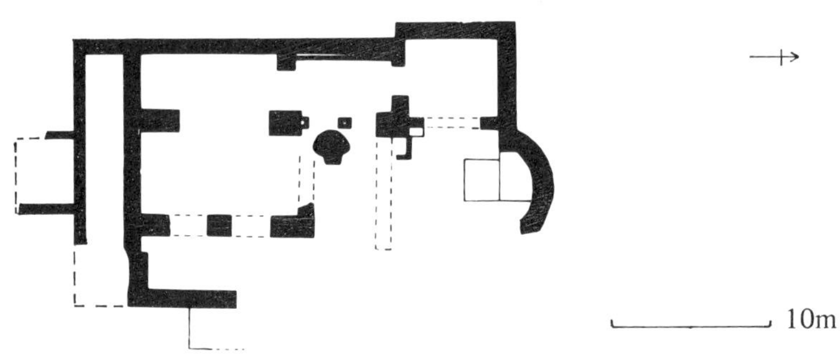

The basic design is the standard three aisled basilica 21m x 15m excluding the apse, which has a diameter of 5.20m; the central aisle is 4.50m wide and the side aisles 3.50m, slightly expanding at the northern end to form pastophoria flanking the bema. Here there are the remains of a mosaic composed of a polychrome mat of interlocking crosses edged by a single guilloche: the mosaic, however, seems to have been partially overlain by the synthronon in the apse. The central aisle is divided from the side aisles by a screen running between piers which stand up to 1.80m high and which vary from oblong to square in proportions. However, these seem to be secondary, for there are also earlier column bases clearly incorporated into the piers; this is especially obvious on the north face of the southern pier on the west side.

---

15. The best illustration of it is pl.xxii in Tiré and van Effenterre, *op.cit.* note 4.
16. *IC.*I.XXII.65.
17. All these capitals were to be seen in 1974 in the main square in Neapolis.
18. Kautzsch, *op.cit.* note 3, nos.46, 210, 291.
19. Basket capital: compare Heilmeyer *Korinthische Normalkapitelle* (Heidelberg, 1970) pll. 11 and 60.1, 1c BC. Lekane: *PAE* 1960, pl.248.
20. *A. Delt.* XXVI. 2.2., 1971, p.529. Personal observation: Dr. N. C. Flemming first brought this site to my attention.

Pl. 43: Architectural fragment from Basilica A. Itanos.
Pl. 44: ***Mosaic panel from the basilica at Olus.***

Pl. 45: Large capital with an oval depression in the top, from the basilica at Olus.
Pl. 46: Depression in the top of the above capital.
Pl. 47: Basket capital from the basilica at Olus.

As it now survives there is no door into the central aisle at the south end, but the church was entered by doors into the side aisles from a narthex 3.20m deep, beyond which are the remains of a vaulted cistern, now much destroyed but at least 5.70m square. Presumably this was set in an atrium as for instance at Panormus. On the east (sea) side, there are the remains of a further room tacked onto the side aisle, but this has been almost completely destroyed by the sea. Of the architectural fragments the finest is a marble single-staired ambo (Pl.48) dedicated by the Deacon Thomas; there are other fragments of the screens also with dedications and finely carved Maltese crosses. In contrast to their material and high quality workmanship there is also one rather crude limestone Corinthian capital of the Leierkapitell type.

It is obvious that this building is of two phases: the first with the side aisles divided from the centre by the normal stylobates implying a conventional roof. It is possible that this building was brought down by the proximity of the sea and rebuilt with the piers which seem to indicate that this phase had a more complex roof of the cross-dome type. There is no evidence to date the first phase. although the mosaic and style of the building make it likely to be late 5c to early 6c, but the design of the second phase should not be earlier than the mid 6c.

Arvi (5/8) (Fig.26) At Ayia Irene, to the east of the main Roman site, possibly in the cemetery area, are the unexcavated remains of a basilica [21]. It is at least 21m long and 14.50m wide with an apse 4.50m in diameter and 2.8m long (internal dimensions), and is constructed of good concrete with a lot of tile in the aggregate. Several white quartzitic marble columns, at least 2m in length, column bases and capitals are lying about near, or on, the site. The capitals are of the Ionic impost type and are very similar to those from the basilica A at Suia (19/17). These are conventionally dated to the reign of Justinian.

Fig.26. Arvi: Basilica.

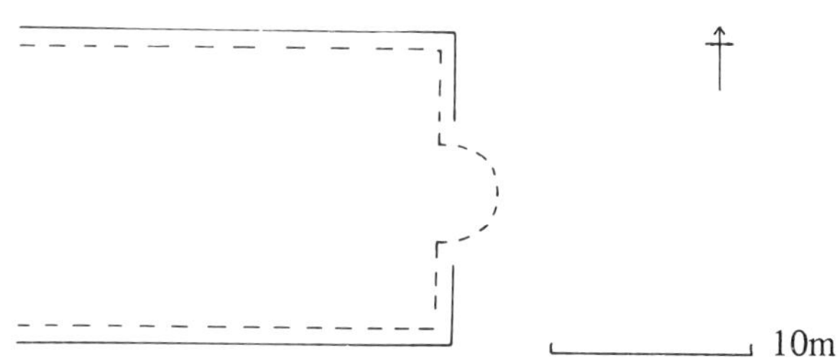

Chersonisos (6/7): Basilica A (Fig.27) About one kilometre to the east of the ancient and modern harbour of Chersonisos is a small headland, surmounted by a chapel of Ay. Nicolaos. This chapel overlies most of the bema of the basilica [22] which in turn may have replaced a temple of Britomartis [23]. The basilica follows the standard plan but it has some unusual additions. Minus the apse, but with the atrium, it is 50.20m long and 18.80m wide. The walls are constructed in fairly coarse mortared rubble. There are fragments of mosaics in the narthex and nave.

Fig.27. Chersonisos: Basilica A.

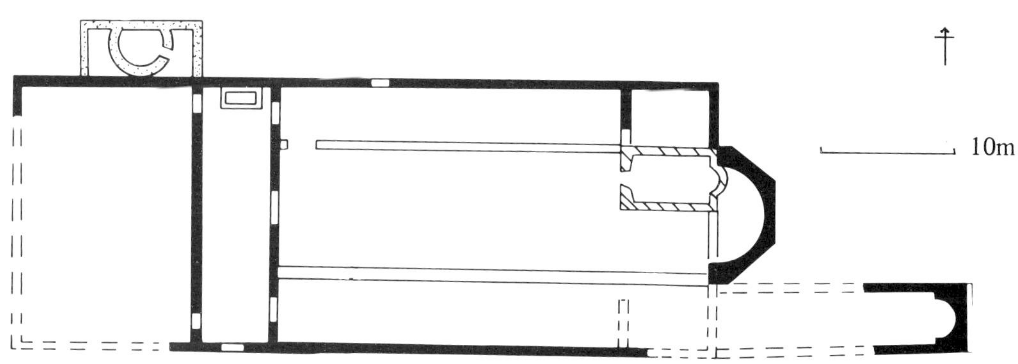

---

21. *Kret. Khron.* X, 1956, p.421, for the cemetery; XII, 1958, p.481, for the basilica. In general *ABSA* LIX, 1964, p.89. Personal observation.
22. Report, A. K. Orlandos, *PAE* 1955, p.327. Platon no.11. Corpus 87, p.110, pl.80-82. The site is most easily located nowadays by the fact that it is in the gardens of the Nova Hotel.
23. S. Marinatos, *A. Delt.* IX, 1924, p.85. *IC.*I.VII.4. The inscription is there dated to the 2c BC.

Pl. 48: Ambo in the basilica at Kolokythia.
Pl. 49: Mosaic of deer and lion, Basilica A, Chersonisos.

The atrium, 12.50m long, was badly preserved with very little of its west or south walls left. However, against the north wall a peculiar building had been added on. It consists of a D-shaped foundation within an oblong 8.40m x 4.00m. From the atrium the narthex, 4.80m deep, is entered by narrow doors at each side of the west wall and from the exterior by a door in the south wall. Within the narthex a late feature was a tomb built on top of the mosaic at the northern end and a similar one by the door into the central aisle. The mosaic floor only survives in fragments with most of the area covered by tile patching. Right against the northern wall of the narthex another tomb cuts through the mosaic, interrupting the pattern. The tomb cover, 2.25 x 0.90m (Pl.7), is made of a large slab of white marble surrounded by diamond shaped pieces of the same material set against a dark blue background. A hole had been pierced through the central slab, presumably for libations [24].

From the narthex, doorways with fine white marble thresholds, complete with grooves for the doors, lead into each of the aisles. The central aisle is 8.15m wide, the north aisle 3.70m, and the south aisle 4.55m wide. The aisles are separated by stylobates 0.60m wide and 0.23m high, carrying columns of grey marble with Ionic capitals. The side aisles are floored with tiles, while the nave has a mosaic which, like the one in the narthex, has been patched with tiles. Further disregard for the mosaic was shown by the placing of the ambo on top of it, on the north side of the aisle, and at some subsequent date more tombs were built against the ambo. The bema and apse are mainly covered by the later chapel and all that can be made out is the distinctive pentagonal exterior of the apse. On either side of the bema, pastophoria 5.40m long complete the two side aisles. However, the south aisle has another building added on to the east [25] the same width as the aisle and 18m long, ending in an apse 3.25m in diameter set into the square end of the building. It would seem most likely that it functioned as a martyrion.

The mosaics are all of a very high quality, using tesserae of grey, white, black, red, yellow and light blue in both geometric and natural designs. Three main areas of mosaic survive in the narthex. In the SW corner a very small part of the border, made up of interlinked semicircles, is left, while further along the west wall the border has become a band of geometric panels that originally may have stretched right across the narthex. The design here consists of a background of linked panels of a derived key pattern in black and white tesserae with alternate panels of varying design (zig zags, a stylised Greek cross and a four-pointed star) in varying colours but all against yellow backgrounds. Beyond this comes the largest fragment made up of a circular emblema of a lion and deer (polychrome) surrounded by a wave pattern in red and white with eight panels acting as spokes from this centre (Pl.49). The panels are of alternate designs of a mat in a scale-like pattern and intricate, slightly varying, knot designs. The spaces between the panels are filled with ivy tendrils and in the sole surviving main corner, in the lozenge formed between the panels and the corner, a simple knot. Finally there is the panel with the elaborate tomb; the mosaic here comprises interlaced circles or compass-drawn crosses, forming four pronged stars in red, yellow and white tesserae.

In the nave the mosaic only survives in the NW corner with a wide border of ivy tendrils in yellow, grey and black surrounding the main design. This begins with a band of geometric panels, similar in overall effect to that in the centre of the narthex, with a derived key pattern alternating with other geometric designs, lozenges, knots and stars, all in polychrome. Beyond this is a great sweep of interweaving strands of varying designs in guilloche or narrow bands with stars, knots or wheel designs in the resulting circles. Within this web are more regular geometric designs of stars or knots set in squares. Filling the spaces left between the web and the outer geometric band are flowers and foliage, including lotus blossom.

Of architectural fragments, apart from the columns and capitals [26], there were parts of the altar screen consisting of unfluted columns with very worn Corinthian capitals.

There is no internal evidence for the date of the church and in fact it is obvious that several phases are represented by the extant remains. Apart from the peculiar building added onto the north side of the atrium, the basic design of the church would seem to be of the same period, the extension of the south aisle perhaps being later. However, within the body of the church there are at least two secondary phases after the construction of the church with the mosaics. The marble tomb in the narthex would seem to be secondary to the mosaic, as is certainly the tile patching here and in the nave. Also in the nave the pulpit base overlies the mosaic and, while the tiles can be seen as casual repairs, the

---

24. The tomb was not opened for fear of damaging the mosaic.
25. Little can be said of this building either from the report or from visiting the site because it is nearly entirely under water, as is part of the main apse.
26. These are not illustrated or described in the report and are not on the site.

new pulpit is a major alteration. Both the tiles and the pulpit, however, in ignoring the design of the mosaic show that at whatever date they were added the church authorities were either not interested in maintaining the mosaic floor or were unable to do so for financial and/or technical reasons. The rough stone tombs found on top of the floors in the narthex and nave may well belong to a period after the collapse of the church building and have been dug down onto the mosaic rather than built up on top of it. Again no date can be assigned to these, as no grave goods had been deposited in them.

Although the church in its various phases cannot be dated internally, there are sufficient parallels to suggest an approximate date at least for the construction. The basic design is of little help chronologically, although the side pastophoria show the ultimate influence of Syria, perhaps via Cilicia[27]; but the possible martyrion beyond the south aisle is rather unusual and so more likely to give a reasonable date when compared to similar structures. The origin of this class of building would seem to be in Syria, where examples have been found at Palmyra[28] and R'safah [29], at the latter dating to 480-520. In Greece there is an example at Vravron [30] where the church is fairly securely dated by pottery and a coin [31] in mint condition to the second quarter of the 6c. The building at Chersonisos is closer than the one at Vravron in plan to the Syrian examples, and so could date to anywhere in the first half of the 6c.

The mosaics would seem to fit this date quite reasonably; they are very close in style to those in Basilica B at Chersonisos, while the layout of the narthex mosaics is the same as at Kera (14/7). The interlocked semicircles forming a border are also used at Suia (19/17), but the mosaics there are not of so high a standard. The dating of Chersonisos B and Kera is no more secure than that of the present site, but Suia A was dated rather later in the sixth century because of its capitals. Outside Crete the same form of border was used at Philippi in the cemetery basilica[32] and there dated to the beginning of Justinian's reign on coin evidence. Combining the evidence from both the design and the mosaics Basilica A would seem to have been built at some point in the first half of the sixth century, perhaps earlier rather than later in the period.

None of the alterations in the church can be dated except that the rough burials do seem to postdate the church and that the other alterations should certainly be placed before the Arab conquest if it was the 'Agarenes' who destroyed the church. Although there is no actual evidence for this it is quite likely unless the little building attached to the north wall of the atrium is more than it seems. The excavator interpreted it as a tower and suggested that it was a lighthouse. This would not seem very likely as the actual port appears to have had one already [33]; moreover the headland here is of no danger to shipping, while if it were, the lighthouse ought to have been at the end by the sea. Towers are known from early Christian churches but normally form part of a facade [34]. The tower here is not part of such a facade, which would normally have twin towers anyway, and does not seem to be of any use at all. A remote but possible interpretation is that it is in fact a minaret of an Arab conversion of the church into a mosque. Such minarets with square bases are known from the 9c [35] and somewhere in Crete Arab mosques of this period must have existed.

Chersonisos: Basilica B (Fig.28) The north side of the harbour at Chersonisos is formed by the headland known as Kastri. This is encircled by a defensive wall of late Roman date within which lies the site of the basilica [36]. The church is among the largest in Crete and was probably the seat of the local bishop. It is 51.70m long and 21.70m wide (internal dimensions) and constructed of fairly regularly shaped blocks of local limestone, mortared together. There are mosaic floors in the narthex, nave, apse and pastophoria, as well as in the later northern wing.

West of the narthex is an atrium or possibly an exonarthex, as its dimensions seem rather cramped for an atrium. It is 5.50m deep and the width of the main church is 17.70m; 3.50m from the north wall there survives part of a wall running EW from the west wall of the narthex which may have divided this area in two. West again of this room is

---

27. Krautheimer, *op.cit.* note 6, p.496, n.20.
28. Lassus, *op.cit.* note 6, p. 168, fig. 7b.
29. Lassus, *op.cit.* note 6, p.39, fig.17; Krautheimer, *op.cit.* note 6, p.162, fig.111.
30. *PAE* 1951, p.55, fig.3.
31. *PAE* 1953, p.74, a solidus of Justinian of 538 in mint condition.
32. *AE* 1955, p.139, fig.16, p.140, fig.17.
33. Gazetteer p.146.
34. Krautheimer, *op.cit.* note 6, p.164-5.
35. G. T. Rivoira, *Moslem Architecture* (Oxford, 1918), p.174. K. A. C. Cresswell, *Early Muslim Architecture* (Harmondsworth, 1958), p.278.
36. Report, A. K. Orlandos, *PAE* 1956, p.241f; *PAE* 1959, p.220f. Platon n.10. Corpus 88 p.111, pl.83-4. Personal observation.

Fig.28. Chersonisos: Basilica B.

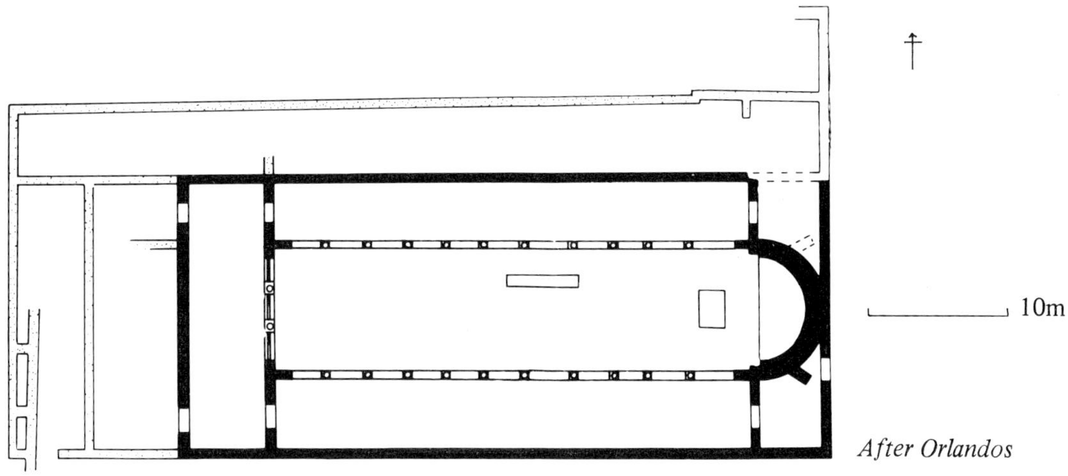

another 4m deep with what are probably a row of cisterns against its west wall. The entrance to this room is by a door in the south wall next to the possible cistern in the SW corner. The stub of wall protruding here might be the foundation of the feed for the cisterns.

This western range was apparently later than the main church which was entered by two doors in the west wall of the narthex. This is 5m deep and originally floored with a mosaic which had been mainly replaced by rather rough floor tiles. After the destruction of the church a wall was constructed above the debris of the collapsed roof cutting off the NE corner of the narthex. From the narthex narrow doors lead into the side aisles which are of unequal width, the south aisle being 4.50m and the north aisle 3.60m wide. The central aisle, 8.40m wide, is entered from the narthex by a tribolon, 6.80m wide. This is made of white marble, as is the more northerly of the two column bases; the other is made of the same grey blue marble as the column bases in the nave.

The nave is divided off from the side aisles by stylobates, 0.60m wide, that run right up to the apse and carry ten columns a side. These were probably at least three metres high, unfluted and supporting Corinthian capitals. Between each column-base the stylobate stands up to 0.98m high; it appears from the relationship of the stones of the stylobate to the moulding of the base that originally the stylobate was much lower and was later built up about the bases. The floor of the nave was originally covered by the mosaic but, as in the narthex, tiles were used subsequently to patch it. Also secondary to the mosaic is the ambo or pulpit base, 4.68m x 0.82m x 0.31m, placed on top of it, half way down the nave on the north side. An Attic sarcophagus-lid [37] is reused as the base of the altar in front of the apse. Apart from the apse there is no area of the central aisle cut off as the bema.

The apse, 7m in diameter, was constructed of somewhat finer blocks than most of the building, and has mosaics covering its floor. It is flanked by pastophoria entered by doors at the end of each side aisle and floored with mosaics. In the south pastophorion these are disturbed by tombs of which two are simple with multiple burials and grave goods. These include pottery dating to the late 6c [38]. The third tomb, which may be original, is far more elaborate and resembles the tomb in the narthex of Basilica A at Chersonisos or the so-called "Bishop's tomb" at Knossos (8/4). It lies against the south wall in the corner and has an elaborate marble cover; at the west end of the cover there is a cross surrounded by a circle of leaves with an inscription,

⳨ ΠΗΓΑΣΙΟΣ ΥΠΕΡ ⳨
ΥΓΙΑΣ ⟜ ΕΑΥΤΟΥ

and at the other end another cross in a circle, surrounded by a larger scalloped-edge circle (Fig.29). As a result of all these tombs little of the floor mosaic survives except the band against the east wall. Close by the join to the apse in the same wall is a small door, masked from the rest of the pastophorion by the 'buttress' of the apse. On the south wall here various Christian symbols, such as fish and a palm tree, have been scratched [39].

37. See p.47. *PAE* 1956, pl.121 α-γ.
38. *PAE* 1959, p.226, fig. 11, with pl.178a. Compare H. Robinson, *Athenian Agora* V, group M (6c), p.116f (Princeton, 1959).
39. *PAE* 1959, p.227, figs.14, 15.

Fig.29. Tomb in Basilica B, Chersonisos.

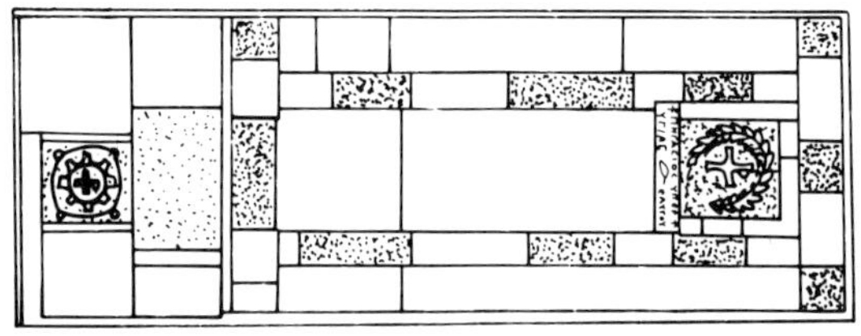

After Orlandos.

Much less survives in the north pastophorion which the excavator claims was extended to the north when the extra range was added all down the north side of the church[40]. However, the north wall of the new range has a dog-leg in it nine metres west of the east wall and a fragment of mosaic of the same design as the rest in the area covers the theoretical position of the 'original' north wall of the pastophorion, so that it seems possible that the north pastophorion always had a northern extension. The whole of this extra range is divided in three, the first room being the extension of the pastophorion, 4.7m wide; the next 4.00m wide, stretching the length of the aisles, and the third, also 4.00m wide, next to the narthex and the additional rooms beyond. These seem to be contemporary with the north range. Back at the east end there is the beginning of another extension to the north.

Little survives of the mosaic in the narthex except for the border consisting of a band of alternating squares in yellow and red outlined in black; and then a row of interlocking semicircles in yellow, red, white and black. This surrounds a geometric pattern of which only a small piece is left in the SE corner. This fragment seems to consist of alternating squares and lozenges in the same colours as the border: the surviving part is made up of a large square about a four-petal flower, or compass-drawn cross. At each corner there are smaller squares, the motifs, in the two that survive, consisting in one of a set of squares in red, yellow and black and in the other a white circle set against a black square with a five pointed red star with a yellow centre as the white circle's centre. The middle of the sides of the large square are just pierced by the points of lozenges, two of which are truncated by the borders of the mosaic, and in only one can the internal design be made out. This is very similar in design to the knot design of the north end of the narthex mosaic at Basilica A.

The mosaic in the nave was originally composed of two rows of geometric panels separated and bordered by a double guilloche band with the outer edge beyond this consisting of interlocked semicircles. There seem to have been at least sixteen panels originally, or perhaps eighteen if they were symmetrically arranged about the fifth panel. Unlike the others this one is not geometric but naturalistic, with fishes, almost certainly symbolic like the ones in the south pastophorion. The geometric panels are all severely damaged, yet enough survives to make out designs of a square of rope-mat set in a circle, and another panel of small squares with stars. The tesserae are in black, red, white, grey and yellow.

The apse mosaic is a purely geometric design with, from east to west, a narrow band of guilloche, then one wave design, a broad band of peltas, a narrow band of lozenges, the widest band of interlocking circles and finally a narrow band of lozenges. The pastophoria mosaics reverse the order, omitting the final lozenges and the circles. Obviously all the mosaics of the sanctuary area were designed as a unity, which reinforces the possibility that the 'original' north wall of the north pastophorion never existed. The mosaics in the later north range are plain large panels of white or pinkish tesserae separated by narrow black bands.

Various fragments of the altar screen were found, including panels showing four- or eight- armed crosses set in circles[41]; this was made of white marble as was a pessiscos from the screen. In the narthex a lekane support was found in the form of a small fluted column 0.63m high and a fragment of the lekane was found in the nave[42]. The excavator suggested that originally these would have stood in the atrium. One very worn Corinthian capital was found[43], but its state is such as to make any closer identification impossible. Apart from the sarcophagus lid other pre-basilica finds include several fragmentary inscriptions.

---

40. No excavations were carried out beyond the south wall as shown, so it is possible that another range could have been added there.
41. *PAE* 1956, p.246, fig.2; *PAE* 1959, p.223, fig.4.
42. *PAE* 1959, p.225, fig.10, with pl.116a.
43. *PAE* 1956, pl.120y.

Passing over the probability of a pre-Christian sacred building on the site, it is obvious that the church is of several phases, apart from the building erected in the narthex above the collapse of the church. The original building of narthex, aisles and sanctuary can be paralleled at a very similar church on Lesbos, at Aphentele [44] . This was dated by Orlandos, who excavated both sites, to late 5c - first half 6c. Within Crete, the church at Lebena (10/23) resembles Chersonisos B in having a similar stylobate and possibly pastophoria flanking the apse. This church may date to the late 5c or early 6c. The mosaics of the main church are very close in some details, especially the border of semicircles, to the mosaics at Chersonisos A and so ought to be close in date, probably the early part of 6c, which on balance seems to be the most likely date for Basilica B.

The later extensions to the building, i.e. the new rooms to the west and north, cannot be dated, nor can the patching of the mosaic with tiles, the new base of the ambo, or the raising of the stylobate. However, the rough tombs in the south pastophorion are dated by the pottery found in them to the late 6c. If the third tomb here is not original, it perhaps ought to date between the building of the room and the placing of these other tombs in that it occupies a much more sensible place in the room in relationship to the overall design. Furthermore, since the tiles, pulpit and tombs all ignore the mosaics to some extent, while the new north range has a mosaic floor, it seems unlikely that the range is contemporary with the other changes and perhaps ought to be earlier.

Chersonisos: Basilica C A third basilica was identified by S. Xanthoudides[45], but its existence has been held in doubt [46] . Its remains were described as an apse, presumably correctly orientated, or roughly so, and part of a wall, constructed of limestone with cement and tile. This building was said in 1918 to be 200m SW of the village. Lying between the ruins of the theatre and the harbour there are still visible remains of a building of stone and tile with column-bases and an apse or section of curved wall[47]. However, the 'apse' is not pointing east and the very massiveness of the wall, 1.50m thick, with its good tile courses, makes it totally unlike the other basilicas here or in the rest of Crete.

Piskopiano (6/8) On the edge of the mountains behind Chersonisos in the village of Piskopiano another large basilica is known but not excavated. It is some 45m long, 20m wide and has an apse 9.40m in internal diameter[48]. Various architectural fragments are known including a very ornate fragment of the screen, showing what looks like a hanging bowl surrounded by flowers, below a pediment set against stylised leaves[49]. From a tomb in the church came a gold coin of Heraclius and Heraclius Constantine, 613-641. Flooring materials included polychrome marble set in geometric designs [50] .

Mallia (6/20) (Fig.30) About 800m west of the Minoan Palace and quite close to the present shore is the site of a small Roman settlement with a partially excavated basilica [51] . Although the entire plan was not recovered, it is obvious that, while the rest of the plan is quite standard, the east end is unique in Crete. The basic church, excluding the rooms beyond the apse, is 35.0m long and about 15m wide, and is of normal stone and rubble construction. There are mosaic fragments in the nave and in the northern of the two annexes beyond the east end.

Fig.30. Mallia: Basilica.

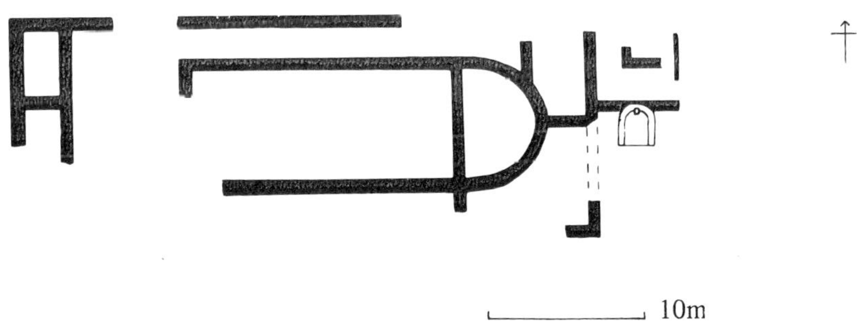

44. A. K. Orlandos, *A. Delt.* XII, 1929, p.44, fig.46.
45. *A. Delt.* IV, 1918, par.31.
46. Platon no.12.
47. Personal observation.
48. *A. Delt.* IV, 1918, par.31. Platon no.8. Nothing is now visible except some column fragments.
49. Gerola, *Mon. Ven.* II, p.53, fig.21. On display in the Heraklion Historical Museum.
50. Corpus p.111, no.45, claims mosaics not mentioned elsewhere.
51. *BCH* LXXXIII, 1958, p.829; *BCH* LXXXV. 1961, p.950f. Corpus 92, p.113, pl.85. *Etudes crétoises* XIX (Paris, 1974), General plan ref. E/F 1.

From the plan [52] it would seem that at the west end there are at least two rooms whose use is unknown; the northern one measuring 4m north-south and 2.50m east-west. East of these, in front of the main part of the church, is an area 7.30m deep and presumably the full width of the building. In that the north wall of the nave is shown as continuous from this point to the apse, the area ought to be the narthex, but it seems to be too large for this. It is perhaps more likely that it is an atrium with rooms on its west side as at Panormos (13/3) and that the narthex is within the 'nave' area.

Of the three aisles there is no evidence for the southern one except that the plan of the east end seems to demand it. The main aisle is 7m wide and the north aisle 4.00m wide. The nave with its mosaic is built above a crypt 5.50m x 6.60m that contained a very fine second century sarcophagus [53] which seems to have been reused in the fourth century to contain two bodies. Associated with this was a building of the same date which lay beneath the basilica [54].

The apse is the full width of the centre aisle and separated from it by a wall, presumably of no great height. Three other walls protrude from the apse; one that seems to be the end of the south aisle; another coming out about two-thirds up the north wall of the apse and the last from the apex of the apse, running EW to meet a NS wall two metres beyond. The resulting plan shows that here again the apse of the basilica is flanked by pastophoria. These, however, do not complete the east end, for beyond them are two more rooms with a common EW wall, 7.00m long and aligned slightly north of the EW wall of the pastophoria. The southern of the rooms seems to have been a baptistery with an apsidal font built into the common wall, in the same way as the font in the south pastophorion at Panormos (13/3). In the apex of the font a pit, 0.40m deep, had been sunk into the floor. The northern room was excavated for 4.25m to the north and up to its eastern wall, which had a doorway at its south end. There are fragments of mosaic against the west and south walls. In the centre of the room is an L-shaped stretch of wall which seems to contain what are possibly rough tombs [55].

The mosaics in the nave are described as being geometric with rose-like designs in three colours. In the north room of the annexe at the east end the mosaic by the west wall consists of a fragment of the border of black ivy-like leaves on a white background. The fragment by the south wall includes a cross set in a circle.

The only architectural fragments recovered from the church are Ionic impost capitals (Pl.50); the volutes are carved to look like decorated scrolls with a stiff linear design between them. The actual blocks are steep sided and square in effect. No cross was visible on the capitals left at the site [56]. In form and style of decoration they resemble Kautzsch's 'ältere Gruppe' from St. John's, Ephesus [57]. These are dated to the reign of Justinian.

As at nearby Chersonisos (6/7), this basilica does seem to honour an unknown deceased Christian but unlike Chersonisos A and B the church here was built on the same site as the 'original' burial in the sarcophagus. Whether or not the objects of this honour died in the second century and were the original occupants of the sarcophagus or whether the two died in the fourth century and reused it cannot be proved, but the latter seems more likely given the rather pagan nature of the ornamentation. The erection of a church on an earlier cemetery site is common and the basilica at Knossos (8/4) is a close parallel for this in Crete, as the building there also seems to have been aligned on an earlier burial. Nevertheless, the basilica at Mallia seems to have functioned as an ordinary church for its village. However, it is possible that the baptistery and the other room at the east end could be additions to the original design.

The sanctuary area minus additions is similar to the Hypslometopon Basilica in Lesbos [58] which was dated to the second half of the 6c, although the capitals there are nearly the same as at Mallia and ought to date to slightly earlier. The only other dating evidence from the site is of no real aid: while cleaning the walls coins of the Vandalic Kingdom of N. Africa were found. Unfortunately, it is not clear what relationship the coins had to the walls. From the capitals and the relationship between Mallia and the other local basilicas at Chersonisos with their complex chancels, the church here is perhaps best dated to the middle of the 6c.

---

52. The excavations were hampered by the water level in the marshes which appears to submerge the site in the winter. The plan is therefore taken from the only published one in *Etudes crétoises* XIX, which is at 1:2000, supplemented by my own observations.
53. See p.47. The sarcophagus is on display in the Roman Room of Heraklion Museum.
54. *BCH* LXXXV, 1961, p.950, fig.17.
55. This area was not fully excavated and it is only from the photograph that I suggest that these are tombs: *BCH* 1961, p.951, fig.18.
56. These are to be found on the main site, north of the custodian's house.
57. Kautzsch, *op.cit.* note 3, p.566.
58. A. K. Orlandos, ' *Αἱ παλαιοχριστιανικαὶ βασιλικαὶ τῆς Λέσβου*', *A. Delt.* XII, 1929, p.5, fig.1.

Pl. 50: Ionic capitals from the basilica at Malla.
Pl. 51: Architectural fragments built into the SE corner of the chapel of Ay. Georgios on the site of Lyttos.
Pl. 52: Bird capital from Lyttos in Heraklion Historical Museum.

Avdhou (6/23) Mosaics found here are described[59] as of geometric design with peacocks; this makes it extremely likely that the building they came from was a basilica.

Piyi (6/24) The early mediaeval church of Ay. Panteleimon undoubtedly stands on the site of an early Christain basilica [60]. There are fragments of walls in stone faced concrete protruding from the SW and NE corners; at the latter there are two walls 2.50m apart supporting an archway, the bottom of which is 2.30m above present ground level. Apart from these walls there are also numerous architectural fragments reused in the church: in the north aisle the penultimate column to the east is composed of four superimposed capitals, three of which would seem to be of the 5/6c Leierkapitelle type, but the other is probably earlier. There are other fragments built into the walls including an Ionic capital of 6c type, as well as earlier inscriptions[61]. This earlier material may well indicate the existence of a pagan predecessor to the basilica, very possibly a shrine to Asklepios [62] since a copious spring rises nearby.

Lyttos (6/25) No plan of any late Roman church has yet been recovered from this vast site, but there is definite evidence for at least one major church below the later church of the Cross (Timios Stavros), in the reputed area of the ancient agora. Mosaics[63] have been uncovered here and protruding from its SE corner there is a large piece of earlier concrete masonry. Apart from this there are architectural fragments built into the other later church of Ay. Georgios and further along the site to the south more fragments seem to have been used in one of the windmills. Although these fragments are scattered over some considerable distance it is not impossible that they all derive from the one church which has the mosaics[64] below the chapel of Timios Stavros. North of here a pessiscos can be observed by the path that crosses the site.

The fragments include an Ionic impost capital and a probable window lintel by the ruins of the windmill. The blocks built into the SE corner of Ay. Georgios seem to come from ornate piers (Pl.51). All these fragments are covered with very finely carved acanthus foliage, either by itself or as a background for a cross. The style would date these to the late 5c when compared to similar material from Nea-Anchialos Basilica A [65] and Corinth Lechaion [66]. The capital probably dates to the same period. A further figured capital with doves comes from the site and again ought to date to the later 5c [67] (Pl.52).

Panayia (6/35) Gerola reports mosaics below the church but no other details are available [68].

Kastelliana (7/30) Near to the cisterns another large building was discovered [69] with mosaics including panels of clematis and guilloche borders. Clematis does occur on basilica-mosaics, e.g. at Suia (19/17) but it is also used on secular mosaics. Whether or not this particular building is a basilica cannot be decided without further excavation.

Inatos (7/31) (Fig.31) On the west bank of the River Mintris a short distance inland are the fragmentary remains of a basilica [70]. All that can be seen is what is left of the east end and even this is being eroded by the river. The remains are constructed of stone-faced cement of a higher quality than most of the other late Roman churches of the island.

Fig.31. Inatos: Basilica.

59. *Kret. Khron.* X, 1956, p.419. Corpus 95, p.114.
60. Gerola, *Mon. Ven.* II, p.192, and tav. 2. Personal observation.
61. *IC.*I.XVIII.77, 80, 90, 125, 130.
62. Spanake I, p.92.
63. *Kret. Khron.* VII, 1953, p.490. Platon no.9. Corpus p.113, 90 Stavros and 91 Ay. Georgios.
64. I am here ignoring the Corpus claim for mosaics below Ay. Georgios for which there seems to be no evidence.
65. Krautheimer, *op.cit.* note 6, p.130 pl.78. Details of the Lyttus material from thesis field work.
66. Krautheimer, *op.cit.* note 6, p.140, pl.92.
67. On display in Heraklion Historical Museum.
68. Gerola, *Mon. Ven.*, p.299, n.1. Corpus p 114, n.47.
69. *Kret. Khron.* VIII, 1954, p.516. Corpus 94, p.114. Nothing of this building or the mosaics could be seen in 1973.
70. Personal observation. I was able to examine the block in the Museum stores by kind permission of the Ephor, Dr. St. Alexiou.

The apse is 4.50m in internal diameter and as far as can be seen is semicircular. Just enough survives on its north side to reveal a possible pastophorion with a second NS wall 2.60m to the west of the end wall. To the south the end wall can be traced for 4.70m beyond the apse, thus suggesting that the south aisle is wider than the main aisle. This does not seem very likely, and it is possible that there is an additional room here. The alternative of a tripartite transept is unlikely in that the north wing here is shorter than the width of the south one, which would result in a very peculiarly shaped transept.

Various column fragments in grey marble or granite which might come from the church can be seen further down the river. Also in the storerooms of the Heraklion Museum is a carved block from Itanos that may well come from the basilica; the decoration includes flowers or stars very similar to ones on architectural fragments from Inatos (1/39) and Panormos (13/3). This decoration would date the Inatos example to the sixth century.

Knossos (8/4): Ayia Sophia The modern church of Ayia Sophia in the village of Makryteichos seems to have been built above an earlier basilica. Its only surviving part is a large apse, or rather its foundations, that joined the present apse on the south[71]. Possible early Christian graves have also been found at the SW corner of the church [72].

Knossos: Sanatorium (Fig.32) The northern boundary of the city at Knossos seems to have been marked by a small stream beyond which lay one of the main cemeteries. Above one part of this a small basilica was built and has been excavated and published in greater detail than any other comparable site in Crete [73]. The church was very badly robbed, but enough survived to show that it was of standard plan, 21.60m long and 12.09m wide. Mosaic floors had originally been laid in the narthex, aisles and sanctuary. The construction was of large but often irregular blocks with earlier tombs filled in to try and prevent subsidence. The filling of these tombs provides accurate dating for the erection of the church.

Fig.32. Knossos: Sanatorium Basilica.

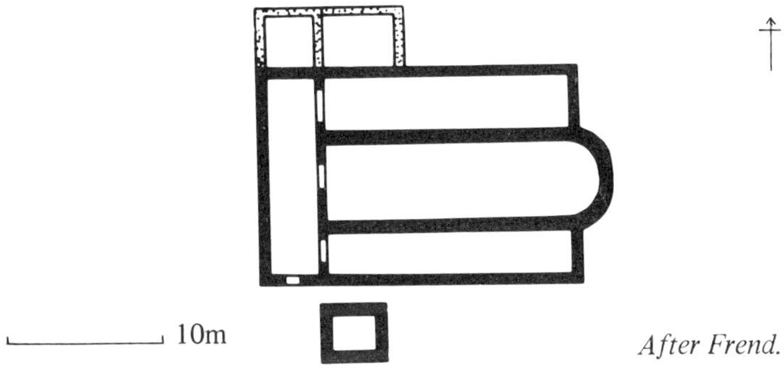

After Frend.

The narthex, 3.12m wide, was entered by a door 1.32m wide in the southern wall, at which point the mosaic had had to be patched because of wear. No entrance was possible from the west because of the way the church had been recessed into the hillside. From the narthex doors led into the nave and side aisles, which seem to have been meant to be of equal width at 3.10m and 3.08m. The north aisle and mosaic had been very badly disturbed by collapse into the earlier tombs and later robbing, even though the north wall had been moved out at one point to avoid going over three tombs.

The nave was 4.50m wide and at a level 0.10m higher than the narthex. It had been floored in marble slabs of different shapes that had probably originally formed a symmetrical pattern. Separating it from the side aisles was a high stylobate, 0.93m, made of some of the largest blocks still *in situ*. These stylobates seem to have been part of the original building in that the laying of the mosaics took into account minor irregularities of the wall blocks, and the excavator states that the masonry of the narthex and the stylobates formed a "single integral feature" [74].

In the NW corner of the nave an earlier tomb[75] stood 0.37m proud of the floor. The sides had been faced with marble slabs and the top with an elaborate cover of *opus alexandrinum* or marble inlay. Covering the head was a

71. Knossos *Survey* 92. This apse was not visible in 1973/74.
72. Report by J. W. Hayes, 12th April 1971 in the Telegraph Post Book, kept at the Taverna of the British School at Knossos.
73. W. H. C. Frend, 'The Byzantine Basilica church at Knossos', *ABSA* LVII, 1962, p.186f. Platon no.6. Corpus 86, p.109, pl.79. Knossos *Survey* 36.
74. It is not clear if this means keyed in or what. The plan p.186 fig.2 is not particularly helpful.
75. Tomb 8, p.194f, in the report with p.149, fig.9a, 9b for the bottles. They are Isings form 105; C. Isings, *Roman glass from dated finds* (Groningen, 1957).

'halo' in yellow-white marble 0.70m in diameter; next to this was the lower part of a Late Minoan ribbed blossom bowl of black steatite with a hole bored into its bottom connecting into the tomb. Beyond this, long hexagons of red, grey and mottled marble were arranged around a central square of porphyry. The last third of this elaborate design had been disturbed and replaced with a rough plaster cover containing pieces of the original marble. Below the top cover three large limestone slabs covered the tomb, the last slab coinciding with the area of disturbance. In the tomb lay one person with two glass bottles as grave goods. The skeleton was intact except for the skull, which, apart from the lower jaw, seems to have been removed, probably when the top cover was ruined. In its final form the tomb was very similar to those at Chersonisos (6/7) A (the tomb in the narthex) and Chersonisos B (the tomb of Pegasius in the south pastophorion). These both probably date to the early 6c and it would seem likely that the *opus alexandrinum* cover at Knossos is of the same date, contemporary with the building of the church. However, the actual tomb must be earlier, for the grave goods in the form of the two bottles date to the late 3c or early 4c.

The division between the nave and chancel was marked by a line of fragments from the screen about 11m up the nave. The floor had been covered with a mosaic of which little had been left by the subsidence and robbing. Only the bottom of the foundations of the apse had been left, but it projected 1.90m beyond the east wall and was apparently divided from the chancel by a narrow wall. Window glass and hollow tile tubes for vaulting were recovered from this area. Below the centre of the apse a small heap of burnt bones was found [76] ; this is interpreted in the report as part of the pre-church cemetery, but when compared to similar deposits from Panormos (13/3) and Kera (14/7) might be some sort of foundation offering.

Apart from the narthex entrance, it is suggested that there was another entrance into the church via an annexe, 4.85m x 3.95m, built against the north wall of the north aisle. The main evidence for the entrance is a column base in this building and a column nearby. This building was joined to an earlier wall to the north. On the west side of this room is another flanking the narthex. On the floors of these rooms and in the levels below, a considerable amount of domestic refuse was found, including hearths. The functions of these rooms cannot really be determined from this evidence, but given the nature of the deposits and the existence of an enclosed courtyard north of them, it may be that they were used for some temporal rather than spiritual role.

The other building whose use is far from clear is the free-standing structure at the SW corner by the narthex door. This is quite small, 2.10m x 3.90m, and separated from the main church by a cobbled passage 1.45m wide. The excavator suggested that this was a tower on the grounds of the width of the foundations, 0.77m, and the amount of rubble. Against this is the shallowness of the foundations, 0.50m, and perhaps the fact that the building seems to have been used after the collapse of the main church despite the fact that a tower would be most vulnerable to the earth-quakes which seem to have brought the main church down. The parallel used in the report for a tower is also not really applicable, as the tower of Ay. Andreas at Eressos on Lesbos is attached to the narthex as a staircase [77]. Possibly this building here was a baptistery standing independently of its mother church, like the possible example at Itanos (1/39). The best actual parallel is the similar structure, 4.1 x 3.5m, at Silchester, outside the main entrance of the narthex [78]. If the building here is a baptistery then the actual font could have been in the area without flooring in the SW corner.

Of the mosaics, those in the narthex and south aisle were the same; composed of white, red, orange, blue, pink and purple tesserae. The main motif is a series of equal-armed crosses composed of lozenges enclosing a design of a circle flanked by semicircles and then 'tongues' protruding beyond these, giving an effect rather like a hair slide. Between the arms of the cross catharine wheels are set within circles and the whole design is set against a background of what looks like fern leaves, and bordered by a guilloche. The mosaic in the north aisle also has a guilloche border within which is a row of three circles with inset squares and separated from the next row by small squares set at each corner of the larger internal square. In these are swastika motifs in red and blue. What was left of the mosaics in the sanctuary area consisted of two wide panels of 'varicoloured interlaces' divided by a central path of orange and pink scallop shells, all enclosed by a 'broad frame of elaborate polychrome interlaces'. In the rubble of the nave there were also a few green and blue glass tesserae which may be evidence for wall mosaics. Other wall decoration consisted of yellow painted wall-plaster with a red slip.

---

76. P.209 tomb 34: the bones are said to have been broken and charred before burial. All the bones in this group of tombs are said to be human but no details are given.
77. Orlandos, *op.cit.* note 58, p.30.
78. G. C. Boon, *Silchester* (London, 1974), p.181.

Architectural fragments [79] included a rather fine grey marble lintel with a peacock relief from the narthex and, from the same area, a lion-head sima in limestone and a marble jewelled cross. Other similar crosses came from the screen. From the apse came a relief in grey marble of a dolphin. Column fragments were of both unfluted pink marble and corkscrew grey marble types. The latter varied in diameter from 0.33m to 0.47m. The narthex crosses are of the same type as that on the mosaic at S. Apollinare in Classe (532-6) but that from the screen may be slightly later, being comparable to a cross from Sant'Apollinare Nuovo at Ravenna (mid 6c). The corkscrew columns should date between the mid 5c and the mid 6c [80].

The excavator deals with all possible parallels for the mosaics, but the important ones include a mosaic from the Procopius church at Gerasa [81] dated 526-7, although it is not as close as the report makes it sound, being different in its details. The 'hair slide' is also found on mosaics on the Greek mainland at Elis [82] and at Amphipolis Basilica [83]. The scallop, or scale design, is not uncommon, the best example in Crete being at Suia, where it is also used to mark the central path down the church. The mosaics in the north aisle can be paralleled from sites from Aquileia to Sabratha and Nea Anchialos [84].

The orientation of the church is NW-SE, determined by the earlier tombs, particularly Tomb 8, in the narthex. Obviously the basilica was built in honour of the early Christians of Knossos who are known from the 2c [85]. The cemetery itself seems to have been in use from the first century [86]. The date of the construction of the church must be the early 6c from the style of the mosaics and architectural fragments, but more importantly some of the tombs had been filled in by the builders of the church and pottery from these tombs confirms the date [87].

After a period of use and the addition of the annexes, the church was destroyed or collapsed. The date of this can be fixed with gratifying certainty; two coins were found:

> "beneath an enormous block of fallen masonry sunk into the natural clay was found a follis of Heraclius I and Heraclius Constans . . . . . . This coin can be dated to 612-3 and was in good condition when lost. Another follis of Heraclius was found nearby" (report, p.197).

In the catalogue these coins, b16 and 17, are said to be from beneath the nave floor, but in the passage quoted above there is no mention of any floor between the destruction rubble and the natural. The coins are admitted as an embarass-ment in the report's conclusions, where again they are assumed to predate the church. However, by the description in the main text it would seem much more likely that they date the end of the church. The cause of this can only be guessed at, but an earthquake would seem most likely. An alternative possibility for which there is no direct evidence is a Slavic raid. The archaeological evidence for such raids at exactly this date is best shown by the distribution of coin hoards in the Aegean as illustrated by Dr. D. M. Metcalf in the same volume of the ABSA [88]. The Slavs certainly did reach Crete a few years later in 623 [89], and so an earlier raid is quite possible. Against this raid hypothesis is the lack of direct evidence from the site, in that all the other sites excavated in Knossos seem to have been abandoned by 400 [90]. This indeed shows the importance of the cemetery to the 6c Christians who bothered to build the church next to a desolate or at least much reduced city instead of in the probable new centre at Heraklion.

Paliani (8/11) A large number of various architectural fragments at this convent marks the site of a previous basilica [91]. The capitals are of several types, including a rather fine 'Leierkapitell' and other rather squarer Corinthian capitals. The most attractive piece, however, is an impost block showing two birds with crossed tails, looking back at each other. The space between their heads is filled in with a leaf set in a circle. In form and style Kautzsch's 618 is quite close; this dates to the Justinianic period and comes from Constantinople. There is a second similar block (Pl.53)

---

79. All the fragments are listed in the report, p.212f.
80. Group 6 in J. L. Benson's 'Spirally Fluted Columns in Greece', *Hesperia,* XXVIII, 1959, p.253f.
81. C. H. Kraeling, *Gerasa, City of the Decapolis* (Newhaven, 1938) pl.lxxxiv a.
82. J. P. Sodini, 'Les mosaiques paléochrétiens de la Grèce', *BCH* XCIV, 1970, p.751.
83. *Ergon* 1964, p.34, fig.33.
84. P.199 of the report.
85. Bishop Pinytus of Knossos in 170 in Eusebius *Hist. Ecc.* IV.21.
86. See gazetteer, p.152.
87. Especially p.221, fig.14, nos.18, 22, which are Late Roman C. Ware Form 3F.
88. P.14 'The Aegean Coastlands under threat: some coins and coin hoards from the reign of Heraclius'; fig.p.15.
89. Land (ed.) *Thomas Presbyter of Emesa,* p.115.
90. See Gazetteer: Knossos (8/4).
91. Gerola, *Mon. Ven.* II, p.181f. and pl.124-6. Platon no.8. Personal observation.

decorated with leaves and α and ω monogram. There are also trabeate fragments decorated with stylised acanthus. The capitals would all seem to date to the first half of the 6c.

Phodele (9/2) The present church on the site dates to 1323, but there is some doubt whether its obvious predecessor is pre- or post-Arab. The design of its east end is not unlike that at Vizari (12/12) and could be close in date to it, but the definitely post-Arab basilica at Viran Episkopi (13/2) provides a better comparison. It therefore seems more likely that the church at Phodele is post-Arab [92].

Gonies (9/7) Below the reputedly tenth century church of Panayia, also known as Palaioklissa, there is supposedly an early Christian basilica [93]. Unfortunately renovation in the form of whitewash and a new concrete yard makes it impossible to see anything.

Ay. Miron (9/12) It has been claimed that there is an earlier church below the mediaeval one as shown by the synthronon in the central apse [94]. There is no real evidence to place this before the Arabs, and Gerola [95] believed it to be post-Arab.

Gergeri (10/3) The probable existence of a basilica here is shown by the reuse of architectural fragments in the churches of Christos Soter and the Panayia [96]. Amongst the fragments in the first church is an inscription recording the restoration of the bema pillars [97].

Gortyna (10/10) As befits the capital of the island and the seat of the archbishop from St. Titus onwards, more churches are known from this site than any other in Crete [98]. They include the most important, St. Titus itself; one of the most unusual, the Mitropolis building; two converted temples, the Pythian Apollo and Mavropapas; the Acropolis basilica and a rather dubious one below the village church of Ay. Deka.

Apollo (Fig. 33) The great Greek and Roman temple [99] of Apollo Pythias was almost certainly converted into a church, if one accepts the addition of the apse and columns not as 'Roman', i.e. pre-Christian, but as evidence for the conversion of a typical Cretan temple into a three-aisled basilical church. Unlike the rest of the building, the apse is constructed of stone-faced cement; the facing is a little crude, like other late buildings in Gortyna. The columns are of marble or granite, and are reused, one of them bearing an inscription to Caracalla [100]. The form of the temple was

Fig. 33. Gortyna: Pythian Apollo.

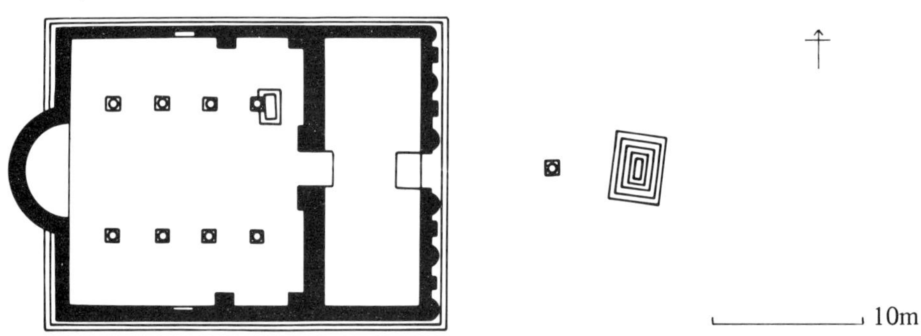

very suitable for conversion, the pronaos becoming the narthex and the naos proper (divided in three by the columns, four a side) becoming the nave, 9m wide, with side aisles *c.* 4m wide. The apse, which had to be at the west end because of the orientation of the temple, is raised 0.45m up from the aisles and is 6.47m wide, protruding 3.32m beyond the west wall. The temple seems to have served as the cathedral until the construction of St. Titus [101].

---

92. K. Lassithiotakes, ' Ὁ Ναὸς τῶν Εἰσοδίων καί μιὰ παλαιότερη βασιλικὴ στὸ Φόδελε', *Kret. Khron.* V, 1951, p.76.
93. *Kret. Khron.* IX, 1955, p.568 . The local and learned guide was very sure about the existence of an earlier church.
94. Platon no.7.
95. Gerola, *Mon. Ven.*, II, p.181.
96. Gerola, *Mon. Ven.* II, 3, p.258, fig. 318-9.
97. *IC.* IV.466.
98. See Fig. 58 for the position of all these.
99. See p.132. *IC.* IV. Praef. ii, p.5. F. Halbherr, *Mon. Ant.* I, 1890, p.9f.
100. *IC.* IV. 280.
101. An inscription, *IC.* IV.460, mentioning Theodorus the Archbishop, was found just to the north of the temple. There seems to be no evidence at all for Platon's idea that there was another church here (Platon no.2).

Mavropapas (Fig.34) This basilica, 26m long minus the apse and 17.80m wide, was also built on the site of an earlier temple [102]. Indeed the only visible remains today are some of the architectural fragments from this [103]. The narthex of the church, 4.35m deep, was entered by doors at either side of the west end or by doors in the middle of the north and south walls. From here there were entrances into each aisle, the north aisle's door being offset from the position of the equivalent door in the narthex west wall.

The north aisle at 4.50m was slightly narrower than the south at 4.85m. Both aisles had doors in their external walls about half way down from the narthex and probably pastophoria; the latter are marked by a wall in the south aisle at *c.* 5.0m from the east end and a pilaster set against the north wall in the north aisle at the same point. The main aisle was 8.45m wide and presumably the sanctuary began at the same point as the pastophoria. The apse was semicircular with a radius of 2.50m.

Of the architectural fragments from the church the most outstanding was a fragment from the screen showing an interlaced figure-of-eight pattern with a dove with an olive branch in the upper part and a scallop shell in the lower. To the left of the figure-of-eight is a cross [104]. A very similar piece comes from the basilica at Vravron which ought to date to the mid 6c [105]. Another fragment bears an inscription [106] on a cross which may be a record of the consecration of the church. Guarducci dates this on letter form to 'probably the 5c'. In that the Vravron parallel is close and dated by pottery and a coin, the later date ought to be accepted. Other fragments include parts of a pessiscos, a much shattered Corinthian capital and more small fragments of the screen.

Fig.34. Mavropapas Basilica.

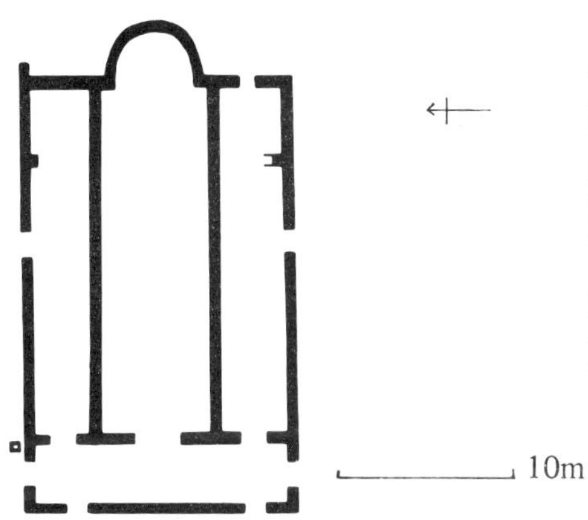

After De Sanctis

Fig.35. Acropolis Basilicas and Temple.

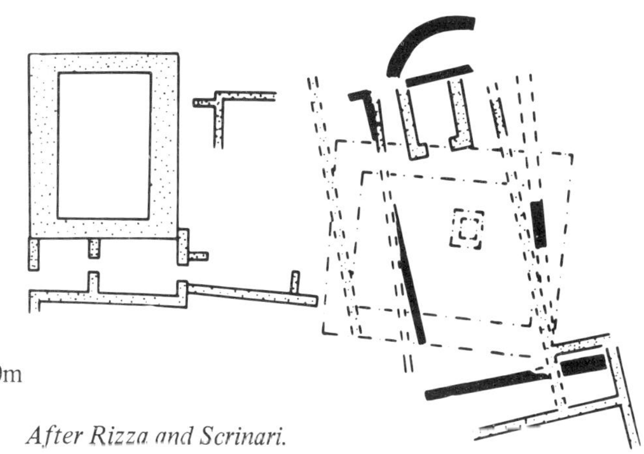

After Rizza and Scrinari.

Acropolis (Fig.35) On the south-east corner of the Acropolis, above the ruins of the temple [107] the remains of two superimposed basilicas [108] are squeezed in between the east wall of the Kastro and the steep edge of the hill. Both basilicas were in an extremely fragmentary state and their plans are far from certain, especially the later and therefore higher of the two.

The earlier church, 20m x 9m plus, seems to be of the normal basilica plan, although its side aisles cannot be traced. It is mainly constructed of limestone blocks reused from the temple below. Despite the excavators' reconstruction there is really no evidence for a wall separating the narthex and nave. The north wall of the nave is fairly definite and on this side there may be a side aisle marked by the excavators' wall Q and, at the east end, wall N. The south wall is more dubious, being only a line of blocks, wall q 1-3, and the fact that a line of NS orthostats, o, stops on this alignment. These stones may mark the division between the nave and the chancel, 12.50m from the church west wall (a). In the nave, approximately in the centre but not on the same alignment as the church, the temple bothros continued in use, perhaps as a font. At the east end a well-built apse, 7m wide, with foundations cut into the rock,

---

102. De Sanctis, *Mon. Ant.* XVIII, 1907, p.277f. *IC.*IV. Praef. iv, p.9. Platon no. 1.
103. Fig.47-9, p.290 of the report. See p.75.
104. Fig.26c. From *Mon. Ant.* XVIII, 1907, fig.52 p.293-4.
105. *PAE* 1951, p.64-6.
106. *IC.*IV.477.
107. See p.71.
108. G. Rizza and V. S. M. Scrinari, *Il sanctuario sull'Acropoli di Gortyna* (Rome, 1968), chap.III, tav.Ac.

completes the church. Various small architectural fragments were recovered showing acanthus leaf decoration. From a deposit associated with the church pottery was found, including a 6/7c African Red Slip Ware bowl, form 104[109]. It is highly likely that this church dates to the later 5c or 6c.

The second church is very fragmentary indeed[110] with only the oblong structure at the east end, walls j and k, and the west wall e/f having any true existence. Furthermore, although the excavator claimed a Justinianic date for this building, one of the 'walls' seems to overlie the deposit containing the 6/7c bowl. Also much of the pottery from the layers of this 'church' which is claimed as 5/6c oriental Byzantine material would seem to be much later in date, 8-11c[111] Furthermore, the only datable tomb, although it was later than some of those associated with the second church, yielded a coin of Emmanuel Commenus, 1143-1180. Given the known reoccupation of Gortyna in the 'Byzantine B' period it would seem most likely that the second church should be assigned to this period.

The 'fortified monastery' to the north of the complex seems to be linked to the later phase and so ought to be of the same date. The dating evidence from here includes pottery claimed to be Arab, a coin of Leo V 813-820, an Arab coin of the 9c, and another coin of Emmanuel Commenus. It is of somewhat better construction than the church and from the dating evidence, none of which is securely stratified, might be of Arab date rather than immediately post Arab.

St. Titus (Fig.36) The most important and best preserved of all the early Christian churches in Crete is the cathedral of St. Titus built in the Agora area of the capital (Pl.54-5)[112]. The church is not quite as long as for instance Chersonisos A or B, being 31m x 19m, but is a far more complex and imposing structure. The three aisled basilica plan underlies the layout, but with the cross dome design built in and dominating it. The entire church is built of large limestone blocks, much more reminiscent of Hellenistic technique than Roman. The only exception to this is the west wall in front of the narthex which is built of tile.

Fig.36. Gortyna: St Titus.

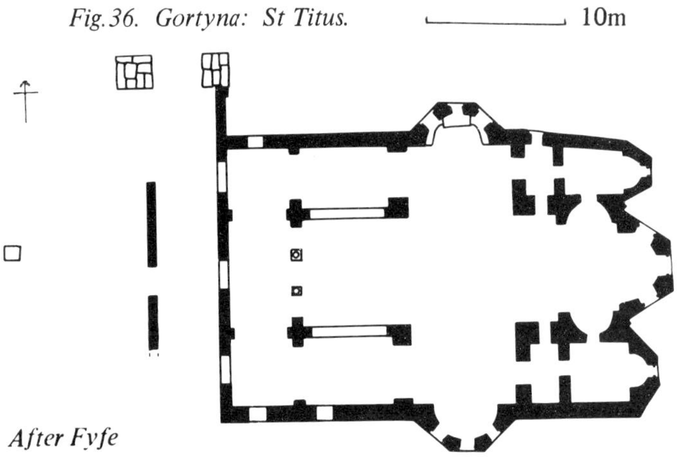

After Fyfe

Pl. 53: Impost capital at Moni Paliani.

The narthex, 4m deep, has three doors in its west wall and doors in the side walls. From the narthex arches lead into the side aisles. The nave, entered through a tribelon, opens out into the crossarms of the main area. The central area was domed, while the nave and side arms were barrel vaulted. These side arms each terminate in an apse. The sanctuary area is very complicated; the chancel is a triconch connected to flanking pastophoria which have their own anterooms. Galleries would have been situated above the narthex and side aisles.

Various fragments of the screen and pulpit were recovered from the church. The pulpit was of the common double stair type. One complete column survived from the tribelon; this was 2.88m high with a cross cut onto it. Its Ionic impost capital (Pl.56) bore a monogram B N with α and ω[113]. The monogram's interpretation, whether a man's

109. Fig. 127 in the report.
110. Tav. C in the report.
111. The parallel material quoted from Jerusalem comes from a muddled rubbish deposit which includes coins of the 8c and is sealed by a 12c layer. The parallels from the Talbot Rice article (*Cahiers Archéologiques* VII, 1954, p.69) are dated there to the 9-11c.
112. T. Fyfe, *Architectural Review* XXII, 1907, p.5-60. A. K. Orlandos, *EEBS* III, 1926, p.301f. Gerola, *Mon. Ven.* II, p.29. Krautheimer, *op.cit.* note 6, p.268 fig.214.
113. *IC.*IV.275.

Pl. 54: Ay. Titos, Gortyna, interior.
Pl. 55: Ay, Titos, Gortyna, exterior

name or the abbreviation of *του νιγκας*, is uncertain. If the latter, it could be compared to dedications to the Heraclid dynasty[114] from the nymphaeum by the Praetorium. The actual capital is dated by Kautzsch[115] to the late 6c. Other fragments seem to date from the post-Arab period, when the church was rededicated. Possibly from the period immediately before the Arab invasion comes a hoard of bronze vessels and fitments including numerous candlesticks. This was found below the nave floor.

At right angles to the main church and to south of it, there is also a building of similar construction. The east wall of this building is aligned onto the west end of the chancel, and its west wall on the west wall of the church. The function of this large building, *c.* 50m x 20m, is unknown. At the west end of the church the tile wall, 4.50m further west, is probably part of the building and forms it exonarthex. Both this wall and the west wall of the church proper end in massive stone piers which are probably supports for a staircase up to the galleries. Beyond this tile wall is a flagged courtyard with a base, 1m square, of uncertain use set 10m beyond the tile wall.

The plan of St. Titus is related to other cross-domed Greek churches, e.g. at Phillipi Basilica B, *c.* 540; on Paros the Hekatonpylai, *c.* 550, and Justinian's Church of the Holy Apostles at Constantinople. However, the capitals and the complex chancel plan seem to date St. Titus somewhat later than these others. Given Heraclius' activity at Gortyna as shown by the inscriptions and the monogram, it seems likely that the new cathedral is another mark of this activity[116].

Mitropolis (Fig.37) At the southern edge of the city a large triconch structure was excavated in the late 1960's [117]. It consists of a basic oblong, 24m x 11m, orientated NE-SW, with its entrances at the west end and large elliptical apses protruding from the centre of each of the long sides. It is constructed of rather poor limestone blocks with a mosaic floor in the south apse and a marbled floor in the north.

Fig. 37. Gortyna: Mitropolis Basilica.

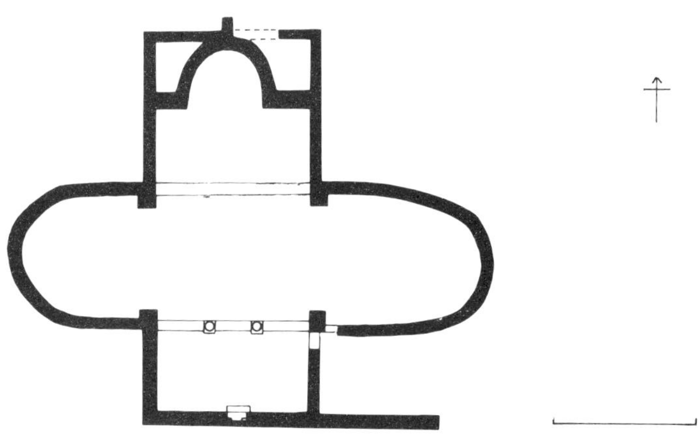

The narthex at the 'west' end of the oblong is 11m wide and 5m deep; it is entered by a single door in its south wall. The west wall continues on to the south, possibly to link with another building in this direction, which would lie under the modern village. From the narthex the main part of the building was entered through a tribelon with its two columns on bases 0.72m square and 0.33m high. The 'nave' is 8m long before the line of the chancel screen is reached. The chancel is 4.75m deep and the apse 3.75m long and 5.10m wide with its apex touching the east wall of the basic oblong. This results in two rather awkward rooms flanking the apse. The construction of this area is of the same material as the rest of the building but of a higher standard. The floor here is of large tiles and there were probably marble orthostats on the walls as in the northern elliptical apse.

The northern apse is of a better build and has a marble floor in addition to a wall-lining in the same material. It is rather more regular in shape than its southern counterpart and not as long: 8.50m as compared to 13m. The southern apse has the only mosaic of the building: this is one of the finest in Crete, in some fifteen colours. The mosaic has a double border of single narrow bands and a double guilloche. Within this is a free design of birds

114. *IC.* IV.512.
115. Kautzsch, *op.cit.* note 3, p.180 no.576.
116. A recent attempt to date the sheil to the late 10c after the reconquest is not convincing. *Acts of the 3rd Cretological Congress* II (Athens, 1976), p.37.
117. *Ergon* 1968, p.111. *PAE* 1968, p.139. Corpus 85, p.108, p.177-8.

wandering amongst a field of flowers. There are no close parallels within Crete, and although the birds at Basilica B at Amphipolis are similar, they are there confined within circles, etc.

There are a number of architectural fragments from the screen in white marble and also from the altar, which was 0.66m x 0.51m. The finest pieces are two Corinthian capitals [118] with Theodosian-type acanthus leaves and a cross between the helices. These must date to the second half of the 5c.

The plan of the building is not common in the Aegean and seems to derive from Africa and the west. Within Crete itself there is another trilobate building at Kato Asites (9/14) but this seems to be a bath building of uncertain date [119]. The closest parallel to the Mitropolis church seems to be an annexe to the Cenchraean Gate Basilica at Corinth [120]. Here a building, almost exactly the same in plan and with the same sort of capitals, was found attached to the main church. There can be little doubt that at Corinth and at Gortyna these buildings served as martyria and it seems very likely that the Mitropolis example did not stand by itself but was attached by its west wall to a church not yet excavated.

The capitals and mosaic date the construction of the martyrion to the later 5c; its decline can be dated from a group of material recovered from on top of the floors. This included bronze vessels similar to those from St. Titus, but also several lamps that very probably date from the time of the Arab invasion [121].

Ay. Deka The present church of Ay. Deka does not appear to be of great antiquity, but Buondelmonte [122] records mosaics of an earlier church below. No trace of these survives today and indeed the only visible remains are the six tile graves in the open crypt, no doubt meant to be the (crowded) resting places of the ten martyrs. It is not impossible that there was an earlier church here, although the Mitropolis triconch seems to be a more suitable building to commemorate the martyrs.

Lebena (10/23) (Fig.38) On the eastern edge of the great sanctuary of Asklepios at Lebena, a small mediaeval chapel dedicated to St. John marks the site of its larger predecessor [123]. The site was excavated early this century but has never been properly published. The early church is of the normal basilical plan but with its narthex at an oblique angle to the nave and aisles. It is 26m long and 14.50m wide (external measurements), constructed of reused material with the main walls of large limestone blocks; the floors were of tile and cement.

Fig.38. Lebena: Basilica.

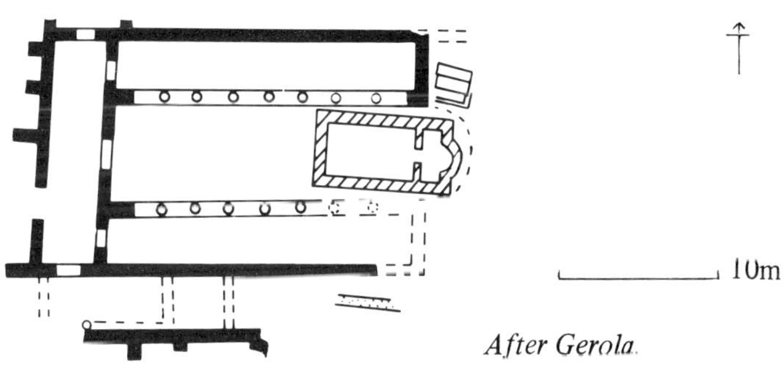

After Gerola.

The first definite room at the west end is the narthex, 3m deep, but a number of stubs of walls projecting to the west and north indicate further unexcavated rooms. To the west the south wall of the church continues and there are three more walls closely grouped at the north end of the west wall. It would seem likely that there was an atrium with a doorway into the narthex and a range of rooms on its northern side. To the north of the narthex two walls flank a doorway in its north wall; this almost certainly led to another room whose west wall in its turn may well have been the east wall of a room off the corner of the narthex. Apart from the atrium none of these putative rooms' functions can be identified, but it is likely that one of them, probably in the north range, was the baptistery.

118. *PAE* 1968, pl. 142a, b.
119. See p.70.
120. J. Shelley, *Hesperia* XII, 1943, p.166. A. Grabar, *Martyrium* (Paris, 1946), p.102 and fig.44.
121. *Ergon* 1968, pl.134.
122. Ap. Cornelius, *Creta Sacra,* p.77f. Platon no.3. Gerola, *Mon. Ven.* II, p.190. Corpus 89, p.112. Personal observation for the tile graves.
123. G. Gerola, *Le antiche chiese di Lebena a Creta* (Venice, 1915). Soteriou, *AE* 1929, p.193 no.22. Platon no.4. Personal observation.

The main entrance into the narthex was through the door in the south wall which may be preceded by a porch. From the narthex doors led into each aisle; as is common the north aisle was slightly narrower than the south, 2.7m as compared with 2.8m. The nave was twice the width at 5.4m. The aisles stretch the entire length of the building, divided off from the central aisle by stylobates carrying seven pink and white marble columns on each side. The sanctuary area is totally covered by the later chapel, although the apse can be seen below its successor.

Later activity has also destroyed the end of the south aisle, but enough survives of the north aisle to indicate that it may have continued beyond the east wall in which there is a possible doorway. If this is the case it would seem that this church too may have had flanking pastophoria. Rough graves were found where the north pastophorion would have been and although they may be associated with the later chapel, graves in one of the pastophoria are known from Chersonisos B (in the south one). Another unusual aspect of the plan is the apsed building linked to the south wall. This building was not fully cleared and is no longer visible; it was at least 10m long and of unknown width. This building is unique in Crete, but there are similar ones at Corinth at the early 6c Cemetery Basilica [124] which contains tombs and at Basilica Γ at Nea Anchialos [125], where it is in the same position as the Lebena example. However, the plan of the main church resembles two other Cretan basilicas quite closely: the west end, as reconstructed in the text, is very similar to Kera (14/7) dated late 5c/early 6c, while the design of the aisles and the possible pastophoria is similar to Chersonisos B (6/7) dated to the first half of the 6c.

The only architectural fragment of any note is built into the south wall of the later chapel and consists of a block decorated with finely cut interlacing acanthus leaves. It is similar to the material from Lyttus (6/25) and ought to date to the late 5c. Given the 6c dates from the similarly designed basilicas, it is not possible to say whether this 5c date is slightly too early for the whole basilica. Both dates really depend on subjective stylistic judgements, and it is safer to assign Lebena Basilica broadly to late 5c/early 6c.

Lasea (10/25) Towards the southern end of the promontory here are the remains of a basilica *c.* 20 x 15m in dimensions[126]. Possibly because of the nature of the site it is orientated NS not EW. There are more rooms to the west which seem to be connected to the church and another wall to the south, but this seems too close to form the further wall of a narthex.

Matala (11/8) It has been claimed that the little church of Panayia at the edge of the modern village marks the site of an earlier church [127]. The only evidence for this now visible is a number of grey marble columns 3-4m high lying next to it. Early this century there were also two capitals of the same type as at St. Titus with the same monogram, but they had disappeared by 1950[128]. In the 16c and earlier a building with mosaics was recorded, as was an inscription from the church [129]. The mosaics have not been recorded since then and the inscription would seem to be of a pagan rather than a Christian nature. However, it is most likely that there was a church here in the late Roman period and that the later church is on the same site; but until this is excavated none of these hypotheses can be proved.

Sybrita (12/4) Below and around the church of the Panayia in the main square of the modern village of Thronos lie the remnants of a rather fine mosaic in red, blue and white[130]. Also lying next to the church is a pessiscos; other architectural fragments have been found, or reused, in the village, including a marble panel, probably from the screen, showing a cross of eight rays or petals set in a lozenge[131]. These fragments prove the existence of an early Christian church, but the mosaic may be earlier and reused in the church. The portion of mosaic surviving, 8m x 2.70m, consists of a border of tendrils, then a strand of guilloche enclosing a pattern of squares containing circles or lozenges. In the surviving portion of the mosaic there are two rows of three lozenges each with a nest of circles within it; in the four triangles formed by the side of the square and the apex of each point of the lozenge is a small circle. On either side of these rows are three rows of the squares with the circles; within the circles are either another nest of smaller ones or a six-rayed star. Kirsten dated this mosaic to the 2c but the corpus prefers a 5c date. When compared to other

---

124. *Ergon* 1962, p.82, fig.92.
125. *Ergon.* 1974, p.25, 7, fig.40, 1.
126. D. Blackman and K. Branigan, 'An archaeological survey of the S. coast of Crete', *ABSA* LXX, 1975, p.30 and fig.8.
127. Platon no.4.
128. *IC.*IV.475.
129. E. Falkener, *Museum of Classical Antiquities* II (London, 1860), p.283. *IC.*I.XX.2. They are included in the Corpus as no. 93, p.114, but there is no evidence at all for their date.
130. E. Kirsten ap. Matz, p.142f., with pl.116.2. Corpus 97, p.116, p.190. Platon no.21.
131. Gerola, *Mon. Ven.* II, p.56, fig.26.

geometric mosaics from basilicas, this one is much simpler in design and is unusual in that the designs are confined to their individual squares rather than interlocking with each other. Also the actual designs do not include the customary types. These, however, do appear in a few fragments to the west of the later chapel, where interlocked circles can be made out [132] within a double guilloche. These fragments would not be out of place in a 5c context although they could be earlier. Overall, an earlier date is perhaps to be preferred for the mosaic, though not necessarily as early as the 2c, perhaps 4c. In this case the early church must have utilised an earlier building in what must always have been a focal area of the city.

Vizari (12/12) (Fig.39) One of the best preserved of all the early Christian basilicas [133] (Pl.57) in Crete is that at Vizari in the Amari valley. It is unusual not only in the amount surviving (the outer walls stand up to 4m high) but also in that it appears to date from the eighth or even ninth century. The church is quite large, 34.20m x 17.30m including the apse, and constructed of mortared rubble of very poor quality. The plan differs from the other pre-Arab basilicas in that the side aisles end in small apses of their own.

Fig.39. Vizari: Basilica.

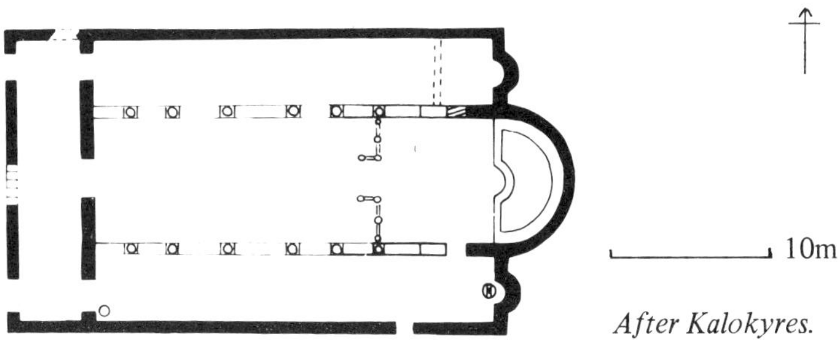

After Kalokyres.

The narthex, 4m deep, was entered by doors at either end of the west wall and one in the south wall. At some date after the initial construction of the building, a window was pierced through the west wall at 1m up. The floor of the narthex, and of the side aisles, was of beaten earth. At an unknown date two tombs had been dug into this floor. Here as elsewhere in the basilica post-Roman material was found including two Arab coins in the burnt layer that seems to mark the destruction of the basilica or its reuse for a secular purpose.

From the narthex three doors led into the aisles: the side doors, at 1.35m, are slightly narrower than the central door, at 2.00m. The two side aisles, 3.50m wide, are at the same level as the narthex, but the central aisle, 7.20m wide, is 0.30m higher and floored with tiles. The aisles are separated by high stylobates, standing 1.00m above the side aisles with six columns a side up to the chancel screen, and then by short walls protruding from the east end. Both side aisles end in small apses, 1.60m wide, and are linked to the bema by narrow doors. The one through to the north aisle was blocked at some date; just before this door, 3.00m from the east end, a wall had been built to cut this part of the aisle off and form a pastophorion. The south aisle was not divided but has an additional exit at 4.60m from the east end. In its SW corner, just to the right of the door from the narthex, a tile-lined hole, 0.52m in diameter and 0.55m deep, had been constructed which the excavator suggested served as a sump, as it was connected by a tile drain to a font at the east end of the aisle in front of the apse. The font (Pl.58) was circular, 1.15m in diameter, and constructed of tile and cement. Within it on either side was a step 0.17m wide, 0.30m deep and running the width of the font.

The central aisle with its tiled floor is divided into chancel and nave by a screen mounted between small columns, fragments of which were found, and the last column of the stylobate. The resulting chancel was 6.80m x 7.20m . The pulpit was situated in the centre of the nave. The apse was the full width of the aisle and had a synthronon together with a small semicircular opening into the apse behind the altar.

Architectural fragments were not numerous: two complete monolithic columns, 2.72m high, from the nave and from the screen various small fragments with geometric designs and from its architrave two fragments with well cut 'fleur de lys' foliage and deep-drilled ovolos framed in a box [134]. Parts of two Corinthian capitals were found as well.

---

132. Personal observation 1973/74. The main portion of the mosaic is barely visible.
133. K. D. Kalokyres, *Kret. Khron.* XIII, 1959, p.7f. Platon no.22.
134. Pl.I.1 in the report.

Pl. 56: Late capital from Ay. Titos, Gortyna.
Pl. 57: Interior view of the basilica at Vizari.
Pl. 58: Font in the basilica at Vizari.

In compensation a great deal of domestic refuse was found, but unfortunately little of it has been published. Among the pottery there is definite late material [135] from the deposit that included the Arab coins. There is some evidence for post-Arab occupation on the site in the form of one 11c coin and 16-17c pottery.

The late date for the basilica proposed by the excavator really depends on the three apsed plan and the *terminus ante quem* of the Arab coins: some of the material recovered, namely the capital fragments and the architrave, could be much earlier, although the capital fragments are very small. The triple-apsed east end is known earlier elsewhere in the late Roman world, commonly in the Balkans [136] and also from Syria [137], but there are no other examples in Crete, before the Arab conquest. However, after Nicephoras' victory there are numerous triple-apsed churches that are very close in plan to this one, e.g. Phodele (9/2), Viran Episkopi (13/2) and Episkopi Mylopotamou (13/13). These churches are probably two centuries after the church at Vizari, but there is a 9c church at Skripou in Central Greece [138] which is triple-apsed; this church, however, probably reflects Bulgarian influences. Although it does seem likely that there may have been an earlier church on the same site at Vizari from which the early architectural fragments were reused, the similarity between this church and the later Cretan ones, and its difference from the other pre-Arab churches on the island, with the exception of St. Titus' very different three apses, makes a late 7c to late 8c date most probable. There is, however, no evidence at all to substantiate the claim by the excavator that this church was the late Roman seat of the bishop of Sybrita. Vizari is more exposed to raids from the sea than Sybrita, not less, and Sybrita has its own church of unknown size. The building of this large church need only be a reflection of the wealth of the Amari valley in the late period which is demonstrated by the number of villas [139].

Ano Malaki (12/20) At this site somewhere in the south of the Amari valley the discovery of an early Christian basilica is mentioned [140], but no other details are added.

Viran Episkopi (13/2) Although the main church of Ay. Eirene here is of 10 or 11c date, sufficient architectural fragments were recovered to prove the existence of an earlier church which had, in its turn, replaced a temple [141]. The main fragments were from three Corinthian capitals, two of which are compared by the excavator with those from Panormos (13/3) dated to the early 6c. The third he dates to the 7c, but it really seems too worn to justify any attempt to classify it further than as within the general class of late Corinthian capitals.

Panormos (13/3) (Fig.40) The basilica [142] is situated on the ridge just south of the new 'motorway' in what seems to have been the main part of the ancient site. The basilica is of the triple transept type and measures 53m x 23m complete with atrium; the basic church is only 34m x 17m. It is built in the normal rather crude rubble and mortar technique with most of the floors composed of slabs or pebbles.

Fig.40. Panormos: Basilica.

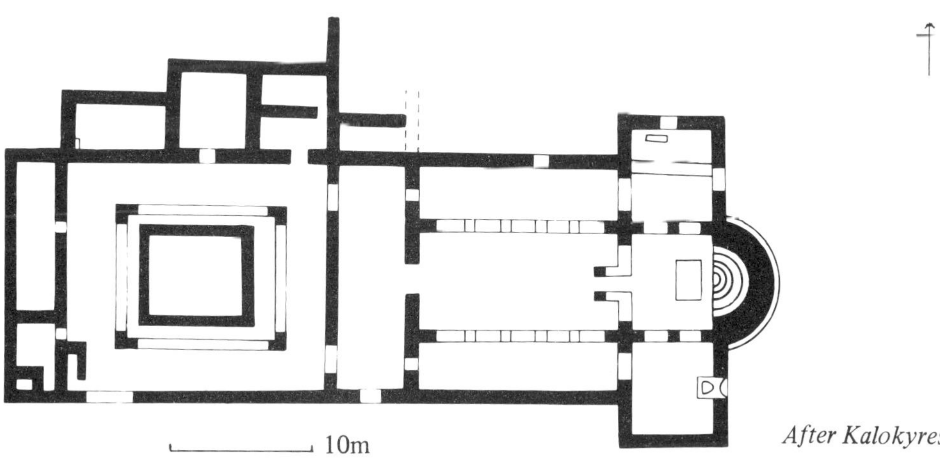

After Kalokyres.

135. Pl. IA.1 in the report.
136. R. F. Hoddinott, *Bulgaria in Antiquity* (London, 1975), passim.
137. Krautheimer, *op.cit.* no.6 p.156, fig.101.
138. Krautheimer, *op.cit.* note 6, p.330 fig.275.
139. See p.48.
140. *A. Delt.* XVI, 1960, p.274.
141. K. D. Kalokyres, *PAE* 1959, p.230. Platon no.24.
142. N. Platon, *PAE* 1948, p.112f., and Platon no.19 with p.424f. K. D. Kalokyres, *PAE* 1955, p.321.

The narthex, 4.4m deep with a pebble floor, is entered from the exterior by a door in the south wall and from the atrium by doors at either side of the west wall. Narrow doors lead into the side aisles and a slightly wider one into the nave. Each aisle is 14m long and separated by a stylobate with 4 Ionic columns per side. The central aisle, 6.50m wide, and the north aisle, 3.4m wide, are floored with slabs; the southern one, 3.2m wide, has a sea-pebble floor.

Protruding into the nave the gateway in the screen leads into the chancel, 5.5m EW x 6.4m NS, which is one step higher than the nave. Below the foundations here what must be a foundation offering was found, consisting of a small container filled with bones. A similar deposit was found at Kera (14/7) and possibly at Knossos (8/4). The apse is 5m wide with a synthronon and a small pit in the centre. From the chancel a double arch leads into each pastophorion, which measure 6.20m EW and 5.5m NS. The more northerly of the two is divided into halves of which the southern, 3.20m wide, is at the same level as the chancel, while the northern half is lower with an earth floor, into which the tile tomb of Theodorus [143], a psaltes, had been dug. Windows pierced the north and east walls of the room. The south pastophorion has a sea-pebble floor and a window in the north wall. This was blocked when a font was inserted into it; the font (Pl.59) is constructed of tile and cement and is of horseshoe shape, *c.* 0.80m x 0.60m x 0.50m deep with, below its lip, a ledge with cut outs at the centre of the base, top and about a third of the way up on each side. Curiously it does not fully fill in the window but only goes half way through, ending in a reverse apse.

The atrium is the only one totally excavated in Crete; it is 18.0m EW x 15m NS (internal dimensions) with a colonnade of Corinthian columns about the central cistern which is 6.65m x 5.65m x 2.50m deep. The entrance from the exterior is at the west end of the south wall. On the north and west sides of the atrium there are ranges of rooms the nature of whose use has raised some debate. The north range consists from east to west, of a small room parallel to the narthex; next a double room 4.4m x 5.0m wide; then a single room of the same size and finally a narrow room, 6.0m x 3.0m. Platon claimed that the first large room was a baptistery when this was in use, but it is possible that it served as one initially, as the font seems to be secondary. Naturally the finds from the room would belong to the latest use of the room when the font was in use and a redundant baptistery could have become a storeroom.

The range of two rooms along the west side of the atrium is again of uncertain purpose; the north room is 10.0m x 2.5m with a door into the atrium and the south room, 4.5m x 2.5m, has a peculiar cut out in its corner that was used as a cistern with a possible second cistern jutting out into the courtyard.

There are no mosaics in this church, but a large number of high-class architectural fragments were found [144]. These include a plain Ionic capital and a fine Corinthian capital of Kautzsch's 'Leierkapitell' type, which he dates to the late 5c - early 6c [145]. Between the Ionic columns in the nave there was a balustrade from which survived fragments decorated with tendrils of both the common ivy leaf and what seem to be fig leaves. Fragments of the screen showed a design of a diamond with a double multi-petalled flower or scallop with scrolls enclosing eight petalled flowers on each side. The pessiscoi from the screen are the only ones known from Crete to be decorated: they bear Greek crosses, flowers and star designs very similar in style to the architectural blocks from Itanos (1/39).

Although there are other tripartite transept churches in Crete, e.g. Kolokythia (3/8), there are closer parallels from the Greek mainland, particularly from Nikopolis[146] where two similar basilicas are dated to *c.* 500, and to the second quarter of the 6c. This date would fit with that for the capitals and is reinforced by the finding of a coin below the floor of the south room of the west range of the atrium. Unfortunately the report[147] only says that it was a bronze coin of the 6c which establishes rather too wide a *terminus post quem* to be of much use. However, the other evidence would all fit a date of the early 6c for the construction of the church. The church was destroyed by an intense fire, and, probably as an aftermath of this, the cistern in the centre of the atrium was filled up with rubbish, including two coins of Leo VI 886-912. These coins are contemporary with the Arab occupation of Crete and so, if they really do date the destruction, it occurred after the initial conquest; alternatively the cistern may have only filled up slowly, in which case the coins may not date the actual destruction, but merely the period of disuse.

---

143. Bandy, *The Greek Christian Inscriptions of Crete* (Athens, 1970) p.71, dated there to the 5c, which conflicts with the other evidence. Robert dated it to 6-7c. Bandy also claims that there is another basilica or part of one visible in the village to the north of the site, but there is no other evidence for this.
144. The fragments are illustrated in *PAE* 1948, p.123, fig.6, p.124, fig.7-8, fig.26a, b.
145. Similar capitals from Constantinople (195), Thessaloniki (225) and Corinth (226).
146. Krautheimer, *op.cit.* note 6, p.137-8 fig.87 and p.496, n.20.
147. *PAE* 1955, p.324.

Pl. 59: Font in the basilica at Panormos.
Pl. 60: Narthex mosaic in the basilica at Kera.

Eleutherna (13/5) At Ay. Irene various architectural fragments have been found including 'Corinthian capitals of 3/4c date' [148] and other Byzantine pieces of 'good workmanship'. The capitals have not been published and do not seem to have been seen since 1896. No details of the other fragments have been published either. Although the date given for the capitals would seem too early for the church, there is no way to verify it; however, the other fragments and the fact of the siting of the later church do favour the existence of an earlier church there.

Episkopi Mylopotamou (13/13) In the apse and south wall of the early mediaeval church of Ay. Ioannis various earlier fragments are reused. It is very likely that these came from a pre-Arab church on the same site[149].

Axos (13/16) (A) Just above the modern village near the summit of the hill, lies the cemetery church of Ay. Ioannis. This church seems to have been built above an earlier one for Pashley saw a mosaic forming most of its floor and there are earlier walls still visible below the east apse and elsewhere [150].

Axos (B) Just before the modern village is reached from Iraklion, the chapel of Ay. Eleutherios and Modestos is to be found on the north side of the main road. The chapel reuses much older material including fragments of columns and actual late Roman stone-faced masonry[151]. It is impossible to say if this earlier building was a church in that walls of stone and cement construction are not commonly reused in the early Christian churches of Crete and there are other examples where probably secular buildings were reused as churches in the mediaeval period, e.g. the possible bath house at Kato Asites (9/14) and the villa at Ayios Ioannis (12/15). The date of the chapel at Axos is probably 10-12c from the pottery built in above the door.

Lappa (14/1): Ay. Phanourgios Below the whitewash and concrete of this church are the remains of what is probably an earlier basilica [152]. The evidence for this is that the present apse is far too large for the width of the standing church and that there are column bases, with neatly whitewashed column fragments on them, that line up with the walls of the church. These bases seem to be *in situ,* although they could have been placed there as ornaments, and the concrete yard makes it impossible to decide. However, combining the evidence of the apse and columns it would seem likely that the present church covers the chancel and sanctuary of its predecessor as so commonly in Crete.

Lappa: Phoundana At the spring of Phoundana on the river Mousela, below Argyroupolis Lappa, a basilica was discovered[153] but backfilled before any detailed examination could be carried out. The only detail published was that it had mosaic floors in the *σχήμα* of a cross. It is unfortunate that the Greek word is ambiguous and can mean either in the shape of a cross, perhaps like the mosaic of Ay. Niketas (16/11), or decorated with crosses like the mosaic at Almyrida (17/9).

Lappa: Pano Chori Here at the church of Ay. Paraskeve mosaics have been reported and so make a third early church possible [154].

Lappa: Unspecified In 1918[155] mosaics were lifted from what has always been claimed as a church. They are now in the store of Rethimnon Museum and have eventually been published [156]; they depict a vigorous hunting scene and seem far better suited to a secular building of the 4c.

Kera-Onythe Goulediana (14/7) (Fig.41) On the heights between the Spili and the Amari valleys one of the more inaccessible basilicas [157] of Roman Crete is to be found at the possible site of ancient Phalanna. It is 31.0m x 15m in basic dimensions with the addition of a porch and a range of rooms at its NW corner; it may also have an atrium at

---

148. L. Mariani, *Mon. Ant.* VI, 1896, p.214. *JHS* XLIX, 1929, p.225. Platon no.18. Gerola, *Mon. Ven.* II, p.57.
149. Gerola, *Mon. Ven.* II, p.79, pl.43. Platon no.20. These fragments are now very difficult to find (1973-4).
150. Pashley I, p.152. No longer visible. Personal observation: the earlier church was larger than its successor but it was not possible to plan the walls because of the density of the graves.
151. Personal observation, 1973-4.
152. Personal observation, 1973-4.
153. *Kret. Khron.* XIII, 1959, p.391. It is reported there under Episkopi but the spring is far closer to Lappa according to local information. Corpus 102, p.120.
154. Corpus 100, p.118.
155. S. Xanthoudides, *A. Delt.* IV, 1918, par.31. Platon no.23.
156. Corpus 99, p.118, pl.90b, 91. See p.54.
157. N. Platon, *PAE* 1955, p.303; 1956, p.229. Platon no.36.

the west end. It is constructed of the normal stone and mortar with mosaic floors in the apse, chancel, nave and narthex. The whole building is on a slope from south to north, so that each aisle is at a different level with the south aisle highest.

Fig.41. Kera: Basilica.

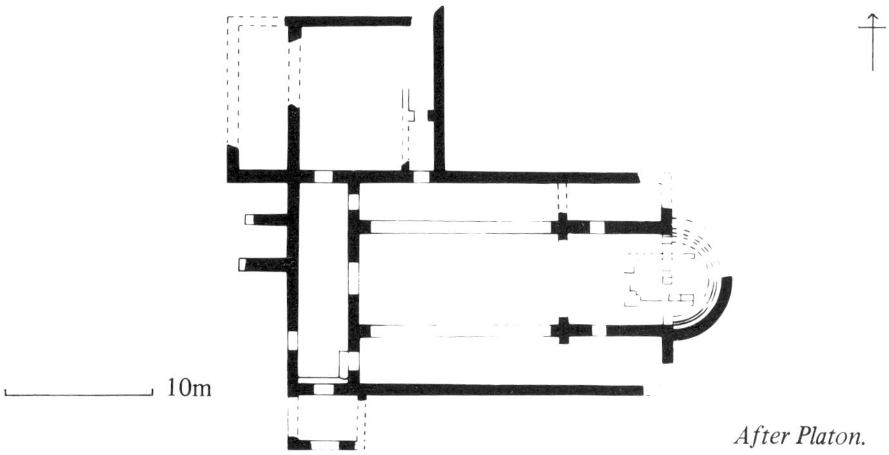

After Platon.

The narthex, 3.20m deep, is entered down a flight of three steps from the porch, 3.0m x 4.0m, with another door towards the south end of the west wall from the possible atrium. Although no south wall of this was found, there are three other walls protruding from the west wall in a very similar arrangement to that at the basilica at Lebena (10/23), where there was a final south wall as well. The final wall to the north is a continuation of the north wall of the church and forms the south wall of the westernmost room of the range beyond it. This room is 3.20m x 9.40m. The main room next to this is 7.00m x 9.40m, and has a door through to the narthex and may have been the baptistery. The final room to the east is a narrow passage, 1.80m wide, with a door to the north aisle.

All three aisles are entered by doors from the narthex with that to the south aisle preceded by a step because of the slope. The north aisle is 2.60m wide, narrower than the south aisle at 3.20m; both aisles end in pastophoria which flank the chancel and both are floored with cement, as is the south pastophorion. The central aisle is 6.00m wide and, as the nave, extends 13.80m up to the chancel; the nave seems to have been separated from the aisles by stylobates, but the chancel or bema is divided from its pastophoria by walls with doors through to them. Much of the chancel and apse had been destroyed by the later chapel, but enough of the latter survived to show that it was 5.80m wide with a synthronon and at its entrance a hole, 0.34m x 0.45m x 0.40m deep, containing a few small bones. This must have been a foundation offering as at Panormos (13/3).

All the mosaics are of varying geometric designs in up to five colours [158]. The narthex mosaic (Pl.60) has a guilloche border with at the north end an eight pronged wheel, the prongs made up of panels of guilloche mat and the central circle the same with its own guilloche border. The southern part of this mosaic is composed of squares separated by smaller ones and containing diamond designs. The nave mosaic is divided into three areas, the centre, another wheel design, and the two bordering panels made up of stars built up from a centre square with triangles as the points set against a background of squares and circles with varying designs within the circles. The chancel has a similar design, the main pattern of larger stars now with eight points, two per side of the central square. The north pastophorion has another wheel-based design.

There are no very close parallels for these designs within Crete, but the composite stars are known from Ay. Paulos on Cos [159] and Basilica Γ from Amphipolis; the former is dated 5/6c and the latter must date to the second half of the 5c on the evidence of its capitals [160]. The layout of the mosaic in the narthex is however similar to that in Basilica A at Chersonisos (6/7), dated to the early 6c. No architectural fragments have been published to help date the building, but the overall design with its pastophoria is obviously related to Chersonisos A and B, Mallia, and possibly Lebena. Lebena also provides a similar west end, possibly even with a porch as well. Given these stylistic parallels Kera is best dated to the late 5c/early 6c.

---

158. Corpus 101, p.119, pl.92-3.
159. *Ibid.* no.28, p.133.
160. *Ergon* 1959, p.41, fig.39 and fig.40 for the capital.

Viglotopi (15/7) Below and incorporated into the mediaeval chapel here are the remains of an earlier and larger building of quite good stone-faced concrete [161]. One earlier wall protrudes from the NE corner of the present chapel. Although the actual quality of the earlier masonry raises the possibility of the earlier building not being a church[162] the physical relationship of the chapel and the earlier walls looks very like the common development of the later building being built above the earlier bema.

Ay. Galini (15/16) Just to the east of the modern village of Ayia Galini the village cemetery with its church of the Panayia may mark the site of an earlier church [163]. Although the graves cover most of the area, fragments of earlier walls can be made out and there are several architectural fragments lying about, including a complete lekane base in local limestone.

Tarrha (16/3) Below the chapel of the Panayia are the remains of a basilica 21 x 12m of typical three aisled design with narthex. Parts of the exterior walls of the basilica still stand up to 3m in height and are of reasonable quality ashlar masonry. The present chapel covers the area of the bema as is normal. Just in front of its west end is a small fragment of mosaic composed of interlocking semicircles in blue, white and red, while in the south aisle is a much larger piece made up of panels divided by strips of interlocking circles; the only panel that now survives is made up of a lozenge with a central petal design[164].

This type of mosaic and the design of the basilica is of the standard 5/6c type, but there is a problem in that another mosaic has been described (by Kristen) as coming from this site, a 'Kiesel' or pebble mosaic showing the head of Apollo[165]. The American excavations [166] along the outside of the south wall failed to establish the date of the structure. The argument there that some of the lower blocks in the wall were reused since they were too rough is not conclusive, since they may well never have been intended to be above ground level and therefore visible. If the pebble mosaic really exists then it does seem possible that there was yet another sacred building here before the basilica, presumably a Hellenistic temple to Apollo [167].

Aradena (16/4) Below the mediaeval church of the Archistrategos, dramatically poised above the 300m gorge, the remains of an earlier basilica were found[168]. The apse of the earlier church is wider than the later one, and part of a wall protrudes at the NE corner.

Phoenix-Loutro (16/5) (Fig.42) On the headland to the east of the harbour the ruined church of the Theotokos would appear to be of late Roman date. Its design is that of the standard three aisled basilica and its internal dimensions (minus the apse) are 18.50m x 11.0m[169]. The narthex, 2.90m deep, is entered by two doors in the west wall,

Fig.42. Loutro: Basilica.

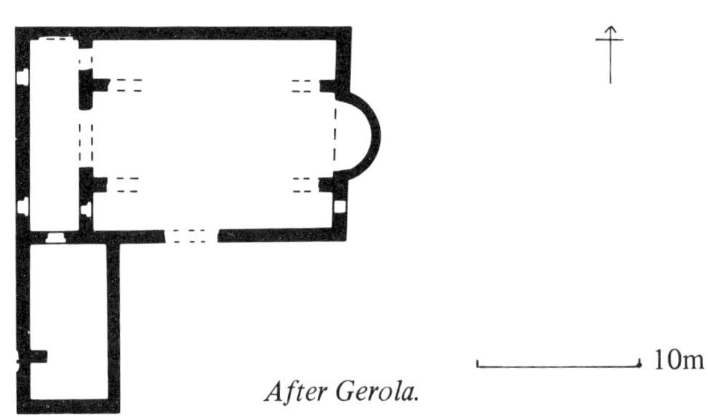

but there is also a possible porch or annexe, possibly the baptistery, on the south side, 9.0m NS x 4.6m EW, with a door through to the narthex. Three doors probably led into the aisles, but only one is recorded. The aisles seem to stretch the entire length of the church, with the northern one at 2.4m wider than the southern at only 2.00m. The

161. Personal observation, 1973-4.
162. See p.120, Axos (13/16) Basilica B, on this.
163. Hood and Warren, *ABSA* LXI, 1966, p.167-8, fig.4, site 1. Personal observation.
164. Platon no.33. Corpus 113, p.125, pl.97b. Information from G. Murray.
165. Ap Matz, p.131.
166. G. Weinberg, 'Excavations at Tarrha', *Hesperia* XXIX, 1960, p.99.
167. My own attempts to visit this site were frustrated by storms.
168. *A. Delt.* XVI, 1960, p.274. Personal observation.
169. Platon no.34. Gerola, *Mon. Ven.* II, p.58-9.

central aisle is 5.00m wide and the apse is 4.00m in diameter. No mosaics or architectural fragments are recorded from the site, but in the nearby church of the Soter part of an amphiskion is reused in the entrance.

Ayios Evstratios (16/10) (Fig.43) Among the numerous late Roman sites on the now desolate plain of Frankokastelli are two early Christian churches. Ay. Evstratios stands on the northern edge of what seem to be the ruins of the settlement or village[170]. The church is a small standard basilica, 19.0m x 12.4m internal dimensions, excluding the apse, and has never been cleared. In the mediaeval period the chancel and apse were rebuilt as a chapel. The construction is of typical stone and mortar with the walls *c.* 0.70m thick and up to 3.0m high where they were reused. The depth of the narthex is not visible, but the two side aisles are both 2.2m wide, while the central aisle is 6.6m wide. The limit of the bema is probably marked by the length of the later chapel, which extends 4.0m down the central aisle. The apse was rebuilt in the secondary phase, but the original one appears to have been 3.60m wide and 2.40m deep. Fragments of several monolithic grey-white marble columns survive, as does one extremely worn Ionic capital. The pottery from the site included 6/7c African Red Slip Ware form 104.

Fig.43. Evstratios: Basilica.

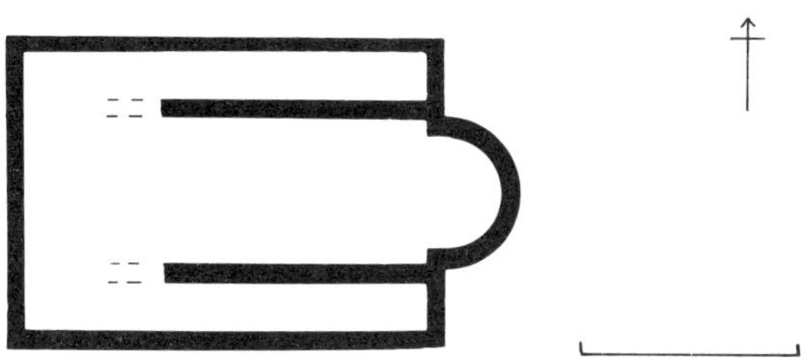

10m

Fig.44. Niketas: Basilica.

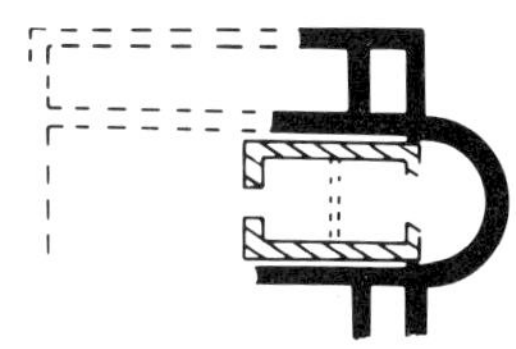

After Lassithiotakes.

Ayios Niketas (16/11) (Fig.44) The other early church[171] on the plain of Frankokastelli lies a short distance away from the previous site, just to the NE of the fort that names the plain. It is the smallest known basilica in Crete, 12.80m long and surviving to 8.10m wide; it has an even smaller chapel on top of its bema. No trace of the narthex survives, but the side aisles, as far as can be seen are each 2.2m wide and end in a pastophorion 2.0m long. The central aisle is 4.40m wide and has fragments of a mosaic floor. The apse is 3.0m deep and *c.*4.0m wide. The mosaic of nine panels appears to be in the design of a cross of five panels with the four corner panels covered by a maeander pattern. The cross itself is largely destroyed, but the north arm seems to have been a panel of a row of zigzags with the centre panel a circle with stylised buds in the corners. All the panels are in red, white and blue tesserae[172]. The fragments of columns are of the same material as at Ay. Evstratios; within the chapel there are very simple block capitals, presumably reused from the earlier church. They bear a Latin cross on their longer side[173].

Aptera (17/2) In the middle of the site of Aptera, a short distance south of the Venetian monastery of St. John, next to the wall of the inscriptions, is the possible site of an early church[174].

The excavator gives no details of the building but mentions tombs with reused fragments of the screen. These tombs must obviously be later than the church which is dated, presumably by the screen fragments, to the 6/7c.

Almyrida (17/9) The basilica here is of the triple transept type with a very fine series of mosaics in the nave and bema. The excavations, in progress, have not yet cleared the narthex[175]. The side aisles are wider than normal in relation to the centre aisle and are floored with stone slabs, as are the pastophoria. The northern pastophorion ends on the same alignment as the screen dividing the chancel and nave, but the southern one continues slightly further down the side aisle; both of them are entered from the chancel through a twin columned tribelon. The only obvious evidence for secondary remodelling in the church is that, as at Chersonisos, the pulpit foundation ignores the mosaic, being placed on top of it half way down on the north side of the nave. The pulpit has two stairs on the long axis and is dated by the excavator to the late 5c; if this date is correct it would seem to indicate that it had been moved from its original position as the mosaic ought not be any earlier, and indeed seems rather to fit a 6c date.

---

170. Hood, *ABSA* LXII, 1967, p.55-6, Site B7. Personal observation.
171. K. Lassithiotakes, ' 'Εκκλησίες τῆς Δυτικῆς Κρήτης ', *Kret. Khron.* XXIII, 1971, p.118, no.140.
172. Corpus 114, p.126, pl.98a, b.
173. Personal observation.
174. *Kret. Khron.* XII, 1958, p.469.
175. *Kret. Khron.* XXV, 1973, p.505. Corpus 109, p.124. Personal observation. No measurements could be taken on the site and none have yet been published.

The nave mosaic consists of six panels surrounded by a single guilloche; the westernmost pair each show a splendid jewelled Latin cross with α and ω surmounted on balls or orbs, in the lower quadrants of the cross surround. On either side of the cross tendrils climb out of a jar and twist round the top of the cross, while in the upper quadrants are two 'eyes'. The tesserae here and elsewhere are in red-brown, blue-grey and white. The next set of panels depict a circle enclosing an eight pointed star, made up of two superimposed squares; in the centre of this is an eight-petalled rose which is surrounded by interlocking ropes that extend around the outer star as well. The final panel before the screen consists of a Greek cross in a circle with offshoots, made up of crescents, going to each corner of the panel. The middle of each side between these is filled with two peltas. Between this set of panels and the screen is a continuous band of small interlocking stars in circles balancing the band of multiple guilloche at the west end of the mosaic before, presumably, the narthex wall.

The mosaic of the bema is composed of a large panel of alternating circles and squares with various motifs of stars, crosses, etc. within them. This is in front of the altar. The large panel and altar are flanked by three panels on each side with the whole mosaic bordered by a single guilloche. From west to east the side panels are a mat of the interweaving ropes; next a panel of the same stars and circles as the final eastern band in the nave and finally a Greek cross in a circle surrounded by a wider circle. The brief preliminary report mentions few finds apart from the mosaics, except that pessiscoi and Corinthian capitals were found; no details of the latter are given.

No real parallels for this mosaic are known from Crete, although some of the minor motifs are quite common, such as the small stars set in their circles. These are known from Chersonisos B and Suia A. The large Latin crosses of the western panels of the nave mosaic would seem to date to the first half of the 6c, with similar ones known from the mosaics of San Vitale and Arian Baptistery from Ravenna[176]. This date would also fit the tripartite transept design of the church, which like the one at Panormos (13/3) ought to date to the early-mid 6c and the date of the minor motifs from the other examples given.

Armeni (17/19) Five columns, three of which were in a row, together with one capital and a small fragment of a mosaic, constitute the evidence for the basilica here[177].

Alikianos (18/8) On the site of the chapel of Zoodochos Piyi mosaics depicting deer, peacocks, vases and other geometric designs are reported[178]. These are no longer visible, but within the church are two reused early 6c 'Leierkapitelle'. The description of the mosaics strongly resembles those at Suia A.

Meskla (18/12) In front of the west end of the old church of the Panayia a mosaic of probable 5/6c date is transfixed by its 'protective' iron railings. The area just visible is about 3.0m square and consists of a geometric design in red, blue and white. The border consists of a series of triangles which encloses bands of linked squares. These contain various typical designs of four rayed flowers or crosses, guilloche knots, circles with crosses, etc. Apart from this mosaic, several very battered pilaster capitals (Pl.61) could be seen by the south wall of the new church, to the east of the old one[179].

Biennos (19/1) Spratt[180] reported seeing columns and a Corinthian capital here and thought it was a church site. More recently Dr. N. Flemming[181] saw the same remains, which from his sketch plan would seem to be a basilica.

Plemeniana (19/9) The church of Christ the Saviour seems to mark the site of a basilica with the usual few architectural fragments, far fewer now than when photographed by Gerola[182]. Two Corinthian capitals with bird-head volutes and deeply cut acanthus-leaf decoration and a small amphiskion are all that now survive. The capitals are dated to the second half of the 5c and although the foliage is not in the Theodosian style there is no horizontal division, and so they ought to belong to Kitzinger's group I[183]. Other capitals seem rather to belong to Kautzsch's Leierkapitell type, but they are crude examples[184].

---

176. F. W. Deichmann, *Frühchristliche Bauten und Mosaiken von Ravenna* (Baden-Baden, 1958), pl.256 Arian Baptistery, pl.314, 369 San Vitale - cf. the cross in Maximinian's hand.
177. *A. Delt.* XXIII.2.2, 1968, p.431. No more details than given above. Corpus 110, p.124.
178. Spanake II, p.46. Personal observation.
179. Platon no.27. Corpus 104, p.121. Personal observation. The mosaic is in a very poor condition.
180. Spratt II, p.237.
181. Personal communication. Details also confirmed by M. S. F. Hood.
182. Gerola, *Mon. Ven.* II, p.54, figs.23-4. Platon no.30, under Kantanos. Personal observation.
183. *DOP* III, 1946, p.18-19.
184. K. Lassithiotakes, ' 'Εκκλησίες τῆς Δυτικῆς Κρήτης ', *Kret. Khron.* XXII, 1970, p.208-9, no.100, pl.297. The latter capitals would seem to be later. Cf. Elyros. It is possible that the others might be early 6c in that their foliage is not 'Theodosian'.

Pl. 61: Fragment of pilaster capital, Meskla.
Pl. 62: Narthex mosaic, Basilica A, Suia.

Kantanos (19/10) The building normally claimed as a Praetorium of 2-3c date excavated by V. Theophanides in 1939 [185] is almost certainly not a Praetorium but a basilica of late 5c to early 6c date. The previous identification relied solely on the inscription [186] found lying in the building, and it was recognised that the structure had been 'reused' in the 5c. The proposed identification is based on the design of the mosaic, which from the rather poor photograph seems to have been very similar indeed to that in the central aisle at Chersonisos A (6/7). If this is the case, the room here with the mosaic would have been the narthex, 7.4 x 3.8m, and the other wall found running 17.4m at right angles the north wall of the central aisle. The stele base mentioned was probably the base of the screen between the naos and the bema.

Elyros (19/16) Just south of the village of Rhodovani the church of the Panayia is built above its late Roman predecessor [187]. The church has never been excavated and the new church of the Panayia has now made this impossible. What is recorded is that it was over 22.0m long and had a badly preserved mosaic with deer, peacocks and flowering tendrils flowing out of kantharoi. Among the architectural fragments are Corinthian capitals of the same crude Leierkapitell type as at Plemeniana and an Ionic impost capital somewhat resembling those from Suia A (19/17) a few miles down the valley. Not only this capital but the mosaic too was obviously very similar, and makes it likely that the two churches were contemporary, being built about the mid 6c.

Suia A (19/17) (Fig.45) By means of the rather unusual prospecting method of revelation by a dream, the basilica here, a little west of the village and *c.* 125m from the sea, was discovered and excavated in 1953 [188]. The mosaics inside and outside the church built after the discovery form the finest group of their date in Crete. The basilica itself is of the normal plan and 20.8m long x 12.40m wide, though slightly narrower at its west end, constructed of rather rough stone bound together with mortar. The entire central aisle and narthex were covered with mosaics [189].

Fig.45. Suia: Basilica A.

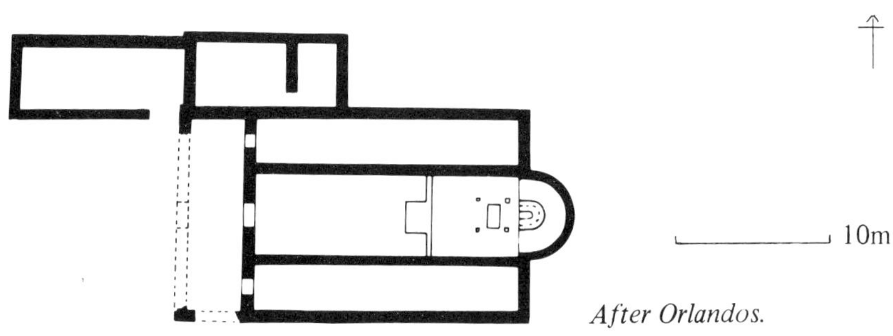

After Orlandos.

The narthex, 3.55m deep, was not sufficiently well preserved above foundation level to tell where its entrances had been. However it seems likely that there had been a door in its north wall through to the range of three rooms here. The two eastern rooms flank the basilica, with the smallest room furthest to the east, 2.40m x 4.05m, and the next room, 7.10m x 4.05m, overlapping the north aisle and the narthex. The third and largest of these rooms, 9.0m x 3.0-3.4m, is beyond the west wall of the narthex and entered by a door in its south wall next to the narthex. The purpose of these rooms is uncertain, but on one of them was probably a baptistery.

The three aisles all have their own doors from the narthex; the two side aisles are both 2.96m wide and the central aisle is 5.03m wide. Stylobates divided them, but no details could be recovered because of the building of the new church, except that it stood 0.23m above the central aisle and slightly higher above the side aisles with their rough slab floors. The nave is 10.08m long with the gate in the screen marked by the cut in the mosaic. The bema is 5.5m long with the altar 1.10m in front of the apse and its foundation 1.54 x 0.87m in size, with the five sockets for the feet surviving. In a square 1.87m^2 about the altar are the four holes for the ciborium. The apse beyond is 4.30m in internal diameter with a synthronon of three rows with the widest, 0.80m, at the top.

---

185. *AE* 1942-4, p.31.
186. *IC.*II.VI.3.
187. *A.Delt.* XVIII.2.2, 1963, p.315. Platon no.32. *Ergon* 1964, p.151. K. Lassithiotakes, *op.cit.* note 184, p.373, no.117, pl.359. Corpus 103, p.120.
188. A. K. Orlandos, *Kret. Khron.* VII, 1953, p.337. For the dream a good account in Spanake II, p.356. Corpus 105, p121, pl.94-6.
189. Slightly more of the mosaic in the narthex and SW corner of the nave is visible on site than shown in the report, fig.7, p.348.

The mosaics in the narthex (Pl.62), so far discovered, cover the northern half of the room in three panels with a surround of interlocking semicircles all round the panels, but the east border has the segments picked out in red. Also on the west and north sides within this border is a further band of interlocking circles of compass-drawn crosses or stars set against a red background. The other colours used in the mosaics are white, yellow and blue-grey. The panel not illustrated in the report but visible on the site must be the central one between the hypothetical door in the outer west wall and the more definite door into the nave. The panel is very similar to the southern pictorial panel in the sanctuary and depicts a peacock or peacocks on a white background with bright red-leaved tendrils intertwining amongst them. The next panel has an interlocking geometric design of four circles set in squares with central designs of a cross, star and leaves with segments of further circles acting as the border. The northernmost panel has a large circle set in a square with a circumference band of guilloche and one large central square of a mat of scallops or scales. From the visible panels it would seem most likely that originally there were, and may still be, five panels in the narthex, two geometric ones on each side of the panel at the door showing the peacocks, symbolising belief in immortality.

The first part of the mosaic after entering the nave comprises three panels of scallops in white, yellow and black with the inevitable surround of interlocking semicircles except on the north side. From here there is a central narrow band of scallops leading to the 'Sacred Gate' with on each side a sequence of geometric and naturalistic panels. Most of these are within the modern church and form its floor. From west to east the panels are a section of interlocking circles or compass-drawn crosses; then a panel with eight circles arranged in two rows with Greek crosses set within them; next the only naturalistic panel showing a kantharos with ivy tendrils coming out of its mouth; then a repeat of the first panel followed by a single larger circle with guilloche circumference and diamond centre with a band of medium-sized interlocking circles stretching right across the mosaic, though not crossing the southern border. On either side of the entrance through the screen beyond this band are panels of scallops.

In the chancel the mosaic has a double border of the semicircles and a double guilloche enclosing two panels separated by a central pathway of small interlocking circles. Each of these panels has a kantharos with ivy leaves, but while the south panel has two peacocks surmounting it, the north panel has two deer. On either side of the altar are panels of a fish on the south and a cross in a diamond on the north. Beyond the altar, before the apse, there is a central panel of interlocked circles flanked by panels of scallops. The tesserae here and in the nave use the same range of colours as in the narthex.

Compared with the mosaics the architectural fragments are disappointing: a pessiscos from the screen, a fragment of a ciborium column, and two columns from the nave. These are in unfluted white marble, 2.06m high and 0.32m in diameter. On the columns are engraved a saint's name, on one Ay. Panteleimon and Ay. Demetrios[190]. It would seem likely that the church was dedicated to these two saints. One capital only was preserved: this is of the debased Ionic impost type with cross engraved on its short side. It is similar to the capitals from Mallia (6/8) and presumably dates to the Justinianic period. The only definite dating evidence from the basilica here must be ignored in this context as it is a block of limestone which is engraved with a cross and the date of 1315. Quite what it is doing in the ruins of the basilica is not clear, but it is not impossible that there had been a chapel of that date on the site that had disappeared.

The Justinianic date would not seem unreasonable for the mosaics. The closest parallels in Crete seem to be the sites at Elyros (19/16) and Alikianos (18/8), although those mosaics have never been properly published. Outside Crete very similar mosaics were found at Hermione[191], but their context and date are uncertain. One of the distinctive features of the Suia mosaic are the semicircular borders which are also used at the early 6c Chersonisos Basilicas A and B (6/7). The central pathway of scallops is known from Knossos Sanatorium (8/4) which is definitely dated to the early 6c. However the Suia mosaics seem slightly cruder than these others and possibly might be a little later in the middle of the century.

Suia: Basilica B (Fig.46) On the east side of the bay numerous late Roman buildings still stand on the slopes above the beach and the river bed, amongst which are said[192] to be two more basilicas, one with a mosaic floor and one just with an apse. It would seem possible that the former is the one here described but no mosaic was visible in

---

190. Orlandos, *op.cit.* note 118, p.340 fig.4.
191. As pointed out by J. P. Sodini, *BCH* XCIV, 1970, p.751.
192. *Kret. Khron.* XI, 1957, p.337. Personal observation. Corpus 106 and 107, p.123. There is no other mention of both of these basilicas having mosaics.

What was left of the other church was the apse and about 15.0m of the aisles, constructed of small blocks of mortared limestone. The north aisle was 3.4m wide and was peculiar in that its end wall joined the apse at an oblique angle. The south aisle was 4.6m wide, leaving a central aisle of 6.0m. Pendlebury describes a lion and deer mosaic from Suia [193] and it is possible that it may have come from this church, as the motif was used in the Basilica A at Chersonisos. Alternatively, in that the motif is common in all periods, there are many other buildings where the mosaics could have been.

One capital which may come from this church rather than Basilica A was published in 1965 [194]. The capital of white marble has a bird at each top corner and in the middle of the sides. Below the birds is a band of rather stiff acanthus decoration topped by a plain fillet grasped by the bird's claws. The base of the capital is another fillet of foliage similar to the main band but much smaller. This must date to the 6c [195].

Fig.46. Suia: Basilica B.

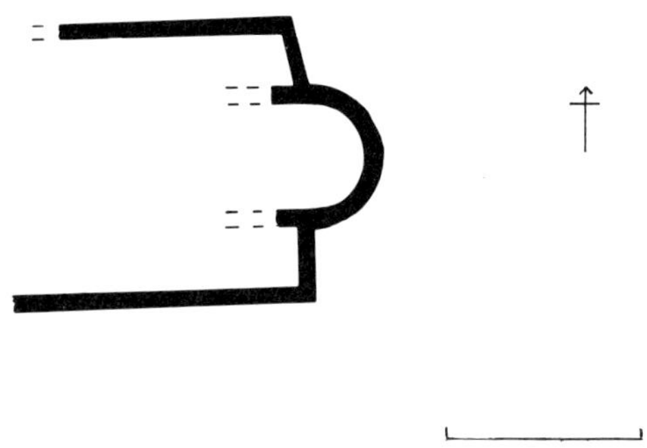

Fig.47. Episkopi: Basilica.

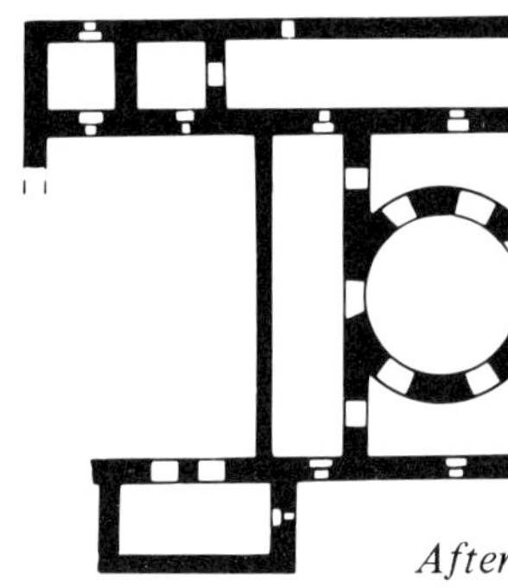

After Gerola.

Lissos (19/18) The two chapels of Ay. Kyriake and the Panayia mark the sites of the early Christian successors to the temple of Asklepios. At the former site the original apse and some of the walls of the earlier church can be made out, the overall dimensions being 22.80m x 11.0m. A small fragment of mosaic in the south aisle is also still visible. At the Panayia, claimed to be the larger of the churches at 23.30 x 13.60m, all that is now visible is one Ionic capital, although here too mosaics have been claimed [196].

Gavdhos, Isle of (19/19) Architectural fragments apparently of late Roman date have been recorded [197] reused in the church of Christ at Vatsiana in the south of the island. Together with the mention of the island in the Tactica of 8-9c [198] this would seem to indicate the existence of an early Christian church on the island, whether at Vatsiana or elsewhere.

Kissamos (20/10) In the recent excavations no actual church has yet been found, but numerous architectural fragments have been reported [199] to add to the previously known Christian tombstones [200].

Skordyliana (20/21) At Glossa a tiled aisle and some architectural fragments are claimed as evidence for a basilica [201].

Episkopi (20/22) (Fig.47) One of the oddest of all the churches [202] of Crete is the church of Ay. Georgios that seems to have been the 10c episcopal seat of Kissamos. As it stands it is normally dated to the 10c, but at the SW entrance into the central rotunda there is a fragment of a mosaic, 0.30m below the present floor level, which ought to date to the 5/6c, being a typical tendril border in black and white. Lassithiotakes claims that the standing church

---

193. *AC* p.368.
194. *A. Delt.* XX.3, 1965, p.570, pl.721a.
195. E. Kitzinger, *DOP* III, 1946, p.17-19, Type II.
196. Spanake II, p.248-9. Corpus p.125 nos 111, 112. Lassithiotakes, *op.cit.* note 184, nos 122-3, p.382. Personal observation.
197. A. Colini, *Boll d'Arte* II, 1925-6, p.423. *IC.* II. VII. Praef. p.90-1.
198. Konidares, ' *Αἱ ἐπισκοπαὶ τῆς Κρήτης μέχρι καὶ τοῦ ι' αἰῶνος*,' *Kret. Khron.* VI, 1953, p.474. 3, p.474.
199. *A. Delt.* XIV.2.2, 1969, p.421-3.
200. *IC.* II. VIII.2, etc.
201. Platon no.28.
202. Lassithiotakes, ' 'Εκκλησίες τῆς Δυτικῆς Κρήτης', *Kret. Khron.* XXI, 1969, p.202. Spanake II, p.164. Platon no.29. Corpus 108, p.123, pl.92.

is of two phases, the original part being only the rotunda and U-shaped bema. This is typical of the N. Syrian tetraconch church[203] to which this church has often been compared[204]; however, Episkopi is totally round and has only the bema breaking the circle, and none of the Syrian examples has quite the same narthex, etc. (this is temporarily ignoring the probability of these outer parts being a later phase). Overall, the Red Church at Peroushtitsa, which is 6c in date, is a closer parallel, although this too has a proper tetraconch [205]. In many ways the closest parallel to just the central or original church is the rotunda of Ay. Georgios at Thessaloniki[206]; but this is so much larger and almost certainly earlier that it may be better to look for the origin of this church in the 10c Balkans, with the round church of Preslav[207] as an example. Indeed, there is no evidence for the shape of the church which contained the mosaic and, if Lassithiotakes is right about the two phases, it would seem unlikely that the rotunda has anything to do with it because the mosaic would have been outside or on the threshold of the church.

Conclusions

The great majority of the churches of Roman Crete are variants on the basic basilica style and date from the mid 5c to the mid 6c, with the majority later rather than earlier in this period, although still before Justinian's reconquest of Vandalic North Africa. There are only two churches that are probably earlier than the mid 5c: they are the first church at Olus (3/7) and the converted temple of Pythian Apollo at Gortyna (10/10), both of which are probably 4c. To balance the two early examples there are two churches built after the mid 6c: these are St. Titus at Gortyna (10/10) dated to the late 6c or early 7c, and Vizari (12/12), probably 8c. Not one of these churches survived intact into the mediaeval period, when many of them had chapels built above their chancels, implying that the position of the earlier church was still known then. If the early church was in or near a later settlement the site often became its cemetery, e.g. Axos A (13/16) and Soulia (15/16). The destruction of the early churches is normally attributed to the Arabs in the 9c, although the only site, Knossos Sanatorium (8/4), where the destruction can be definitely dated is earlier. However, Arab coins seem to be associated with the destruction or secular reuse of Vizari (12/12) and Panormos (13/13) and the sequence of buildings on the Acropolis Basilica site at Gortyna (10/10) would fit an Arab destruction of the first basilica there.

The churches themselves obviously replaced the pagan temples and were often built on the same site, as at the Acropolis at Gortyna (10/10), probably Chersonisos A (6/7), Viran Episkopi (13/2), etc. More rarely the actual temple was converted into a church: the only definite example of this in Crete is the basilica of Pythian Apollo at Gortyna (10/10). Itanos A (1/39) reuses the temple podium and possibly the outer walls as well. Another type of site favoured by builders of the early churches was the cemeteries of the earliest Christians, as at Knossos (8/4), Arvi (5/8) and possibly Mallia (6/20).

With the exception of the triconch martyrion at Mitropolis (10/10)[208], all the other churches of Roman Crete can be divided into three groups of basilicas. The smallest group embraces those churches with tripartite transepts: there are only three examples, Panormos (13/3), Kolokythia (3/8) and Almyrida (17/9). The other groups are the very simple basilicas like Suia A (19/17), Knossos (8/4) or Olus phase ii (3/7), and the others of more complex design with pastophoria, etc., culminating in the design of St. Titus at Gortyna (10/10). The first group are probably all early to mid 6c, but the others have no particular chronological distribution. They do, however, have a slight geographical bias in that the most obviously 'foreign influenced' designs like Chersonisos A and B (6/7), Mallia (6/20) and Lebena (10/23) are on the coast and, except Mallia, at major ports on the trade routes from the East 'whence came these influences'. This must not be overemphasized, as Suia A (19/17), Phoenix (16/5) and Olus (3/7) are all simple basilicas at major ports, while Kera (14/7) with its more complex east end, ranks as almost the most inaccessible basilica in Crete.

The influences borne along these trade routes were mainly from the east, in particular N. Syria. Although it has been claimed [209] that the influence was transmitted via Cilicia, details like the possible martyrion at Chersonisos A which are best paralleled from Syria itself make it likely that to a certain degree the influence was direct from Syria.

---

203. See W. E. Kleinbauer, 'The origin and function of the aisled tetraconch in Syria and N. Mesopotamia', *DOP* XXVII, 1973, p.91.
204. Most recently, A. Novello, 'Tipologia delle chiese bizantine della Grecia', *Corso di cultura sull'arte ravennate e bizantina* XXII, 1975, p.27 tav. vi.
205. R. F. Hoddinott, *Bulgaria in Antiquity* (London, 1975), p.293f., fig.83.
206. R. F. Hoddinott, *Early Byzantine Churches in Macedonia and Southern Serbia* (London, 1963), p.110, fig.47.
207. Krautheimer, *op.cit.* note 6, p.337 fig.283.
208. I am here assuming Episkopi (20/20) to be post-Arab in the form now known.
209. Krautheimer, *op.cit.* note 6, p.114-5.

The only actual evidence for direct religious links between Crete and Syria is the mention of the death of Syrian monks in Crete in AD 622/3 in the Slavic raid[210]. The resemblance between certain basilicas on Lesbos[211] and those about Chersonisos is probably best explained as similar but independant results from the same source rather than diffusion between the islands. However, there was also influence from the Greek mainland, where the best parallel for the triple transept is found in NW Greece. Also, the ultimate roots of the triconch at Gortyna came from the west in Italy or N. Africa, but apart from this the latter area does not seem to have influenced, or been influenced by, Crete. This is somewhat surprising in that Crete had for several centuries been a joint province with Cyrene.

Whatever the design of the east end there seems to have been a great deal of other minor variations of building design in the basilicas that does not seem to resolve into any particularly meaningful pattern. Many have an atrium, one at Panormos (13/3) being well known; but others do not. There is a slight tendency for the simpler basilicas to predominate among the latter. The actual church is entered either by two doors in the west wall or by a single door in the south wall, which may have its own porch, e.g. at Kera (14/7). The aisles are entered by doors from the narthex or by a tribelon: the only example of this in an ordinary basilica is at Chersonisos B, but St. Titus and Mitropolis at Gortyna (10/10) also have them. The use of the tribelon as opposed to doors must have been of liturgical significance, and it has recently been shown that they seem to be confined to the churches within the Praefecture of Illyricum as opposed to the Orient. Since the external parallels for Chersonisos B include the basilica of Aphentele in Lesbos in the latter Praefecture, this shows an interesting clash in influences in Crete. The side aisles can either be equal in width, e.g. at Itanos A and B (1/39), Knossos (8/4), Vizari (12/12) and Suia A (19/17), or unequal; when this happens the south aisle is normally the wider of the two, e.g. at Chersonisos A and B (6/7), Mavropapas (10/10), Lebena (10/23) and Kera (14/7). Those with a wider north aisle are Olus (3/7), Panormos (13/3) and Phoenix (16/5).

Only at a few sites have the stylobates been well enough preserved to discuss their original height, but at Knossos (8/4) they were originally just under a metre high; possibly at Itanos A (1/39) they were about the same, and in their second phases at Chersonisos B an unknown height. Low stylobates are known from the first phase at Chersonisos B, at Chersonisos A (6/7) and Lebena (10/23). At Panormos there were balustrades instead of high stylobates. These high stylobates are a feature of Aegean churches[212], and it is interesting in Crete on the edge of the Aegean to note a mixture and even conversion of stylobate types. The liturgical reason for them is unknown. Possibly connected to this a further phenomenon is observed at Chersonisos B, as well as Chersonisos A (6/7) and Almyrida (17/9): here the pulpit position is half way down on the north side of the nave and is obviously secondary. This position of the ambo seems like the tribelon to be linked to an administrative division of the church[213]; in this case the area of Achaea where the ambo tends to be on the north side as distinct from the practice in areas further north where it is on the south side, and that in Asia Minor, where it tends to be central in the nave. Here and at nearly all the other basilicas the original position of the pulpit is not known.

In the central aisle the chancel or bema normally takes up its last third, except at Chersonisos B and possibly Lebena (10/23), where there seems to be no division before the apse. In the side aisles pastophoria are common at at least twelve of the sites, either in front of the apse or flanking it. The apse normally has a synthronon with varying numbers of benches or steps (one to three) and is semicircular or more rarely U-shaped, showing again eastern influence as at Itanos B (1/39).

The baptistery of the Cretan churches tends to be in one of the ancillary rooms, often to the north or north-west of the narthex, e.g. at Kera (14/7),possibly Panormos (13/3) and Suia (19/17). But it is located in the south pastophorion at Panormos in a later phase and at Mallia in the room which may be secondary beyond the south pastophorion; at Vizari (12/12), which is later than the other churches, it is at the end of the south aisle. As all these three examples of a baptistery at the east end of the church are later, it seems possible that there was a change during the period from a western to eastern baptistery. At Itanos B (1/39) and Knossos (8/4) there are freestanding buildings that may well be baptisteries[214]

Apart from its use as a baptistery the pastophorion also served as the last resting place for certain clerics: in the south pastophorion of Chersonisos B is the tomb of Pegasius, who may be a bishop, and two other graves; at

---

210. E. W. Brooks (ed.), *Chronica Minora* II, p.147. I owe this reference to Dr. S. Brock.
211. A. K. Orlandos, *op.cit.* note 58.
212. See T. F. Matthews, *The Early Churches of Constantinople* (Pennsylvania, 1972), chapter V, p.117: the divisions of the church.
213. J. P. Sodini, *BCH* XCIX, 1975, p.581.
214. A. Khatchatrian, *Les baptistères paléochrétiens* (Paris, 1962).

Panormos in the north pastophorion the psaltes Theodolus is buried. Such commemorative tombs are known from elsewhere in the churches: in the narthex at Chersonisos A; at Knossos (8/4) an earlier tomb had been incorporated into the nave, while at Mallia the tomb was in a crypt below the nave. In the latter two cases the church was obviously serving as a martyrion; specific martyria other than a main church are also known at Mitropolis (10/10) and possibly Chersonisos A.

Many of these churches had mosaic floors; decorative marble inlay floors are known from Piskopiano (6/8), Knossos (8/4) and Mitropolis (10/10). At the last two sites there are also mosaics elsewhere in the church. The mosaics vary greatly in quality and design, but there seem to be some that may come from one school or workshop. The mosaics at Chersonisos A and B are of the same high quality and share several minor motifs, and also the rather unusual border of the interlocking semicircles. This border is also used at Suia A and probably at Elyros and Alikianos, as these mosaics appear to be identical to the Suia example. Obviously the last two mosaics were laid by the same workshop and it seems very likely that Chersonisos A and B were the work of another. Whether the unusual border is sufficient evidence to link the two together must remain in doubt, especially considering the physical and possible chronological distance separating the two groups.

There are other similarities between various mosaics, including the design of the narthex mosaic at Kera (14/7) and Chersonisos A. These churches are further linked in a rather roundabout way in that the west end of Kera may resemble that at Lebena (10/23) whose basic design is very similar to Chersonisos B, where the mosaics were probably laid by the same workshop as at A. All four churches belong to the group with complex east ends. In general, the mosaic designs fit into the common patterns used all over the late Roman world, with specific parallels coming largely from the Greek mainland and islands[215], but also from Syria. None of the mosaics from Crete are later than the mid 6c, but the two later churches of Vizari and St. Titus have no mosaics. Also at several of the earlier churches the mosaics either could not be repaired because of a lack of financial or technical resources, or they had gone out of favour in church decoration.

Within the various types of architectural fragments found in the basilicas there do not seem to be any significant groups. The commonest types of capital are the Corinthian Leierkapitell and the Ionic impost type. The quality of these can be high, as may also be that of the screen fragments.

The only one of all these churches that is really important is St. Titus at Gortyna: the rest all fit into the general pattern of Aegean churches of their period, granted that the influence from the east is more obvious in Crete than most of the rest of the area, leading to the clash of influences in the use of the tribelon, the position of the ambo and the high stylobate. Their fittings again fit into this general framework, with mosaics and architectural fragments of a reasonable to high quality. This all reflects the wealth and position of Crete in the Late Roman Empire up to *c.* 600. For the remaining *c.* 200 years up to the Arab conquest, only one new church is yet known; but when we remember that only a dozen churches of this period are known[216] from the entire empire this is no disgrace for Crete.

---

215. This may be partially due to the large amount published about the early churches of the area.
216. Krautheimer, p.299: dated 1973.

CHAPTER 8: CONCLUSIONS

The Hellenistic period in Crete was one of almost constant internecine warfare, marked by the consolidation of power by the larger cities like Cydonia, Knossos, Gortyna and Hierapytna. At the same time it seems that many, if not most, of the archaic social customs had also dwindled away by the time of Metellus' conquest. This was no straight-forward 'national' war but a rather nasty, vicious Romano-Cretan civil war, culminating in Metellus' victory aided by the Gortynians and Polyrrhenians. For the remaining years of the Republic Crete's history is reasonably clear but, like the rest of the Roman world, rather confused, allowing no time for settlement and peace.

With Octavian's victory at Actium, Crete together with Cyrene became one of the senatorial provinces, although it seems that the two halves of the province had little to do with each other. Archaeologically very little is known of the first century AD but the organisation of the island becomes clearer with the activities of the Cretan Council marked by the establishment of its coinage, ousting most of the city mints under Caligula. The Julio-Claudian period is mainly marked by earthquakes and corrupt governors: on the other hand the progress of Romanisation is clear from the number of citizenship grants, which under Claudius was quite high. This process continued under the Flavians, aided by the creation of the Cretan auxiliary units. In the same period the issues of the council mint became closer in size and weight to the regular imperial issues. This increasing 'binding' of the island within the Empire is also illustrated by the rise of the Flavii Sulpiciani of Hierapytna from city magistrates to failed emperor by the end of the next century. The family probably gained their citizenship via the patronship of Aulus Larcius Lepidus Sulpicianus, who was quaestor in Crete at the end of Nero's reign and afterwards served with Vespasian in Judaea. During his quaestorship his mother, on the vote of the city council at Gortyna, put up a massive statue base to him there [1].

The first century closed with further earthquakes, which may well have spurred on the tremendous building programme all over the island started under Nerva or Trajan, with buildings like the civil basilica at Knossos, the palace at Gortyna, and continuing with the numerous theatres and new roads, etc., being constructed right up into the Severan period. The wealth of the time is also illustrated by the increasing number of mosaics of the 2-3c, and sarcophagi of all the major schools of the same date. Some of this material is later in date than the building boom, extending up to the middle of the third century, which emphasizes the need to be cautious in interpreting the cessation of the building programme as evidence of an economic decline; obviously mosaics and sarcophagi were not as expensive as large public buildings and were also more personal, but by the end of the second century it is perhaps questionable whether any more public buildings were needed or whether there was any remaining space for them in the cities.

The source of the wealth that created both buildings and mosaics must have been derived from agriculture, but unfortunately almost nothing is known about this, and even less of what is known can be dated. The importance of the Mesara estates is clear, and there are other substantial farmhouses known, commonly with built-in pithoi for the storage (presumably) of corn or oil. However, the majority of what would seem to be villas rather than simple farms are later, dating to the 5-6c. Another important localised source of wealth were the trade routes passing by the coasts of Crete, especially the southern coast, with the corn fleets on their way from Egypt to Rome. These routes also brought new gods like Isis and Serapis, and possibly also new customs in the form of the necropoleis of free standing tombs found along the south coast, most noticeably at Lissos. Generally in religious affairs, however, the Cretans

1. *IC.* IV.292.

appear to have been extremely conservative: obviously Minoan divinities like Diktynna maintained their importance and there was comparatively little building of new temples, but rather the continued use and adaptation of archaic structures. One such temple, that of Pythian Apollo at Gortyna, eventually was converted into Crete's first cathedral and served as such probably up to about AD 600.

In contrast to their religious attitudes, the Cretans showed themselves more than willing to be influenced in their art and architecture by the prevailing trends. In the 1-3c the most important source seems to have been the great cities of the coasts of Asia Minor, with clear evidence for the import of actual material like marble and also general ideas. There were also strong links to Greece proper, with the domination of Attic sarcophagi and strong resemblances between many of the mosaics in Crete and those on the mainland. In the Hadrianic period there was also a boom in the export to Crete of statues of the Emperor, manufactured probably in Attica. In more mundane matters, the bulk of the fine pottery imported into Crete seems to have come from the east in the form of Eastern Sigillata, Çandarli ware and later LRC. Some pottery, especially Arretine early on and ARSW later, did come from the west, but never in the same quantities as the eastern material. One aspect of western influence may be the extensive use of brick-faced concrete, despite the fact that Crete has a plentiful supply of good building stone, and the advanced design of certain of the buildings such as the shrine at Lebena, and the bath house at Lappa may be another. In addition, there are certain strays from the west, most remarkably the superb 'Triumph of Dionysus' Italian sarcophagus from Arvi.

In all this, it is very noticeable how little Crete seems to have been influenced from Africa, even though Cyrene formed the other half of the province, and the Diocletianic reform under which Crete eventually became a single province in the Praefecture of Illyricum seems far more logical. The 150 years following this event are rather obscure. The major event in the second half of the 4c was yet another series of earthquakes. Nearly every major site excavated produces evidence of this event: at Gortyna there is wide-scale rebuilding by the governor in the 380's, Oecumenius Dositheus Asclepiodotus, for example of the Praetorian palace[2], and there are destruction levels at Mochlos, Kastelli Kissamou and Knossos. One of the earthquakes responsible must have been that recorded in 365 by Ammianus Marcellinus [3], but this is too late for the Kastelli destruction and for the final abandonment of the site at Knossos, where it seems that the city was deserted at the end of the century. Why the city was not rebuilt is simply not known, but the preference for the coastal site of Heraklion can be paralleled on the southern coast, where again a port, this time Inatos, replaced the inland city, Priansos, as the local major centre.

However, the most dramatic change came in the next century with the vast numbers of basilicas built in the period roughly 450-550; previously Christianity had made almost no archaeological impression except for the conversion of the temple of Pythian Apollo and probably the early church at Olus. Accompanying this great church building programme there was also a change in burial customs, and the simple cist burial became the practice even presumably for the rich, who previously would have used chamber tombs. This must represent a real change in beliefs on an island where at the end of the fourth century the dead Zeus was still being worshipped[4]. The number, the size and the decoration of the new churches is evidence not only for the piety of the builders but also the available wealth, and it is at the same date that rural villas are found for the first time in Crete in any number.

Like the earlier buildings, the design of the churches reflects Crete's geographical position, for although the basic design is the standard three aisled basilica, there are strong Syrian influences, particularly in the design of the east end. Such designs are commonest in basilicas on the coast and again illustrate the role of trade routes in transmitting culture. After the middle of the 6c very few churches were built: only the new cathedral of St. Titus at Gortyna, which may well reflect Heraclid interest in the island, and in the 8c the basilica at Vizari. Again, as with the earlier public buildings, it is not clear how far this change reflects a simple fulfilment of needs or an economic decline, for many of the churches were patched up in rather inferior materials. There can be no doubt that Crete was increasingly exposed from the early 7c both to Slavic and later Arab raids, but for as long into this century as the pottery can be identified, the rural and coastal sites which ought to have been the first to be affected seem to have flourished, even those on the south coast. Nevertheless, St. Andrew of Crete provides literary evidence for awareness of the danger from the Agarenes and archaeologically the reaction is revealed in a new militarisation of the island, with fortifications built at Mochlos, Pseira, Chersonisos, Gortyna, Lyttus and possibly Heraklion and Eleutherna. It is unfortunate that

---

2. *IC.*IV.284b.
3. XXVI.10.15.
4. Julius Firmicus Maternus *De Err. Prof. Rel.* 19.

the only one of these circuits that can accurately be dated is that at Gortyna, where there is a secure *terminus post quem* of Heraclius' reign, but the other defences are of similar style and method of construction. How effective all this was may be questioned, for the Arab fleet wintered on Crete in 674[5] and other raids are known from the Arab sources in the 8c. However, the almost total lack of archaeological evidence for the last 150-200 years before the final fall of the island in 827 is probably misleading, and revealing only of the present ignorance of the material, especially the pottery, rather than a decline in occupation. To support this view, Genesius[6] claims that there were still 29 cities when the Arabs took Crete, and although it is not known what this was based on, nor quite what he meant by a city, this evidence for a flourishing island is also backed by the words Cedrenus[7] puts into the mouth of the Arab leader, Apochaps,

'Lo, behold a land flowing with milk and honey'.

---

5. Theophanes 354.21.
6. II p.47.
7. P.509.

GAZETTEER

The gazetteer attempts to include all Hellenistic and Roman sites known to me: the list is basically compiled from that in Pendlebury and by checking all the relevant publications since 1939, which has more than doubled the number. There are also a few sites published prior to 1939 that were missed in the earlier list. The gazetteer is arranged by eparchy east to west and within the eparchy approximately west to east (see map Fig. 64).

I have visited as many of the sites as possible to check the unpublished information and collect new ('Personal observations' in footnotes); generally, Pendlebury is accurate but without much detail, and he also had a tendency to date certain sites as Hellenistic rather than Roman. Recent British work with its published pottery is very reliable. I had difficulty in verifying M. Faure's work both owing to the inaccessibility of many of his caves and also a confusion in place names, always a problem in Crete. In general, it is difficult to date much of the pottery, with the exception of the fine wares, and many sites known to be Roman from other evidence, e.g. epigraphical, have no pottery visible that can be dated more accurately than Graeco-Roman, i.e. not Minoan or Mediaeval. The remaining problem here is that in the later period there appears to be a re-emergence of shell gritted wares that look horribly like these two other periods!

The dating terms used in the gazetteer are as follows: early and late Roman are my own terms meaning from the Conquest to *c.*400, and then from *c.*400 to the Arab conquest. This rather abrupt division has resulted from the difficulty in dating pottery found on the sites, other than the fine wares. These roughly divide into two groups each confined to their period: the early wares cover Arretine, E. sig. A and B and Çandarli, and the late wares ARSW and LRC, although there are a few less important wares in each period, like Cypriot, 'true' Samian, etc. Strictly speaking, ARSW does occur in the earlier period, but it only becomes common in Crete from the mid 4c. This is also the date for a series of devastating earthquakes in the Aegean whose consequent destruction levels form a real break on several of the important sites that have been excavated. Later, in the mid 5c, the emergence of the basilica church also marks a new departure in the archaeology of the period. In general, then, the period 350-450 marks a real change in the archaeology of the island and so forms the dividing point for the early and late periods; these terms are used following the general usage of Late Roman Empire, although in Crete for the reasons given I have preferred a later starting date than is common, e.g. 324 or 284; in addition, the continuance of the term into the 9c may be stretching it, but there is no clear break in the island's history or archaeology before that. The use of 'early' is simply a corollary to 'late', and follows Hayes' use of the term to cover the wares mentioned above, although he would include Çandarli as a late ware rather than early. Of other terms just Roman is vague: Graeco-Roman is a term quoted from others indicating that the pottery was of the ubiquitous undatable coarse wares mentioned above, which may mean that the site is not very late. Byzantine is again only quoted when it refers to the pre-Arab period and seems to be the same as my Late Period, but I suspect also covers the Mediaeval, i.e. post-Arab period.

Finally, buildings and mosaics described in detail in earlier chapters are merely referred to, and not discussed again.

EPARCHY 1 - SITEIA

(1/1) MOCHLOS Just east of the Gulf of Mirabello is the island of Mochlos[1], about 150m offshore and, contrary to published reports, not joined to it in any recent period[2]. The Roman town here was both on the island and on the mainland slightly to the east. All that can be seen of the latter is a group of fishtanks about 70m east of the present village. There are two tanks separated by a low wall: the larger one is roughly 4.0m^2, the other slightly smaller. In the larger of the two a fragment of a stone filter was found which would originally have been in place across one of the channels connecting the tanks to the sea. No absolute date can be given to these tanks, but by their type and parallels, especially from along the coast at Chersonisos (6/7), they are most likely to be Roman[3]. Seager also records remains near the church of Ay. Andreas, but gives no details.

On the southern slopes of the island there were numerous houses, but many of these were removed by Seager without being recorded. Among the finds he mentions coins of Hadrian (1), Diocletian (1) and Constantine the Great (several). He also notes lamps and a rhyton in the form of a satyr which he thought was earlier. On top of the island above the sheer northern cliffs, which are about 50m high, the fortifications recorded by Seager can still be seen (Fig.48): they comprise a central building 8.20m

Fig.48. Mochlos: plan of the island and fortifications.

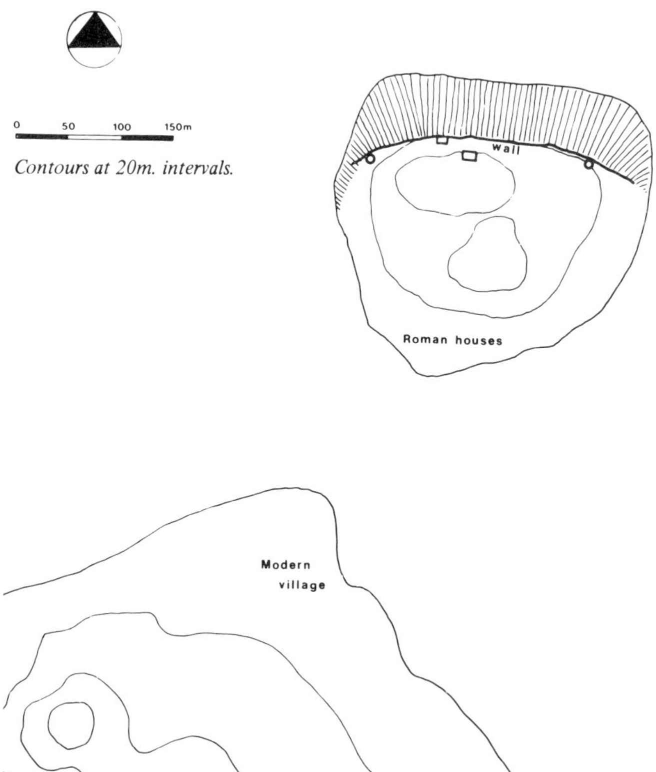

x 11.20m lying 14m behind a curtain wall that runs along the entire crest of the island. On this wall to the NW of the first building is another, possibly a tower 4.0m x 8.4m, and at either end of the wall are round towers with possible flanking walls running down to the sea. All these works are constructed of rough masonry with concrete which cannot be pre-Roman but could be Byzantine B rather than Late Roman[4]. If they are Late Roman their date is most likely to be 7-8c, erected as a reaction to the Arab raids of that period; a 5c date is possible, with the Vandal threat as the cause, but in the historical context this seems less likely.

1. R. Seager, *AJA* XIII, 1909, p.273f. M.S.F. Hood and J. Leatham, *ABSA* LIII-LIV, 1958-9, p.273f. *AC* p.364. Personal observation.
2. Personal observation, with exact depth of 4.50m from Dr. N. C. Flemming. Even given the rise in sea level this channel can never have been an isthmus: see Appendix III.
3. The fish tanks are dealt with in greater detail in Hood and Leatham, *op. cit.* p.275, note 1.
4. Byzantine B is used for the post-Arab period.

(1/2) TOURLOTI At Khordakhia sherds were found by Bosanquet[1].

1. *AC* p.376.

(1/3) MESA MOULIANA A Roman grave was recorded from this village[1] in 1938.

1. *Arch. Anz.* 1938, p.473. *ABSA* XLII, 1947, p.369.

(1/4) KHALKOMATAS Outside this cave[1], north of Chamezi, 'Byzantine' sherds have been found.

1. P. Faure, *BCH* LXXXVI, 1962, p.39. It is not clear exactly what he means by Byzantine; these may be glazed wares, i.e. Byz.B or Venetian, or Late Roman wares as classified by Dr. J. Hayes.

(1/5) LEOPETRO On the ridge above the sea here[1] are the remains of a fortress of uncertain date. It was built of stone and concrete of rather rough character and so could be Late Roman or Byzantine B/early Venetian. It was in ruins by 1538[2]. Pendlebury however claimed to have seen sherds of Classical to Roman date here.

1. Gerola, *Mon. Ven.* I p.88, Fig. 44-5. Spratt I, 158-9. E. Falkener, 'Antiquities of Candia I', *Museum of Classical Antiquities* II (London, 1860), p.269. *AC* p.385.
2. The date of the MS ed. by Falkener where the ruins are mentioned.

(1/6) SKOPI A large stone oil press claimed to be of Hellenistic or Roman date has been found here[1].

1. *A.Delt.* XXIII.22, 1968, p.404.

(1/7) ROUKAKA Sherds have been found in a field south of the village[1].

1. *AC* p.376, *ABSA* XXXIII, 1932-3, p.95.

(1/8) GRAS At Kato Vigli a tombstone was discovered[1] dated from the letter forms to the 4c. On the stone is a crude bust of the dead woman surrounded by a mirror, what may be a shuttle and two other objects, probably a distaff and spindle. Nearby at Forteza the headland is fortified with a wall that may be Late Roman or Mediaeval[2].

1. *IC* III.IX.3
2. Gerola, *Mon. Ven.* I, p.90.

(1/9) KOUTSOURAS In front of the church of Ay. Antonios a scatter of Roman sherds was found, and built into the church a tombstone of possible 3c date with a mirror depicted in relief[1]. There are also sherds from a nearby cave.

1. P. Faure, "Επιγραφαί έκ Κρήτης", *Kret.Khron.* XXI, 1969, p.316, no.3. P. Faure, *BCH* LXXXVI, 1962, p.40.

(1/10) MAKRYGIALOS Below the modern village[1] is a large Roman site of which very little is known, but during recent construction work the remains of many Graeco-Roman houses were noted. Pendlebury saw a cistern on the pensinsula to the west, where there is a large scatter of sherds, including ARSW, combed amphorae and LRC form 3. Also, he recorded a tombstone, probably of late date. It is very likely that this is the site of ancient Stalis[2].

1. *ABSA* XXXIII, 1932-3, p.100. *AC* p.376. *PAE* 1959, no.34, p.219. *Kret.Khron.* XIII, 1959, p.391. *IC* III .IX.6 for the tombstone. Personal observation.
2. *IC*.III.VI.7 and above p.16.

(1/11) PILALEMATA A 2/3c tombstone has been found here[1].

1. *A.Delt.* XXII.2, 1967, p.487.

(1/12) SITEIA The only major ancient structure known from here is the basilica[1] of late 5c/early 6c date. In the museum at Ay. Nikolaos there are a few lc A.D. lamps on display, as well as a number of Hellenistic pots. A small number of early Roman inscriptions are also recorded as coming from the site[2]. Recently a series of ten fishtanks were found below the Custom House: the larger of these was at least 7.0 x 4.25 x 3.5m in height, with a series of secondary channels. Evidence was also found in the form of rock-cut holes for some form of roof to protect the fish. Contrary to the general situation in Central-E. Crete the sea level here appears to be lower than when the tanks were cut, presumably in the early Roman period[3]. Roman pottery has also been observed north of the modern town[4].

1. For the basilica with refs., see above p.89.
2. *IC.* III.VIII. Personal observation (Museum).
3. C. Davaras, 'Rock-cut Fish Tanks in E. Crete', *ABSA* LXIX, p.87.

4. Information from M.S.F. Hood.

(1/13) PETRAS Vases are recorded from the Kephala here[1] but more importantly, from just past the Kephala, on the east of the headland Karavopetra or Trypete is a ship shed cut into the natural rock. It is 30m long, 5.50m wide and 5.0m deep at an angle of 15°30′ to the sea. However, it ends on the present edge of the sea, indicating perhaps a drop in local sea level since its construction. It cannot be dated, but the type of structure is either Greek or Roman. No Roman material was seen here by M.S.F. Hood[2].

1. *AC* p.376, quoting *A.Delt.* IV.2, 1918, p.23. K. Davaras, 'εἰς νεώσοικος παρὰ τὴν Σητείαν', *AE* 1967, p.84.
2. Personal communication.

(1/14) EPISKOPI PISKOKEPHALOU Remains of a small settlement were found here[1]; part of a Roman building with a concrete floor and occupation debris consisting of pottery and bones was the only structure identified, but a group of tile graves was also found. One of these graves was a flat vessel containing a corpse aligned SE-NW, and what were claimed to be bird bones. A 3c tombstone is also known from here.

1. *PAE* 1956, no.34, p.239. *Kret.Khron.* X, 1956, p.413. *IC*.III.VIII.4.

(1/15) PISKOKEPHALI This site[1] may just be an outlier from the previous one; two tombstones of 2/3c date are known, and a group of seal stones. A mosaic was recorded as being found in a nearby field, perhaps indicating the presence of a villa.

1. *AC.* p.376. *Arch. Anz.* 1938, p.474. *IC.* III.VI.20; VIII.2.

(1/16) KATO EPISKOPI Remains of Graeco-Roman buildings which contained two Roman coins are recorded from near this village at Ellenika[1].

1. *Kret.Khron.* VI, 1951, p.477.

(1/17) ROUSSA EKLISSIA A lamp signed by Romanensis was found here[1]. This dates to the 2c; the potter worked at Cnidos.

1. *IC.* III.IX.9. The lamp is no.3824 in Heraklion Museum Pottery Catalogue.

(1/18) MARONIA A 1c B.C. tombstone to Maxima decorated with the feminine symbols of a comb and mirror was found here at Plakakia[1].

1. K. Davaras, ' Ἐπιγραφαί ἐκ Κρήτης I', *Kret.Khron.* XIV, 1960, p.462.

(1/19) VOURLIDORIZA This cave[1] at the foot of Mount Gallou 'to skopeli' contained Roman-Byzantine sherds.

1. P. Faure, 'Sur trois sortes de sanctuaires crétois II', *BCH* XCIII, 1969, p.174.

(1/20) KATSIDONI Near this village[1] a cave also contained Roman-Byzantine sherds.

1. P. Faure, 'Cultes de sommets et cultes de cavernes en Crète', *BCH* LXXXVII, 1963, p.496, cave no.2.

(1/21) TOURTOULI Tile graves of Hellenistic or Roman date are known from this site[1].

1. *Kret. Khron.* XIII, 1959, p.389.

(1/22) PRAESOS This once powerful city[1] seems to have become deserted in late Hellenistic times, but later occupation or at least use of the same cemeteries is shown by a 3c A.D. tombstone and a tomb containing Roman coins from the necropolis.

1. R. Bosanquet, 'Excavations at Praesos I', *ABSA* VIII, 1902, p.231. *IC.* III.VI. passim, no. 22 for the tombstone. *Kret. Khron.* XIII, 1959, p.390.

(1/23) SKLAVI A solidus of Constantine III 641-668 found here[1] is now in the Heraklion Historical Museum (Catalogue no. 1816).

1. The collection is unpublished but on public display.

(1/24) LITHINES Half a kilometre SE of Lithines[1] built into the church of Stavromenos is a 4/5c tombstone; nearby is a scatter of late Roman sherds.

1. P. Faure, 'Ἐπιγραφαί ἐκ Κρήτης', *Kret.Khron.* XXI, 1969, p.315.

(1/25) CHANDRAS A fragment of a crude, possibly late, tombstone is built into a village house here[1].

1. *IC.* III.IX.5.

(1/26) APIDI In the Heraklion Museum coin catalogue a silver issue of Julia Domna, 193-217, is recorded, no.1991. A Roman-Byzantine site was noted at Mesa Apidi[1].

1. *Arch. Anz.* 1938, p.480, for the site.

(1/27) ZIROS The Roman site identified by Faure is probably the same as the one found before the war. A 3c tombstone is also known from the area around the village[1].

1. *IC*.III.VI.21. *AA* 1938, p.478. P. Faure, 'Nouvelles recherches sur le peuplement des montagnes de Crète', *BCH* LXXXIX, 1965, p.29.

(1/28) KHAMETOULO A Roman site at Sto Dokhi, but no other details known[1].

1. *AC* p.385

(1/29) PHARMAKOKEPHALO Roman sherds were found on this headland[1] south of Ampelos.

1. *ABSA* XXXIII, 1932-3, P.100; mentioned *AC* p.365, 375, where it is identified as Ampelos as opposed to the site at Xerokampos to the north.

(1/30) AMPELOS-XEROKAMPOS On the beach and headland, Ellinika, to the south, Hellenistic-Roman sherds and some tombs hollowed out of the cliffs were found by Pendlebury and others. Spratt saw some actual ruins. Among the sherds was a stamped Rhodian amphora fragment[1].

1. *IC* III.I. passim. Spratt I, p.238-9. *AC* p.362 and 364, as *ABSA* XXXIII, 1932-3, p.99.

(1/31) KOUPHONISI ISLANDS The remains[1] on the main island of this group, the ancient Leuke islands, have recently been described by Leonard. The island is not large, *c.* 2 x 4km, but has considerable remains of a town of some wealth and a statue on the summit of the island at its southern end. Spratt and others recorded a platform for the statue: in 1903 it was described as a pyramid with 20 steps of well-cut limestone. Leonard could only see a modern base for a datum point of roughly mortared stone; it would seem most likely that this is simply a modern rebuilding of the presumably ruined platform. On the platform sat a more than life-sized seated statue in Parian marble, of which two fragments still survive on the site. This might have been a beacon of Roman date rather than a statue of a Ptolemy as previously suggested, since the remaining material from the site must be Roman because of the concrete used, and there is also a similarity between this statue and that at Porto Rafti[2]. North of the summit are the cisterns and aqueducts recorded by Spratt and Leonard. There are four cisterns fed by two aqueducts; apart from cistern 3 they are all built of stone, brick and mortar and are of varying sizes, with cistern 1, *c.* 14.0m x 65.0m, being the largest. The two 'water systems' are quite small, being no more than 0.50m high and the channels 0.30 and 0.20m wide. Leonard could find no trace of the 650ft cistern seen by Spratt and suggests, probably correctly, that in fact the latter took cisterns 1-3 as being all one. Both water systems end at an area *c.*65.0m x 350.0m, which appears to have been artificially levelled with walls on its east and west sides. It is impossible to say what this was without excavation, but a forum is possible, as suggested by Leonard. Closer to the coast north of the 'forum' are remains of several buildings including a small theatre. East of this are the ruins of various buildings, originally quite pretentious, with columns of marble and what sounds like granite and fragments of three mosaics: one of black and white, the others only of white tesserae. Most of the walls were of stone and mortar, but one used fine brickwork. Finally, on a small islet there are more walls, with another black and white mosaic in fragments and painted plaster.

Leonard sees this obviously wealthy site as a reaction to the piracy endemic in the Aegean, and following Spratt considers it unlikely that pirates would have erected such buildings. This seems to me to fail to realise that it is obvious that the Cretan pirates of the Hellenistic period were extremely successful and at the same time there is no reason why they should not have been prepared to adorn their own towns with expensive buildings[3]. Secondly, and more importantly, it is clear that the bulk if not all of the remains on the island described by Leonard are of Roman date. Although no doubt some piracy always existed, this site must be connected to the trade route from the east, especially the corn trade, and have gained its wealth from its strategic position, like the other cities on Crete's south coast.

1. Spratt I, p.241. R.C. Bosanquet, 'Dicte and the temple of Dicteaean Zeus', *ABSA* XL, 1940, p.71. Albert Leonard Jnr., 'Kouphonisi Revisited', *Archeologia classica XXIV,* 1972, p. 353, tav. *CIV-CX.*
2. see p.17.
3. For the pirates, H.A. Ormerod *Piracy in the Ancient World* (Liverpool 1924)

(1/32) PELEKYTA Roman sherds in this cave[1] one hour NE of Kato Zakro.

1. P. Faure, 'Cavernes et sites aux deux extrémités de la Crète', *BCH* LXXXVI, 1962, p.38ff.

(1/33) EPANO ZAKRO At Kali Strati is a possible site of a villa with the remains of a hypocaust found here in 1896[1]. Previous Hellenistic occupation may be indicated by a stamped amphora fragment; this is probably 4/3c B.C. Rhodian[2]. Finally from a cave 120 m up from the village at Katsimpourdou are Roman sherds.

1. L. Mariani, *Mon. Ant.* VI, 1895, p.293. P. Faure, *op.cit.* 1962.
2. *A. Delt.* XXI, 1966, B, p. 417. Stamp of Apatourios, cf. *Délos* XXVII, p.300, E 253.

(1/34) KAROUBES At 'Elliniko Piyadi' is a Roman-Byzantine site, and nearby at the end of the gorge in the cave of Speliara Roman sherds were found[1].

1. P. Faure, *op.cit.* 1962, p.38.

(1/35) KOCHLAKIES Roman sherds[1].

1. *Arch. Anz.* 1938, p.477.

(1/36) AY. NIKOLAOS The site here[1] was discovered and excavated on a day's excursion from the work at Palaikastro. A rough building was found with much Minoan material, but also some sherds 'which looked Hellenistic or Roman'.

1. *AC* p.364, A. M.N. Tod, 'Excavations at Palaikastro II', *ABSA* IX, 1902-3, p.339.

(1/37) PALAIKASTRO Above the Minoan town[1] in block X were the fragmentary remains of the Temple of Dictaean Zeus. No plan could be recovered, but the architectural fragments dated it to 6c B.C. However it would seem to have lasted well into the Roman period, since the famous hymn is dated to the 3c A.D. by letter forms[1]. Apart from this there is slight evidence for the period, consisting of a cup and three jugs from the Kastri below, in which a small number of Classical or Hellenistic black glaze sherds were visible. More important is the statue found by Spratt but now lost of a seated figure in Parian marble just like that from Kouphonisi. As has already been suggested these are most likely to be beacons of Roman date, positioned on suitable heights above the sea. This one had obviously fallen off the Kastri down onto the beach. Finally, in the Historical Museum at Heraklion there is a lamp (no.1269) that is provenanced as Palaikastro, Siteia, which ought to date to the very end of Roman Crete before the Arabs.

1. R.C.Bosanquet, 'Excavations at Palaikastro IV', *ABSA* XI, 1904-5, p.298. Spratt I, p.210. *IC* III.II.2 for the hymn. *A.Delt.* XVII.2.2, 1961-2, p.290. Personal observation.

(1/38) SAMONIUM SHRINE I South of the actual site of the shrine[1] at 'sto Verneyadi' are a large number of graffiti scratched on the rocks, including some of Roman date. These may be dedications or mere scribbles.

1. *IC* III.VII.2-27

(1/39) ITANOS This is the largest site[1] in the east of the island after Hierapytna; it covers two acropoleis and the land between. The necropolis appears to be situated to the north. From the story in Herodotus[2] Itanos must have been a flourishing city by the mid 7c, and it would seem most likely that it replaced Palaikastro as the main site of the area when that declined. The most obvious remains are those of the two basilicas on the main acropolis and on the slopes to the south[3]. The first one reuses a Hellenistic temple to Athena Polias[4]. Itanos' continuing prosperity into the Roman period is shown by the dedications to Caligula and Severus[5] and also by the ruins of well-built concrete structures of unknown function on the SW slopes of the southern (inland) acropolis. Little is known of the rest of the Roman site, although some late houses were uncovered on the main acropolis. As with so many of the sites the date of its abandonment or destruction is unknown, but the pottery recovered from the surface includes a large percentage of 7c forms[6] but no glazed wares normally dated to the early mediaeval period.

1. *IC* III.IV passim. *BCH* LXXV, 1951, p.193f. Personal observation.
2. IV.151f.
3. See p.89ff.
4. *IC* III.IV. Praef.p.78.
5. *IC* III.IV. 19 and 20.
6. African Red Slip Ware forms 104-6 (6-7c) . Late Roman C Form 3 E (5c), 3F (6c). Cypriot RSW Type C (7c). There was more of the latter ware here than at any other site seen by me.

(1/40) SAMONIUM SHRINE The only real evidence for the shrine[1] here is its mention in the *Stadiasmus Maris Magni*[2] and the inscription built into the later chapel. Spratt saw a small submerged building with only one level of stones above water.

1. *IC* III.VII. passim Praef. and no.1. Spratt I, p.189.
2. 318-9.

(1/41) ANDRAS A building of Graeco-Roman date was found here[1].

1. *BCH* LXXXIV, 1960, p.822.

(1/42) AY. KONSTANTINOS Hellenistic sherds[1].

1. *AC* p.362 (site not located within Eparchy).

(1/43) ACHLADION On the hill Platyskinou remains dated to the Graeco-Roman period were found. Also nearby at Ellenika there were rock-cut tombs[1].

1. *Kret.Khron.* VI, 1952, p.477.

EPARCHY 2 - YERAPETRA

(2/1) CHRISTOS Above the chapel and spring of Ayia Paraskeve just before the village[1] coming from Malles, are the remains of Roman buildings where several lamps were found. One of the buildings had a floor of sea pebbles. About 20m below the spring, built into the present rough track, are the remains of a more substantial wall of concrete and tile. Several inscriptions have been found here but these do not seem to have been *in situ*.

1. *A.Delt.* XVI, 1960, p.262. *Kret. Chron.* XIV, 1960, p.527. *A.Delt.* XXI. 3, 1966, p.554-5. IC. IXIX. 3, 8. Personal observations.

(2/2) MALLES Little is known of the site of Malla[1], modern Malles; I was unable to identify the site at Khlia mentioned by Pendlebury, but the most likely place for the ancient site seems to be underneath the now deserted lower village, south of the track to Christos, around the church of Ay. Georgios. Although later occupation has obliterated any definite evidence here, the church stands on older foundations, which include reasonable concrete, including tile.

1. *AC* p.376. *IC.* I.XIX. Personal observations.

(2/3) MYTHI 100 m south of the source of the river here are the remains of a Roman site[1] including tile work and 2/3c pottery. Also behind the village in the mountains is the cave Souvloto which contained Roman sherds.

1. P. Faure, *BCH* LXXXIX, 1965, p.36.

(2/4) MYRTOS Below the modern village are the remains of a small Roman town[1]. The only visible ruins are to the west of the village on the northern side of the coastal track; they consist of a brick-faced concrete building with hypocausts and a fragmentary geometric mosaic. The building, which is normally identified as a bath house, although as yet no definite evidence for this has been produced, was obviously of some importance, but to claim it as potentially one of the most interesting monuments of Roman Crete[2] is exaggerated. It is dated to the Late Antonine period.

Within the village area there were more similar buildings recently revealed by drains cut down the main street. These were again of brick-faced concrete and one had a white tessellated pavement. Several inscriptions have been found here of early Roman date, all of which are probably tombstones, possibly coming from the cemetery reported from the other side of the river.

1. Hood, *ABSA* LIX, 1964, p.93. *Kret.Khron.* XVIII, 1964, p.284. *Ergon* 1967, p.127. *PAE* 1967, p.214. *A.Delt.* XXIII. 2.2, 1968, p.404. *AR* 1973-4, p.39. *IC.* III.III.32, 39, 53-4. Personal observations.
2. *AR* 1973-4, p.39.

(2/5) KALAMAFKA At Sellia sherds and a lamp[1].

1. *AC* p.375.

(2/6) PSATHI In the cave Psathochampasos a lamp was found with a relief of Artemis, therefore probably dating to 1/2c.

1. P. Faure. *Fonctions des cavernes crétoises* (Paris, 1964), p.177.

(2/7) OLERUS On the northern edge of the plain opposite the modern village of Meseleri is the site of ancient Olerus[1]. Famed for its shrine to Athena, all that survives today are sherds, including ARSW, and one small building at the foot of the hill a short way east of the pipeline coming along the slope. This is probably what is left of a bath house; it has an apsidal end, 2.50m in radius, floored in *opus signinum*, and a 3m square room beyond with another wall going off to the west. Local tradition claims that there is another site under the village of Meseleri, but nothing is visible there.

1. *IC* III.V, passim. Only two inscriptions. *AC* p.362, 376. Personal observations.

(2/8) HIERAPYTNA (Fig.49) The ancient city here seems to have been larger than the modern town, stretching from the stream to the west of the modern town and to the east approximately as far as the present settlement, excluding the very recent development here[1]. Very little can now be seen of the city with its 'naumachia, amphitheatre, two theatres, temples, thermae, and aqueducts'[2]. There is now no trace of the first of these, but the remains of the moles of the outermost of the triple harbours can still be made out, one running from the jetty by the Venetian castle, and the other from the jetty a little to the east. They also show very clearly on Spratt's illustration of the town[3] The amphitheatre lay in the western part of the town, near the larger theatre[4]; it was sited between two low hills with six buttresses at each end to complete the circuit Its construction was of concrete, partially faced with white marble. It probably dates to the 2c, like the other major buildings known from the city. However, in the same area recent excavation has revealed a large stone structure with numerous pink marble columns. Associated with this building and another to the east were groups of pottery mainly of Augustan date[5]. The only other known building from the city is the smaller theatre on the eastern part of the site near the modern church of Timios Stavros[6]. However, the largest surviving Roman structure is a wall that runs along the top of the beach, west of the fort, for several hundred metres towards the stream, delineating the western edge of the city. The wall was constructed on top of the natural rock, possibly deliberately cut as a foundation. The material used for the wall was stone faced concrete on a base of levelling courses five tiles thick; the wall survives to a height of 2.0m, with a second similar levelling at 1.50m. Initially, the wall was 1.25m thick, but after a short forward-projecting portion it was doubled in width by the addition of another width of wall. At one point there remains what may be a simple gate or tower with an internal width of 2.50m, but since only part of the side walls survived it was impossible to determine the exact function of the structure[7].

The wealth of the city is also clear from the various finds, particularly from the group of sarcophagi from here[8], all of which seem to have come from near the larger theatre, indicating that this was on the edge of the city on the western side. They include two very fine Attic examples, and the famous Isis sarcophagus. The latter is now in Istanbul together with the statue of Hadrian[9] trampling on a Jewish boy: there is a further fragment of what may be another cuirassed Hadrian in the Museum, and also a possible head of Augustus. Other finds include a very good bronze of a boy in a cloak, seemingly from a sepulchral monument, again of Augustan date.

Fig.49. Hierapytna: plan of the area of the ancient city.

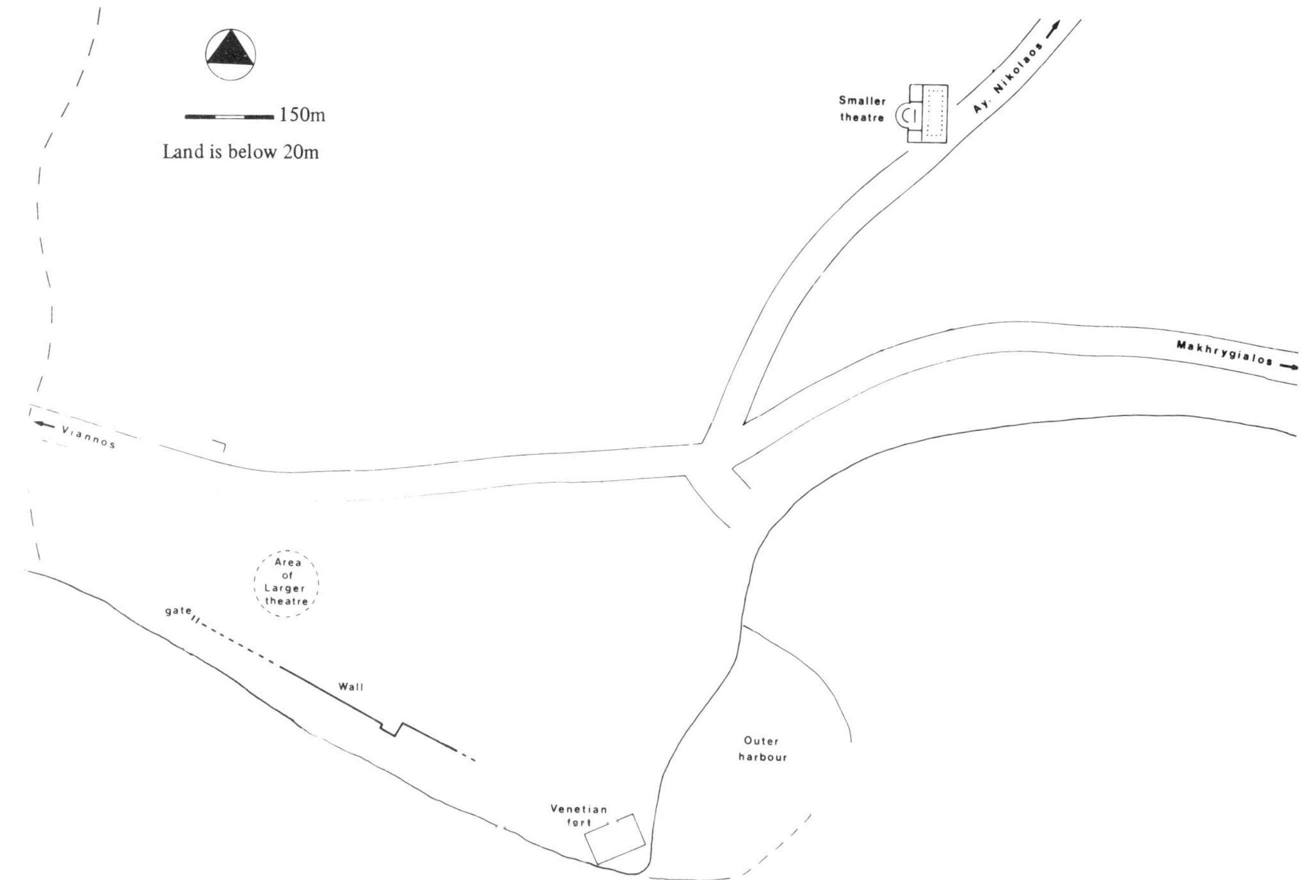

1. *IC* III.III. passim. Spratt I, p.256f. Belli ed. Falkener, p.11f. C. C. Vermeule *Roman Imperial Art in Greece and Asia Minor* (Harvard 1968), p.442. K. Lehmann-Hartleben *Die antiken Hafenanlagen* 1923, p.201, pl. XXXVII. Falkener *Museum of Classical Antiquities* (London 1860), p.271-2.
2. Belli ed. Falkener, p.11f.
3. Op. cit., p.255.
4. See above p.59.
5. Personal observations. Arretine Service II sherds and Eastern Sig.A. There were also a few fragments of ARSW and Late C Form 1 4/5c.
6. See above p.57.
7. Personal observation. The wall initially forms the wall of a school, then part of the veterinary centre, where it is double width, and then proceeds through a cement factory to become the boundary, including the possible tower, of an area of plastic greenhouses. Spratt I, p. 283, mentions this wall where it was re-used as part of the tomb containing the two Attic sarcophagi.
8. See above, p.47.
9. *Berytus* XIII, 1959, p. 55, no. 182. The other statues are

unpublished. The bronze is in the Heraklion Museum. See also *Kret.Khron.* XII, 1958, p. 481.

(2/9) KENTRI Hellenistic figurine[1].

1. *AC* p.362, Heraklion Museum catalogue no.4642.

(2/10) KATO CHORIO A group of inscriptions from here: three concerning land disputes and one other[1]. Possibly this marks a boundary between estates.

1. *IC.* III.III.28-9, 57 and 62.

(2/11) EPISKOPI The main remains here are those of the late Roman Christian basilica[1], but an earlier site is also possible because of the Augustan inscription from here[2].

1. See above p.91.
2. *IC.* III.III.63.

(2/12) PAKHYAMMOS About 200m from the sea here a large Roman building (Fig.50) was cleared and backfilled between June 4th and 6th 1903[1]. It was built in the same way as the structure at Tholos, but better, i.e. of stone-faced concrete on the exterior, tile-faced on the interior. The main building, *c.* 17.0m x 42.40m with the long north side facing the sea, had two long narrow corridors on the north and south sides running from the east end up to a range of three rooms at the west. Between these rooms was the central block, which included what seem to be two storage rooms divided into six sections, each with its own entrance. It is possible that this plan represents only the basement of a villa or alternatively it may be only a complex warehouse. The fact that there is a complicated system of cisterns and aqueduct on the eastern side of the complex may be evidence for the former interpretation. The aqueduct was traced 75m inland up to another cistern, from which it headed south towards Vasiliki. The only dating evidence recorded were two AE coins; one of Byzantine date and the other of Antoninus Pius. A 2c date for the structure is quite possible from the type of construction.

1. H.A.Boyd, 'Gournia', *Trans. Penn. Univ.* I.1, 1904, p.13. *AC* p.364 as a Graeco-Roman building.

Fig.50. Pakhyammos: plan of building with aqueduct.

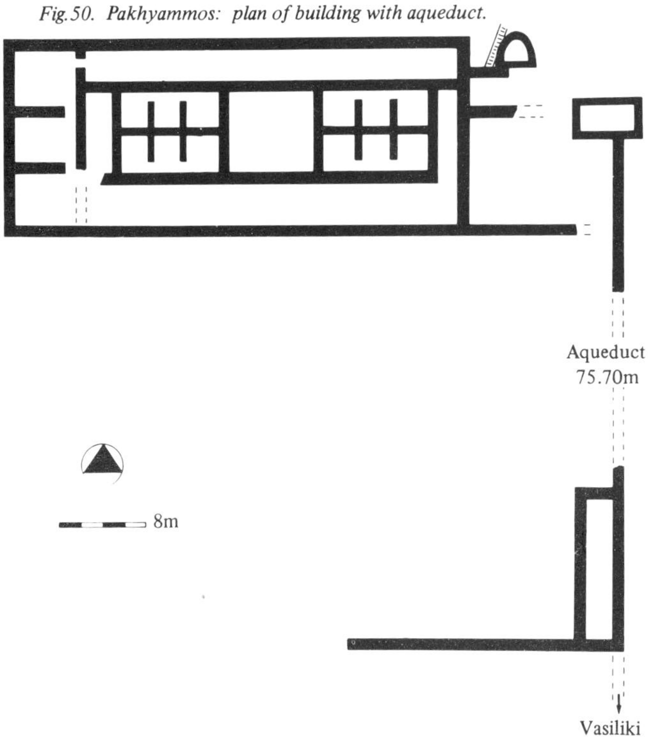

(2/13) VASILIKI Above the famous Minoan site are the remains of a small Christian basilica[1] together with some poor late tombs. The basilica was built on top of an earlier important building, which may be associated with an aqueduct coming down from the hills. It is possible that this is the same system that fed the building at Pakhyammos. Roman sherds also exist to the south of the site, including Çandarli ware.

1. R. Seager, 'Excavations at Vasiliki', *Trans. Penn. Univ.* I, p.207; II.2, p.113. *Ergon* 1972, p.113-118, for Zoes's recent work. Personal observation.

(2/14) MONASTERAKI Roman remains including walls[1].

1. *Arch. Anz.* 1938, p.470.

(2/15) AY. IOANNIS A 3c tombstone is known from here[1], but, of more interest, Pendlebury claimed to have seen a stretch of Roman road running from here to Skinokapsala. He does not say why he considered it to be of this date.

1. *IC.* III.III.48. *AC* p.385.

(2/16) AY. PHOTIA At the mouth of the stream here is a small cistern lined with pink cement. Round about there was a quantity of pottery of indeterminable date.

1. *AC* p.375, as *ABSA* XXXIII, 1932-3, p.100 'late Roman site'. Personal observations.

(2/17) KAVOUSI Below the village on the west of the Tholos road Marinatos excavated a walled tomb containing over 30 lamps of 2-3c[1] and two AE coins of Maximianus (235-8) and Probus (276-282).

1. Marinatos, *AJA* XL, 1936, p.373.

(2/18) THOLOS About 100m south of the church of Panayia, which may be the successor to a late Roman basilica, stands the building (Fig.51) that gives the place its name[1]. This structure is 52.50m long and 5.25m wide (internally); the walls are of concrete, faced on the exterior by

Fig.51. Tholos: plan of building near the shore.

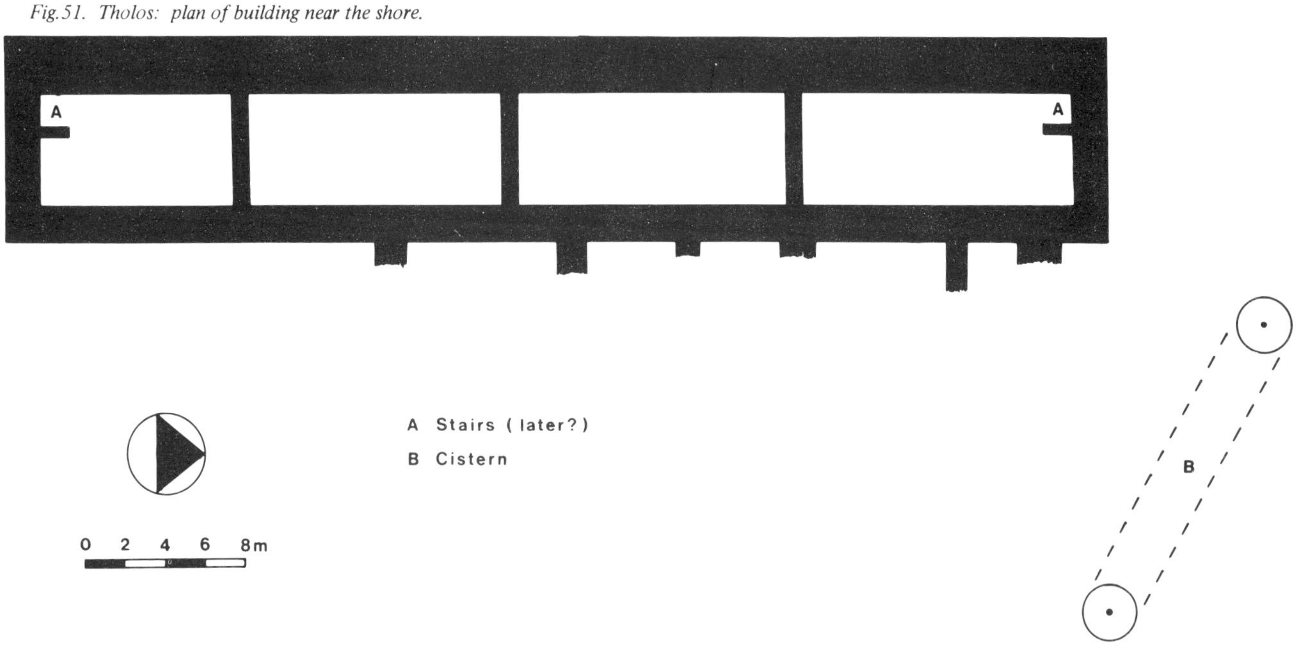

squared stones and on the interior with tiles, and stand up to 3.0m high. The floor is of cement incorporating crushed tile and sea pebbles. The interior is divided into four by partition walls, set at roughly equal distances. The west wall is far thicker, at 2.40m, than the eastern one at 1.63m; this latter wall is buttressed at ten points at slightly irregular intervals; the buttresses vary in thickness from 1.1 to 1.6m. In the SW and NW corners there are later additions and in the NW corner there are also signs of a staircase rising 1.50m. Finally there are no traces of any doorway surviving, although the SE corner is too ruined to be certain that there was none. Beyond the NE corner there is a cistern with two well heads 2.8m in diameter and 15.50m apart.

In the area Roman gems have been found, and there are late Greek/Roman lamps from Ay. Antonios. At Khoriodhakia a limekiln and a cistern with poor house foundations to the south of it are known, but the only direct dating evidence comes from two graves here which contained a coin of Gallienus. From Tholos itself there was a sherd of Eastern Sigillata B, of its earlier phase *c.*10 B.C. to *c.*A.D.75. There was also a quantity of early mediaeval glazed pottery.

Obviously none of this affords a secure date for the building itself, but its style of construction and the evidence from the 'villa' at Pakhyammos down the bay makes a date any earlier than *c.* A.D.100 very unlikely, but a 2/3c date is quite possible. Its function must also remain uncertain, but it seems to have been the basement of a massively built structure, possible some sort of warehouse on this sheltered bay.

1. H.A.Boyd, 'Excavations at Kavousi, Crete', *AJA* V, 1901, p.155f. Personal observations.

(2/19) PSEIRA On the top of this island Seager found what he describes as 'the remains of a Roman military camp, probably a beacon station', and above the Minoan site there were further Roman remains[1]. More recent work[2] has added some concrete 2m below present sea level, perhaps the remains of Roman harbour works. Amphorae fragments were also noted. The pattern of occupation here would seem very similar to that at Mochlos (1/1) with an earlier Roman civilian site succeeded by a military presence.

1. Seager, 'Excavations of the island of Pseira, Crete', *Trans. Penn. Univ.* III. 1, 1910, p.6-7.
2. Leatham and Hood, *ABSA* LIII-LIV, 1958-9, p. 277-8.

(2/20) KHARAKAS Stones and sherds, including Roman material, were found[1] on a little hill on the south side of the old main road between Ierapetra and Myrtos, just west of the stream running down the valley to the plain of Trouli.

1. Hood, *ABSA* LIX, 1964, p.96.

EPARCHY 3 - MIRABELLO

(3/1) MILATOS The main visible remains of the site are on the coast to the west of the present settlement, in the area of a short modern quay. Here there are stretches of concrete walling of good quality, utilising tiles; no facing survives. A little way inland a heap of stone work had been cleared from a field; this included several pieces with ¾ round moulding[1]. On the shore the pottery included a probable piece of ARSW, but inland there was more Hellenistic black glazed ware. Other reported finds from this area of what are presumably houses include an erotic lamp and what is described as Terra Sigillata[2]. From this evidence it would seem unlikely that the destruction of this site, probably in the 2c B.C., mentioned by Strabo, had any long term effect except in the political status of the city.[3]

1. Personal observation.
2. *Kret. Khron.* XXIII, 1971, p.498.
3. Strabo X.4.14 and *IC.* I.XXI. Praef.

(3/2) VRACHASI Below the village at Stavromenos two rectangular rock cut graves were discovered when a water pipe was being laid. Each grave held a skeleton with a bronze (unidentified) coin by the head. Other grave goods included a bronze stud and some sherds, including a fragment of what was identified as 1c Samian[1].

1. *A.Delt.* XX.3, 1965, p.565.

(3/3) ORNIAS Sherds seen by Pendlebury in 1937[1].

1. *AC* p.373.

(3/4) SKHINIAS Sherds on Koprana[1].

1. *AC* p.373.

(3/5) DORIES A tombstone dated to 3 or 4c coming from near the church of Ay. Constantinos may indicate a site here[1].

1. *IC.* IX.2.

(3/6) DREROS The occupation of this site seems to date mainly to the Hellenistic and earlier periods or the Byzantine B period[1]. However, a small group of nine Caligulan coins of the Knossos colony were found on the hill of Ay. Andonios, indicating a degree of activity here in the early 1c A.D.[2] A crude cross scratched onto the Hellenistic cistern in the Agora area ought probably to be associated with the definite 12c occupation in the area[3].

1. S. Marinatos, 'Le temple géometrique de Dreros', *BCH* LX, 1936, p.214f. P. Demargne and H. van Effenterre 'Recherches à Dreros', *BCH* LXI, 1937, p.5f. *IC.* I.IX.9.
2. The coins are of the types Svoronos Knossos 202-6, issued by Pulcher Varius as *IIvir.*
3. The evidence is a group of Comnenid coins. The cross was seen during thesis fieldwork.

(3/7) OLUS The site of the city of Olus stretches from the mainland, over the former isthmus, onto the peninsula beyond. The only building that has been excavated is the basilica[1], but the size of the site and the quantity of sherds of all periods reveals its importance[2]. The large number of inscriptions from the site and area, including dedications to Tiberius and the 4c restorer of the Governor's Palace at Gortyna, Oecumenius Dositheus Asclepiodotos, again reinforces the impression of the city's wealth. Apart from the basilica there are remnants of other buildings visible both on the peninsula and the mainland; on the latter, close to the sea, and approximately opposite the basilica, there are the remains of a large concrete structure covering an area *c.*26.0m x 22.0m with walls *c.* 1.0m wide. Without excavation it is impossible to determine its function or date within the Roman period. Apart from the material from the basilica the major finds are two statues of early Imperial date, one of a woman and one palliatus[3].

1. See p.91.
2. On the site in general, *IC.* I.XXII. The sherds included Çandarli, possibly Late Roman C Ware, ARSW Form 104B (Personal observat.).
3. Vermeule, *op. cit.* (2/8) note 1, p.443.

(3/8) KOLOKYTHIA On the opposite side of the peninsula from Olus there is a large site facing the island of Kolokythia. The basilica here has been cleared[1] but there is also a reasonably dense scatter of sherds both north and south of it. The only material visible was either Late Roman (LRC 3 and Cypriot RSW9?) or Minoan. However, Hellenistic material has also been reported[2].

Leading from this site over the saddle towards Olus are the remains of a road with a slight agger (Pl.63): it is 3.50m wide with an irregular paved surface with large edging stones. It would seem most likely to be Roman in date or possibly Hellenistic, given the nature of the two sites it linked. On the actual saddle there was a quantity of Roman pottery of indeterminate character, probably indicating a minor site here[3].

1. See p.92.
2. *AC. p.* 363 for the Hellenistic. Personal Observation.
3. Personal observation.

(3/9) ELLINIKA West of the present village is the site of a small Hellenistic temple dedicated to Aphrodite and Ares[1]. It was built at the end of the 2c B.C. after the frontier dispute with Olus had been settled. The temple comprises two chambers, each with its bench altar, but with no communicating door between them. Its total size is 12m square, and it is constructed of the local limestone. Beyond the temple is the hill of Mt. Oxa, where there was a site with defensive walls of uncertain date.

1. J. Bousquet 'Le Temple d'Aphrodite et d'Arès à sta Lenika', *BCH* LXII, 1938, p.386-408.

(3/10) LAKKONIA A 2/3c tombstone may indicate a site here[1].

1. K. Davaras, ' Ἐπιγραφαί ἐκ Κρήτης II', *A.Delt.* XVIII.I, 1963, p.158, no.13.

(3/11) PATARAKI METOCHI Here in the mountains above Kritsa there seems to have been a sanctuary to Pan, Watcher of the Woods, to whom in the 2/1 c B.C. Timon dedicated his promised statue. There were also sherds in the area[1].

1. *AC* p.376. *IC* I.XVI.7. *BCH* XXV, 1901, p.304.

(3/12) KAMARI At the chapel of Aphendi Christou at Ellinika a concrete wall and Roman coins were found. Although this site is high in the mountains in the area of Lato such material ought to be evidence of a villa rather than a minor farm or village[1].

1. *AC* p.375. *BCH* XXV, 1901, p.384.

(3/13) LATO The city of Lato is the most intensively excavated Greek site in Crete[1] with extensive remains of the Hellenistic period, especially the buildings of the Agora area. However, hardly any Roman material has been found apart from three early 4c coins reported in 1903[2].

1. *IC* I.XVI, including three tombstones of Roman date reused in Kritsa (no.8-10). For the site see now the new series of reports in *BCH* XCIII, 1969 onwards, 'Recherches à Lato 1-'.
2. *BCH* XXVII, 1903, p. 232.

(3/14) AY. NIKOLAOS This was the site of the other Lato 'pros Kamara'; it is possible that this refers not to any building with a vault but rather to the overhanging cliffs above the Lagoon which form the most memorable feature of the town. The ancient site seems to have been mainly SE of the Lagoon on the hill. There was obviously an important building on the corner of the roads Koundhourou and Sphakionake, where at 1.50m depth three walls were found and associated with this were a marble statue of a female in himation (date unknown), a limestone Corinthian capital, lamps of 1c B.C - A.D. 3c, loomweights and amphora fragments including Coan ones[1]. Further out of the town to the east on the Odos Lato tile graves of Roman date have been found[2]. From the site of the mill on the hill have come a lamp of 3/4c date and a LRC stamp of late 5c date[3]. There are numerous inscriptions[4] up to 3c, mainly sepulchral but including one dedication to Augustus.

1. *A.Delt.* XX.3, 1965, p.564, and *Kret.Khron.* XXI, 1969, p.534.
2. *PAE* 1971, p.301.
3. In the Museum: the stamp is Hayes' 41a or b.
4. *IC* I.XVI.15ff.

(3/15) PRINIATIKOS PIRGOS Above the Minoan site on this small peninsula jutting out into the Gulf of Mirabellou, there were walls and sherds of the Roman period[1].

1. E. Hall 'Excavations in eastern Crete, Vrokastro', *Trans. Penn. Univ.* III.3, 1914, p.84.

(3/16) NISI Between the above site and the next peninsula of Nisi there seems to have been a scatter of settlements on the coast, but only reaching any size on the peninsulae[1]. At Nisi the site stretches all over the peninsula and back onto the mainland, with the densest concentration of sherds on the southern slopes facing inland[2]. There would seem to be rather more Hellenistic material than Roman, including large numbers of coins of Olus.

1. *ABSA* XXXIII, 1932-3, p.95. *AC* p.365, 376.
2. Hall, *op. cit.* (3/15), p. 79. Personal observations.

(3/17) KALOKHORIO There was obviously an important site here, with a major building at Elliniko which had marble columns and coffered ceiling[1]. It is not known if this was Hellenistic or Roman. Pottery of the former period has been found here[2], while of the latter period an actual kiln has been excavated. This was of the updraft type, surviving up to 3.15m high, circular in shape, 4.0m in diameter, and built of tile and stone. The floor had 36 vents supported on 10 arches. The ware produced was described as typical grooved Roman, presumably meaning the common cooking pot ware. East of the kiln was a fragmentary second structure which may have been a drying oven[3]. One inscription is known from here, and also a lamp of Romanensis (of Cnidos, 2c in date)[4].

1. Boyd, *op.cit.* (2/12), p.13.
2. *Kret.Khron.* XIII, 1959, p.388.
3. *A.Delt.* XIX.2.3, 1964, p.440, and *AE* 1973, p.80, n.4. K. Davaras, 'Κεραμεικὴ κάμινος εἰς Ἴστρωνα ἀνατολικῆς Κρήτης', *A.Delt.* XXVIII.1, 1973, p.110.
4. *IC* I.XIV.5-6 under Istron.

(3/18) TAPIS Graves seen at Kamarais[1].

1. *AC* p.376.

EPARCHY 4 - LASITHI

The Lasithi Plain has recently been surveyed by L. V. Watrous, (see bibliography), in whose work more detail is available.

(4/1) KARPHI Hellenistic sherds seen at Ta Mnemata[1].

1. *AC* p.361. H.W. and J.D.S. Pendlebury and M.B.Money-Coutts, 'Excavations in the plain of Lasithi I: The cave of Trapeza', *ABSA* XXXVI, 1935-6, p.10, site 3b.

(4/2) TRAPEZA CAVE The deposits in the cave contained a certain amount of 'Byzantine' pottery[1]. Some Hellenistic sherds were also found.

1. *AC* p.361. Pendlebury and Money-Coutts, *op.cit.* (4/1), site 3f.

(4/3) PINAKIANO (2) This site is about the chapel of Ay. Georgios, above and west of the main road from Chersonisos[1]. Large amounts of pottery of indeterminate character, together with walls of rough stonework mark this site, which seems to be the largest on the plain.

1. Possibly site 2a in Pendlebury and Money-Coutts, *op.cit.* (4/1). Information also from L.V. Watrous.

(4/4) PINAKIANO (1) In the fields near the Vidhiani Monastery Roman sherds and glass have been found[1].

1. Pendlebury and Money-Coutts, *op.cit.* (4/1), site 1a.

(4/5) LAGOU At Kolonna 5 minutes east of the village, Hellenistic graves have been found and further east at Kerasa another tomb of the same period and nearby Roman remains[1].

1. Pendlebury and Money-Coutts, *op.cit.* (4/1), sites 2b and d.

(4/6) TZERMIADHA At Ponta or Ayia Anna 10 minutes SE of the village Hellenistic sherds and coins and Roman coins have been found[1].

1. Pendlebury and Money-Coutts, *op.cit.* (4/1), site 3i.

(4/7) TZERMIADHA At Megalos Potamos or Vounos 10 minutes south of of the village on the plain, Roman sherds[1].

1. Pendlebury and Money-Coutts, *op.cit.* (4/1), site 3k.

(4/8) KATHAROS Towards the east end of this extension of the main plain, Roman sherds were found near a spring[1].

1. Pendlebury and Money-Coutts, *op.cit.* (4/1), site 13a.

(4/9) KROUSTALLENIA In a road cutting by the Monastery here Roman remains were observed[1].

1. *EEKS* II, p.533. *ABSA* XLII, 1947, p.192.

(4/10) AY. KONSTANTINOS, KEPHALA On the NW side of the hill is a large site with Roman and Hellenistic sherds and coins[1].

1. Pendlebury and Money-Coutts, *op.cit.* (4/1), site 7b.

(4/11) AY. KONSTANTINOS, AVGOUSTE Large 'Byzantine' site. Possibly really part of the previous settlement[1].

1. Pendlebury and Money-Coutts, *op.cit.* (4/1), site 7c.

(4/12) AY. GEORGIOS At tou Vasilikou 15 minutes east of the village a Roman imperial coin and sherds were found[1].

1. Pendlebury and Money-Coutts, *op.cit.* (4/1), site 8a.

(4/13) XEROKAMBOS Roman site: no other details[1].

1. Information from L.V. Watrous.

(4/14) KAMINAKI Another reasonably large site appears to have been at Magatzedhais, where walls, an aqueduct and sherds are reported. Further sherds from Koutsounaria 5 minutes to the south are probably part of the same site[1].

1. Pendlebury and Money-Coutts, *op.cit.* (4/1), site 9b and a.

(4/15) PSYKRO 15 minutes north of the village, at Skallia and Stavri, Roman sherds and walls were found[1] and more recently a fragment of a sarcophagus[2].

1. Pendlebury and Money-Coutts, *op.cit.* (4/1), site 10b.
2. *Kret. Khron.* I, 1947, p. 637.

(4/16) PSYKRO-DICTAEAN CAVE A small amount of Roman material has come from this cave, but it is uncertain whether this represents Roman tourism or a continuation of the cult[1]. The material includes several lamps, a number of bronze objects and an iron ring with a green glass bezel[2].

1. Compare Apollonius of Tyana's visit to the Idaean cave as a religiously motivated tourist. Philostratus IV.34.
2. The material is collected in J. Boardman, *The Cretan Collection in Oxford* (1961). Also *IC* I.I.

Boardman p.36-7 no.161, Bronze Fibula, possibly Roman.

p.41 no. 194, Iron ring Intaglio of standing figure, possibly 1c A.D.
p.51 n.l. Heraklion Bronze Buckle, Heraklion Bronze Ear Scoops, Heraklion Silver Christian Cross, Heraklion Bronze Zoomorphic fibula.
p.52 no.226, Wickholder, Late Roman or Mediaeval,
p.52 no. 232, Bronze plaque,
no. 234, Two Hellenistic bronze coins of Aptera,
p.57 no. 247, Lamp fragment, 1-2c cf. *IC* I.I.1.
p.74 no. 360-1, Glass beads,
no.366, Glass beads,
no.369-70, Glass Beads.

(4/17) PLATI Roman site on the plain[1].
1. Information from L.V. Watrous.

(4/18) KATO METOKHI At Roussanos 10 minutes SE of the village, Roman sherds[1].
1. Pendlebury and Money-Coutts, *op.cit.* (4/1), site 12.

EPARCHY 5 - BIANNOS

(5/1) KHONDROS The main site here, or at least its cemetery, was at Arkalies or Ampeliou Poros, where a number of early Christian tombs have been excavated[1]. These were typical simple graves cut into earth and covered with slabs of rock: the grave goods were few, including an ampulla with a cross (unfortunately not illustrated), a bronze buckle, earrings and some small pots. Further down towards the sea a jug of what was claimed to be Roman date was found[2]. However, the most interesting site is on Roukouni Korfi, where a building (Fig.52), probably of Hellenistic date, was excavated[3]; this was a circular structure

Fig.52. Khondros: plan of building.

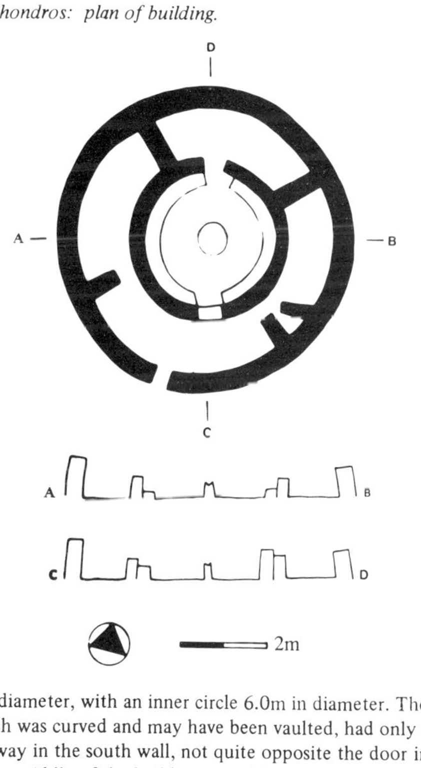

12.0m in diameter, with an inner circle 6.0m in diameter. The outer wall, which was curved and may have been vaulted, had only one narrow doorway in the south wall, not quite opposite the door in the inner wall. In the middle of the building, possibly open to the sky, was a fireplace, and beyond this another door leading into a chamber between the two circuits and cut off from the remainder of this space by cross walls linking the two walls. It is possible that this was some sort of watch tower, although its position here makes it difficult to connect to any major centre. Alternatively, it was a well built shepherd's bothie.

1. *Kret.Khron.* X, 1956, p.417.
2. *A. Delt.* XX.3, 1965, p.556.
3. *A. Delt.* XV.1, 1960, p.258. *Kret Khron.* XIV, 1960, p.512, *AR* 1960-1, p.24, fig. 25.

(5/2) BIANNOS Very little is known of the ancient city here, but sherds of Classical to Roman date have been found, especially to the NW of the present village[1]. Roman and Byzantine coins are also known and there is evidence for a church from the 6/7c tombstone of Anastasios the underdeacon[2].
1. *AC*, p.374; M.S.F.Hood, 'Travels in Crete', *ABSA* LIX, 1964, p.83, no.35. 2. Coins Le Rider p.233, Inscriptions *IC*.I.VI.
2. Coins Le Rider p.233, Inscriptions *IC*.I.VI.

(5/3) LIGARAS Small Roman site near the church of the Panayia, 150m south of the road from Viannos to Arvi, 2.9 km south of Viannos[1].
1. Hood, *op.cit.*, p.83, site 36(2).

(5/4) KERATON Although Roman sherds have been found on the summit of the mountain[1] the fortifications here would seem rather to be early Mediaeval from the type of construction[2]. From the summit the view in every direction is superb, making the site ideal as a vantage position. Below the summit there is an extensive spread of pottery of very indeterminate character, probably Mediaeval.
1. *AC* p.374. Hood, *op.cit*, p.84, site 37. Boardman, *op.cit* (4/16) note 2, p.100, n.469.
2. On the defences, *Mon. Ven.* I p.81-2. Personal observation as to their date. I assign them to the later period particularly because the cisterns are not of the normal Roman type but much rougher, with a stone and mortar vault rather than concrete.

(5/5) TROKHALOI On the plain where the Viannos-Arvi road reaches the sea there are the remains of a Roman concrete building and sherds[1]. Presumably this is the site of a villa farming the rich coastal plain.
1. Hood, *op.cit.*, p.84, site 38. *AC* p.380.

(5/6) PEFKOS Two Hellenistic coins from here may indicate a site[1].
1. *AC* p.363.

(5/7) AMIRAS A group of small Roman sites are located on the fertile land on the slopes of the valley leading down to Arvi[1]. There is a scatter of sherds south of 'Khori' (D on Fig.17, *ABSA* 59), a more substantial site north of this (E and F) with a fragment of Arretine, CRES TI in *planta pedis* (AD 20-40), and about ½km to the east on the hill Arkalokefalo a possible shrine (G and H), and finally another occupation site to the south of the last hill on Korifi Lepreas (J).
1. Hood, *op.cit.*, p.86, site 40.

(5/8) ARVI The main site here appears to be below the modern settlement and extending somewhat further inland[1]. Little can be seen but there is a tradition that the church of the Panayia is on the site of an earlier building; concrete foundations were visible at about 1.0m depth, exposed by modern construction. The cemetery area was to the east, with graves of late date known[2] as well as fine sarcophagi of the 2c and 3c[3]. The only partially visible structure is in this area, being the basilica at Ay. Irene, dating to the early-mid 6c[4]. As at Knossos, this church might well be on the site of the earlier Christian cemetery.
1. *IC* I.IV. Hood, *op.cit.*, p.89, site 42. Personal observations.
2. *Kret.Khron.* X, 1956, p.421, *ibid.* XVII, 1963, p.399.
3. See p.47. Both in Fitzwilliam Museum, Cambridge (Pl. 10).
4. See p.95.

(5/9) KATO SIMI This shrine to Hermes and Aphrodite, high up in the mountains, is extremely important, as here there really does seem to be a continuation of the cult from MMIII to the 3c A.D.[1] In the late Hellenistic and Roman period the shrine is quite small, being a rectangular building 2.65m x 2.85m, but with walls surviving up to 2.0m high. It was entered through the south wall, while opposite, against the north wall, was an altar-bench 1.10m high. Surrounding the building on its eastern and southern sides was a wide wall, of which only the foundations survived. The date of the building is given by a coin of Lyttus sealed by the floor, 2/1c B.C., and a reused inscription of 2c B.C. Lamps of 1-3c A.D., together with the 3c A.D. dedication to Hermes tell of the shrine's continuation up to the Christian period.
1. *PAE* 1973, no.19, p.188, A. Lembesis with all references to her earlier preliminary reports. The coin, of Lyttus, is Svoronos 133.

(5/10) KALAMI About 1km south of the village on a shoulder above the gorge, sherds and stones of walls, possibly Roman[1].
1. Hood, *op.cit.*, p.93, site 43 (1).

(5/11) KATALAGARI (site not located within eparchy) A figurine, apparently of Roman date, was found here[1].

1. *A.Delt.* XX.3, 1965, p.556.

(5/12) NESI/MESI From Nesi[1] Hellenistic and Roman coins are recorded as well as terracotta fragments of a gorgon head and bucrania. This place cannot be located within the eparchy but may be the same as Mesi, where a Hellenistic house is recorded[2].

1. *A.Delt.* XXII. 2, 1967, p.488.
2. *Kret. Khron.* XXV, 1973, p.475.

EPARCHY 6 - PEDHIADHA

(6/1) KALLITHEA In the cave here claimed[1] to be a shrine of Eileithyia Roman material has been identified.

1. Faure, *BCH* XCI, 1967, p.133.

(6/3) KATO VATHEIA At Sochera a Roman lamp and small ribbed jar were found[1].

1. *Kret.Khron.* XIX, 1965, p.291.

(6/4) GOURNES Roman tile graves[1].

1. *Kret.Khron.* II, 1948, p.531.

(6/5) SKOTEINO In the cave here a 2c erotic lamp, together with some other pottery, was found[1]. The identification of this cave as the Labyrinth seems highly fanciful, even given the impressive setting and stalactites[2].

1. *A.Delt.* XVIII.2, 1963, p.312. *Kret.Khron.* XVII, 1963, p.398.
2. Faure theory, *Kret. Khron.* XVII, 1963, p.315.

(6/6) AGRIANA Tile graves containing some glass and lamps were destroyed by roadworks here[1].

1. *A.Delt.* IX, 1924-5, par.13.

(6/7) CHERSONISOS (Fig.53) Although the present village of this name lies a short distance inland, there is no doubt that the ancient city of Chersonisos lies below and about Limani Chersonisou. As befits the name the most important remains are those of the harbour[1] (Pl. 64); this is formed by the headland Kastri to the north and a series of three moles on the eastern and southern sides, forming a well-sheltered anchorage 270 x 150m in size. The east side of the harbour is formed by mole A, which runs from the headland south for about 150m before meeting a short east-west mole (B) *c.* 30.0m long. The final mole (C), 2.60m wide, forms the southern edge of the harbour about 80m beyond mole B. Moles A and B are between 5.20m and 5.30m wide, built of concrete with a facing of small squared stones. Their original top surface is only preserved on parts of A, where rectangular stone bollards can be discerned. In the inner face of A there are also rectangular recesses, probably for protective timbers to prevent ships damaging themselves against the mole. Beyond the moles there are breakwaters of large rough boulders and it is possible that these may be earlier than the moles, since there is a slight difference in alignment; they may be related to Classical or Hellenistic harbour works, of which there are traces to the south of C.

Fig.53. Chersonisos: plan of the area of the ancient city.

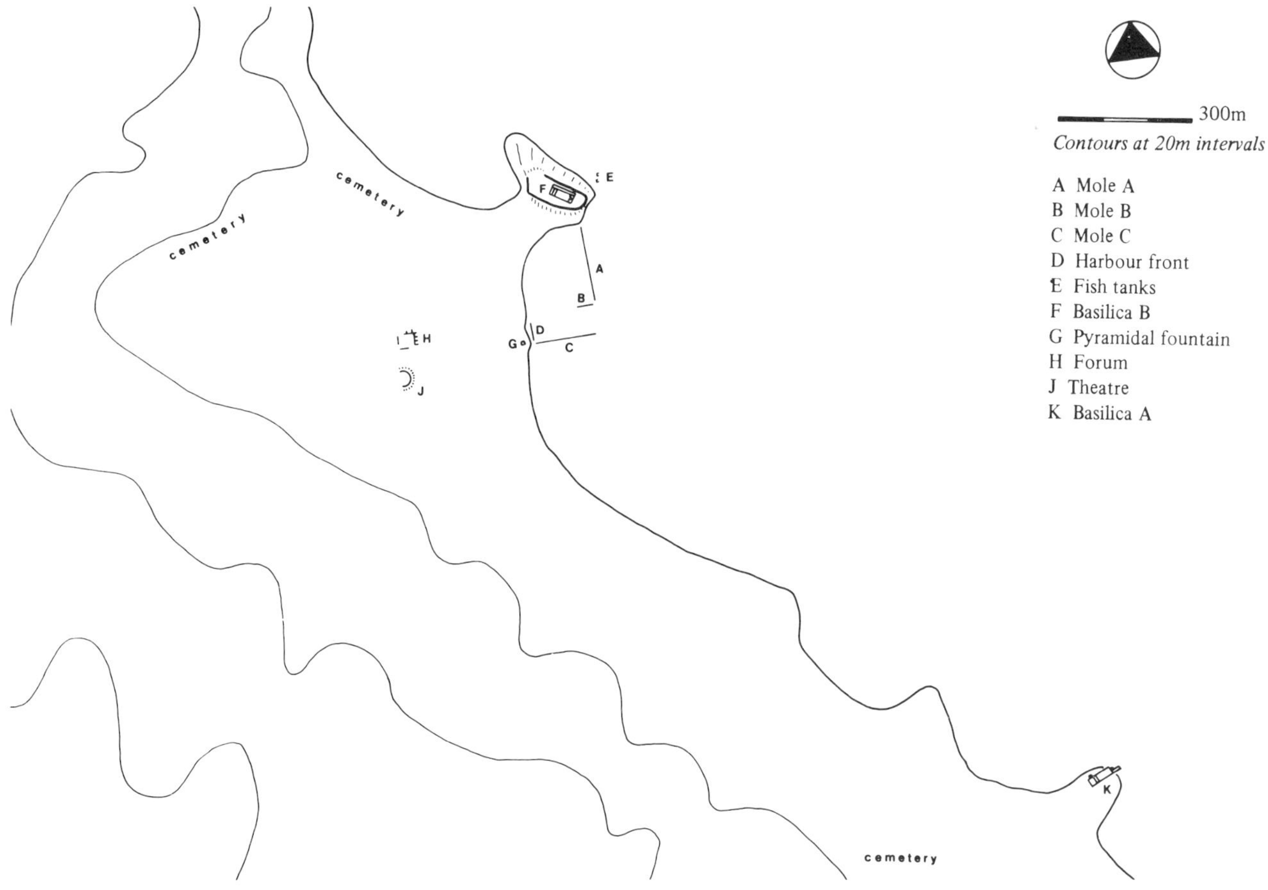

(6/2) AMNISSOS Above the Minoan levels and reusing the walls a temple was built in the Archaic period dedicated to Zeus Thenatas[1]. This shrine continued in use into the Roman period and by the Hadrianic period the worshop of Sarapis had become part of the cult[2]. Apart from these gods Eileithyia was also worshipped[3], possibly in the temple but definitely in the cave a little way up the hillside where material, mainly lamps, up to the late Roman, i.e. Christian, period was found[3].

1. *PAE* 1933, p.93f. Willetts. *Cretan Cults and Festivals* (London 1962), p.249.
2. *PAE* 1934, p.132.
3. *IC.* I.II. Praef. for all the literary evidence. *PAE* 1929, p.95, for the lamps, etc.

Pl. 63: Road between Kolokythia and Olus, running east.
Pl. 64: Harbour front and mole C (below water) at Chersonisos. The Nora Hotel, the long building further down the coast, marks the site of Basilica A.
Pl. 65: Capital in a garden at Chersonisos.

The harbour is completed by quays on the land side (west) which run for about 30 m north from C. The *Stadiasmus Maris Magni* mentions that there was a tower here, and it is possible that there was a lighthouse at the junction of the moles A and B[2]. At present the top of the moles are awash, and it would seem from this, combined with the evidence of the fish tanks (see below), that the Roman sea level was about 1m lower than the present level.
The headland forming the northern side of the harbour was occupied from the Minoan period, but the earliest known Roman activity is a series of fish tanks on the SE corner. There are three tanks, at present 1.95m to 2.20m below sea level (floor depths), and varying in size between 4 x 3m and 2 x 1.25m. They are connected to the sea by a series of channels, allowing a constant flow of fresh sea water into the tanks. There are traces of concrete walls between the tanks and on the edges of the complex which suggests both that the sides of the tanks were raised above the cut rock and also that there may have been some form of roofing, essential to prevent too great evaporation, particularly in the summer.
On the top of the Kastri are the remains of the large Basilica B[3], dating to the early part of the 6c, which may have replaced a temple here. There are no architectural remains of this temple, but there is an inscription recording the gift of 500 dr. to the most sacred treasury. The most famous temple of the city was that of Britomartis[4], but the inscription dedicated to her came from the other basilica, 1km to the east of the Kastri site, well outside the area of the city. However, there was no other definite evidence for a temple found at this site either, and a comparatively small inscription can be moved. Overall, it seems more likely that the temple of Britomartis was on the Kastri, dominating the city and acting as a mark for sailors in exactly the same setting as the Temple of Diktynna at her shrine beyond Cydonia. Finally on Kastri, there is a wall of concrete with stone facing that follows the edge of the 'acropolis'. There is no dating evidence for it, but it would seem likely to be part of the system of fortifications probably dating to the 7c[5].
The main area of the city lies south and west of the harbour area, possibly stretching round the bay to the east as well. On the harbour front the remains of several buildings of concrete or stone can be seen exposed on the shore, but the only coherent structure is a square pyramidal fountain with mosaic sides. When this was restored it was found to be in the courtyard of a large building of unknown function[6]. The mosaic[7] probably dates to the 2c or 3c A.D. Further west behind the modern houses are remains of several very large concrete structures. About 200m beyond the shore is a building of concrete faced with stone and tile; an apse 1.50m thick can be made out and it is this feature that seems to have led to its identification as a basilica[8]. For the reasons given in the discussion cited it seems more likely to be some possibly public building of the 2/3c. NW of this is an area *c.* 30 x 50m covered with a mass of tile faced concrete; it is immediately north of the theatre and might be part of the Forum or Agora that presumably existed here. All that can be made out of the plan is a corner with a series of walls coming off it as buttresses or possibly small rooms or shops. South of this is the theatre[9], 46.0m in diameter and presumably 2c in date.
The wealth of the city is also evident from the finds, particularly the statues: they include a life-sized one possibly of Julia Domna[10], several heads, one of which may be imperial[11], a statuette of Aphrodite[12] and from Basilica B comes a reused 2c Attic sarcophagus[13]. The latter is still on the site, as are several capitals: one 2c Pergamene-Ephesian type could be seen (1975) by a cafe on the harbour front, and another very fine late one (Pl.65) between the main village and Basilica A.
Apart from the Britomartis inscription there is no earlier material from the 6c Basilica A, but it is in this general area that one of the cemeteries of the city lay, with tombstones from the village of Koutouloupharі[14]. On the other side (west) of the city a cemetery is known from the site of the Creta Maris Hotel, round the bay NW from the Kastri[15].
The Aqueduct Although the city has such a good harbour, its development may have been limited until the Roman period because of a lack of water[16]. There can be no doubt that this was rectified by the aqueduct built at an unknown date ? 1-2c. The actual source tapped is uncertain: Belli[17] thought it was part of the same system that supplied Lyttus, but it is more likely that it made use of the spring at Ay. Panteleimon (Piyi) (6/24) as Spanake suggests[18]. However, nothing appears to survive until the aqueduct crosses the present-day road from the coast to Kastelli 5km (by road) north of Piyi. Here the aqueduct coming north is on the west side of the road, which has actually destroyed what must have been a *caput aquae,* 7.50m x ?(destroyed); the aqueduct then crosses the stream/gorge (Pl.66) and continues down to the coast on the east side of the gorge. The height of the arch as surviving is about 12.0m, and this is about a further 7.0m below the level of the *caput.* The aqueduct in the gorge is 3.0m wide, constructed of stone-faced concrete with levelling courses of large masonry dividing the arch into 5 blocks. The central part of the 4 upper blocks, from which the actual arch sprang, are not stone but tile-faced. The present-day gap between the surviving sides is about 15m.
The aqueduct then continues along the hillside with no major arches visible until it reaches the valley of Potamies at Xerokamares. At this point (just a short distance after the Lassithi road leaves the road to Kastelli) the gorge is about 60m deep; the number of arches needed to cross this gap can no longer be definitely ascertained, but there were at least six. The major piers are 8.0m wide at their base, narrowing down to a mere 1.0m where the aqueduct rejoins the hillside. The tallest pier still stands about 25m high. The length of the aqueduct over the ground is not known, but from its first major visible remains to Chersonisos is 10km on the map 'as the crow flies'.

1. In general *IC.*I.VII. For the harbour and fish tanks, J. Leatham and M.S.F. Hood, 'Sub-Marine Exploration in Crete, 1955', *ABSA* LII-LIV, 1958-9, p.266ff.
2. 349 'it has water and both an island with a tower and a harbour'.
3. See p.99.
4. Strabo X.479.14. The inscription *IC.*I.VII.4 and Sp. Marinatos, ' Ἐπιγραφὴ εἰς Βριτόμαρτιν ἐκ Χερσονήσου', *A.Delt.* IX, 1924-5, p.79.
5. See p.133.
6. *Kret. Khron.* X, 1956, p.419.
7. See p.51.
8. See p.101.
9. Personal observation for the Forum and see p. 59 for the theatre.
10. On display in Heraklion Museum no.334.
11. *Kret. Khron.* XII, 1958, p.479.
12. *Kret. Khron.* XXII, 1970, p.518.
13. See p.47 for the sarcophagus. Personal observation for the capitals.
14. *IC.*I.VII.6, 15, 18, 23.
15. *Ergon.* 1974, p.121.
16. Spanake, *Crete: a guide* I, p.196. This, however, clashes with the account in *Stad.* 349 (*op.cit.* n.2) where water is specifically mentioned. Possibly the shortage of water was not acute until more modern times or possibly that part of *Stad.* was written after the aqueduct was in use, although I believe that much of that guide is Hellenistic in origin.
17. Belli ed. Falkener, p.16.
18. Belli ed. Spanake, p.161. The details of the aqueduct are from personal observation at both sites.

(6/8) PISKOPIANO Apart from one inscription which may well have come from nearby Chersonisos, the only evidence for a site is the basilica below the present church[1].

1. See p.101 for the basilica; the inscription is *IC.*I.VII.16, 1c B.C.

(6/9) DIA, ISLAND OF There appear to be two main sites on the island of Roman date: the first is round the bay at the SW corner of the island[1], where Graeco-Roman sherds are reported, and slightly NE of this, where late Roman pottery has been identified, including LRC 3 E. The second site is on top of the island, where the pottery included ARSW 106.

1. Information from M.S.F.Hood. Also *AC* p.361 and 372; *AC* 's Ay. Pelagia is not marked on the maps but if it corresponds with the Panayia on the British Military map there is a third site here.

(6/10) EPISKOPI West of Episkopi at Alonaki Roman house foundations were found: one house had three large pithoi sunk into the floor, together with a vat[1]. The rock-cut graves on the Kephala are probably post-Arab.

1. *Kret.Khron.* VI, 1951, p.474f.

(6/11) GALYPHA Graeco-Roman pottery from here recorded in the Heraklion Museum[1].

1. *AC.* p.363.

(6/12) KOUNAVOI Between here and Zagourianoi various remains have been found of the city of Eltynaia[1]. The main site was at Kenderi or Ellinika, where house foundations have been uncovered. At the turning out of Kounavoi to Zagourianoi there was a small Doric temple at which the inscription naming the site was found. Near here were graves constructed of tiles with stone slab coverings, which might have been Roman, although all the other material mentioned seems to have been Classical-Hellenistic in date. The only other later material from the area is a number of Byzantine coins.[2]

1. *IC* I.X. *A.Delt.* IV, 1918, par.24. *Kret.Khron.* II, 1948, p.537; X, 1956, p.418.
2. Le Rider, p.232.

(6/13) ANISARA On the coastal plain east of the River Aposelemi before Chersonisos a Roman building, possibly a farm, was found during road works[1]. A large pithos was found set in the floor of the building.

1. *Kret.Khron.* XXV, 1973, p.463.

(6/14) KOMES Graeco-Roman deposit[1].

1. *AC* p.384.

(6/15) AY. PARASKIES A fragment of pithos with ']ρικου' was found here; from its form it probably dates to the 4c[1].

1. *Kret.Khron.* XXI, 1969, p.540. Illustrated *PAE* 1968, pl. 165a. Parallel forms *Athenian Agora* V, pl.28-9, M235, 272.

(6/16) ASTRITSI Hellenistic sherds and a 3c B.C. figurine have been found here[1].

1. *AC* p.361. Figurine, *Kret.Khron.* XVIII, 1964, p.284.

(6/17) SABA Hellenistic and 'Graeco-Roman' vases are recorded from this site, and a probable cemetery at Ellinika[1].

1. *AC* p.361, 364, and Mariani, *Mon.Ant.* VI, 1895, p.237.

(6/18) THRAPSANOS Byzantine material, including lamps, have been found here and also a silver ring.[1]

1. *EEKS* IV, p.273 and *AC* p.373; the ring is no.442 in the Heraklion Museum.

(6/19) VIGLA Near Stalis west of Mallia and south of the chapel of Ay. Ioannes Chrysostom, three parallel graves were excavated. Two were lined and covered with stone slabs and contained an individual with grave goods. The third tomb, although its two sides were lined with stone, was covered with tiles, and the two bodies were contained by tiles. The pottery was probably of 1-2c date[1].

1. *A.Delt.* XXI.2, 1966, p.407, pl.436 g-d.

(6/20) MALLIA On the western edge of the Minoan site there is an extensive Roman settlement, perhaps a large villa or wealthy village[1]. There are various concrete walls scattered over several hundred metres from the present shore inland to the site of the basilica. The basilica itself is built on top of a 4c structure of unknown extent, which included the 2c Attic sarcophagus[2] reused possibly as some sort of martyrion. Other 2c/3c material has been found in the area[3] and it is likely that it is to this century that the concrete buildings should be assigned. In the immediate area of the basilica, there are various walls west and north of the church which unfortunately do not make any coherent plan. Due north of the same spot, right by the sea shore, there are obvious rooms, while to the west at Klozani a tile-lined cistern, 1.70m x 2.05m x 1.50m deep, was excavated[4] together with an associated room. East of the basilica on the edge of the higher ground above the marshes there stands 2.70m high the remains of a bath house[5]. All that is left is a rectangular building built up against the natural rock, it is 5.0m wide and at least 10.0m long, with a heavy *opus signinum* floor above a space that may have acted as a cistern. A drain passes through the outer wall from the bath - i.e. the area of the floor - and is continued by a channel on the outside of the wall.

1. For the basilica see p.101-2. The earlier material is very briefly reported in *BCH* LXXXII, 1958, p.829 – tile graves above House Theta. *BCH* LXXXIX, 1965, p.1005 for the cistern. *Etudes Crétoises* XIX, p.18, with the overall plan; the Roman settlement is in the area C-F 1-2.
2. See p.47.
3. *BCH* LXXXIX, 1965, p.1005.
4. *IC* I.VII.31, 2c tombstone. Various coins in Heraklion Museum, no.1992 (Decius), 1993 (Salonina).
5. Personal observations.

(6/21) MOCHOS Hellenistic and Roman sherds are recorded from the area at Mouri and Kalimniokhori[1]. There is also a tombstone, possibly 3c, and a dedication to Trajan[2]. It would seem unlikely that the latter really comes from what must have been only a small site: it is more likely that it was brought up from Chersonisos.

1. *AC* p.361, 363, 373. 2. *IC* I.VII.29, 30.

(6/22) POTAMIES Remains from Khalikias in Heraklion Museum[1].

1. *AC* p.373, Catalogue 8990-2. *IC* I.XVIII. 187. An inscribed clay base.

(6/23) AVDHOU The mosaics of a probable Christian basilica were discovered here[1].

1. See p.104. *Kret. Khron.* X, 1956, p.419.

(6/24) PIYI Built into the early mediaeval church of Ay. Panteleimon are numerous fragments of its early Christian predecessor[1] and a number of inscriptions of Hellenistic and early Roman date. These inscriptions, together with one reused Corinthian capital of Imperial date, make the possibility of an earlier sanctuary likely[2].

1. See p.104.
2. *IC*.I.XVIII.77.80.90.125.130. The capital is reused with the other later capitals described p.104.

(6/25) LYTTUS (Fig.54) The site of ancient Lyttus is awkwardly placed on a ridge of hills jutting out from the Lassithi massif, overlooking the Pedhiadha plain. It is this relationship to the plain that must have been the reason why the site was originally chosen. No large-scale excavation has ever been conducted here, and so our knowledge of the site is very fragmentary, based on chance finds and two small excavations[1].

The centre of the ancient city seems to have lain in the area of the present church of Timios Stavros; it was here that a number of inscriptions dedicated to the Emperor were found. Close by are the remains of a sizeable building constructed of stone-faced cement, 14.0m wide and 16.50m at least in length[2]. The church of Timios Stavros stands on the site of a large basilica of late 5c date and further down the ridge there may be a second basilica at the present chapel of Ay.Georgios[3]. There is definitely a major 2c building here with painted wall plaster, but the excavator's suggestion of an altar on the grounds of the quantity of ash about seems a little far-fetched. At the other end of the site, on the SE slopes overlooking the plain, is possibly the site of the theatre[4] which in its final form may date to the mid 1c A.D. Further up the slope here, just below the top, stands a cistern, 4.0m high, constructed of tile-faced concrete with walls *c.* 1.0m wide and measuring 12.0m x 7.0m with four buttresses on the side facing down the slope. Presumably it was supplied from the aqueduct (see below). The comparatively small area at the top of the site stretching from just north of Timios Stavros to a little way down (south) from Ay.Georgios is enclosed by a massive wall constructed of a rubbly concrete with quite good squared stone facing. It is at least 1.0m thick and survives up to 2-3m in height as viewed from the exterior; internally it barely reaches above the present ground level[5]. There are no definite towers standing out from the wall, but as it follows the contours of the top of the hill at the angles there are towers on bastions of irregular design. Some are semicircular, up to 7.0m in diameter (Pl.67), but others are concave or concave with a following triangular projection. The design and style of this circuit is very similar to the defences on the Acropolis at Gortyna[6] and it would seem likely that the defences here at Lyttus also date to the 7c.

However, the importance and wealth of the city is better illustrated from the large number of inscriptions found, mainly by chance, and in particular the series of imperial dedications to Trajan and Hadrian with their families[7]. These come from the statues dedicated by the new chief magistrate each September: over thirty bases are known, but only one statue, a bust of Trajan[8]. The wealth of the site is also illustrated from its cemetery, which was below the site to the south in the area of the modern village of Xydas; one tomb here[9] contained goldleaf and an intaglio of the Emperor with a lance.

The aqueduct[10] About 1km SE of the city are the massive remains of its aqueduct at the aptly named village of Teichos. The aqueduct here leaves the flank of the Lassithi massif and crosses a narrow valley east of the village; at the point where it springs from the mountain side it is 4.60m wide; it then continues straight for Lyttus to the NW. At no point here is the actual channel preserved, but the average width is 2.40m and it stands up to 10.0m high. The source appears to be 10 km away (direct map distance from Teichos) in the Krasi/Kera area at the head of the Potamies valley: fragments of an aqueduct were found at Kera, where its channel was 0.40m wide, and at Krasi, where the channel was 0.35m on top of a supporting 6.0m high wall against the mountain side.

1. In general *IC*.I.XVIII. Agora area, *Kret. Khron.* VII, 1953, p.490.

Pl. 66: Aqueduct to Chersonisos crossing the valley 5 km north of Piyi.
Pl. 67: Exterior facing and core of the defensive wall at Lyttos, northwest corner.

The 'Altar', *Kret. Khron.* XXV, 1973, p.475. *A. Delt.* XXVI. 2.2, 1971, p.493f.

2. Agora area report (very brief note) and personal observation.
3. See p.104.
4. See p.61. The cistern - personal observation.
5. *Mon. Ven.* I, p.72, and personal observations.
6. See p.71.
7. *IC.* I.XVIII, 15-50 and Vermeule, *op.cit.* (2/8) note 1, p.443.
8. *Kret. Khron.* IV, 1950, p.534, *AJA* LXI, 1957, p.250, group A no.5.
9. *Kret. Khron.* VI, 1952, p.480, and *Kret. Khron.* XIII, 1959, p.386.
10. Belli ed. Spanake, p.161. L. Mariani, *Mon.Ant.* IX, 1898, p.406. Personal observations.

1. *AR* 1957, p.17.

(6/30) ARMACHA A 1c A.D. tombstone dedicated by Helen to her husband Sotas was found here: its interest lies in the three objects engraved on it – there are an axe, sickle and a third object that has been interpreted as a suspended cauldron on a stand. However, the other two objects are both agricultural implements and so this third one logically ought to be one as well. Possibly it is in fact a representation of a donkey mill. The very existence of this fine tombstone implies that the deceased was not just a 'mere peasant' and so his owning such a mill is far from impossible[1].

1. P. Ducrey, 'Trois nouvelles inscriptions crétoises', *BCH* XCIII 1969, p.843. Parts of such a mill have been found at Knossos built into the Roman building above the Unexplored Mansion.

Fig.54. Lyttos: plan of the area of the ancient city.

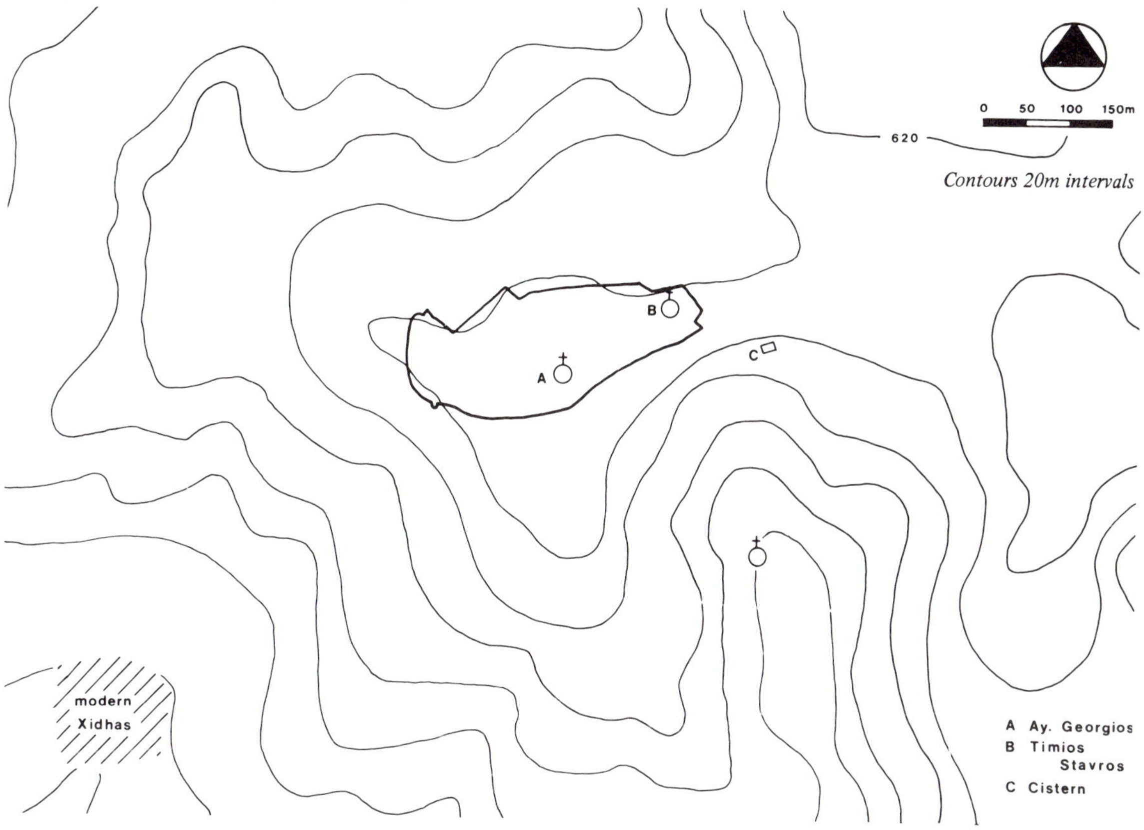

(6/26) KASTELLI PEDHIADHOS Part of a cemetery of tile graves covered with stone slabs was found here at Kera[1]; they presumably are of early Roman date. Also in the cave of Aphendi Christos Roman sherds have been claimed to be found[2]. Finally, in the Historical Museum in Heraklion there is a coin of Heraclius whose find spot is given as Kastelli[3]. The last object could of course have come from Lyttus, as could the various inscriptions of early Roman date reused in the village[4].

1. *EEKS* I, p.616 (*AC* p.384).
2. Faure, *BCH* XCI, 1967, p.133.
3. No.381.
4. *IC.* I.XVIII, passim.

(6/27) MOUKTARO At Panayia a Roman lamp with a cupid on the disc[1].

1. *Kret.Khron.* XIV, 1960, p.525.

(6/28) LILIANA A Roman tombstone to Aphrodisios was found here[1]; as was a denarius of Hadrian[2]. 2km to the east in the cave '*τοῦ Γαρέφαλλου*' a 3c B.C. unguentarium and fragments of 1/2c lamps were found[3].

1. *Kret.Khron.* VII, 1953, p.515. Perhaps the man did come from Aphrodisias.
2. Heraklion Museum Catalogue no. 1651.
3. A. Kanta, '*τὸ σπήλαιο τοῦ Λιλιανοῦ*', *Kret.Khron.* XXIII, 1971, p.425.

(6/29) KATALIMMATA A Roman farmhouse with a so-called wine press above a Minoan site, and so ill-recorded[1].

(6/31) RUSSOCHORIA At Stavromenos tombstones of 2-4c date have been found[1].

1. *IC.* I.V.51. *A.Delt.* XXV.2.2, 1970, p.460. Both mention Cossutii, possibly a local family.

(6/32) NIPITIDOS A group of 1-3c tombstones comes from this village[1].

1. *IC.* I.V.47-50.

(6/33) AVLI A solidus of Justinian II (685-695 1st reign) is recorded from here[1].

1. Heraklion Historical Museum, no.1228.

(6/34) KASSANI There are two 2-4c tombstones from here[1]; the second is of interest as being of a probable Jew, Iudas aged one.

1. *IC.* I.V.16, 17.

(6/35) PANAYIA Apart from the possible basilica[1] there is a 2c tombstone built into the church.

1. See p.104 for the basilica. *IC.* IV.18 for the tombstone.

(6/36) AFRATI There are a number of inscriptions from this site[1], mainly from closer to the modern village than the Geometric city. Most of them are dedications to Artemis, whose small shrine was excavated here; they include a dedication to Fortuna on behalf of Trajan of a heifer. A Gnostic gem was also found here.

1. *IC.* I.V.2 etc. D. Levi 'Arkades', *Ann.Sc.At.* X-XII, 1927-9, p.27-8.

(6/37) EMBAROS Roman and earlier material is recorded from about the ruined chapel of Ay. Petros to the SW of the village[1]. There are tombstones engraved with agricultural implements and animals from the village[2].

1. *AC* p.363, 372 from Halbherr, *AJA* 2nd series, V, 1901, p.281. Personal observation did not reveal any sherds that were particularly helpful in dating the site here. The chapel may be on the site of an earlier building.
2. *IC* I.V.11-13.

(6/38) KARAVDOS There is a 2/3c tombstone from here and a 'boundary stone' is also recorded[1].

1. *IC* I.V.15 for the tombstone. *AC* p.372 for the other.

(6/39) XENIAKOS A 3/4c tombstone is reused in the church; it may well have come from nearby Embaros originally[1].

1. *IC* I.V.14.

(6/40) MILIARDO A number of Roman coins and a conical weight of spotted stone were found here[1].

1. *Kret.Khron.* XIII, 1959, p.386.

EPARCHY 7 - MONOFATSI

(7/1) PARTHENI A deposit of Hellenistic and Roman sherds by the road[1].

1. *AC* p.373, as *ABSA* XXXIII, 1932-3, p.84.

(7/2) AY. THOMAS This site is basically below the modern village, which, situated on its hill, overlooks the northern plain and controls the pass from there over to the Mesara, like Prinias on the other side of the pass. Unlike that site, however, there seems to have been a sizeable Roman settlement here, with some remains visible at the northern end of the village on the rock where the modern cemetery is to be found[1]. Various tombs are also known from here associated with a cave dedicated to Demeter and Kore[2].

1. Spratt II, p.56f, *AC* p.364, 374. The latest evidence from the site is a coin of Gallienus (Le Rider, *op.cit.* p.233).
2. *Arch. Anz.* 1933, p.314. *Kret. Khron.* XXI, 1969, p.317. *IC*.I. XXXI, 2-3 for the dedication. Also in Faure, *BCH* XCI, 1967, p.133.

(7/3) MEGALE VRYSE Cement foundations of a Roman building were found here[1].

1. *BCH* LXXXV, 1960, p.833.

(7/4) LOUTRA Cisterns and an aqueduct were seen here in 1916[1]; it may possibly be the same site as the above.

1. *Arch.Anz.* 1916, p.156; *AC* p.374.

(7/5) MELIDOCHORI On the heights of Kasteriotes above the modern village of Melidochori are the remains of a large city, seemingly mainly of Classical and Hellenistic date[1]. Spratt roughly surveyed the fortifications here which seem to be both Classical (the two Acropoleis) and Hellenistic (the linking wall between the Acropoleis) with square projecting towers. On the southern slopes are the remains of numerous houses with two springs of water; before the one below the west Acropolis Spratt saw the remains of 'artificial basins and conduits'. The extent of Roman occupation is uncertain; coins have been found on the site[2] and from the modern village below comes an inscription of 63 A.D. about the boundaries of Gortyna's public lands[3]. The ancient name of the site is unknown since its previous identification with Arcades is wrong, that city definitely being at Ini (7/25).

1. The best account, Spratt I, p.319; also *ABSA* XXXIII, 1932-3, p.84.
2. P. Faure, 'Roman and Byzantine coins', *BCH* LXXXIV, 1960, p.198.
3. *IC* I.XXVI.3.

(7/6) VAGIONIA At Ellenika a rectangular building and sherds were reported; at Niphadhi a cistern and wells[1]. Only the latter now seems to be visible just east of the village, south of the new road. The cistern is of concrete with a tile inner face and stone outer face; the walls are 1.0m plus in width[2].

1. *AC* p.375.
2. Personal observation: only one corner survives.

(7/7) KOUMASA Above the Minoan tomb Tholos B there was a grave covered with two tiles, one of which had R stamped on it. In the grave was a skeleton of a man with three small pottery flasks. In between Tholoi A and B was a similar grave with another skeleton accompanied by a glass flask and a lamp[1].

1. S. Xanthoudides, *The Vaulted Tombs of the Mesara* (Liverpool 1924), p.4.

(7/8) STAVGHIES South of the road, on the western side of the stream that marks the eastern edge of the village, there is a hillock on top of which is a Venetian well-head. This seems to be built on top of earlier foundations and there are fragments of a spiral column and other architectural pieces in the area. It seems quite possible that in fact there is a cistern here, with perhaps a building nearby[1].

1. Personal observation. The village cemetery is on the opposite side of the road.

(7/9) PHOURNOPHARANGO Coins, sherds and Graeco-Roman terracottas were found here[1].

1. *AC* p.374, 364.

(7/10) PANAYIA Various coins have been found at the Patela[1] including two of Gordian, and to the west of the village a burial claimed to be of Roman date. 35 minutes south of the village is a cave with Roman sherds[2].

1. *Kret.Khron.* IX, 1955, p.567. *AC* p.374, from *ABSA* XXXIII, 1932-3, p.86.
2. Faure, *BCH*, LXXXIV, 1960, p.199.

(7/11) DIONYSI At Leivadi a 'Terra Sigillata omphalos bowl with a central relief of a Medusa'[1]. Possibly this is a bowl of 3/2c B.C. Calene Ware.

1. *Kret.Khron.* XVII, 1963, p.406.

(7/12) AY. IOANNIS On the south coast near Ay. Ioannis, Roman sherds[1].

1. Faure, *BCH* LXXXIV, 1960, p.199.

(7/13) STOUS AGIOUS A Roman site near Cape Poda with a cave with Roman sherds[1].

1. Faure, *BCH* LXXX, 1956, p.9.

(7/14) STERNES To the west of the village a cistern was seen in 1916: it no longer appears to be visible[1].

1. *A.Delt.* II, 1915, par.p.24.

(7/15) SOKARAS The site here has yielded sherds and coins[1] and from a grave a large glass vessel 0.24m high, a gold ring with an onyx intaglio of Hermes and four coins, all silver, of Vespasian (1), Domitian (2) and Trajan (1)[2].

1. Faure, *BCH* LXXXIV, 1960, p.199.
2. *Arch. Anz.* 1933, p.314, and *A. Delt* XV, 1934-5, p.59.

(7/16) ASIMI A Hellenistic or Roman head of a satyr and a sard scarab were found here[1].

1. *Kret.Khron.* XII, 1958, p.480.

(7/17) ARGEION A site on the actual plain with a few Hellenistic and more Roman sherds[1].

1. *ABSA* XXXIII, 1932-3, p.86.

(7/18) AY. PHOTIA The entire squalid modern village is constructed on top of a group of 10-12 tile-faced cisterns, approximately 12m x 4m each. The cisterns were probably originally entirely above ground level as at (7/30), but now only the vaulted portion is uncovered[1]. There is also a 1/2c tombstone from the village[2].

1. *A.Delt.* II, 1916, par. p.24. Personal observations.
2. *IC*.I.XXIX.2.

(7/19) DORAKI Roman tombs were found here[1].

1. *BCH* LXXXI, 1957, p.618.

(7/20) PYRGOS No actual remains have been found here, but Pyrgos is mentioned as part of a joint Kome with Rhytion in early 2c A.D.[1]

1. *IC* I.XXIX.I, 120 A.D.

(7/21) ROTASI On the Kephala above the village is the site of ancient Rhytion; there is no definite Roman material visible, but numerous walls of roughly squared masonry and some Hellenistic and earlier pottery exist. However, the inscription mentioned above (7/20) is evidence that in the early 2c there was a shrine to Zeus Skylios here[1].

1. *AC* p.373. *IC* I.XXIX.I and Praef. Personal observations.

(7/22) PRAITORIA A few sherds and some possible pithos burials are known from here[1].

1. *ABSA* XXXIII, 1932-3, p.86. *AC* p.374. The Roman date for the burials is assumed by Pendlebury, who did not actually see them.

(7/23) VELOULI At 'stes Vakiotes ten Kephalan' there are a number of rock-cut chamber tombs from where presumably came the various finds in the Heraklion Museum recorded by Pendlebury[1]. A 2c B.C. tombstone of some literary pretensions comes from here[2].

1. *AC* p.362, 375, *ABSA* XXXIII, 1932-3, p.85.
2. *IC.* I.V.40.

(7/24) PARTIRA There is a 2/3c tombstone from here decorated with pruning hook and axe or mattock of the dead man[1].

1. *IC* I.XXVI.I.

(7/25) INI SE of the village of Ini on and about the hill Kephala is the site of Arcades, celebrated by Theophrastus and Pliny for its springs[1]. This tradition has been maintained by the church of Zoodochos Pighi to be found by the spring on the northern edge of the hill. The site seems to have spread off the hill on the north and east sides, where the slope was gentler than the abrupt cliffs of the south and west. Little can be seen over most of the area, but the pottery includes E Sigillata, Çandarli Ware and even Gaulish Samian; interestingly no late ware was seen, which may indicate a decline in prosperity in this period[2]. Just a short distance east of the church of Zoodochos are the remains of a vaulted building of uncertain function, constructed of concrete faced with stone for the first visible six courses and then by tile; it survives up to 3.0m in height and covers an area 9.40m x 5.90m with at least three rooms[3]. Further to the SE are the remains of the bath house, where the recently published inscription[4] about separate bathing hours for the sexes was found. All that survives is a rectangular room 7.70m x 3.70m, with a little niche in the interior SE corner. It is very similar in construction to the other building, all tile faced except a stretch of the west wall: this may indicate a different phase. Approximately 30m to the south are the remains of an aqueduct with piers 2m square, running out from the hill towards the east. Too little survives of the system to be sure whether it was taking water from the springs of the city out or bringing more in from the mountains of the Lassithi Massif to the east. The date of the bath house and the other buildings is uncertain, but the inscription is dated to the early imperial period, pre-late 2c, and given the type of construction and the similar Hadrianic regulations noted in the article, an early 2c date seems very likely. Given the number of inscriptions known from the vicinity few other finds have been reported: they include a few coins[5], an inscription to Asklepios[6] and a tomb at Agoutsakia[7].

1. Collected references, *IC* I.V.Praef.
2. Personal observations.
3. Personal observations.
4. P. Ducrey and H. van Effenterre, 'Un règlement d'époque romaine sur les bains d'Arcades', *Kret. Khron.* XXV, 1973, p.281. Also personal observations.
5. *Kret. Khron.* XIX, 1965, p.291.
6. *Ibid.* X, 1956, p.420. Cf. *IC*.I.V.20 for another.
7. *Ibid.* XIII, 1959, p.387.

(7/26) PYRANTHOS All that survives of this city, possibly a Kome of Gortyna, are a few sherds reported at Trokhalais and an inscription of 63 A. D. about Gortyna's public lands[1].

1. *AC* p.375, *IC* I.XXVI, 2.

(7/27) LIGORTYNOS On the southern edge of the village, overlooking the eastern end of the Mesara, are the ruins of a cruciform building. In its final form it was obviously an early Mediaeval church, but there are reused columns of marble and granite and also a cistern nearby. It is possible that as at Kato Asites (9/14) a Roman bath house has been reused as a church[1].

1. *Kret.Khron.* VI, 1952, p.479. *Mon. Ven.* II, p.216, fig.220. Personal observations.

(7/28) NEO CHORIO A Graeco-Roman cemetery. No other details[1].

1. *Kret.Khron.* VI, 1952, p.479.

(7/29) KASTELL BELVEDERE Below the Venetian castle are the remains of the city of Priansos; very little of it has survived because of the later occupation, but Pendlebury saw remains in the SE corner[1]. From nearby comes an official monument to a veteran of the Augustan Civil Wars restored by the proconsul[2]. In the later period Priansos appears to have lost in importance to its port Inatos.

1. *AC* p.374.
2. *IC* I.XXIV.5.

(7/30) KASTELLIANA The main visible remains here are the cisterns (Fig.55) on the southern edge of the village, east of the road to the coast. They are constructed of tile-faced concrete with walls 1.40m thick. There are four cisterns built in one block 18.40m x 12.60m (internal measurements), each cistern 12.60 x 4.0m, standing about 3.0m high to the spring of the vault, which has not survived. The northern wall has four buttresses. The possible mosaic and basilica is no longer visible[1]. Other finds from here include a lamp showing a centaur on the disc, a gold earring and a Hellenistic head[2].

1. *Kret Khron.* VIII, 1954, p.516, and personal observation. See p.104 for the basilica.
2. *A.Delt.* XX.3, 1965, p.555.

Fig.55. Kastelliana: plan of the cisterns.

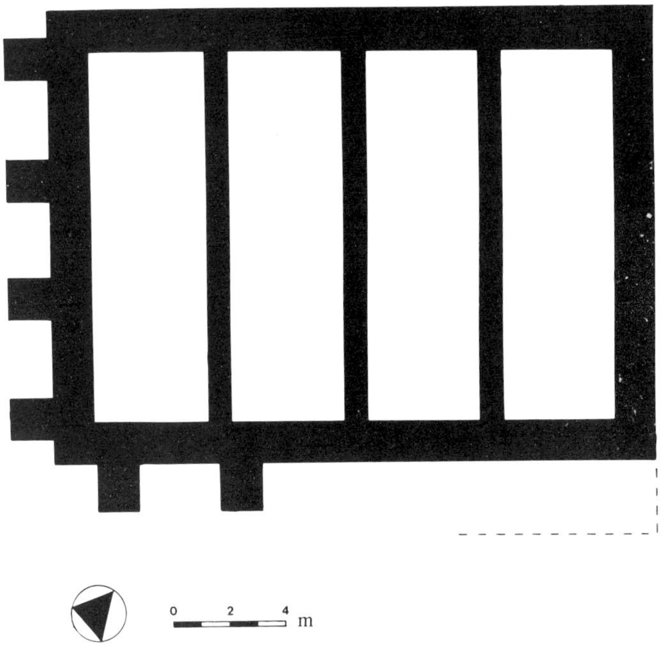

(7/31) TSOUTSOUROS The main area of the ancient city of Inatos lay about the river Mintris; the winter flooding of this stream has revealed several houses between the cliffs and the shore. From one of these came the rather crude group of Artemis and Niobe[1] which is probably of late 2c date, as is the associated material, including a lamp with a Medusa head. Other houses here included one with a peristyle with both smooth and fluted columns[2]. Further down the stream are the remains of the 6c basilica[3] and right by the beach are the possible remnants of another major building marked by a number of fragmentary monolithic granite columns. Further to the west are the remains of the theatre, partially cut out of the rock of the cliffs and partly built of stone-faced concrete; all that can be made out is that the external diameter of the cavea was about 32m. Fragments of concrete walls survive to the west end of the bay but form no intelligible plan except one possible small cistern. Pottery from the Hellenistic to Late Roman period is scattered profusely over the site, with a higher than normal percentage of ARSW as opposed to LRC in the later pottery[4]. In the cliffs that limit the site inland is the cave of Eileithya, in which Roman material was found; there is also an inscription to her of Roman date from the site[5].

1. S. Marinatos, ' Οἱ Νιοβίδαι τῆς 'Ινάτου ', *AE* 1934, p.1. Heraklion Museum, no.265-6.
2. *Kret. Khron.* XXIV, 1972, p.492; *PAE* 1971, p.286.
3. See p.104.
4. Theatre etc., personal observations.
5. Inscription, *Kret. Khron.* X, 1956, p.421. Cave, *Kret. Khron.* XVII, 1963, p.397.

EPARCHY 8 - TEMENOS

(8/1) HERAKLION No actual Roman building has been found here, but a large number of tombs, dating 1c-3c, either rock-cut chamber or cist, have been found in the area between Odos Evans and the Museum[1]. With one possible exception all these lie outside the line of the Byzantine B/1st Venetian walls[2] and it is possible that in fact there may have been a late Roman circuit on much the same line. There is one inscription, probably late 7c, that may refer to such a wall[3] but this was found within the line of the Byzantine B walls, built into another wall parallel to them. Whether this was its original position is far from clear. Within the city late Roman material has been found below the Arab layers at Ay.Petros[4], down by the shore within the old circuit.

1. *Kret.Khron.* VIII, 1954, p.515. Tile graves opposite the Museum. *Kret.Khron.* IX, 1955, p.565, the one possible exception, but the report is unclear: opposite the Museum. *A.Delt.* XX.3, 1965. Cist Grave p.562, near the Museum. *A.Delt.* XXI.3, 1966, p.408. Chamber Tomb: east of the cinema Astoria. *Kret.Khron.* XXI, 1969, p.539. Odos Evans, 2c B.C. tomb.
2. The line of these walls is marked by Odos Khandakos and Odos Daidalos. See *Kret. Khron.* I, 1947, p.238, *ibid.* IV, p.353. Part of a tower is still visible at the east end of Odos Daidalos.
3. *Kret. Khron.* XV-XVI, 1961-2, (1st Cretological Congress), II, p.47. The interpretation of the inscription taking OPOI as meaning walls and the ΔΙΑΒΟΛΟΣ as a reference to the Arabs is not certain as is made clear in the discussion after the article.
4. *A. Delt.* XXIII.2.2, 1968, p.427. G.C. Miles, 'Excavations at Ay. Petros, Heraklion 1967', *Acts of the 3rd Cretological Congress* III, (Athens, 1975), p.225. G.C. Miles, 'Coins from the excavations at Ay. Petros, Heraklion, Crete', *American Numismatic Society Museum Notes* XVII, 1971, p.163.

(8/2) MASTABA Hellenistic and Roman sherds were seen in this modern suburb of Heraklion[1], about a kilometre south of the main site above.

1. *AC* p.363, 372; *ABSA* XXXIII, 1932-3, p.91.

(8/3) AY. IOANNIS Various finds from this village half way between Heraklion and Knossos indicate a small but long-lived site: Roman lamps[1], early Byzantine grain storage pits[2] and 1c A.D. coins have all been found here. Recently an altar dedicated to Artemis has been found here, as well as another inscription recording the repair of the road, presumably from Knossos to Heraklion[4].

1. *A. Delt.* XXI.3, 1966, p.410.
2. *Kret. Khron.* XI, 1951, p.336.
3. Heraklion Museum Catalogue, no.2002.
4. *Ergon* 1975, p.199-200.

(8/4) KNOSSOS (Fig.56) The Hellenistic and Roman city occupied the area west of the Kairatos and north of the Palace, covering about 1 sq. km (100 ha)[1]. Since the Minoan Palace has claimed nearly all the archaeological attention very little is really known about the later periods, but recently enough work has been carried out to enable a rough outline of the site's history in the Roman period to be attempted.
The centre of the city is marked by the remains of the 1c/2c basilica[2] and about 100m to the NW the remains of the theatre. This was built of concrete, but has been so badly destroyed by the modern road that nothing else can be said of it apart from the fact that there is no evidence that it was an amphitheatre as it is normally called. The only evidence for such a building at Knossos is an inscription mentioning Ludi. From the existing visible fragments of buildings and the known mosaics it is obvious that the favoured residential areas of the city were on the level area north of the centre extending up to the northern limit of the city, and west of the centre up to the bottom of the Acropolis. No excavation has been carried out in the first of the areas mentioned, but there are numerous lumps of concrete marking the position of buildings, and a great deal of fine pottery, including much Arretine, on the surface. Only one mosaic has yet been uncovered, however: the Apollinaris mosaic dating to the early 2c[3]. West of the centre the Villa Dionysus, of early 2c construction, has been excavated and shown to have had but a short life, destroyed in the period 160-180. There are numerous other mosaics known from the field here, including one depicting the four seasons[4]. Known mosaics extend as far as the Taverna of the British School, which has a mosaic under the steps leading to its roof![5]
South and east of here the quality of the houses seems to drop, with the recent excavations above the Unexplored Mansion[6] revealing rather crowded houses bordering streets that were first established in the Geometric period. Very scrappy remains of the Hellenistic period were found, which came to an end about the mid 1c B.C., presumably with the capture of Knossos by Metellus. The first period of Roman building is Augustan, presumably when the *colonia* was founded, but again little survived the later rebuilding, especially north of the street that divided the site roughly in two. All these rooms were quite small and cannot represent a house of any particular standing, built as they were of mudbrick on stone socles or rubble construction. These buildings were finally destroyed in the mid or third quarter of the 1c[7] although there had been an earlier partial Augustan destruction as well. In the 2c more substantial houses were erected north of the street, and in the SE part of the site. The latter had mainly been removed by Sir Arthur Evans, but one room, 5.90m x 3.35m, survived complete with frescoes with a panel design of large diamonds, and below them a band of imitation marble slabs. This room was damaged in the 2c, but rebuilt, finally going out of use in the 3c, when a group of full size plaster heads was dumped in the extreme SW corner of the building. North of the street a more complex house was erected, consisting of a series of rooms grouped round a courtyard or yards. This too was damaged in the 2c, about the middle of it, and in its final form with a central column in the main yard dates to the early 3c. The whole area was abandoned soon after this, however, and no 4c structures were found. A similar picture was revealed by the Hellenistic and Roman levels from the excavations on either side of the Royal Road[8], but here there seems to be less 3c material and a more definite 4c occupation. Little is known about the NE quarter of the site except the actual, concrete, Makryteichos, possibly a stoa.
None of these sites continued into the late period, and apart from the 6c basilica by the modern Sanatorium outside the limits of the city and the possible basilica below Ayia Sophia in the modern village[9], the only evidence for post-4c occupation are a few tombs and the Arab building by the Kairatos[10]. No late pottery is visible anywhere on the entire site, so it seems that basically Knossos was deserted after the 4c. This may have been caused by the series of earthquakes known in the 4c, perhaps particularly the massive one of 365[11].
The cemeteries of Hellenistic and Roman Knossos are well known and lie on all sides except the east, where the slopes rise sharply up from the Kairatos. There was a bridge across the stream leading over to this side, but there are no definitely Roman remains on its eastern side. The northern cemetery stretches from the Zafer Papoura hill - on top of which is a 4/3c B.C. tower, the only sign of any defences - to the area of the cemeteries at the Fortetsa turn[12]. Most of the tombs are Hellenistic to 4c A.D. and of the cist type, but there are later ones, including a 6/7c osteotheke with at least 36 secondary internments[13]. There was also the 'Tomb of Caiaphas'[14] which may have been a 4c Mausoleum. The western cemetery uses the Acropolis area and nearly all the burials are in chamber tombs cut into the rock and dating again up to the 4c, but one 5/6c tomb is known from near Ay. Kyrillos[15]. The southern area consists of two parts: firstly, the burials on the Gypsades, both cist or slab graves and chamber tombs, and secondly the very fine chamber tombs further down the valley before Spelia[16]. Cutting across this southern end of the valley the route of the aqueducts that supplied Knossos from an unknown point to the south can still be partially traced up to the gorge south of Ay. Kyrillos[17]. There are no definitely Roman roads leading from the city, but it seems very likely that the Venetian road to Heraklion down in the valley, as opposed to the modern road, may cover its Roman predecessor leading as it does straight from the Fortetsa turn to the Morosini Square in Heraklion. Additional evidence is provided by the recent find of an inscription from Ay. Ioannis (8/3).
On top of Gypsades is the only definite temple known from the site, and even that is rather undistinguished[18]; here there seems to have been a very small 5c B.C. Doric temple which probably continued in use into the Roman period. Possibly connected to the establishment of the *colonia* are a series of ovens, to the north of the temple, which in

Fig.56. Knossos: plan of the ancient city and the immediate area.

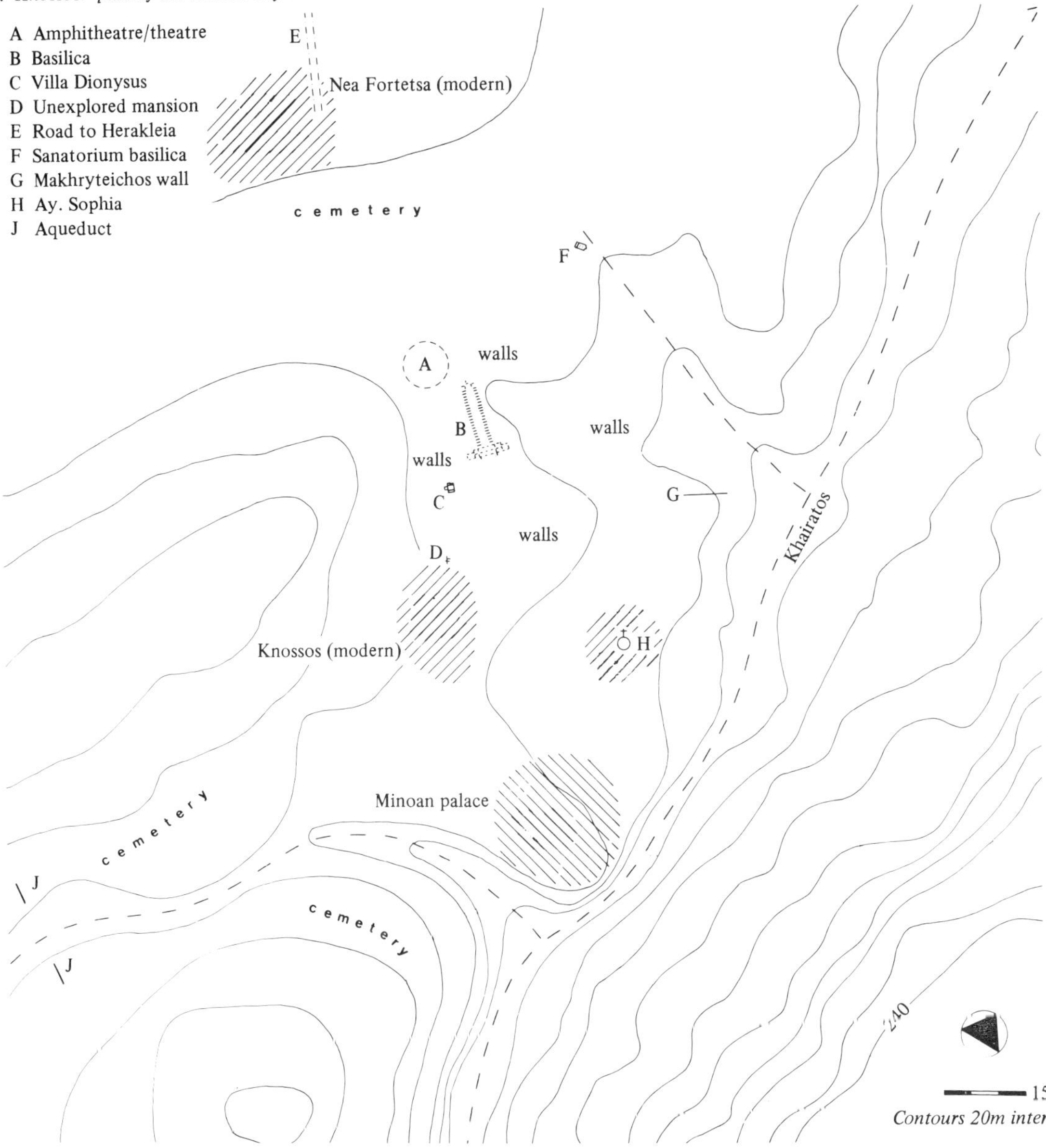

:heir turn were disused by the late 2c. There is no evidence for 3c activity on the site, and by the 4c the site was occupied by what is interpreted by the excavator as a farmhouse, although there is a possible Mausoleum of concrete nearby whose floor seals a pit containing a Hellenistic Kore from the earlier temple. The only other temple from Knossos is the possible temple of Rhea on top of the palace[19]; the latter appears to have been totally deserted in the later periods, apart from this temple and some stone robbing[20].

1. For all sites known to the mid-1950's, M.S.F.Hood, 'Archaeological survey of the Knossos area', (London, n.d.).
2. See p.67.
3. See p.53. On display in the Heraklion Museum.
4. See p.53 for the mosaics. The mosaics are all referred to in the *Survey*, no.68. Also the mosaics revealed by the sewer trench in 1971 from the Villa, *Kret. Khron.* XXIV, 1972, p.492. There were two in section, personal observation.
5. No.82.
6. Extensive preliminary; L.H. Sackett, *AR* 1972-3, p.62.
7. Possibly the earthquake mentioned in Dictys of Crete in the reign of Nero, if one can trust Dictys as historical evidence. Quoted in Praef., *IC*.I.VIII, p.53.
8. Preliminary reports: S. side, *AR* 1971-2, p.20; N. side, *AR* 1958, p.20.
9. See p.105ff.
10. P. Warren, 'An Arab building from Knossos', *ABSA* LXVII, 1972, p.285.
11. Ammianus Marcellinus XXVI.10.15.
12. J. Brock, 'Fortetsa', *ABSA* Suppl. Vol.2, 1957, p.39.
13. *AR* 1973-4, p.35-6.
14. *Survey* no. 23, p.11-2.
15. *Survey*, nos. 65, 75, 78, 106. *Kret. Khron.* XX, 1968, p.325, Ay. Kyrillos.
16. *Survey*, nos. 142, 144-5, 158.
17. *Survey*, no.136, 157. Now mainly destroyed by a new water main.
18. J.N. Coldstream, 'Knossos, the sanctuary of Demeter', *ABSA* Suppl. Vol.8, 1973, p.6.
19. Diodorus Siculus V.66.1. *POM* II.i.6.
20. Although even this appears to have been very limited; cf. *ABSA* X, 1903-4, p.51-3. Also the Dictys story for Roman knowledge of the Palace.

(8/5) AY. VLASIS Tombs seen in 1933[1].

1. *AC* p.372.

(8/6) AY. SYLLAS Pottery of Hellenistic or Roman date was found at Koutsourelia[1].

1. *Kret.Khron.* XIII, 1959, p.386.

(8/7) ARKHANES Remains of Roman buildings were found at Troullos[1], including some reasonably substantial tile built structures. Also at Tsami a late Hellenistic building was excavated[2].

1. *Kret.Khron.* XI, 1957, p.335; *ibid.* XII, 1958, p.479.
2. *Ergon* 1974, p.118.

(8/8) STRABOMYTE SW of Iuktas is the cave of this name, which contains Roman pottery[1]. Also there is Roman material in the cave of Chisto Nero [2].

1. Faure, *BCH* XCI, 1967, p.133. Also *BCH* LXXIV, 1950, p.311.
2. *Op.cit.* n.I.

(8/9) IUKTAS No Roman remains have actually been found on the summit, but the Tomb of Zeus was definitely still being worshipped in the late 4c[1] and it is very possible that the Roman shrine was on the site of the later church of Afendi Christos[2].

1. Julius Firmicus Maternus, *De. Err. Prof. Relig.* 19.
2. For the topography of the summit, *POM.* I.p.151f.

(8/10) KANLI KASTELLI South of the village the hill of Rocca is crowned with massive remains of the castles of Nicephorus and later the Venetians[1]. This site is, however, almost certainly ancient Lykastos, and there is one tile-lined cistern at the northern end of the hill by the chapel of Panayia that may be Roman, as opposed to the other much cruder cisterns elsewhere on the hill[2]. It is quite likely that the main Roman settlement here was below the hill on the site of the modern village.

1. Gerola, *Mon. Ven.* I, p.181.
2. Personal observation.

(8/11) MONI PALIANI At the convent here there is the basilica of the first half of the 6c.[1].

1. See p.107.

(8/12) MIKHANES West of Heraklion a Roman farmhouse with associated tile graves was found[1].

1. *AR* 1957, p.16.

(8/13) AY. THOMAS, HERAKLION Possibly a separate site with a tile grave with glass vessels, a tear vessel and silver rings of 1c B.C./1c A.D. date[1].

1. *A.Delt.* XX.3, 1965, p.555.

(8/14) KARNARI An inscription from here about the imperial settlement between Capua and Knossos over a land dispute[1] in A.D.84.

1. P. Ducrey, 'Trois nouvelles inscriptions crétoises', *BCH* XCIII, 1969, p.841.

EPARCHY 9 - MALEVISI

(9/1) AY. PELAGIA The main remains here at the site of ancient Dium or Cytaeum are of the Hellenistic period (4/3c), and include what is claimed as the remnants of a prytaneion[1]. There are also houses constructed of rough stone walls built on terraces cut out of the rock, which are later 3/2c B.C., and last into the early Roman period.

1. *AAA* V, 1972, p.230. *Kret.Khron.* XXV, 1973, p.461 and 472. Much of the site has been destroyed by the new hotel. Dr. Alexiou's later view is that the site was Panormos Apollonia, rather than Cytaeum.

(9/2) PHODELE Although Roman remains have been claimed from here at Elliniko[1] there is no material from the site of the ruined village that need be pre-Mediaeval. The earlier church[2] could be pre-Arab, but is more likely to be 11-12c.

1. Faure, *Kret.Khron.* XVII, 1963, p.19. Personal observation.
2. See p.108.

(9/3) DAMASTA 5/4c vases from here[1].

1. Le Rider, p.257.

(9/4) MARATHOS A possible Graeco-Roman farm[1].

1. Hood *et al*, *ABSA* LIX, 1964, p.55, site1.

(9/5) ARKALOSPELIO A cave at 475m on Mt. Arkalokephala containing late Roman, 'Byzantine' and Mediaeval sherds[1].

1. Faure, *BCH* LXXXIX, 1965, p.48.

(9/6) KAMARAKI In the foothills a so-called late Roman refuge cave with a humidity of 98%[1].

1. Faure, *BCH* LXXXIX, 1965, p.47.

(9/7) GONIES A building and sherds of Roman date were found at Kanassos and it is claimed that the Palaioklissa in the actual village is built on top of an earlier basilica[1]. Roman imperial coins are also reported from Sklavokampos down the valley[2].

1. *Kret.Khron.* IX, 1955, p.568, and see p.108 for the basilica.
2. *AC* p.369.

(9/8) GAZI There seems to have been a substantial site here, possibly ancient Apollonia or rather one of the Apollonia of Crete. A possible villa was found here[1] with finds including a Doric capital, millstone, and associated tile graves.

1. *Kret.Khron.* XI, 1957, p.336. Another tomb, *A. Delt.* XIX.2, 1964, p.438-9. Pottery noted, *ABSA* XXXIII, 1932-3, p.92.

(9/9) KAVROCHORI At Marathokephala, a Hellenistic building was found[1].

1. *Kret.Khron.* XXIV, 1972, p.492; *PAE* 1971, p.300.

(9/10) TYLISSOS On the site of the famous Minoan settlement were found scrappy remains of its Greek and Roman successor[1]. The few remains were basically of Classical or Hellenistic date, including the 5c altar, although there were undated Byzantine coins in the topsoil and a stone bowl which the excavator dated to the Roman period. In 1965 at Doniana Roman pottery, loomweights and a stone lekane were found, perhaps indicating a slight shift of the site[2].

1. J. Hazzidhakis, 'Les villas minoennes de Tylissos', *Etudes Crétoises* III, 1934, p.66 and p.109, with Pl.XXXI-II for the post-Minoan.
2. *A.Delt.* XX.3, 1965, p.556.

(9/11) KASTELLI MALEVYZIOU Nothing substantial remains of the castle here but a rectangular building was seen on the summit[1] and claimed to be Roman, associated with Roman/Byzantine sherds. It would seem quite possible that this was in fact part of the castle. A cave is now visible[2] on the NW side of the hill not far above the road, which may have been a chamber tomb in origin.

1. *ABSA* XXXIII, 1932-3, p.92.
2. Personal observation, 1974.

(9/12) AY. MIRON Unlike most of the hilltop sites of central Crete, e.g. Kanli Kastelli, Prinias, Melidochori, that at Ay. Miron is still occupied by the modern village, and consequently little is known of its predecessor, Rhaukos[1]. A number of Hellenistic inscriptions exist, together with an inscribed Roman water pipe, and some sherds were seen to the SE of the village, on the slopes of the hill. The best evidence of its existence in the Roman period is really the *Life of St. Miron*, *c.*250-350 A.D., who came from the city of Rhaukia, which must be an alternative form of the name[2]. The existence of an earlier basilica below the church of the saint in the centre of the village is not really proven[3].

1. *IC* I.XXVII, for the inscriptions. *ABSA* XXXIII, 1932-3, p.91 for the sherds. *A.Delt.* XXII.3, 1967, p.487, for a Rhodian stater from here.
2. On the saint, Th. Detorakes, ' *Οἱ ἅγιοι τῆς πρώτης βυζαντινῆς περιόδου τῆς Κρήτης* ', 1970, p.132.
3. See p.108.

(9/13) KROUSSONAS There is an extensive site on the hill above the modern village situated on a spur of the foothills of Mt. Ida, overlooking the coastal plain, but nearly all the pottery seemed to be earlier than Roman, in particular Hellenistic. Closer to the village some of the pots could have been Roman coarse ware, so it seems very likely that as at Kanli the main Roman site is conveniently situated on the spur below the hill, below the Mediaeval and modern village[1].

1. *ABSA* XXXIII, 1932-3, p.92, just sherds, Geometric-Roman. Personal observation.

(9/14) KATO ASITES On the SW edge of the village stands the remains of the Roman trilobate bath house reused as the church of Ay. Katerine[1]. Another building is known from the village itself, but all that was recorded was that it had a pithos built into it—?into the floor as a storage vessel[2]. Also from here is another water pipe stamped with the same name as the one at Rhaukos, *οὐαγῶν*[3]. It would therefore seem likely that there was a sizeable Roman 'town' here, possibly Pannona.

1. See p.70, fig.13.
2. *A.Delt.* XX.3, 1965, p.555.
3. K. Davaras, ' *Ἐπιγραφαί ἐκ Κρήτης* II', *A.Delt.* XVIII.1, 1963, no.3, p.152.

(9/15) ANO ASITES A stone slab cist grave was excavated here at Papoura Kephalas[1], which contained one skeleton aligned EW and no grave goods; it could be of late Roman date by its type. Also a glass bottle, likely to have been part of grave goods, is recorded as coming from here[2].

1. *A. Delt.* XXIV.2.2., 1969, p.420.
2. In Heraklion Museum; *AC* p.372.

(9/16) PRINIAS PATELA This flat topped acropolis dominating the routes from the Mesara to the north is most famous for its archaic temples with their sculpture[1]. It was probably ancient Rhizenia and was taken by Gortyna in the Hellenistic period[2]. There is no definitely Roman occupation on the hill, where the final building, late Hellenistic, is a splendid 'toy fort' 36m x 40m (internally) with corner towers. NW of the site by the modern road are two well-preserved chamber tombs that could be early Roman or Hellenistic[3] but Roman material has been reported from Peze[4] nearby, and an inscription of A.D.63 about Gortyna's public lands is known from the actual village[5].

1. Most conveniently, *Italian Guide* p.75. A.K. Lembesi *Οἱ στῆλες τοῦ Πρινιά* (Athens 1976).
2. *IC*.I.XXVIII, as Rhizenia? No.28, two lead sling shots inscribed ΓΟΡ.
3. Personal observation. *Mon.Ant.* IX, 1899, p.331.
4. *AC* p.372. Coins of Trajan and Div. Faustina presumably from here. Heraklion Museum Nos. 1994-5.
5. *IC*.I.XXVIII.29. *Cf.* *IC*.I.XXVII.2-3.

EPARCHY 10 – KAINOURGHIO

(10/1) ZAROS NW of the modern village at the spring of Sternes ('the cistern') in the valley of Vrontisi, are the remains of the *caput aquae* of of the aqueduct that supplied Gortyna (Fig.57).[1] The actual *caput* still exists, though since Taramelli surveyed it the roof has collapsed. It is built of concrete walls 1.40m wide, with a stone facing and tile levelling courses, 37m x 5m wide, and 4m high up to the vault. It was built next to the mountain side to which it is linked by a wall 0.70m wide. The wall of the cistern next to the mountain (the northern) was 2.30m higher than the southern as extra protection against stone falls. Parts of the actual aqueduct survive lower down the valley as a stone-faced concrete wall up to 4.70m high, with the now exposed water channel 0.80m deep and 0.50m to 0.35m wide at the bottom. The fabric of the aqueduct was protected from surface waters coming off the mountain by a system of drains, arched channels 0.45m high and 0.60m wide, piercing the line of the wall. These channels were at 20-25m intervals and some are still visible.

Apart from the aqueduct a major building was also noted by Taramelli near the spring: it was built of tile-faced concrete with one room 30m x 9m; this is no longer visible. Roman coarse wares can be seen in the area north of the cistern[2] and coins of Theodosius (gold)[3] and Julia Augusta[4] (silver) have been found here. There is also one stamped tile[5] with the same name as the ones from Lebena (10/23) and Gortyna (10/10) known from Zaros.

1. A. Taramelli, *AJA* 2nd series VI, 1902, p.120ff.
2. Personal observation.
3. *Kret. Khron.* XIX, 1965, p.291.
4. *AC* p.375, Heraklion Museum no. 1273.
5 *IC*.I.XXXI.10. Julius Fusculus.

Fig.57. Zaros: Caput aquae, *plan and section.*

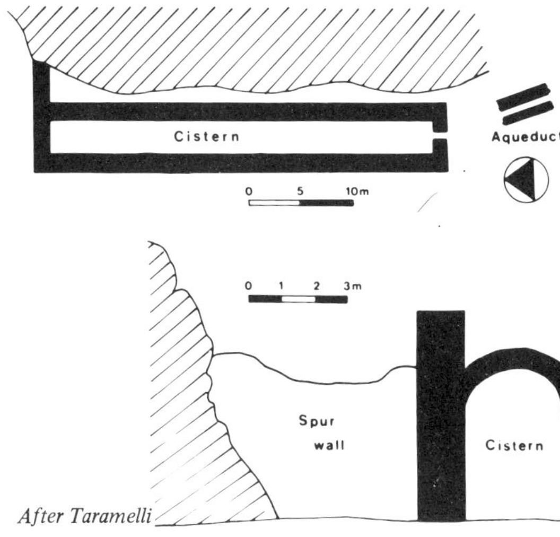

(10/2) NIBRETOS On the opposite side of the valley from the main village is the deserted hamlet of Droson; a building of Graeco-Roman date with marble floors and exedrae was found here. The finds included a bronze lekane, glass lacrimaria and fragments of two marble lekanae depicting scenes from the Labours of Heracles– the apples of the Hesperides and Cerberus. It is uncertain whether the building with such objects was a bath house or some sort of shrine to the hero[1].

1. *A.Delt.* XVII.2, 1961-2, p.289.

(10/3) GERGERI Apart from the possible basilica[1] there are also late coins from here: one of Heraclius[2] and the other of Michael II in whose reign Crete was lost[3]. There is also a crude architectural fragment of uncertain date in Heraklion Museum basement[4].

1. See p.108.
2. Heraklion Historical Museum, No.383.
3. Heraklion Museum, No.1498.
4. Personal Observation.

(10/4) PANASSOS A griffin handled bronze lamp from here is on display in the Heraklion Historical Museum[1]. It may well have come from any of the Christian basilicas of the area, e.g. Gergeri, and does not necessarily indicate another from this village.

1. No.224. Such lamps are very common, dating to the 5/6c.

(10/5) MOULIA 'A large well-preserved Graeco-Roman lamp'[1].

1. *A.Delt.* XVII.2, 1961-2, p.289.

(10/6) APOMARMA An inscription recording the construction or perhaps repair of an aqueduct was found here near an ancient aqueduct, according to Guarducci[1]. She connects it to the Zaros-Gortyna system. If the inscription is really from Apomarma, as she indicates by referring to inscription no.5, then it is too far up the valley to be connected to the Gortyna system, but if it is really from the same place as the preceding inscription, no.8 from Pluti, then it would be on the line of the Gortyna aqueduct.

1. *IC*.I.XXXI.9.

(10/7) MOIRES Two early tombstones have been found here[1] and also a late 7c solidus of Constantine IV[2].

1. 1c A.D. tombstone of Thychaon, *Kret.Khron.* XXII, 1970, p.518. Roman tombstone of a daughter of Anteros, *Kret.Khron.* XXV, 1973, p.463.
2. Heraklion Historical Museum, No.414.

(10/8) KASTELLI On the site of the Venetian castle a group of 3c B.C. coins was found, including some unusual issues with AINA on them. It is suggested that this site may represent the place of exile of the contemporary family of Ainaones from Gortyna[1].

1. Faure, *Kret.Khron.* XIX, 1965, p.222-3.

(10/9) KHOUSTOULIANA 'Hellenistic vases from the pit at Gerolakkos in the Gortyna Museum'[1].

1. *AC* p.362.

(10/10) GORTYNA (Fig.58) The site of the largest city and capital of Roman Crete[1] is now almost totally deserted and covered by olive groves. It extends for about 150 ha from the mountains on the northern edge of the plain, for about 1km southwards and from the modern village of Ay. Deka on its eastern edge to beyond the R. Lethaeus to the west. The work of the Italian School has revealed many of the public buildings of the Roman period, and chance finds with consequent rescue excavation have delimited the main cemeteries on all three non-mountainous sides of the city.

After the Sub-Minoan period the Acropolis was never a place of regular habitation, but rather a place of religious or, later, military functions. The temple (Fig.58.1) and altar[2](Fig.58.2) were probably the earliest religious structures in the city; the former dating possibly from the Protogeometric period, the latter to the 8c B.C. The altar seems to have gone out of use by the 3c B.C. but the temple continued into the Roman period. Unlike the Temple of Pythian Apollo, however, this temple, possibly dedicated to Athena[3], was not basically altered, but remained a simple rectangular building 8.80 x 12.40m, with a central bothros right until its demise as a temple some time before the Christian basilica was constructed on the site, perhaps in the 6c A.D.[4] The other buildings on the Acropolis are the so-called Kastro[5](Fig.58.3), the sunken hall 59m x 24.50m, of uncertain though definitely Roman date and function. This was incorporated and extended when the Acropolis was fortified in the late 7c or early 8c.

Fig.58. Gortyna: general plan of the ancient city.

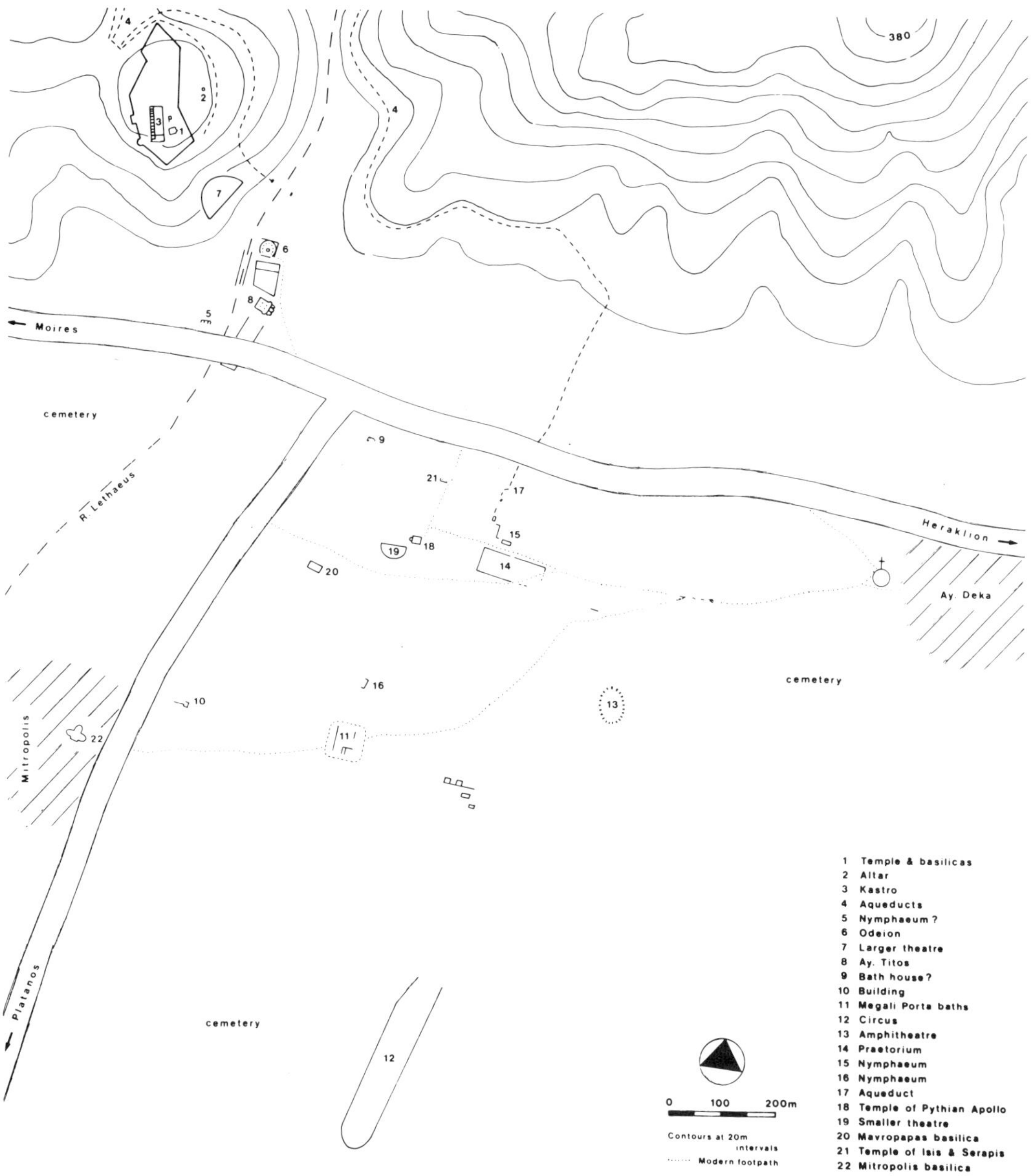

The Acropolis dominates the valley of the Lethaeus as it comes out of the mountains and, following its course, the aqueduct, (Fig.58.4) which started off at Zaros, can be traced coming down into the city[6]. Initially there are two branches, both on the right bank of the river, and about 43m apart; the higher of the two was slightly larger than the lower, both in the actual size of the aqueduct, up to 1.70m and 1.80m wide as compared to the lower at *c.* 1.10m x 1.00m, and in the size of the channel–higher 0.65 x 0.56m, lower 0.55 x 0.45m. Some distance before they approached the Acropolis the lower one sent off a branch which crossed over the river and continued on the left bank down into

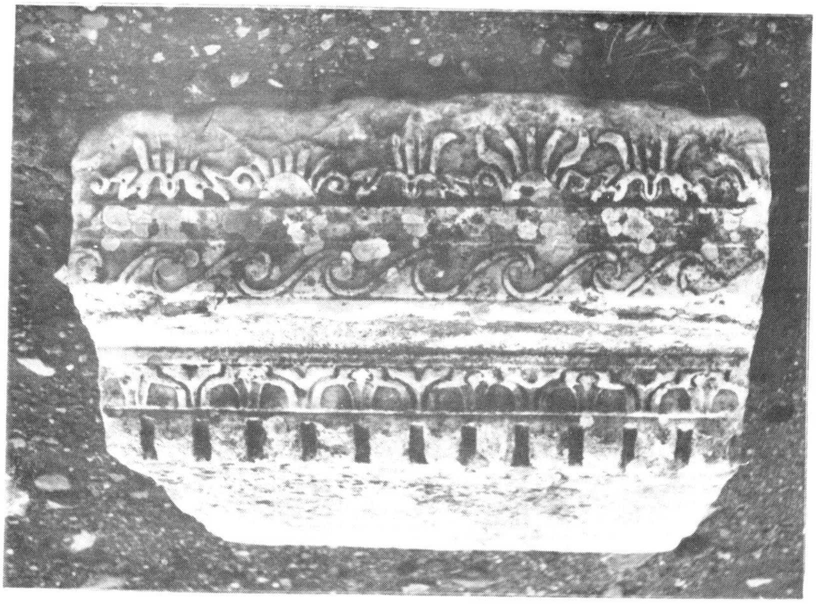

Pl. 68: Architectural fragment at Ay. Titos, Gortyna.
Pl. 69: Largest fragment of wall, Megali Porta baths, Gortyna.

the city. At the point of crossing there are visible remains of a *caput aquae* to maintain pressure in the system as it crossed over and rose up the other side. The aqueducts remaining on the right bank continued along the gorge but came together to cross the valley by another bridge on two levels on the west side of the Acropolis before separating again to flank it. The lower branch finally left the other just before the Larger Theatre and crossed down to the area of the Forum and the Odeion. The higher branch continued down to the plain on the west side of the Lethaeus, partially underground, where it was ventilated by wells. It is possible that it finally finished at the series of vaulted concrete structures (Fig.58.5) just west of the river and north of the modern road, which may have been a nymphaeum.

The suggested Forum area lies below the Acropolis and has been partially excavated: the northern edge must have been limited by the Odeion (Fig.58.6) that in its final form dates to the early 2c A.D.[7] but must be on the site of similar structures going back to the 5c B.C. Immediately to the S W and across the river the ruins of the Larger Theatre (Fig.58.7) of the city are present[8]. This was not separated from the rest of the area, for here the river ran through a culvert that remained intact at least up to the late 16c[9]. The area between these buildings and the great cathedral of St. Titus (Fig.58.8)[10] which probably dates to the late 6c or early 7c, has not been excavated, but there are architectural fragments preserved on the cathedral site which must date to the second half of the 2c[11]. It is not known from what building these came or exactly where this building stood, but there are dedications from the area to Asklepios, the 'highest God', and the imperial family[12] which imply the existence of temples at least to the gods and possibly to the Emperor. The dedication to Severus would fit the date of the fragments very reasonably, although the inscription is more likely to refer to a statue than a building.

Little is known about the remaining area east of the 'Forum' and between the mountains and the modern main road: presumably there was housing here, perhaps of the poorer classes whose dwellings would not have survived as well as the concrete built structures to the SW between the main road and Mitropolis. Here there are several unexcavated visible buildings of stone and tile-faced concrete, including a possible bath house (Fig.58.9) in the east angle between the main road and that to Mitropolis. All that survives is a lump of masonry including several tile-lined niches and areas of waterproof cement lining. Further south and on the same side of the Mitropolis road are the remains of a large building (Fig.58.10) built in a rougher concrete with very little tile used except at the west end; the only discernible room was 7.2 x 2.6m[13]. Also in this area a polychrome mosaic was found, obviously from an important building which may have been public rather than a private dwelling if the dedication to Trajan is really associated with it[14]. Between here and what is probably the public baths a small part of a rather curious structure was excavated[15] revealing a short length of an aqueduct running up to what appeared to be the end of a small stadium with a width of 25.10m and at least 24.43m (length excavated). No spina was found, but there was a square structure near the end.

The baths mentioned lie about 350m NE of Mitropolis and are known as the Megali Porta (Fig.58.11) (Pl.69). The remains consist of a great jumble of tile-faced concrete with one wall still standing about 7-8m high. In places there are secondary supporting walls faced in stone alone which may be considerably later than the original building that presumably dates to the 2c by the style of construction. The building covers an area of about 60m x 60m and although no plan can be made out, the general assumption that it was a large public bath-building would seem reasonable. There are fragments of buildings to the south of here, but more substantial remains about 150m to the east, where there are several buildings just visible, including one with many fragmentary columns in a grey granite, some unfluted and others spiral. All these structures and also the baths seem to be planned on a grid aligned on the main compass points, and if this is really so this is the only example of such planning from Crete[16]. 300-400m SE of this area are the scanty remains of the circus, 374m long (Fig.58.12) and a maximum of 68m wide: some of the piers are still visible, but for most of its length it is under cultivation[17]. 200m north of this is the amphitheatre (Fig.58.13), 66m x 50m (internal arena) and dating to the late 2c; from its remains it was obviously an ornate building of some pretensions[18].

In the centre of the city and so separated from the administrative centre in the Forum, are the ruins of the Praetorium (Fig.58.14) covering at least 10,000 sq.m[19]. This was a building of considerable splendour, constructed basically in the 2c succeeding an Augustan palace and rebuilt in the 4c after the earthquakes of that century. It continued in use right up into the post-Arab period as a monastery[20], but it was finally abandoned like the rest of the site at about the time of the Venetian conquest. In the immediate area of the Praetorium there were several fountains in the courtyard to the west and a large nymphaeum immediately to the north (Fig.58.15)[21]. This dates to the 2c, and may well be linked to the rebuilding of the Palace at that time. Another nymphaeum of similar plan and date lies to the south, closer to the baths (Fig.58.16)[22]. All these waterworks must have required a tremendous flow of water and the remains of one of the aqueducts can be traced coming down towards the Praetorium: it is in a very fragmentary state but it was obviously carried on arches with small cisterns at the bottom of the arch for distributing water en route (Fig.58.17). There is also a possible third large nymphaeum about 50m north of the Praetorium. The only dating evidence for the aqueduct itself in the area is supplied by its relation to a building next to the praetorium nymphaeum. Here the water tower at the end of the aqueduct overlies this building, which is rectangular, 10m x 15m, and constructed of porous blocks; from the material found with it it would seem to be a little temple of Augustan date dedicated to a female deity[23]. It is obvious that there were other major structures in this area from inscriptions found round about: one probably from a temple to Roma and Augustus, and the other commemorating the restoration in 169 A.D. in marble of a cross roads adorned with imperial statues[24].

Directly to the west of this complex is the main temple of Gortyna, the Temple of Pythian Apollo[25] (Fig.58.18). It was built in the 7c B.C. as a simple temple like that on the Acropolis, but in the Hellenistic period was extended by the addition of a pronaos. At the same time a small Heroon was constructed near its entrance. It continued in use right through the Roman period, being converted into a church, perhaps as the first cathedral, of Gortyna[26]. Immediately west of the temple is the Smaller Theatre (Fig.58.19) which is the best preserved of all the theatres in Crete; constructed on the level plain, it is built entirely of tile-faced concrete, with a double tiered cavea 50m in external diameter[27]. Some distance west again of the theatre is the site of the 6c Basilica at Mavropapas (Fig.58.20)[28], which is no longer visible, except for a few architectural fragments lying in a field. These, however, come from the temple that preceded the church. The fragments include Ionic capitals and composite pilasters that date to the 2/3c A.D. but there are also Doric fragments that could come from an earlier Hellenistic temple associated with the large group of proxenia decrees of that date found on the site[29]. The final temple in this central area is that of Isis and Serapis[30] (Fig.58.21) to the north of the Pythian Apollo. The temple now revealed is 1/2c A.D. in date, but again there seems to have been a Hellenistic predecessor.

The limit of the city is basically marked out by the position of the cemeteries on the three sides not bounded by three mountains. To the west the known cemetery is about 400m beyond the Lethaeus although there are stray tombs closer, like the chamber tomb in the west flank of the Acropolis[31]. The main cemetery[32] here obviously lay by the main road out, which was found in one section with a good paved surface 5.30m wide. In the area there were some houses forming a suburb along the main road, one with a white pebble mosaic floor and others continuing up to the 6c. The graves however were numerous, basically either of the stone cist and slab type or more complex enclosures built of stone with partitions for the individual burial, or in one case a clay sarcophagus[33]. On the south side the cemetery lay in the Mitropolis area extending eastwards; here Taramelli excavated a chamber tomb constructed of tile-faced concrete and noted in the area many fragments of sarcophagi and plain coffins[34]. Other well-built stone tombs have been found more recently[35] in the same area. In the actual village of Mitropolis lies the site of the probable Martyrion (fig.58.22)[36]. Finally, on the east side the cemetery was in the area of the village of Ay.Deka, where below the church a group of six tile graves in one enclosure are venerated as the burial places of the martyrs. Similar grouped tile graves have been excavated dating to the 1-3c, and at the turning of the Vagionia road a tile and stone chamber tomb of the 1c A.D. has also been found[37].

1. Basic studies, *IC* IV.Praef. A. Taramelli, *AJA* 2nd series VI, 1902, p.101f.
2. G. Rizza and V. Scrinari, *Il sanctuario sull'acropoli di Gortyna* (Rome 1968).
3. *Ibid.* for the temple, p.23f. The only identifiable terracotta was of Athena but there were many other female ones.
4. See p.71, and p.109 for basilica.
5. See p.71.
6. Taramelli, *op.cit.* note 1, p.118f.
7. See p.65.
8. See p.63.
9. Belli ed. Falkener, p.21.
10. See p.110ff.
11. Personal observation: one Corinthian capital of the normal 2c type and a fragment of architrave (pl.68.) that resembles the style of the Severan architecture at Lepcis that in its turn is probably closely related to contemporary work in Greece and Asia Minor. See M. Lyttleton *Baroque architecture in Classical Antiquity* (London 1974), p.292.
12. *IC*.IV.239, 240, Asklepios. 241, 242, Highest God. 269, 272, 276, 278 (Severus), 281. Also see p.37ff. for emperor worship.
13. Personal observations.
14. *Kret. Khron.* XIV, 1960, p.460 and 508.
15. *Ann Sc. At.* XIV-XVI, 1955, p.479.
16. The baths have never been investigated; very short note in *Italian Guide* p.17. Also personal observations.
17. See p.70-71.
18. See p.63-65.
19. See p.79-80.
20. *IC*.IV.468, but dating the lid to the post-Arab period.
21. See p.75-76.
22. See p.75-76.
23. Personal observation for the aqueduct, etc. *Ann.Sc. At.* XXXI-I' 1969-70, p.449, and *Kret. Khron.* XXV, 1973, p.470 for the temple.
24. *IC*.IV.270, 333.
25. See p.79.
26. See p.108.
27. See p.61.
28. See p.109.
29. *Mon. Ant.* XVIII, p.284f. The pilaster is no. 570 in E. von Mercklin *Antike Figuralkapitelle* (1962), p.233. Dated to 2/3c in the eagle group.
30. See p.73, 75.
31. Taramelli, *op.cit.* note 1, p.158.
32. *PAE* 1971, p.292. 1c A.D. houses, *Ergon* 1975, p.197.
33 *Kret. Khron.* XXV, 1973, p.474.
34. *op.cit.* note 1, p.160.
35. *Kret. Khron.* XXV, 1973, p.464.
36. See p.112-113.
37. *A. Delt.* XVII.2,1961-2, p.285. *A. Delt.* XXVI.2.2, 1971, p. 500. *PAE* 1969, p.241.

(10/11) KOUSSES Graves and sherds have been found here[1].

1. Graves, *BCH* LIX, 1925, p.474. Sherds, *ABSA* XXXIII, 1932-3, p.90.

(10/12) POBIA Nearby, at Alithine, a group of graves constructed of mortared stone walls and covered with stone slabs was discovered in the course of laying a pipeline. They probably are Christian from their alignment and lack of grave goods. Nearby, Roman houses with pithoi and other pottery have been located.[1] Other material from the area includes a denarius of Domitian[2], a 1/2c tombstone and a 4c inscription which may have some religious significance[3]. In the same area at Kouroupes is a cave 'τσή Μεϊρες ή τρύπα' which contained Roman lamps[4].

1. *Kret.Khron.* XXIV, 1972, p.492. *PAE* 1971, p.286.
2. *Kret. Khron.* XIX, 1965, p.291.
3. *IC*.I.XXIII.20 and 22.
4. Faure, *BCH* XCI, 1967, p.135.

(10/13) PERI In the course of road works a Roman building was discovered containing a row of twelve pithoi sunk into the floor up to their necks, presumably as storage vessels. Three smaller pithoi were also found to the north of the first row[1].

1. *Kret.Khron.* XIV, 1960, p.525.

(10/14) PLATANOS Although more famous for its Minoan remains, minor excavations were also conducted on a Roman site at Siderogourna[1] where a 'country dwelling' was excavated and the existence of a kiln noted.

1. *A. Delt* II, 1916, par.25.

(10/15) PLORA The site of ancient Pyloros seems to have been around the modern villages of Plora and Apesokari, rather than to the west, as Pendlebury suggested[1]. Between the villages there are substantial remains of concrete walls forming a cistern 10.50m x 6.00m linked to another building by a wall or aqueduct[2]. From Plora itself comes a marble head of a male assigned to the Roman period[3].

1. *AC* p.374.
2. Personal observations. The remains are to the south of the road about halfway between the villages.
3. *A. Delt.* XXVI.2.2, 1971, p.500.

(10/16) APESOKARI Pendlebury recorded massive walls at Ellinika 5 minutes NW of the village. Although the remains recorded above under Plora are a reasonable distance away from Apesokari, taking into account Pendlebury's famed walking rate it is likely that these two sites are the same or possibly the two ends of the same site[1].

1. *ABSA* XXXIII, 1932-3, p.88.

(10/17) LOGAROTOPOS 35 minutes SW of Plora, Pendlebury reported numerous walls and columns on this summit, with further sherds below[1].

1. *ABSA* XXXIII, 1932-3, p.89.

(10/18) AYIOS SIDHEROS Roman sherds[1].

1. *ABSA* XXXIII, 1932-3, p.88.

(10/19) VASILIKI There seems to have been a small site here in the low hills above the plain, with sherds[1], walls[2], and a possible olive press[3] found here.

1. *ABSA* XXXIII, 1932-3, p.87.
2. *Arch. Anz.* 1938, p.470.
3. *A. Delt.* XX.3, 1965, p.555.

(10/20) GOULOPHARANGO GORGE At Ay. Savvas a rectangular stone building was noted[1] associated with Roman pottery and plaster, and also Minoan material.

1. *ABSA* XXXIII, 1932-3, p.87.

(10/21) TRYPETE At the mouth of the above gorge are the remains of a small Roman site where Evans saw a cistern[1] which however could not be located by Pendlebury[2], who only found sherds. Nearby is a cave which is claimed to have yielded Roman material[3]. Presumably the site was a small port or fishing village.

1. *POM* II.i p.82.
2. *ABSA* XXXIII, 1932-3, p.87.
3. Faure, *BCH* LXXX, 1956, p.100 no.8.

(10/22) MIAMOU At Makry Livadhi are the remains of a small settlement[1] and sherds in the nearby cave[2]. It may be that this site is connected to possible exploitation of the mineral resources of the Asterousia Mountains, in particular the copper and iron ores[3].

1. *A.Delt.* IV, 1918, par. p.10. Minor finds, *Kret.Khron.* XVII, 1963, p.406.
2. *AJA*, 2nd series I, 1897, p.292.
3. See p.22.

(10/23) LEBENA (Fig.59) The site here seems to have been entirely devoted to the cult of Asklepios[1] until the construction of its very much less impressive Christian successor in the form of the basilica[2] to the east. Apart from these religious buildings with the associated guest houses, etc., the only remains are those of a cemetery of tombs to the east[3] constructed of stone and tile and covered with stone slabs. One tomb contained a fine golden finger ring with a sard intaglio of Zeus Serapis.

1. *IC*.I.XVII, and p.79. See p.80ff for the buildings.
2. See p.113-114.
3. *Ergon* 1971, p.261-2, pl.321-3.

(10/24) ANTISKARI A Roman bronze and a silver Hellenistic coin of Gortyna are meant to have come from here[1]. Also, Roman sherds are claimed from close by some possible copper ores here[2].

1. *AC* p.362, 374.

Fig.59. Lebena: general plan of the city.

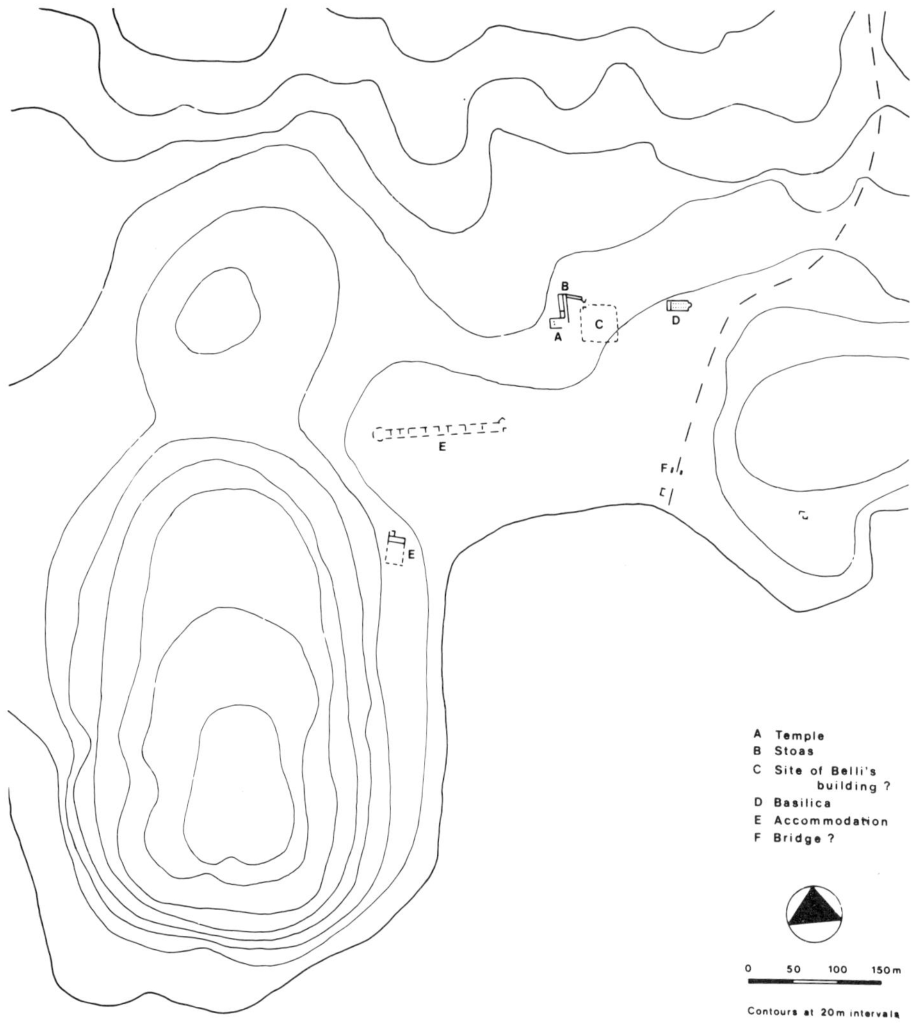

2. P. Faure, 'Le problème du cuivre dans la Crète antique', *Acts of the 2nd Cretological Congress* II, (Athens 1968), p.182.

(10/25) LASEA 8km west of Lebena is the site of ancient Lasea, covering a considerable area on the mainland. No excavation has been carried out here but Hellenistic tombs[1], various inscriptions[2] and amphorae off the coast have been found[3]. The site itself is covered with pottery[4] and remains of concrete walls, including one section lined with *opus signinum:* the recent survey has identified a possible temple, basilica and aqueduct system. A breakwater extends towards the island of Traphos, but leaves a channel 10-15m wide between the island and its south end. On the next headland to the west a built, vaulted, freestanding tomb of the same type as at Lissos (19/18) and Suia (19/17) can be seen.

1. *Kret.Khron.* XVIII, 1964, p.284.
2. *IC*.I.XV.
3. *A. Delt.* XXII.2.2, 1967, p.488
4. Personal observation. Pottery, ARSW 104-5, LRC 3 E. Eastern Sigillata. D.J.Blackman and K. Branigan, 'An archaeological survey on the S. coast of Crète', *ABSA* LXX, 1975, p.28-32, site SC10.

(10/26) AGIOPHARANGO GORGE This gorge was intensively surveyed[1] and five late Classical-Hellenistic sites and nine Roman were located. Apart from one larger site that was no later than the 1c B.C., all these sites were small farmsteads.

1. *AR* 1971, p.23.

(10/27) BEDIADHOS A lead figurine is recorded from this unlocated place on the Mesara[1].

1. *Kret.Khron.* VII, 1953, p.492.

(10/28) KALOI LIMENES 2km west of Lasea is the bay where St. Paul landed[1]. By the chapel of the Saint there is a considerable scatter of Roman sherds, early and late, with further Roman occupation NW of the modern village[2].

1. *Acts* 27.8.
2. Blackman and Branigan, *op.cit.* (10/25), p.24.

EPARCHY 11 - PIRGIOTISSA

(11/1) TYMBAKI Between the modern village and Kokkinos Pirgos a substantial Graeco-Roman building was found with walls up to 1.80m high, marble columns and tile floors[1]. Closer to the village on the site of the aerodrome, three tile graves were found containing skeletons without grave goods[3].

1. *Kret.Khron.* XII, 1958, p.481.
2. *Kret.Khron.* XI, 1957, p.339.

(11/2) KALYVIA Hellenistic burials and some Roman pottery in a well are known from here[1].

1. *AC* p.362, 374.

(11/3) AYIA TRIADHA Above the Minoan levels were found the remains of a Hellenistic shrine to Zeus Velchanos, the main finds being a mass of tiles with dedications to the god. Above this and slightly to the NE were the ruins of a Roman farm with a main room 12.60 x 3.15m divided into various compartments, containing what seemed to be an olive press[1]

1. F. Halbherr, *Rend.Linc.* XIII, 1905, p.378-9.

(11/4) PHAESTOS Reasonably substantial remains of Hellenistic and earlier buildings were found above the Palace here[1], including a defensive wall taking in the area of the palace and westwards. The Roman occupation of Phaestos was limited to some buildings on the SE slopes[2] and a group of late graves on the actual hill. The main Roman site may have been under the village of Ayios Ioannis below the hill to the south. This change in the site may be connected to the Gortynian capture of the city in the 2c B.C.[3] At Ayios Ioannis on the eastern edge of the village are the remains of what is probably a bath house, with the vaults of two rooms still intact; the building covers about 10m x 8m, with four rooms, now nearly entirely filled with earth[4]. Beyond this was the area of the cemetery in the Roman and Hellenistic periods, as numbers of tombstones have been found in this area, and two actual graves[5].

1. *Italian Guide* p.64f. Most recently, *Ann. Sc. At.* 2nd series XXVII-XXVIII, 1965-6, p.312f.
2. *A. Delt.* XIX.2, 1964, p.448.
3. *IC*.I.XXIII. Praef.
4. Personal observation.
5. Tombstones; *IC*.I.XXIII. 7-15. Graves; *Ergon* 1974, p.117.

(11/5) KAMILARI I At Palaioekklesia there seems to have been an earlier religious building which from the dedications[1] was a temple to Artemis of Hellenistic date. A small part of the building has been excavated.

1. *IC*.I.XXIII.6. Also for the excavations, *Kret.Khron.* XI, 1958, p.290. *A.Delt.* XXI.2, 1966, p.410 for a marble head from here.

(11/6) KAMILARI II All around the turning to Kamilari from the road to Matala is a site *c.*400 x 350m, with a lot of pottery and one fragment of a stone-faced concrete wall[1].

1. Pottery – E. Sigillata, Çandarli, much ARSW, LRC, including a stamped base, Hayes 72. Also a very late lamp with a funnel filler. Earlier material included black-glaze and what was probably earlier pithoi fragments. Personal observation. Map reference, BM. Sheet 25/815023.

(11/7) SIVA A hoard of coins from here included various Greek and Roman issues but also some Mediaeval ones, making it somewhat unlikely that this find actually indicates a Roman site[1].

1. *Kret.Khron.* XII, 1958, p.480.

(11/8) MATALA Apart from a stone building[1] of uncertain function near the sea shore, no Roman building is known from this, the main recorded harbour of Gortyna. There is also a possible basilica and temple[2] but these are both rather uncertain. One of the most important aspects of the site is the ship shed on the south side of the cove; this is 38.0m x 5.85m and was possibly roofed[3]. It cannot be dated since there was no associated material, but is probably Hellenistic or Roman. However, Matala is most famous for its numerous tombs cut into the soft rock on the north side of the bay and further up the coast to the north. A few have been excavated and date to the 1/2c A.D.[4] They are all variants on the designs of a single or double with side rooms chamber tomb. The design of the niches also varies slightly from rectangular with a loculus to semi-circular without.
The role of Matala as a harbour and equally the difficulty of entering it under certain conditions is illustrated by a wreck just north of the bay of a Roman merchantman with a cargo of Rhodian amphorae[5].

1. *EEKS* II, p.536.
2. See p.114.
3. D.J. Blackman, 'The Neosoikos at Matala', *Acts of the 3rd Cretological Congress I*, (Athens 1973), p.14.
4. *PAE* 1969, p.242.
5. G. Grile and C. Davaras, 'The possible site of Menelaus' Shipwrecks', *Kret. Khron.* XVII, 1963, p.47.

EPARCHY 12 – AMARI

(12/1) KASTRI A small defended site at the mouth of the gorge of Patsos with short stretches of surviving walls and towers. Contrary to Pendlebury, the recent survey could only find Classical-Hellenistic material and no Roman.

1. *AC.* p.369. M.S.F.Hood and P.Warren, 'Ancient sites in the Province of Ayios Vasilios, Crete', *ABSA* LXI, 1966, site 36 p.188.

(12/2) PATSOS Of the group of caves near this village the most important is that of Ay.Andonios, from which came a dedication to Hermes Kranaios[1] dating to the 1c B.C.; however, there does not seem to be any other material of Hellenistic/Roman date from the cave. From the slope in front of another cave[2] to the north there was one sherd of ARSW, form 105.
From the hill Kefalia west of the village came some sherds of Graeco-Roman date[3].

1. Hood and Warren, *op.cit.* (12/1), site 32(1) p.186. *IC* II.IX.
2. *Ibid.* no.32 (2), p.187.
3. *Ibid.* no.35, p.188.

(12/3) AY. GEORGIOS Just south of here[1] and north of Apostoli, there are two ruined chapels of early Mediaeval date with Sgraffito ware bowls built into the walls. It is possible that the westernmost of them may utilise an earlier structure.

1. Personal observation at BM Sheet 8/665827.

(12/4) SYBRITA The site of Sybrita extends from the Acropolis above the modern village of Thronos, under the village and for a considerable distance to the south. Very limited excavations have been carried out here[1] establishing part of the line of the Classical-Hellenistic walls along the crest of the Acropolis and then east of Thronos down perhaps towards the modern road and then west towards the chapel of Ay.Photini north of Yena, probably the site of one of the cemeteries of Sybrita by the number of tombstones found in the area[2]. The most important Roman features from the site are the mosaics from the square at Thronos, where there seems to have been a basilica and possibly an earlier important building[3] and the mosaic, possibly 4c in date, from the area 'ta Marmara' to the SW[4]. In the first area in the village other fragments of Roman buildings were found, including part of a hypocaust system. No temple is known, but dedications to Hermes[5] and the 'Highest God'[6] presuppose such buildings.

1. E. Kirsten, in Matz, p.135f.
2. *IC*.II.XXVI passim.
3. See p.114.
4. See p.54.
5. *A. Delt.* XXIII.2.2, 1968, p.420.
6. *IC*.II.XXVI.3.

(12/5) YERAKARI A group of small sites west of Yerakari: at 'Ston Platano' sherds and walls; at Psares a larger site, possibly a village; at Ayios Ioannis another farm and at Palaioklisia sherds[1].

1. Hood *et al*, *ABSA* LIX, 1964, site 26, 3-6, p.75.

(12/6) YERAKARI Some Roman material is known from the village itself, but the main site in the area was about 0.9km SE, where substantial concrete walls were exposed in the road cutting on the road to Vrises and Ano Meros[1].

1. Hood *et al*, *op.cit.* (12/5), site 26, 1-2, p.75.

(12/7) ELENES The cave at Maryieles contained Graeco-Roman sherds and nearby at Merodhiana was the site of a Classical-Hellenistic farm[1].

1. Hood *et al*, *op.cit.* (12/5), no.24, 1 and 3, p.73-4.

(12/8) MERONAS There is a group of small sites about the village, mainly consisting of sherds and tiles probably marking the remains of farms, but at Stavros 3km south of the village there was a possible shrine with many animal figurines found here during road works[1]. Also from here are three 1-3c tombstones[2].

1. *AC* p.370; Hood *et al.*, *op.cit.* (12/5), site 23, p.72.
2. *IC*.II.26.19, 22, 25.

(12/9) ASOMATOS A concrete wall and sherds mark the site of another possible villa[1].

1. Hood *et al.*, *op.cit.* (12/5), site 27(5), p.76. No longer visible.

(12/10) SKOUFIA Vaulted building seen in 1933, possibly a cistern[1].

1. *AC* p.371.

(12/11) MONASTIRAKI Just north of the modern village is a site with many stones from walls and sherds with black and red 'glaze'[1]. Also, SW of the village a concrete wall and sherds, possibly the site of a villa[2].

1. Hood *et.al*, *op.cit.* (12/5), site 27 (30), p.76.

(12/12) VIZARI Although this site is most important for the late basilica here[1], of 8/9c date, there is also an extensive town site extending between the basilica and the village about 1km to the east. The only excavated site is a possible bath house to the SE of the basilica, where Kalokyres[2] found a black and white mosaic in a niche: this probably dates to the 3c[3]. There are other concrete built walls standing in the area, but it is not known of what date or function these are.

1. See p.115ff.
2. *PAE* 1956, p.251, pl. 127b, 128a, b.
3. See p.54.

(12/13) VIGLA A small Classical and Hellenistic town is situated on this hill about 1km south of Vazari[1].

1. Hood *et al, op.cit.* (12/5), site 30, p.77.

(12/14) KOUROUTES Roman sherds and a lamp[1].

1. *AC* p.370.

(12/15) AYIOS IOANNIS In the village itself the church of Ay.Ioannis reuses the site of a Roman concrete building[1]. Ayia Sofia about 1km to the west also reuses such a structure, which stands about 3m high at the SW corner. Pottery spreads about 50m down the slope, including LRC 3 C[2].

1. Hood *et al, op.cit* (12/5), 31(1), p.78. Nothing visible 1974.
2. *ibid.,* 31(2). Personal observation.

(12/16) APODHOULOU About 1km to the NW are the traces of a small Roman site, possibly a farm, including a stone olive press[1].

1. Hood *et al, op.cit.* (12/5), site 32(3), p.78.

(12/17) ARDHAKTOS Sherds seen in 1935[1].

1. *AC* p.369.

(12/18) RIZIKAS Roman lamp[1].

1. T. Dunbabin, 'Antiquities of the Amari', *ABSA* XLII, 1947, p.189.

(12/19) KASTRI On this ridge controlling the southern entrance into the Amari is the site of a small 'city': there is a profuse scatter of stones and Classical to Late Roman pottery[1]. On the plain south of the hill is another smaller site of what may have been a sanctuary, the finds from it being predominantly lamps and pots of odd forms. A dedication to Athena Wadia might well have come from here[2]. Finally in this area, about 1km south of the Kastri, at Mandhres, are the remains of a small Roman settlement and cemetery of slab and tile covered graves with one tombstone[3].

1. Hood *et al, op.cit.* (12/5), site 32(4) p.79. The site appears to have suffered considerably from landslips since then.
2. *Ibid.* site 32(5) p.80. *Kret. Khron.* XI, 1957, p.337. *IC.*II.XXX.2.
3. *Ibid.* site 32(6) p.80. Tombstone to Kotulos: K. Davaras, ' Ἐπιγραφαὶ ἐκ Κρήτης II', *A.Delt.* XVIII.1, 1963, p.141, no.2.

(12/20) MALAKI Possibly the site of a basilica[1].

1. See p.117.

EPARCHY 13 - MYLOPOTAMOS

(13/1) STAVROMENOS At the eastern edge of the coastal plain of Rethimnon there is a large site stretching between the sea and the first hills inland for about 1km along the coast. It is not known what its ancient name was, although Allaria has been suggested. The main Roman site appears to have been east of the stream in the area known as Palaiokastro, and there is a large building of concrete exposed on the east side of the stream itself[1]. Other building fragments have been noted for about 200m east but the suggested tombs[2], considering their position within the built-up area, are more likely to be further buildings. The actual cemeteries seem to be west of the stream, where tile and slab covered graves have been found, and further inland, where rock-cut tombs of the normal type with niches have been seen. A large amount of pottery of Hellenistic black-glaze, true Samian, Eastern Sigillata, Çandarli, Late Roman C, and African RSW, can be seen on the site. Several tombstones are known to have come from here as well, and mosaics are reported from the site, but no other details are known[4].

1. Main account, Hood *et al, op.cit.* (12/5), site 12(1), p.62. Also Personal observations.
2. *Ibid.* fig. 9, nos. 2, 3. 3 appears to be modern work.
3. *IC.*II.XXIV.1. Faure, *Kret. Khron.* XXI, 1969, nos. 7-9, p.318.
4. *A. Delt.* IV, 1918, par. p.15.

(13/2) VIRAN EPISKOPI In the actual village below the 10/11c predecessor to Ay. Eirene there was not only a Christian basilica[1] but also a temple probably dedicated to Diktynna, if the milestone recording the repair of the road with her money which was found associated with the building is to be taken as evidence for its dedication[2]. Apart from the inscription a statue of an ephebe was also found here. Possibly connected to this temple is the early Roman Ionic capital reused in the church of Ay. Demetrios to the SW of the village by the river[3]. Alternatively there may be another earlier building here as the church is a full 1km to the SW of the village. There is another small Roman site 1.50km east of Viran Episkopi on a small hill 'Roussa' next to the stream on the main road[4].

1. See p.117.
2. *AE* 1962, 129. *Cf. IC.* II.XI.6.
3. Personal observation.
4. Hood *et al, op.cit.* (12/5), site 7, p.59.

(13/3) PANORMOS Apart from the 6c basilica [1] very little is known about this site, which is mainly situated on the low ridge above the narrow coastal plain here. The area is covered with stone heaps from the buildings, but there are no excavated or standing remains other than the basilica. The length of occupation of the site, 1c B.C. - 9c A.D., is shown by the coins recorded from here in Heraklion Museum[2].

1. See p.117-8.
2. Nos. 1428 Issue of Knossos (Kydas) ae. 1430 Diocletian, ae. 1431 Probus, ae. 1432 Caligula, ae. 1433 Michael I, Follis.

(13/4) BALI Probably the ancient Astale; there are remains on both sides of the bay[1] with the most intensive pot scatter in the northernmost cove on the west side. Unfortunately none of the pottery observed could be closely dated. Faure[2] claims late Roman sherds in a nearby cave.

1. *AC* p.363. Personal observations.
2. *BCH* LXXXIX, 1965, p.46.

(13/5) ELEUTHERNA Now totally deserted, this is one of the most impressive sites in Crete, dominating the surrounding countryside from its promontory between two streams[1]. The site is approached from the south along a rock-cut road complete with drains which leads onto a courtyard about 10m wide and cut to resemble paving stones. At the actual entrance into the city there are the ruins of a massive tower (P1.3) still about 8m high and 5m square. It was constructed of concrete rubble, faced with squared stone and a little tile, but the interior appears to be solid, with no internal chamber like that of the bastion in the Acropolis circuit at Gortyna. The date of the Eleutherna tower is uncertain and might be either late Roman like the Gortyna circuit or early Mediaeval, when the city was still occupied. Other fragments of late Roman or Mediaeval defences were found by Payne in his explorations on the slopes to the NE.

No other building survives on the site, although there is a possible basilica at Ay. Eirene[2] and Spratt thought he could identify a temple on the east slopes where he saw a statue of Parian marble[3]. However, on the west side rock-cut cisterns supplied by an aqueduct from the mountains to the south are still visible. There are two groups each of three cisterns divided by rock pillars: the cisterns are overall both about 40 x 25 x 5-6m, with the pillars either 2m or 3m square. Although the recently discovered aqueduct would seem to be Roman, the cisterns are probably earlier, for on the eastern side of the site there is a fine water supply system of small cisterns and conduits that is definitely of Hellenistic construction[4]. Of similar build are the two bridges in the valleys to the east and north, illustrating the wealth of this city in the Hellenistic period[5]. Near the northern bridge was one of the cemetery areas, with the tombs cut into the cliffs of the main site.

Numerous inscriptions are known from the site, mainly reused in the village of Prines, including dedications to Augustus, Tiberius and Severus, together with Caracalla[6]. Various statues have also been found[7].

1. Best description, Spratt II, p.89f. Also *IC.*II.XII. Spanake II, p.158f. *JHS* XLIX, 1929, p.224 for Payne's trenches. Personal observations.
2. See p.120.
3. *Op.cit.* note 1, p.94.
4. Personal observation for the latter. Cisterns: Spanake, *op.cit.* note 1. Aqueduct: *A. Delt.* XXII.2.2, 1967, p.500.

5. E.N. Petroulake, *AE* 1914, p.230, basically repeated in S. Parnicki-Pudełko, 'Starozytne mosty w Grecji', *Archeologia* XI, 1959, p.128.
6. *IC*.II.XII. 27-9.
7. *A. Delt*. XXII.2.2, 1967, p.500. *Kret. Khron.* X, 1956, p.422.

(13/6) PRINES A larger than life headless marble statue possibly of Hera was found here, presumably originally from Eleutherna[1].
1. *A.Delt.*XX.3, 1965, p.570.

(13/7) ALPHA A cave with Byzantine sherds[1].
1. Faure, *BCH* LXXXIX, 1965, p.48.

(13/8) PLAKA KALIS A Roman building with a hypocaust with round tile columns, limestone floor and marble facing slabs was excavated here, probably a bath house[1].
1. *Kret.Khron.* XI, 1957, p.337.

(13/9) PERAMA Pendlebury reported Roman sites at Palaioklisia and Ta Grivila, but nothing was seen in 1962[1].
1. *AC*, p.370 and Hood *et al., op.cit.* (12/5), sites 3-4, p.56.

(13/10) KHOUMERI At Megas Dhris, on top of the hill, are traces of a Roman site with reported concrete buildings and a cistern. Below this site is a large rock-cut chamber tomb[1].
1. Hood *et al., op.cit.* (12/5), site 2(3) and (2), p.55-6.

(13/11) MELIDONI More famous as the scene of a particularly effective massacre in the 19c, the cave was previously dedicated to Hermes[1] as shown by the inscriptions carved on the rock face at the entrance into the cavern.
1. *IC*.II.XXVIII for the inscriptions etc.; Spanake II p.260 is the best description of the cave itself.

(13/12) KERAMATA 4c B.C. graves[1].
1. *Kret.Khron.* VII, 1953, p.490.

(13/13) EPISKOPI Reused architectural fragments in the church of Ayios Ioannis probably indicate an earlier basilica here[1].
1. See p.120.

(13/14) SISES On the coast north of this village road works destroyed a small Hellenistic and Roman site; amongst the material recovered was an inscription naming the Sisaioi, demonstrating the continuity of the placename[1].
1. Faure, *Kret.Khron.* XIX, 1965, p.229 and 284.

(13/15) ALOIDES Marble statue of a seated female and a lion protome ought to indicate a site of some wealth or a shrine[1].
1. *Kret.Khron.* III, 1949, p.595-6.

(13/16) AXOS The ancient city of Axos spreads off the hill dominating the modern village and extends some distance NE towards Livadha. However, little excavation has been carried out here except for the two temples dug at the turn of the century[1]. The main temple on the Acropolis was of the normal Cretan archaic type, possibly dedicated to Apollo or Athena. The smaller of the temples was situated off the hill and was more conventional in plan, with pronaos, naos and opisthodomos, this probably dated to the Hellenistic period, but continued in use into the Roman era. A third temple might have existed at Yerakaro, where a Roman relief of Demeter together with numerous figurines was found, but no actual temple structure could be located[2]. In the Christian period there was at least one basilica, on the same site as the later church of Ay. Ioannis, and possibly another at the site of the chapel of Eleutherios and Modestos[3]. Given the high proportion of Hellenistic and earlier finds from the site in general, e.g. in 1965 20 Roman and Byzantine coins as opposed to 155 Hellenistic[4] were reported, it would seem that the city declined somewhat in importance in the Roman period. Nevertheless, such Roman tombs as have been found generally have contained quite rich grave goods in terms of jewellery, etc.[5].
1. *IC*.II.V. *Mon.Ant.* IX, 1898, p.308f.
2. E.N. Petroulakes, 'Finds from Axos', *AE* 1915, p.43.
3. See p.120.
4. *A. Delt.* XX.3, 1965, p.566-7.
5. *Ibid*. Also *A. Delt*. XVII.2, 1961-2, p.300.

(13/17) LAMIA In the mountains behind Axos, a cave with Roman sherds[1].
1. Faure, *BCH*, LXXX, 1956, p.100.

(13/18) ANOGEIA Roman silver coin[1].
1. *Kret.Khron.* XIX, 1965, p.291.

(13/19) SISARKHA Pendlebury saw a small fort at Santiri[1].
1. *AC* p.371. In 1974 the locals denied any knowledge of the place or any antiquities in the area.

(13/20) IDAEAN CAVE The cult of the Cretan Zeus continued into the Roman period with inscriptions, lamps and a house below the cave, evidence of continued interest[1]. Possibly the wish to visit the cave in this period was as much from tourist motives as religious ones.
1. *IC* I.XII. Convenient summary in R. F. Willetts *Cretan cults and Festivals* (London 1962), p.144. For a religous tourist, Philostratus' *Life of Apollonius of Tyana* IV.34.2.

(13/21) KALAMA Graeco-Roman tomb[1].
1. *Kret.Khron.* III, 1949, p.595.

EPARCHY 14 - RETHIMNO

(14/1) LAPPA Standing on the hill between the rivers Petre and Mousella is the site of Lappa, below the modern town of Argyroupolis. Because of the intensive later occupation on the site very little is preserved of ancient Lappa, one of the two 'free' cities of Roman Crete. The most important building is that recorded by Belli as a temple but was probably a 3/4c bath house, the scanty remains of which can still be seen on the slopes of the hill to the NW by the springs that supply the Mousella[1]. On the northern edge of the hill itself there is a further possible bath house reused in the church of Ay.Nikolaos[2] with surviving tile-faced concrete walls and exedra outside. The apse of the latter feature is about 1.50m in diameter and 2.0m high. In front of it is a possible plunge bath 2.50m x 1.40m, with further rooms in front and to the north. Of the later part of the period there are three possible churches, at Phoundana below the hill, on the Mousella at Pano Chori, and at Ay. Phanourgios in the actual city[3]. The mosaics found somewhere in the town in 1918 seem to be 4c Hunting Mosaics, and more likely to come from a secular building, possibly the main bath house[4] mentioned above. Various other architectural fragments have been reused in the later buildings, the most important being an Ionic capital of Roman date which can be seen just down the hill from Ay.Phanourgios. There is the normal quantity of fragmentary statuary[5], but also one complete statue of Aphrodite 1.61m high in the Hellenistic tradition but dating to the Neronian period[6]. Dedications to Augustus and Hadrian survive, but the statues that probably originally accompanied them have not[7].
1. See p.83.
2. Gerola, *Mon. Ven.* II, p.51-3. Personal observations.
3. See p.120.
4. See p.54.
5. *A. Delt*. XXIV.2.2, 1969, p.448. *A. Delt.* XVII.2, 1961-2, p.300.
6. D. Papastamos and K. Staehler, ' ῎Αγαλμα ᾽Αφροδίτης ρωμαϊκῶν αὐτοκρατορικων χρόνων', *Kret.Khron.* XXIV, 1972, pp.93-106.
7. *IC*.II.XVI.12, 13.

(14/2) ZOURIDHI Remains at Ay. Georgios and Ay. Ioannis north of the village and at Christos to the south[1].
1. *AC* p.371.

(14/3) MONOPARI Although the later Venetian fortifications[1] dominate the site, there are also traces of earlier defences, possibly Hellenistic. Sherds of that period and of the Roman period have been found here[2].
1. Gerola, *Mon. Ven.* I, p.265. Spratt II, p.114.
2. *AC* p.370, 360.

(14/4) RETHIMNON There can be little doubt that this was the site of ancient Rhithymna[1] but almost nothing is known of the older town except one late Roman building from the Plateia Kiouloubase[2]. It is very likely that most of the ancient site lies below the Fortetsa on the hill dominating the town. Belli saw a temple on a hill near the town[3] but it is not known where this was. The only visible ancient work is the ship shed to the west of the Fortetsa.
1. *IC*.II.XXIV. K. Kalokyres Ἡ ἀρχαία Ῥίθυμνα (Athens 1950).
2. *Kret. Khron.* VII, 1953, p.490.
3. Belli ed. Falkener, p.25.

(14/5) MOUNT VRYSINAS Faure claimed to have seen Hellenistic and Roman houses at this sanctuary site[1], but recent excavations[2] do not seem to have found any material of this date.

1. *BCH* LXXXVII, 1963, p.504.
2. C. Davaras, *AAA* VII, 1974, p.210-3.

(14/6) PRASES South of the village at Ayios Kosmas, Roman sherds[1].
1. Hood *et al, op.cit.* (12/5), site 18, p.69.

(14/7) KERA (ONITHE GOULEDHIANA) At Onithe, situated on a plateau above the valley linking the Spili and Amari valleys, are the remains of a large early Greek city, possibly Phalanna. On the northern edge of the site are the ruins of a large 6c basilica[1], but apart from this there is very little evidence for any Roman or even Hellenistic occupation[2].
1. See p.120-121.
2. *AC* p.360, 370. In early 1975 practically all the pottery on surface of the site seemed to be early -? Archaic.

(14/8) AMPELAKIA Graeco-Roman sherds in a field at Livadhos south of the village[1].
1. *AC* p.363.

(14/9) SELLI At Agromouli south of the village and below (14/7) an extensive site with walls[1].
1. *AC* p.371.

(14/10) MIRTHIOS Roman sherds at Petres and Ay. Theodoros[1].
1. Hood *et al, op.cit.*, (12/5), site 20, p.70; *AC* p.370.

(14/11) PYRGOS Sherds, including wavy-lined amphorae[1].
1. Hood *et al, op.cit.*, (12/5), site 11, p.61.

(14/12) PIYI Road works destroyed a cemetery of tile covered graves, some of which were partially cut into the limestone[1]. Also from here comes a tombstone of a Christian[2].
1. *A.Delt.* XXV.2.2, 1970, p.476.
2. *IC*.II.XXIV.12. Dated there by letter form to 4c.

(14/13) PANKALOKHORI Sherds and a headless statue seen here[1].
1. *AC* p.370.

(14/14) ARSANI Tile grave[1].
1. Hood *et al, op.cit.*, (12/5), site 13, p.66.

(14/15) PIKRI Two rich tombs have been excavated here: one of a woman with glass vessels, bronze chain and mirror, the other with ten pots[1].
1. *A.Delt.* XXIII.2.2, 1968, p.419. *Kret.Khron.* VIII, 1954, p.517.

(14/16) AMNATOS A reasonably sized settlement on top of the hill Perisakia with Classical to Roman material, including quern fragments and the circular orbs from an olive crusher. In the cliff marking the eastern side of the site were several rock-cut chamber tombs[1].
1. Hood *et al, op.cit.*, (12/5), site 16, p.67-8. In 1974 the site had been almost destroyed by agricultural activity.

(14/17) TZIDHAIS Small 'fort' and cistern[1].
1. *AC* p.371.

EPARCHY 15 - AY. VASILIOS

(15/1) APOLLONIA This elusive ancient site[1] may be the Graeco-Roman site at Sellia Soudha.
1. *IC* II.p.192. M.S.F.Hood and P. Warren, 'Ancient sites in the Province of Ayios Vasilios, Crete', *ABSA* LXI, 1966, site 27, p.186. Matz p.126.

(15/2) SELLIA FINIKIAS Classical to Late Roman site high up in the valley[1].
1. Hood and Warren, *op.cit.*, (15/1), site 26, p.184. Pottery includes LRC 3.

(15/3) SELLIA AY. MARINA Small site near the ruined church with slab covered graves, sherds and tile. Again LRC 3 amongst the pottery[1].
1. Hood and Warren, *op.cit.*, (15/1), site 29, p.185.

(15/4) SELLIA KAMBOS Small Roman site on the mountain plain above Sellia, with LRC amongst the pottery[1].
1. Hood and Warren, *op.cit.*, (15/1), site 30, p.185.

(15/5) SELLIA VOUKELARI Sherds on the high ground above the beach.[1]
1. Hood and Warren, *op.cit.*, (15/1), site 28, p.185.

(15/6) PLAKIAS In the area of the church of Ayios Georgios a small Roman site marked by tile and sherds[1]. North of the church are reported slab covered graves.
1. Hood and Warren, *op.cit.*, (15/1), site 25, p.183. Tile is reused in the church but there is no other sign that it might be on the site of an earlier building. The Roman concrete masonry reported in *ABSA* is natural conglomerate. Personal observation.

(15/7) VIGLOTOPI On the side of the valley overlooking a fertile area to the east are the ruins of a Mediaeval chapel that is on a site of a larger structure, possibly a basilica[1]. There is some pottery about, but none need be earlier than Mediaeval.
1. See p.122. Personal observation at BM8/532287. The hill behind the site (to NW) is named Viglotopi.

(15/8) KOXARE AMBELO Graeco-Roman site on the hill above the entrance into the Gorge of Preveli[1]. Sherds and tile can be seen on the site, but nothing distinctive. On the other side of the valley here at Ayios Markos another Roman site yielded a comparatively unusual sherd of LRC Form 10 (6/7c).
1. Hood and Warren, *op.cit.*, (15/1), site 19 and 17, p.180. Ay. Markos; no.13, p.177.

(15/9) AY. PELAYIA On a knoll above the valley a concrete and tile wall with associated sherds marks the site of a probable villa[1].
1. Hood and Warren, *op.cit.*, (15/1), site 11, p.176.

(15/10) PREVELI On the east bank of the Megas Potamos about 250m north of the larger of the 19c bridges are the remains of what Platon[1] correctly thought must have been a bath house. It is a circular building with a central room 'petal shaped' with other rooms off it. It obviously is related to the bath building at Lappa and the temple at Lebena. On the west bank of the tributary, i.e. to the SE of the above site, are further sherds and tiles, indicating a smaller building here[2].
1. *Kret.Khron.* I, 1947, p.638. Hood and Warren, *op.cit.* (15/1) site 20 (1), p.180.
2. Hood and Warren, *op.cit.*, (15/1), site 20 (2), p.181.

(15/11) AYIOS SAVVAS At the bottom of the gorge of the same river stands the church of Ay. Savvas with a Roman site between it and the sea[1]. S.E. of the church is a wall of concrete with steps on its south, or seaward, side. The pottery includes ARSW 105 and Cypriot Ware forms 2-3 (all 6/7c).
1. Hood and Warren, *op.cit.*, (15/1), site 21, p.181.

(15/12) AY . PHOTIA Roman walls[1].
1. Matz p.134.

(15/13) CAPE MELISSA Roman sherds and possible houses here may mark the site of Psykheion[1].
1. Hood and Warren, *op.cit.* (15/1), site 3, p.170.

(15/14) SAKTOURIA At Ellinikon SW of the village a few possible Graeco-Roman sherds together with some slab covered graves nearby indicate a possible site. Further south, about 500m from the sea, another mainly Minoan site also yielded some Roman pottery, including a stamped base that from its design is probably ARSW[1].
1. Hood and Warren, *op.cit.*, (15/1), site 5-6, p.171-2.

(15/15) MELABES 2km below the village above the junction of two streams is the site of what was probably Korion[1]. The site has a small acropolis, possibly the site of a temple to Athena, and remains of stone walls to the east.
1. *Kret.Khron.* XIII, 1959, p.391. Two inscriptions, one to Athena, one mentioning the Korioi. G. Huxley, 'Stephanos of Byzantion *s.v.* Κόριον', *Greek, Roman, Byzantine Studies* XI, 1970, p.53. Hood and Warren, *op.cit.*, (15/1), site 2, p.169-70. Nothing later than Hellenistic seen.

(15/16) AYIA GALINI Very little survives at this site, ancient Soulia[1], but in front of the church of Tessares Martires stand two monolithic columns, 4.10m high, of Egyptian granite. It is likely that they came from the temple of Artemis which stood on the right bank of the stream near the sea and was destroyed by building at the turn of the century. Fortunately it was seen by Halbherr[2], who described it as being of late date with Ionic columns of an artificial and bad style, probably contemporary with the Roman inscriptions found on the site. Apart from this the only Roman remains in the village are a stretch of concrete wall near the sea and a Corinthian capital sitting on a roof.

However, about ½ km east of the village on the west side of the River Platis at the cemetery church of Panayia, are the remains of an earlier church and possibly an associated settlement higher up the hill[3].
1. *IC* II.XXV. Hood and Warren, *op.cit.*, (15/1), site 1, p.167, with

full references. Personal observations.

2. *AJA* XI, 1896, p.594.

3. See p.122 for the putative basilica. Sherds included LRC.

(15/17) AY. GALINI WRECK Off Kokkinos Pirgos lie the remains of a vessel wrecked in the late 3c[1]. Apart from the coin hoard dating the wreck it also held a large amount of very miscellaneous bronzes: they include statuettes, lamps, vase attachments, but also two ingots and assorted 'rubbish'. It is a matter of doubt what this cargo means: suggestions include a bronze worker's hoard or a lot of loot from one of the Gothic raiders who attacked Greece in the reign of Probus. If the latter is true, the pirates' taste would seem to be eclectic and odd at that; if the former some of the material neither seems to be junk suitable for melting down nor 'all his own work'.

1. Hood and Warren, *op.cit.* (15/1), site 1, p.169, collects all references. It is of course quite likely that apart from probably calling in at a Cretan port the vessel and its cargo had nothing to do with Crete at all.

(15/18) KERAME On a hill above the coast between Cape Melissa and Preveli is the site of a fortified 'city' with fragments of polygonal and isodomic walls and towers that seem to be mainly Classical rather than later in date. There was no material of definite Roman date. The identification of the site is uncertain; it may be Bionnos[1].

1. Hood and Warren, *op.cit.* (15/1), site 8, p.173. *IC* II.XXX.1.

EPARCHY 16 - SFAKIA

(16/1) POIKILASSOS One of the most remote of the ports on the southern coast of Crete was here, at modern Trypete. Spratt observed[1] various remains in the valley about 1 mile inland, including an inscription to Serapis illustrating the importance of the trade route from Egypt to the settlements on this coast.

1. Spratt II, p.244. *IC* II.XXI.1.3c.

(16/2) SAMARIA In the cave of Ay.Nicolaos in the gorge, Byzantine sherds have been reported[1] and Pashley saw what the locals claimed to be the last refuge of the Greeks sited at Ellenais an hour above the actual village of Samaria[2].

1. *BCH* LXXXVI, 1962, p.55.

2. II.85, 268.

(16/3) TARRHA At the bottom of the gorge on either side of the stream are the ruins of Tarrha; its cemeteries have been excavated[1] and some work done on the site of the church of Panayia. Contrary to the excavator's opinion, it seems that this could be on the site of an earlier temple, which in its turn was converted into a basilica[2] before the whole structure was destroyed at an unknown date, to be rebuilt in the late Mediaeval period. The cemeteries on the other side of the stream are all composed of slab covered graves dating from the Classical to the Late Roman periods. In the same area several buildings of Roman date were located, and also a stretch of the defences, with a round tower linked to a double wall. An extensive spread of burnt glass waste was in the excavator's opinion indicative of glass manufacture nearby but not actually on the site.

1. *IC* II.XXIX. G. Weinberg 'Excavations at Tarrha', *Hesperia* XXIX, 1960, p.90f. T.S.Buechner, 'The glass from Tarrha', *ibid.* p.109f. *A. Delt.* XXV. 2.2., 1970, p.473: XXVI.2.2., 1971, p.511.

2. See p.122 for the basilica and mosaic.

(16/4) ARADENA Perched above a spectacular gorge lies the ancient city of the same name as the modern village. Little can be seen except the remains of the earlier and larger basilica reused in the church of the Archangel Michael[1]. Apart from this there are reputed to be tombs, and north of the village a cistern, 23 x 13m.

1. See p.122 for this. General, *IC* II.IV. Spanake II, p.72.

(16/5) LOUTRO Although this site is almost entirely hemmed in by the mountains behind, the promontory of Loutro accommodated the major Roman city of Phoenix because of its harbour, which provides the only all-season port of Crete's south coast[1]. No real excavation has been carried out on the various tile-faced concrete remains here, but at least one basilica has been identified[2], at the church of the Theotokos. The importance of the harbour is illustrated by the inscription set up by the captain of the 'Isopharia', of Alexandria, in the early 2c[3].

1. Spratt II, p.249. *IC* II.XX.

2. See p.122.

3. *IC*.II.XX.7.

(16/6) ANOPOLIS 600m above Loutro is the plain of Anopolis with several small villages set on the fertile land. Dominating the southern edge of the area is the church of Ay. Aikaterine, controlling the path down to Loutro, and immediately to the west of the church is a large site with numerous collapsed houses of stone (Pl.70) and much pottery, including E. Sigillata[1].

1. *AC* p.360. Only mentions Hellenistic. *IC* II.II. for the few tombstones; also *A.Delt.* XVIII.2, 1963, p.315; *A.Delt.* XXIII.2.2, 1968, p.418. Personal observations.

(16/7) NIBROS A limestone column drum and fragments of other marble columns were observed here, unearthed during the construction of a house. There was also some pottery of an indeterminate character[1].

1. Personal observation, 1974.

(16/8) KOMITADES Column fragments also seen here[1].

1. Personal observation, 1974.

(16/9) PATSIANOS On the western edge of the Frankokastelli plain and just off the higher ground here are a group of Late Roman villages/farms marked by the fallen stone walls of the houses, etc., and pottery[1].

1. M.S.F.Hood, 'Some ancient sites in South-West Crete', *ABSA* LXII, 1967, p.47-57. Sites B4: pottery LRC 3F and 10; 6-7c.
B5: pottery LRC 3c; late 5c.
B6: pottery LRC 10; 6-7c.

(16/10) AY. EVSTRATIOS Between the above sites and the castle is a small site similar to the others and, slightly further east, the larger site of Ay. Evstratios with a basilica[1] and associated village. From the visible remains the site may at one time have been surrounded by a rough wall, but whether this ought to be linked to the Late Roman or Early Mediaeval phase of occupation is uncertain.

1. First site: Personal observation. Ay.Evstratios: Hood, *op.cit.* (16/9), site B7, pot ARSW 105, 67; 4-7c. Basilica, see p.123.

(16/11) AY. NIKETAS The final site on this now desolate plain is just NE of the castle, where the little chapel of Ay. Niketas reuses the earlier (? 6c) basilica here[1]. Unlike Ay. Evstratios there is no obvious village here, and what pottery lies about looks to be Mediaeval.

1. See p.123. Personal observation.

(16/12) ASFENDOU Roman pottery is known from the cave of Skordollakia and from Pigadholakkos, with a vaulted cistern at the latter place as well.[1].

1. Information from M.S.F.Hood.

EPARCHY 17 - APOKORONAS

(17/1) KISAMOS This Kisamos was the port of Aptera[1], but its location is a matter of doubt: it should either be immediately below Aptera at Kalami, where ancient moles are marked below water level on the 1843 Admiralty chart[2] and where Roman and Hellenistic sherds are known, or further to the east at Kalyves.

1. *IC* II.III. Praef., p.11. Faure, *BCH* LXXXIV, 1960, p.209.

2. Reproduced *Mon. Ven.* 1.2, p.512-3, fig.309.

(17/2) APTERA (Fig. 60) 200m above Souda bay, dominating it and the country inland, are the extensive ruins of the city of Aptera, sited on a plateau and defended by its Classical-Hellenistic walls 3.80 - 3.90 km long[1]. These are built in either a polygonal or pseudo-isodomic style, up to 2.80m thick and surviving up to 3.0m high. On the western side one gate survives of Winter's Type II[2], i.e. a gate formed by overlapping the walls; in addition there is a square tower or bastion on the outer, overlapping, wall, with further such towers along the wall, including one to the south 'looking straight' into the gate. Although these walls are

Pl. 70: View over the site of the city of Anopolis.
Pl. 71: North end of the L-shaped cisterns, Aptera.
Pl. 72: Tower at Polyrrhenia.

Fig.60. Aptera: plan of the ancient city site.

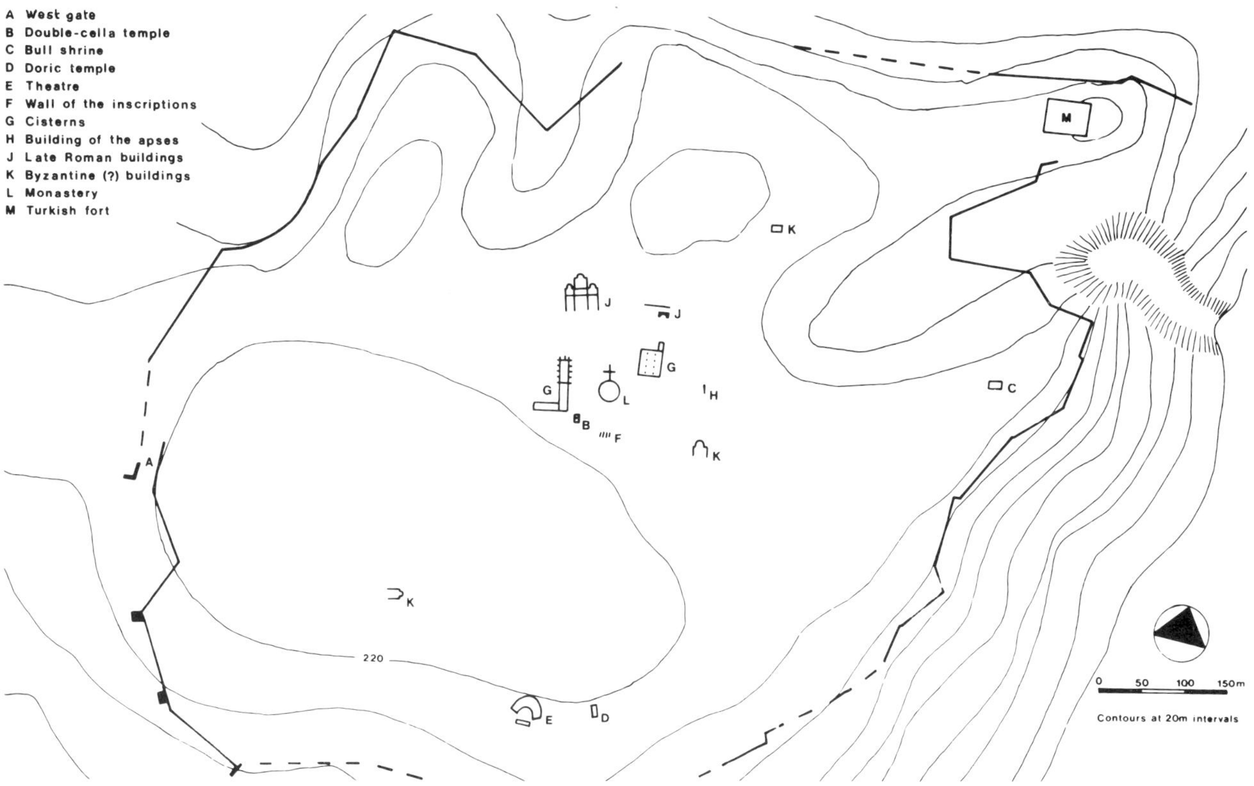

earlier, it is obvious that they could have been a considerable obstacle if needed in the Roman period.

Approximately contemporary with the later parts of the walls are a group of temples, the theatre and a public building known from inscriptions. The temples are all small: the best known is just south of the monastery in the centre of the site and consists of a double cella 6.32m x 3.96m constructed of fine squared ashlar joined together with clamps but no mortar. It is probably of 2c B.C. date like the similar temple at Naxos (3/9), and, like that shrine and also that at Kato Simi (5/9), dedicated to a pair of divinities. The pottery from here continued into the late Roman period and there were some secondary walls, perhaps forming a porch, tacked onto the front (east) side of the building[3].

Near the eastern edge of the city is the site of the second temple: this is the so-called Bull Shrine, named after the statues of these creatures found nearby[4]. On excavation it was found to date to the late 1c B.C., and to be distyle in antis with two statue bases in front[5]. From the nature of the offerings the excavator suggested that the temple was dedicated to Demeter and Kore, although their connection to bulls is not clear. The final Hellenistic temple is a short distance east of the theatre in the southern half of this site: this has not been excavated, but is known from the quantity of fragments of Doric capitals and columns here[6].

The theatre[7] is unique in Crete in that apart from some minor rebuilding it is of pre-conquest date, probably late Hellenistic from the style of the Doric capital found associated with it. It is basically built of stone with only a little brickwork of later date: the cavea is 55m in diameter, the orchestra 18m; the stage building is 25 x 6m. The possible public building is that from which the proxeniae inscriptions[8] forming the Wall of the Inscriptions just south of the Monastery and east of the double temple came. Nothing is known of it except the length of the wall, 15m, and the date of the decrees, mostly 2c B.C.

The Roman buildings fall into three groups: the cisterns, the late buildings scattered round the site, and the possible basilica of 6/7c date near the Wall of the Inscriptions[9]. The cisterns are in two groups[10]: the first is L-shaped, built of stone and tile faced concrete *c.* 60 x 35m (long sides) and 6.30m wide. The long stroke of the L is tile faced and stands entirely above ground level, surviving up to 6m high, with buttresses at its north end (Pl.71), while the short base of the L is stone faced and built up against the slope; this may indicate that the structure is of two phases. This cistern complex is just to the west of the monastery, while the second group is immediately to the NE. This is a triple cistern, 24.70 x 18.50 x 8.20m, divided by two rows of four columns massively built of stone. However, the roof is vaulted in concrete and the reservoir and feed system that still partially survives at the NE corner of the complex is of tile faced concrete. From this difference in construction it is likely that these cisterns were initially built in the Hellenistic period but extended under the Romans. The water source for both these complexes is not known, but must lie in the mountains some distance to the SW.

The remaining buildings vary from very fragmentary walls to the large mass of rooms north of the cisterns. Of the small buildings the only one probably of much importance is the so-called Building of the Apses[11] just east of the Monastery: like all these buildings it is constructed of concrete faced with rather rough stone work and so is likely to be of late date; all that survives is one wall with three large internal niches rather than apses: the purpose of the building is unknown. The buildings north of the cisterns[12] still stand two storeys high but in very ruined condition. From the building on the west masses of vaulting lie in ruins on the ground, but enough of the ground plan can be made out to see the triple apsed north end of the building, which from its position in relation to the cisterns and its design could well have been a large bath house. The building on the east of this area also includes an apsed room with windows overlooking the bay. Whether it was part of the same overall complex as the west building or separate, it is obvious from these structures that Late Roman Aptera was of considerable wealth and importance.

Aptera's cemetery seems to have been to the west of the city at Megalo Chorafia, from which a large number of tombstones and a few actual tombs are known[13]. Various statues, including a female possibly of the Imperial house and a representation of Hygieia have been found here[14], and also three stelae showing Demeter, Athena and another female[15].

1. *IC*.II.III. H. Drerup ap.Matz p.89f. The walls, Matz p.90f.
2. F. Winter *Greek Fortifications* (London 1971), p.215f.
3. Matz p.99f, no.4.

4. Matz no.8.
5. *Kret. Khron.* XII, 1958, p.469.
6. Matz no.7.
7. Matz no. 6. See p.57f. for theatres in general.
8. Matz no.4. *IC*.II.III. 4-15.
9. See p.123 for the basilica.
10. Matz no.1 and 2. Personal observations.
11. Matz no.5.
12. Matz no.9. Personal observation.
13. *A. Delt* XVII.2, 1961-2, p.299. *IC*.II.III. passim.
14. Possible Imperial female, *IC*.II.III.45. G. Mendel *Musées impériaux ottomans, Cat. des sculptures* II (Constantinople 1912-14), p.340, no.604 (In Istanbul).
15. *A. Delt*. XX.3, 1965, p.570.

(17/3) AZOIRES Traces of Graeco-Roman occupation on a hill[1].
1. M.S.F.Hood, 'Minoan sites in the far west of Crete', *ABSA* LX, 1965, site D3 p.111.

(17/4) STYLOS At Sellia a possible Roman farm with pithoi[1] was found. At Sternaki the Minoan tholos tomb[2] was found to contain 12 Hellenistic vases in the relieving triangle above the doorway, possibly indicating the date of its robbing and reuse of it in a cult.
1. *A.Delt.* XXVI, B2, 1971, p.511.
2. Hood, *op.cit.* (17/3), site D3.2, p.111.

(17/5) TA MARMARA Faure records a Byzantine village here: it is not clear quite what this means[1].
1. Faure, *BCH* LXXXIV, 1960, p.209.

(17/6) RHAMNI Faure has a Byzantine/Venetian village here[1], probably a Deserted Mediaeval Village.
1. Faure, *BCH* LXXXIV, 1960, p.206.

(17/7) MELIDONI Two caves in this area had Roman pottery in them, at Gourgouthia and at Geranes. There is also a rock-cut tomb with vases and glass near the latter cave[1].
1. Faure, *BCH* LXXXVI, 1962, p.42.

(17/8) PEMONIA In the cave of Skolakas, Roman sherds in an occupation level[1].
1. Faure, *BCH* LXXXVI, 1962, p.43.

(17/9) ALMYRIDA On the western edge of the bay here is the site of the partially excavated basilica[1].
1. See p.123-4.

(17/10) DRAPANOKEPHALA Roman - ?Byzantine sherds on the northern part of the plateau[1].
1. Faure, *BCH* LXXXIX, 1965, p.56.

(17/11) LITSARDA A group of several small Roman sites are reported from here: at 'sta Ellinika' to the north, at Lousothoros to the west and at Stavros to the south[1].
1. Faure, *BCH* LXXXIV, 1960, p.207. In 1974 I was unable to find these places.

(17/12) VRYSES East of the village spanning the Almyros are the remains of a Classical-Hellenistic bridge with a span of 11.10m and width of 4. 80m[1].
1. *AC* p.350 under Philippos. Spanake II, p.125.

(17/13) AMPHIMALLA Georgioupolis at the mouth of the Almyros is probably the site of this ancient town. Although nothing is now visible, Pendlebury saw a 'heavily walled building'[1].
1. *AC* p.369.

(17/14) ASPROSIKIA In the cave Korakia, Roman sherds[1].
1. Hood, *op.cit.* (17/3), site D7 p.112.

(17/15) KORAKIA Roman sherds in cave[1].
1. Faure, *BCH* LXXX, 1956, p.98.

(17/16) HYDRAMIA The village of Dramia at the mouth of the river Mousella is on the site of ancient Hydramia, the port of Lappa. Apart from a scatter of indeterminate pottery between the village and the river nothing is now visible, but a lead water pipe was recovered from 'Roman buildings' here and there is a statue of Heracles from the site in the Museum at Chania[1].
1. *IC* II.XIV. Personal observations.

(17/17) KAVALLOS On the sourthern slopes above Lake Kournas there is an extensive scatter of sherds and stones, but some of the pottery is definitely 10-12c (heavy brown-yellow glaze on orange fabric), and much of the rest is shell-gritted, which could be Late Roman or Mediaeval.[1]
1. Faure, *BCH* LXXXIV, 1960, p.206, 'Roman village'. *AC* p.370. Personal observations.

(17/18) ASI GONIA A stuccoed chamber tomb is known from here[1] together with Roman coins found in the vicinity, including issues of the provincial series[2].
1. *BCH* LXXIX, 1955, p.306.
2. Le Rider, p.261.

(17/19) ARMENI A possible basilica here[1].
1. See p.124.

EPARCHY 18 - CYDONIA

(18/1) MODIA Roman and Byzantine coins are known from this village, and it is likely that the name preserves that of the city of Moda, which issued coins in the Hellenistic period[1].
1. Le Rider, p.264. Svoronos, p.243.

(18/2) ANTHROPOTRYPA In this cave in Mount Troulos, Roman pottery has been found[1].
1. Faure, *BCH* XCIII, 1969, p.203.

(18/3) VRYSES The possible site of ancient Pergamon may be found on the heights of Ayios Georgios above Vryses[1], although there is no definitely Roman material from here. Nearer the village Roman pottery has been found in the cave Kera Spiliotissa and also at Timios Stavros by a spring east of the village.
1. Hood, *op.cit.* (17/3), site C3, p.106 collects all references.

(18/4) PLATANIAS Roman sherds seen west of the village at Amoutsa and Hellenistic sherds at Riza to the east[1].
1. *AC* p.360, 371. Local information insisted that Amoutsa was the name of the beach to the east where nothing could be seen in 1974.

(18/5) AY. MARINA In the cave of Nerotrypa 2.5 km south of the village, Roman to Modern pottery[1].
1. Faure, *BCH* XCIII, 1969, p.203.

(18/6) STALOS On the hill Vouno west of the road to Stalos are stones from house-walls and sherds, including Graeco-Roman[1].
1. Hood, *op.cit.* (17/3), site C.5, p.107.

(18/7) GALATAS Roman sherds on a knoll near the sea[1].
1. Hood, *op.cit.* (17/3), site C6.2, p.108.

(18/8) ALIKIANOS A tile bearing a male bust of Roman date was found here[1]. West of the village, the church of Zoodochos Piyi is on the site of a 6c basilica[2].
1. *Ergon* 1964, p.149. 2. See p.124.

(18/9) KASTELLOS VARYPETRO The Venetian fortress above the plain here conceals a large Classical to Late Roman site including Hellenistic houses of 3c B.C., tombs and a gold issue of Justinian II (685-711, except 695-705)[1].
1. *A. Delt*. XXII.2, 1967, p.500: Roman jugs.
A. Delt. XXIV.2.2, 1969, p.431: 3c house and Roman levels.
A. Delt. XXV.2.2, 1970, p.468, 473: tombs and the coin.
A. Delt. XXVI.2.2, 1971, p.511: general layers, Late Classical to Byzantine.

(18/10) KRITHARES Near the fortress of Kastellos is the cave of Krithares with Roman to Mediaeval sherds[1].
1. Faure, *BCH* XCIII, 1969, p.203.

(18/11) DEBLA On a spur of the White Mountains above Varypetro a small watch tower, or rather its foundations, was found above the EM settlement[1]: it was dated to the 30's B.C. by a coin of Lollius of his Cyrene issue. It is very likely that the placing of a tower here was connected to the civil wars, as suggested by the excavators.
1. P.Warren and Y.Tzedakis, 'Debla: an Early Minoan settlement in Western Crete', *ABSA* LXIX, 1974, p.299.

(18/12) MESKLA The main remains of the site here consist of the 5/6c basilica mosaic in front of the church of the Koimesis Panayia[1]; there are also a number of architectural blocks behind the church which presumably come from the basilica. Apart from these there are several inscriptions[2] and reported buildings from the hills above the modern village. Coins from here include issues as late as Theophilos, 832-9. Some of the Hellenistic coins include issues of Keraia and this together with the name of the river here – Keritis – has led Faure to suggest that the city here was Keraia: however, Guarducci prefers Polichna and the literary evidence for both names would suggest that Keraia was closer to Polyrrhenia, while Polichna was definitely in the area of Cydonia.

1. See p.124.

2. *IC*.II.XXII. *Kret. Khron.* XVII, 1963, p.393. Faure, *Kret. Khron.* XXI, 1968, p.320-1, no.13-15. In general, Faure, *BCH* LXXXVI, 1962, p.49f.

(18/13) SKORDYLIANA Here in the foothills of the White Mountains a building with columns 1.50m in diameter dated to the Hellenistic-Roman period was found. It was presumably either a shrine or possibly a villa[1].

1. *Kret.Khron.* VI, 1952, p.480.

(18/14) KONTOPOULA Faure claims[1] to have located a Roman village and cemetery at Mouri to the north and to have seen Byzantine tombs at Tsougkariana to the NE. In 1974 I was unable to find out where these places were. The village is set on a fertile plain.

1. Faure, *BCH* LXXXIV, 1960, p.208.

(18/15) MOURNIES The cave of Mavre Trypa contains Roman sherds[1].

1. Faure, *BCH* XCIII, 1969, p.203.

(18/16) MARATHI Cave of Marathospelios with Roman sherds[1].

1. Faure, *BCH* XCIII, 1969, p.203.

(18/17) MINOA Behind the islet of Marathi, immediately opposite Aptera on the other side of the bay, is the site of Minoa at Limni[1]. On the heights above the little harbour are the remains of a tower, 6.0m in diameter, built of isodomic masonry. Spratt thought that this was part of a defensive circuit, but Pendlebury and Theophanides preferred the theory that it might have been a lighthouse since they were unable to see any connecting walls. Spratt, however, is quite definite about the existence of such walls running from the sea's edge up to the tower, and if this is true it is likely that he was right about the function of the tower.

However, the major structure known from this site is that excavated down by the sea by Theophanides in 1939. He thought that it was part of the quay and its installations, but it is most likely to have been part of a large seaside villa (fig.61). Traces of concrete walls were traced for about 85m along the shore, 2m back from it and only 0.70m above present sea level. An area at its eastern end about 25m square was totally excavated, to reveal a range of rooms set behind a verandah which ended in an apsed room. It is likely that there was a colonnade along the range from several bases found here. Within the room at the end was a square portion of uncertain use; in the report this is interpreted as a guard room with an arms store. Behind this first set of rooms there is a bath suite with one small plunge bath with two steps down into it and an apsed end. The water for this and the building in general was no doubt supplied by a large well 2.22m in diameter surrounded by a massive 1.50m thick wall with a drain. The construction was basically of stone, but *opus signinum* and tile were used when appropriate. Finds included a Doric capital and several coins; one a Cydonian issue of Trajanic date, an Imperial issue of Marcus Aurelius, and an Athenian issue. The capital was of Hellenistic date, but the coins, the type of building and the use of *opus signinum* etc., make it likely that this building was early Roman, ? 2c, and perhaps replacing an earlier Hellenistic one.

1. Spratt II, p.130. V. Theophanides, *AE* 1950-1, par. p.1.

(18/18) CYDONIA, CHANIA (Fig. 62) The continued importance of the city of Cydonia-Chania has inevitably resulted in a lack of information about its past. It would seem that more remains existed up to the 16c, when the refortification resulted in the destruction of the theatre[1] which Belli planned, but unfortunately this too has been lost. Belli also records the existence of an aqueduct and a temple with a Doric portico, both of which have also disappeared. The destruction caused by the Venetians is clearest on the Kastellos where recent excavations have established the Minoan site beyond doubt, but no later levels survived the Venetian activity here. The old Venetian wall at the bottom of the hill, however, proves the existence of Classical-Roman buildings by its reuse of numerous column drums.

Fig.61. Minoa: plan of the villa.

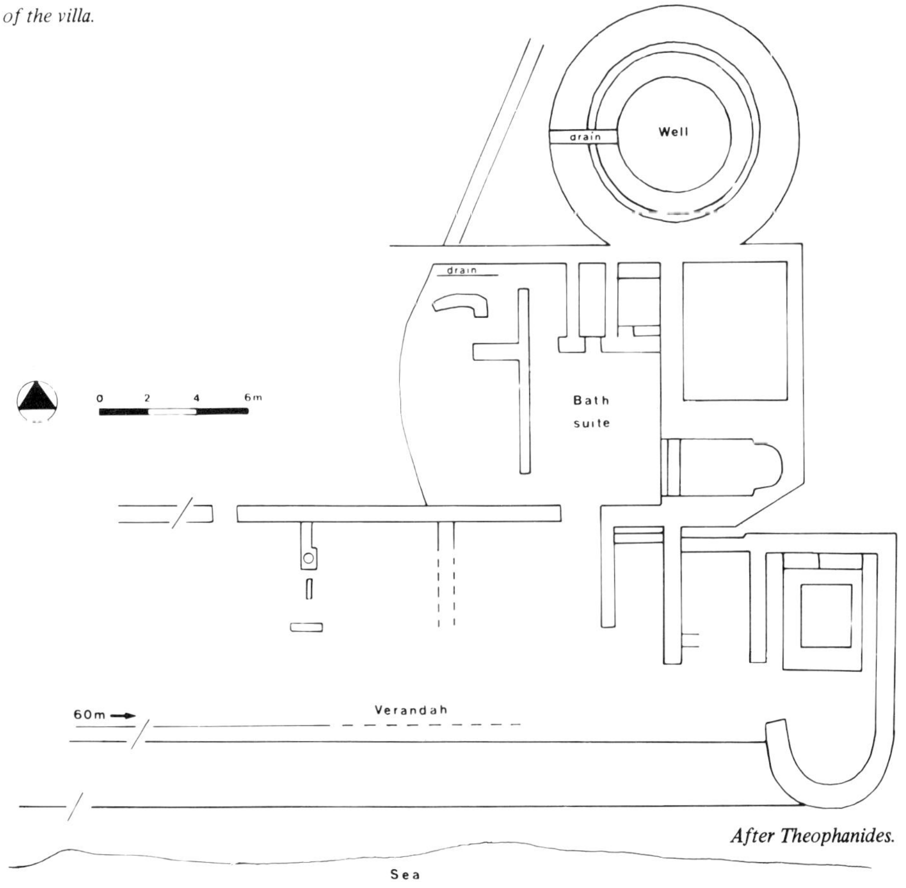

After Theophanides.

Fig.62. Cydonia: plan of Roman finds from Chania.

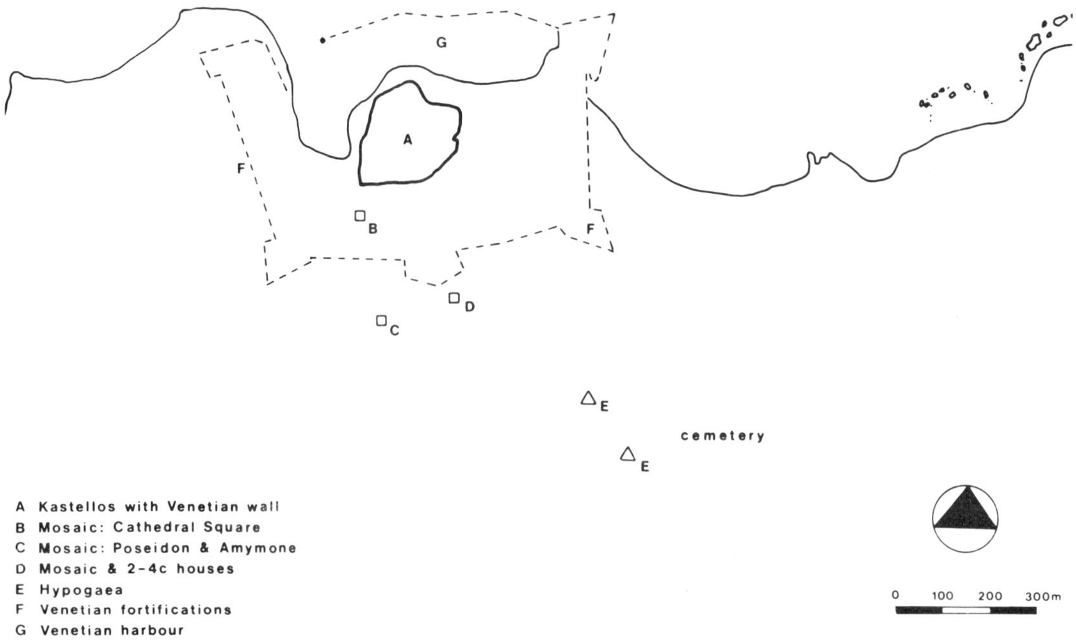

However, more definite proof of the wealth of Roman Cydonia survives in the form of a large number (for Crete) of mosaics known from several sites in the city[2]. The best known mosaic is that of Poseidon and Amymone, dating to the 2c, found off the Odos Korakas; another plain mosaic may come from the same house. A short distance NE, 8.0m under the National Bank, another mosaic was found with further houses of 2-4c date from close by[3]. It would seem from this concentration of mosaics that this was the 'upper class' suburb of Roman Cydonia. The most recently discovered mosaics come from the cathedral square from a bath building which is dated by the style of mosaics to the first half of the 2c. The interest of these rather commonplace mosaics with their designs of Tritons, are the letters ΛΑ which may well be an invitation to have a good bath.

SE of the above areas between the modern park and the Law Courts is the area of the cemeteries. These have the normal types of tombs, but also two Hypogaea[4] with up to 14 chambers, 7 on each side of an elevated central passage; each individual chamber was closed off with a large slab. Unfortunately the larger and better published of the two was robbed in antiquity but the other smaller one with nine chambers was dated to the 1c B.C. This type of grave would not seem to be a type usually found in Greece.

A final problem about Cydonia is that of the harbour; Ps-Scylax mentions[5] a harbour closed to the north. It is uncertain to what this refers, but contrary to Guarducci's opinion it seems possible that the present Venetian harbour, with its mole to the north, might be reusing an earlier installation.

1. Belli ed. Falkener, p.26.
2. See p.54. for the mosaics.
3. *A. Delt.* XXV 2.2, 1970, p.471.
4. *A. Delt.* X, 1928, p.44, for the larger Hypogaeum. *Kret. Khron.* XIV, 1960, p.515 for the other. *Kret. Khron.* XIII, 1959, p.376, slab covered cist graves at Mazale. *Kret. Khron.* VI, 1952, Roman graves in Ay. Ioannis area. *A. Delt.* XXV.2.2, 1970, p.473, Tile graves. Matz, Taf.63, chamber tombs.
5. *IC*.II.X.Praef.

(18/19) LERA Pottery from the Neolithic to the Late Roman period was recovered from this cave: many of the Classical sherds had graffiti proving the worship of Pan and the Nymphs here[1].

1. *A.Delt.* XXII.2.2, 1967, p.496-7 Hood *op.cit.* (17/3), site C17, p.110.

(18/20) KHAVYIARAS Roman sherds from around the cave[1].

1. Faure, *BCH* LXXXIV, 1960, p.213. Hood *op.cit.* (17/3), site C16, p.110.

(18/21) AKHYRO Hellenistic or Roman sherds from the cave[1].

1. Faure, *BCH* LXXXIV, 1960, p.212; Hood, *op.cit.* (17/3), site C18. 5, p.111.

(18/22) ARKOUDHOSPILIA Roman sherds reported from here by Jantzen but not noted in the excavations[1].

1. Matz, p.4. *A.Delt.* XXII.2.2, 1967, p.495. Hood, *op.cit.* (17/3), site C18.2, p.110.

(18/23) PLATANI SOUDAS A bath building consisting of three rooms, the central one being a plunge bath, was excavated here[1]; all three rooms were of tile-faced concrete and were 6 x 3m in dimensions. There was a hypocaust in the southern room.

1. *Kret.Khron.* VIII, 1954, p.517.

(18/24) LIMNI Hellenistic cist tombs with slab coverings were found at Limni on the Akrotiri[1]: it seems likely, although the notice does not say so, that this is the Limni which is the site of Minoa and the tombs are therefore part of the site.

1. *Kret.Khron.* III, 1949, p.595.

EPARCHY 19 - SELINO

(19/1) BIENNOS Just north of Cape Krio in the bay of Biennos are the remains of a partially submerged basilica[1]. One of the sherds from the area, however, looks earlier.

1. See p.124. Information from M.S.F.Hood about the pottery.

(19/2) PANAYIA A considerable scatter of sherds about the church may mark a Roman village[1].

1. Hood, *op.cit.* (16/9), site A6, p.51. Pottery includes ARSW 67 (5c), LRC 3C (5c).

(19/3) ARCHANGEL MICHAEL The small church here reuses architectural fragments, including a column of blue veined marble 0.30m in diameter. The cleft of rock in the hill where the church is sited has been artificially levelled and other building platforms are visible. It is obviously not possible to date these, and unfortunately all the pottery in the area could be either Mediaeval or Roman. However, given the nature of the work the rock cuttings are more likely to be Classical-Roman than later and the existence of a small shrine here is quite likely[1].

1. Hood, *op.cit.* (16/9), site A5, p.51. Personal observations.

(19/4) AYIOS YIORYIOS (i) Just west of the river Pelekaniotikos are the remains of a massive concrete wall 1.0m wide running EW: this has been interpreted[1] as a quay but as the relevant change in sea level has probably been mis-dated[2] it is more likely to be part of a house[3], perhaps a villa on the other side of the river to the village (19/5).

1. Hood, *op.cit.* (16/9), site A3, p.49. Pottery includes ARSW 104/5, LRC 3F (6-7c).
2. See p.182, Appendix III.
3. Personal observations. Also Savignoni, *Mon. Ant.* XI, 1901, p.467.

(19/5) AYIOS YIORYIOS (ii) West of the river are the scattered traces of a site extending off the knoll north of the road, over the road towards the sea[1]. The pottery included some late combed amphorae fragments but also much other 'Graeco-Roman' material.

1. Hood, *op.cit.* (16/9), site A2, p.49. Personal observations.

(19/6) SKLAVOPOULA Three Roman tombs were excavated here[1] containing a range of fine glass and pottery ranging from the 1c B.C. to early 4c A.D. The reason for the settlement from which the tombs' occupants came was probably the copper ores which were worked here, malachite being extracted from small adits each *c.*30 cu. m; the only dating evidence from the workings were four sherds of possible Classical-Hellenistic date[2].

1. *A.Delt.* XVII.2, 1961-2, p.299.
2. O. Davies *Roman Mines in Europe* (Oxford 1935), p.267.

(19/7) KONTOKINIYI (PELKIS) A small site here with little pottery, none of which was necessarily Roman, may be ancient Pelkis[1].

1. *IC.*II.VI, Praef. p.84. Information from M.S.F.Hood.

(19/8) GREGORIANA A cist grave of rough stones was found here. Its contents belied the poor construction in that it contained a diadem of gold leaves, three glass vessels and two probable Rhodian amphorae[1].

1. *A.Delt.* XXIV.2.2, 1969, p.434.

(19/9) PLEMENIANA Just below Kantanos in the village of Plemeniana the church of the Saviour is on the site of a late 5c/early 6c basilica[1].

1. See p.124.

(19/10) KANTANOS Sited at the head of the valley of the river Kakodikianos is the modern village of Kantanos, the place of the Hellenistic and Roman city of the same name[1]; it is possible that Kadros (19/20) further down the valley was the earlier city, but there is really no need for this well established theory[2]. The main remains at Kantanos are the remnants of extensive metal working NE of the village[3]. These comprise adits going into the quartzitic veins of chalcopyrites and galena and the actual furnaces for processing the ore. These were *c.*0.60 x 0.60 x 0.90m high, constructed of concrete with associated cisterns and pipes for washing and cooling. The ore still contained 44.32% iron, which may indicate that the miners were primarily interested in the other metals, copper and gold. The pottery described in the area – coarse red wares – was probably Roman. The only building from the site is the so-called Praetorium associated with the statue base of Septimius Severus[4], but it is almost certain that this building was not just converted in the 5c, as suggested by the excavator, but was in fact a basilica of 5/6c date[5]. However, the inscription of A.D. 100 at least provides evidence of official building activity then[6]. At least one wealthy tomb is known from Kantanos[7].

1. *IC.*II.VI.
2. Started by Pashley II, p.116, already queried by Savignoni, *Mon. Ant.* XI, 1901, p.400.
3. O. Davies, *op.cit.* (19/6), p.267.
4. V. Theophanides, *AE* 1942-44, par. p.31. *IC.*II.VI.3.
5. See p.126.
6. *IC.*II.VI.2.
7. *Kret. Khron.* XVII, 1963, p.393.

(19/11) PALAIOKHORA The only evidence for a site actually on the site of the modern village and Venetian fort is one 6c buckle bought by Sir Arthur Evans and now in the Ashmolean Museum[1]. The most recent account of the area[2] denies a site here on two grounds: firstly that no ancient remains are known from the obvious site, ie. the fort; but the same is true of the undoubted site at Rethimnon (14/4): and secondly that the peninsula would have been an island in the Roman period; but this is based on a late dating of the sea level change.

1. Boardman *The Cretan collection in Oxford: the Dictaean Cave and Iron Age Crete* (Oxford 1961), p.128 no.558 (1909.828).
2. Hood, *op.cit.* (16/9), site A1, p.48-9.

(19/12) KALAMYDE An extensive spread of Roman pottery is known[1] from the east bank of the River Vlithias, just before it reaches the coast. This may be the ancient Kalamyde, but if there was a more substantial site below the fort at Palaiochora itself, as suggested above, it would seem likely that this site would have been one of its dependencies, Kalamyde being at Palaiochora.

1. Hood, *op.cit.* (16/9), site A1, p.48-9.

(19/13) AZOGYRES At Loutra there were traces of a building with a scatter of Roman and Hellenistic sherds.

1. Faure, *BCH* LXXXIV, 1960, p.217.

(19/14) HYRTAKINA On Kastri above Temenia is the site of Hyrtakina[1]; there are traces of walls in polygonal masonry, therefore probably of late Classical or Hellenistic date. The excavated buildings include several Hellenistic houses and a sanctuary of Pan dating to 4/3c B.C., 22.70 x 6.0m in dimensions, with a column altar in the centre. There are numerous rock-cut chamber tombs with material mainly from the 5/4c. It would seem that the site declined in the Roman period, although the statue of Pan is dated to the 1c A.D.

1. *IC.*II.XV. Savignoni, *Mon.Ant.* XI, 1901, p.408. V. Theophanides, *AE* 1942-4, p.38.

(19/15) KAMPANOS Tombs at Kamini and Kaloyiannis[1] are known, but more importantly there are traces of mining with galleries 1m square to extract the malachite ore.

1. *AC* p.369. Davies, *op.cit.* (19/6), p.268.

(19/16) ELYROS Just south of Rhodovani on a promontory of the hills is the site of what was probably the largest of the cities in SW Crete. No large scale excavation has ever been carried out here and very little can now be seen. Previously part of the cavea of the theatre could be made out[1] and also a portion of the aqueduct coming in from the direction of Rhodovani; this was of stone-faced concrete 1.80 x 2.20m. This may be the mass of concrete still visible at the crossroads at the northern end of the site. On level ground near the centre of the city is the present church of Panayia marking the site of the 6c basilica known here[2] and the theatre site is nearby. Pottery on the site included Hellenistic wares and one fragment of Arretine[3], but curiously no late wares were visible. Tombs of the Roman period are known from stelae[4], and Hellenistic ones also.

1. Savignoni, *Mon.Ant.* XI, 1901, p.424.
2. See p.126.
3. Personal observations.
4. *Ergon* 1964, p.149. *Kret. Khron.* IX, 1955, p.569, 4c B.C. tombs.

(19/17) SUIA The port of Elyros was down the valley at Suia (Pl.4), where there are extensive remains of the Roman city, mainly to the east of the river bed which divides the site in two. Here there are a series of buildings of tile or stone faced concrete, but with the exception of a probable basilica[1] it is not possible to make out any plans; there is, however, a massive structure at the top of the present beach. At the eastern edge of the site part of the necropolis survives, with the typical built vaulted-tombs of the south coast sites. West of the river bed the modern village obscures the little that is left here, but a large house can be made out perched on the edge of the raised beach. This building, now reused as a pigsty, covered an area *c.* 20 x 40m, with a small apse on the sea side which contained a mosaic of which only one red leaf survives[2]. The date of this structure might be 6c in that the style of the mosaic leaf is very similar to those from basilica sites. On the far western edge of the site is the only excavated building from Suia, the 6c basilica with its fine mosaics[3].

1. See p.127.
2. Personal observation. Savignoni saw a hypocaust here which has since disappeared. Also *IC.*II.XXVII for the few inscriptions. *A. Delt.* XX.3, 1965, p.570, for a funeral stele from the site.
3. See p.126f.

(19/18) LISSOS 3km west of Suia is the site of Lissos, nigh on inaccessible except by sea, but which nevertheless seems to have flourished from the Hellenistic period right down to its abandonment with the other south coast sites in the post-Roman period. The site is hemmed in by cliffs on all sides with only a very narrow exit to the sea and a narrow gorge leading up into the mountains; at the rear of the site below the eastern cliffs is the small Doric temple of Asklepios[1] built in the Hellenistic period and adorned with a mosaic floor in the 1c A.D. The reason for this shrine with its portico is the therapeutic spring which still flows in front of the temple, down into the centre of the site alongside the steps to the temple. In the centre are the remains of the concrete built theatre, c. 15m in internal diameter of the cavea, and just north of this are the remains of a basilica[2] below the chapel of Ay. Kyriake. South of this complex there are numerous fragmentary buildings of stone- and tile-faced concrete, until one reaches the sea and the chapel of Panayia. It has been claimed that there is another basilica here, but there is no visible evidence for this, although there is a fine Asiatic sarcophagus, or rather its fragments, reused in the building[3]. Perhaps the most impressive remains of the site are the large number of built vaulted tombs which exist on the slightly more gentle western slopes of the site: most are about 2 x 3 x 2m in height with arcosolia in the three doorless walls[4].

1. See p.84.
2. Personal observations. Also Spratt II, p.241. Savignoni, *Mon. Ant.* XI, 1901, p.448. *IC*.II.XVII.
3. See p.128 for the basilicas and p.47 for the sarcophagus.
4. Spratt II, p.241 and above p.42 for the discussion of this type of tomb.

(19/19) GAVDHOS On this, the most southern part of Europe, *c.* 20km south of Crete, there are two sites at least, one on the northern cape at Ay. Ioannis[1] and one on the southern end of the island at Vatsiana. There may also have been a basilica at the latter site[2], for architectural fragments are recorded from the church. From the northern site Spratt recovered a statue of a seated life-sized female in Pentelic marble which he presented to the British Museum[3].

1. Spratt II, p.277. *IC*.II.VII. A.M.Colini, *Boll.d'Arte* II 1925-6, p.424. *AC* p.360, 370.
2. See p.128.
3. A.H. Smith *A catalogue of sculpture in the Department of Greek and Roman Antiquities, British Museum III* (London 1904), p.201 no.2062.

(19/20) KADROS This is the suggested other, earlier, site of Kantanos, and indeed there are walls of polygonal masonry and other Classical and Hellenistic material[1]. There are also Roman sherds and tombs with some fine glass of the 1-3c[2].

1. *AC* p.370 under Vlithias. Savignoni, *Mon.Ant.* XI, 1901, p.395f.
2. C.Isings *Roman glass from dated finds* (Groningen 1957). Forms 12, 82, 108.

EPARCHY 20 - KISSAMOS

(20/1) AGNEION The *Stadiasmus*[1] mentions a shrine to Apollo here, but the last person to have seen anything here appears to have been Buondelmonte in the 15c.

1. *Stad.* 338. Buondelmonte ap. Cornelius *Creta Sacra* I (Venice 1755), p.87.

(20/2) PHALASARNA This harbour on the west coast of Crete is important because all the ancient remains are above the notch that marks the dramatic change in land-sea level that is a feature of Western Crete[1]. The structures here consist of a dried-up harbour of Hellenistic date, a large number of graves no later than the 4c B.C.[2], and on the Acropolis several buildings of polygonal masonry which may include a temple. There is no definitely Roman material from the site either in the form of concrete or pottery[3]. From the evidence of this site and others it would seem very possible that the date of the land-sea level change occurred in the Hellenistic period rather than later[4].

1. N.L.Flemming (ed.) *Science Diving International* (London 1974), p.51.
2. *A. Delt.* XXIV.2.2, 1969, p.433.
3. Personal observations.
4. Fuller discussion in Appendix III. *IC*.II.XIX for the literary references to the site down to the 2c B.C.

(20/3) KASTELLIANA At Ellinika a small site with mosaics may indicate a villa[1].

1. *AC* p.369. I have been unable to identify the exact site but it is probably above the plain of Phalasarna north of Platanos.

(20/4) MESOGEIA Sherds and coins from Teresgona Ellinika[1].

1. *AC* p.370. Remarks as above (20/3).

(20/5) PATELLA Small site near a large rock cutting south of (20/2): it is possible that the cutting could be a ship shed[1].

1. *AC* p.370. Ship shed suggested by Mrs P. Martin.

(20/6) PERIVOLIA A tomb containing a bronze ring and buckle as well as a coin of Claudius was found here, while at Plokamiana a little further down the valley four 2c B.C. graves were found[1].

1. *EEKS* II, p.528. Presumably these are what Faure, *Kret.Khron.* XVII, 1963, p.25, refers to when he places Innachorion here.

(20/7) PLOKAMIANA See above (20/6).

(20/8) MONI CHRYSOKALITISSA By the little harbour north of the monastery there is a scatter of sherds: some were definitely Minoan[1] but others could have been later, in hard orange or shell-gritted fabrics.

1. Hood, *op.cit.* (17/3), site A1, p.101-2; all Minoan. *AC* p.369; Roman. Personal observations.

(20/9) SELLI On the promontory west of Kastelli extensive Hellenistic and earlier remains were excavated and published[1]. They included a house 10 x 9.40m with six rooms dating to the 4/3c B.C.

1. *AE* 1942, 4, par. p.1.

(20/10) KISSAMOS Recent excavations[1] in the northern part of the modern town of Kastelli Kisamou have revealed a series of buildings which include what may be part of the theatre mentioned by Belli[2], who also states that there had been an amphitheatre here. West of the possible theatre a fragment of the aqueduct coming into the city from Krya Vryse 2 km SW was found, together with fragments of houses; the coins found here would date these structures to the mid 3c. In the same area 40m to the west part of a large house with at least two mosaics was found: the mosaics were polychrome with black and white surrounds[3]. From the plan it is obvious that these two rooms, 7.60 x 6.80 and 7.50 x 3.70m, together with the smaller rooms and to the west a conduit supplying the water, form part of a larger structure, but it was not possible to excavate the rest. The date of this building was given by a series of coins of the mid 3c, which seem to fit the style of the mosaics. It was destroyed in the mid 4c, a hoard of coins, the latest dated to 346, giving the *terminus post quem.* However, it was rebuilt, the doors blocked in between the large rooms, pithoi built in to one of the minor rooms, and the conduit no longer used. The standard of building in this second phase was poor and the mosaics were disregarded; a tomb was cut into one. This phase lasted into the 7c, when the coin series came to an end. Other buildings of the earlier phase were found in the town, including one where the tile faced walls were still 3.0m high, complete with a hypocaust, and in the northern part of the town a bath house with marble floors, orthostats and columns. Among the finds were fragments from a Christian basilica[4] and several statues, including a fine Satyr.

However, the finest statue is the inevitable cuirassed Hadrian[5], complete with a Barbarian boy. West of the town at Mavro Molo are the possible remains of an ancient mole which may mark the site of the harbour of Kissamos, but it is now nearly entirely on dry land.

1. *A.Delt.* XXII.2, 1967, p.498-9. XXIII.2.2, 1968, p.416-7. XXIV.2.2, 1969, p.431-2. XXV.2.2, 1970, p.471. Most of the excavations took place on the line of the new 'motorway'.
2. Belli: ed. Falkener, p.26.
3. See p.55.
4. See p.55. *IC*.II.VIII for the inscriptions, Christian and others.
5. Vermeule *Roman Imperial Art in Greece and Asia Minor* (Harvard 1968), p.442.

(20/11) POLYRRHENIA Inland from Kisamos the Acropolis of Polyrrhenia dominates the countryside and so not suprisingly was used as a stronghold by the Venetians[1]. Their fortifications are the most prominent ruins on the hill, but they may include parts of earlier circuits of late Roman date. The southern part of the circuit is of a different construction to the definitely Venetian high acropolis on the northern end of the hill, but this may only reflect different reused masonry rather than a difference in date, for the walls here are still far cruder than the walls of definitely Roman date at Lyttus and Gortyna. The only excavation ever conducted on the site took place by the church of the ninety-nine Martyrs on the level ground on the south of the hill: here a large Hellenistic building was revealed, or at least two parallel walls 6.73m apart and up to 49.25m in length[2]. In the church there are numerous dedications[3], so it is very likely that these walls of superb pseudo-isodomic masonry are something to do with a temple. Lower down the hill east of the above building there is a well-chamber cut into the rock and traces of other house platforms above the modern village. In the village itself there is a tower of part of the circuit in the better style (Pl. 72), which contains a cistern in its base, probably linked to further cisterns in the village[4]. Of the early Roman period the only real evidence for the wealth of the site is a series of inscriptions to Metellus, Augustus and one recording something done by Hadrian[5].

1. *Mon. Ven.* I, p.72-9. *Mon.Ant.* XI, 1901, p.314.
2. Theophanides, *AE* 1942-4, p.17f.
3. *IC*.II.XXIII. 23f.
4. Tower as n.1. Also *Kret. Khron.* X, 1956, p.237.
5. *IC*.II.XXIII.14, 12, 66.

(20/12) KHOREVTIANA Roman sherds in a field[1].

1. Faure, *BCH* LXXXVI, 1962, p.55, no.22.

(20/13) TOPOLIA A Denarius of Volteius of 78 B.C.[1]

1. J.C.Myres 'On some bronze coins from Crete', *NC* 3rd series XIV, 1894, p.89.

(20/14) AY. SOPHIA 2km south of Topolia, the cave of Ay. Sophia[1] contained Roman pottery.

1. Hood, *op.cit.* (17/3), site A 3 p.104-5.

(20/15) DRAPANIA On the coastal plain here three cist graves and a building of Roman date were found[1]; the finds included a Doric capital, indicating a building of some status.

1. *Kret.Khron.* XVII, 1963, p.394.

(20/16) NOPIGIA This may be the site of Methymna, with fragments of limestone and marble columns, together with possible Roman pottery, NW of the village just before the actual coastal plain[1]. The chapel of Ay. Georgios here probably reuses an earlier building[2].

1. *AC* p.360, 370. Personal observations.
2. Pashley II, 32.

(20/17) PHALELIANA A Roman building with six storage vessels found on a tile and stone floor[1]. Pendlebury claims to have seen a fort at Tramontana here: it is uncertain what he means.

1. *A.Delt.* XVII.2, 1961-2, p.300.
2. *AC* p.371.

(20/18) RHOKKA The rock from which the site derives its name looms over the eastern end of the Kisamou plain and also controls the passes coming down into the plain from the mountains. The main site is on the plateau and slopes on its southern side, extending under the present village. Where it is not obscured by modern housing, many house platforms cut into the rock can be seen complete with roadways and drains. On the summit of the rock itself there are two 5 x 3m buildings of rough concrete with a cistern; it is uncertain what date these are[1]. Pottery from the site includes Hellenistic Black Glaze and E. Sigillata B[2]; contemporary coins are also known from the site, as are tombs of the same date[3].

1. Personal observation. *Mon. Ven.* I, p.92.
2. Personal observation, including a stamp UM, 10 B.C. - A.D. 75 (Hayes p.10).
3. Myres, *op.cit.* (20/13). *AC* p.371; *Kret. Khron.* XIV, 1960, p. 515, tombs.

(20/19) TRIALONIA 1.8 km south of the above site is a smaller settlement with rock-cut chamber tombs and remains of buildings[1]. Coins of late 1c-2c date are recorded from here[2].

1. Spratt II, 209-11. Faure, *BCH* LXXXIV, 1960, p.218.
2. Svoronos, Domitianic provincial issue no.61, Cydonia issue 153, Trajanic. Also Trajanic issue from Caesarea in Cappodocia. Myres, *op.cit.* (20/13).

(20/20) GAVALOMOURI 3/2c B.C. pot[1].

1. *EEKS* IV, p.268.

(20/21) SKORDYLIANA Possible basilica at Glossa[1].

1. See p.128.

(20/22) EPISKOPI There is a probable basilica at Ay. Georgios and in the area about the church there are several stone-faced concrete walls that are probably late Roman[1].

1. See p.128-9, and personal observations.

(20/23) NOKHIA About the church of Ayia Varvara SE of the village a site has been variously dated from Minoan to Roman[1]. None of the pottery visible in 1974[2] was necessarily Roman, but much could have been.

1. Hood, *op.cit.* (17/3), site A6.3, p.105.
2. Personal observation.

(20/24) PHALELIANA PROF. ILIAS On this hill just before the Kastelli Kisamou plain, north of the motorway, a large Roman site with walls, columns, etc. has been located[1].

1. *A.Delt.* XXII.2, 1967, p.499.

Fig.63. Diktynnaion: plan of the sanctuary area.

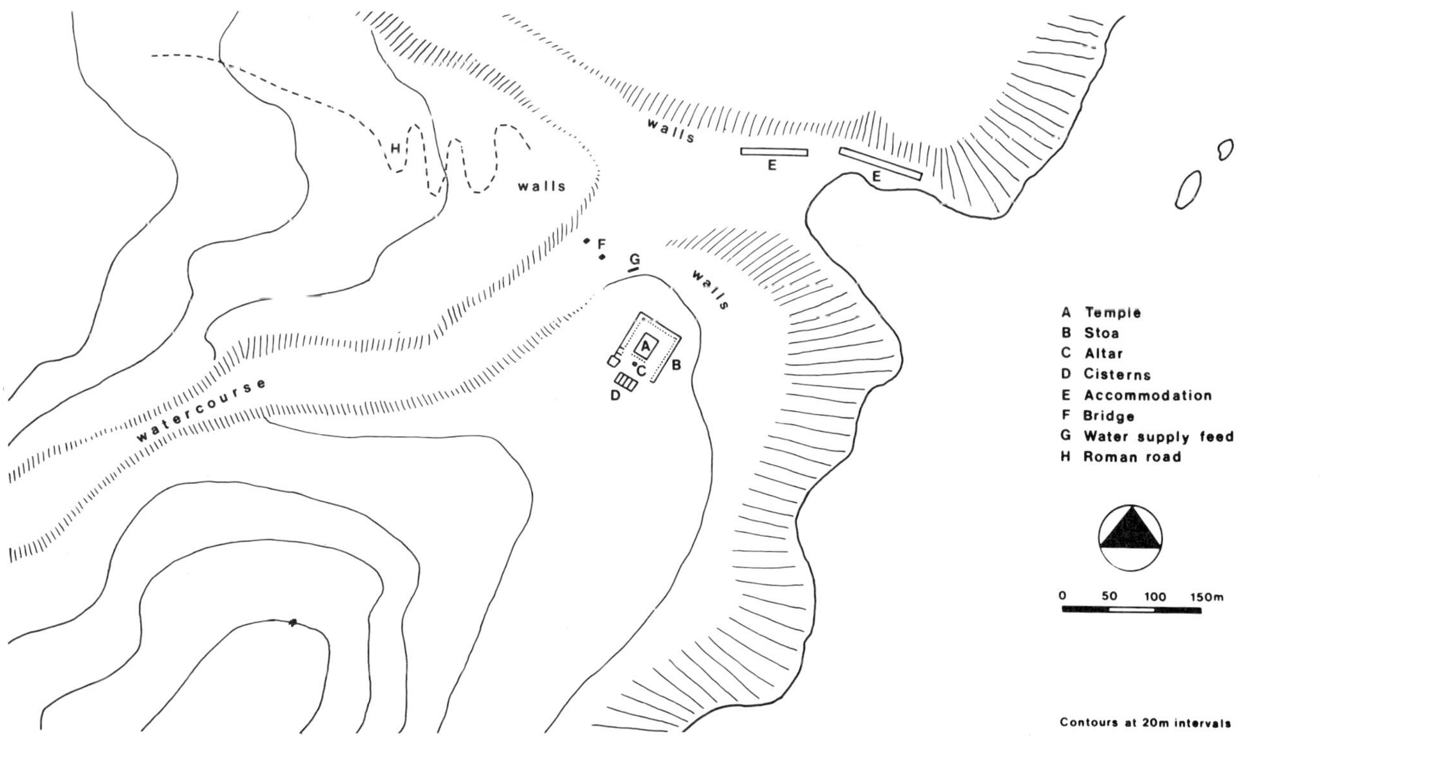

(20/25) KOLENI KAMARA While installing water works part of a possible Roman bath house was discovered[1].

1. *A.Delt.* XXV.2.2, 1970, p.473.

(20/26) MARATHOKEPHALA On this ridge overlooking the Chania Plain Faure[1] identified a Byzantine site.

1. Faure, *BCH* LXXXII, 1958, p.498. 1974: nothing to be seen.

(20/27) RHODOPOU There is a Hadrianic milestone set in front of the church of Ay. Georgios which of course is unlikely to be in its original position, but there is a site '20 minutes south' of the village. The stone is XI miles from somewhere, possibly the shrine that paid for the road, or Kissamos the local polis[1].

1. *IC* II.XI.6. Faure, *BCH* LXXXII, 1958, p.497.

(20/28) MT. ONYKHAS 4 miles NW of Rhodopou Faure[1] claims to have found Roman sherds on top of this mountain.

1. Faure, *BCH* XCVI, 1972, p.399.

(20/29) DIKTYNNAION (Fig. 63) The site was centred on the sanctuary of the Goddess which was situated on the promontory on the southern side of the bay[1]. In the sheltered little cove on its northern side there were ranges of buildings undoubtedly serving to house the temple priests, etc., and also to serve the 'pilgrims'. None of these were excavated, but they are still quite well preserved, built of stone-faced concrete. There are two long ranges; one above the modern landing stage on the north side of the bay and one EW orientated up the beach. It was in the westernmost room of this building which had a podium that the statue of Hadrian burnt in Chania Museum was found[2]. Other buildings have apses and one was identified as an Odeum, but with really no supporting evidence. All this complex is divided from the temple by a winter flood course over which there are still fragments of a bridge: this may also have carried water down from the cisterns, for halfway up the slope there is a rough stone-faced concrete wall out of which project four pipes, possibly to supply a basin here, hence possibly down into the main city. Although access from the sea must always have been important there are the remains of a Roman road twisting up out of the valley.

1. Matz, p.106-117. *IC* II.XI. Personal observations.
2. Vermeule, *op.cit.* (20/10), p.443.

(20/30) LATZIANA (Not located within eparchy) Byzantine ruins[1].

1. Faure, *BCH* LXXXVI, 1962, p.55.

SITES NOT LOCATED BY EPARCHY

NF 1 ASIROTOI Denarius of Trajan in Heraklion Musuem[1].

1. Cat. No.1274.

NF 2 LOUNTRI Figurine in Heraklion Museum[1].

1. *AC* p.360. Somewhere in western Crete.

ALPHABETICAL INDEX OF SITES

APPENDIX I: The Imperial Officers

The Governors

CN. TREMELLIUS SCROFA: 50 B.C. Quaestor of Crassus 71, Trib. Pleb., Praetor, Procos. Cret. et Cyr. Cicero *Ad.Att.* 6.1.13.
M. IUNIUS BRUTUS: 43/2 B.C. Exceptional appointment never taken up. Cicero *Phil.* 2.97 etc.
L. LOLLIUS: *c.* 39 B.C. Only known from his *c.* 39 coins. *BMC Cyr.* Group III.
CRASSUS: *c.* 37/36 B.C. Known from his coins, *BMC Cyr.* IV. Possibly Cos 30 B.C.
AULUS PUPIUS RUFUS: between 30 and 27 B.C. Known from his coins but these are restricted to Cyrene *BMC Cyr.* V, and it is possible that his governorship may have been there only.
C. CLODIUS VESTALIS: in 30's or 20's B.C. IIIvir, and later Procos. Creta et Cyr. *IC.* IV.327, *PIR* [2] C1192.
FLAVIUS or FABIUS: between 27 and 13 B.C. Josephus *Ant. Iud.* 16.169.
LOLLIUS PALIKANUS: in period 23 to 17 B.C. *BMC Cyr.* VII. *PIR* [2] L319.
SCATO: in period 23 to 12 B.C. *BMC Cyr.* VI.
L. PLOTIUS VICINAS: ?4/3 B.C. *IC.* IV.200, 289, 328. *PIR* P395.
Q. LUCANIUS PROCULUS: in period 12 B.C. to A.D. 14. *AE* 1927,140. *PIR* [2] L348.
M. NONIUS BALBUS: Augustan. Trib. Pleb. 32 or his son. Patron of the *Commune Cretensium. PIR* N102.
C. RUBELLIUS BLANDUS: Augustan. Either the Rubellius who was a Triumvir AAAFF, *PIR* R81 or less likely the Cos. Suff. of 18 A.D. *PIR* R82. *IC.* IV.293.
P. SULPICIUS QUIRINUS: Augustan. The only reason to attribute the Procos. to this notable officer is his campaigns against the Garamantes and the Marmaridae (Florus 2.31); see B. Levick *Roman Colonies in Southern Asia Minor* (Oxford 1967), p.203.
PANSA: Possibly Vibius Pansa Leg. P.P. in Vindoliciis. *IC.* IV.294.
P. OCTAVIUS: Tiberian, before 29. Seneca, *Ep.* 95. *PIR* 015.
CAESIUS CORDUS: early 20's A.D. Convicted of extortion. Tacitus *Annals* III.38,70. *PIR* [2] C193.
CORNELIUS LUPUS: 20's A.D. Cos. Suff. 42. Cities of Crete issued coins under his authority: Svoronos Cydonia 110, Eleutherna 40 etc. *PIR* [2] C1400.
OPPIUS/OCCIUS FLAMMA: Tiberian, pre-26. Seneca, *Controv.* 9.4.19. *PIR* 05.
P. VIRIASUS NASO: 28-31. Trib. Pleb. Curator Locorum Publicorum Iudicandorum. Governor for three years, putting up dedication on Seianus' downfall. *IC.* IV.272. *PIR* V475. *ILS* 158.
LACHES: 30's. Coins, Svoronos Cydonia 109, Hierapytna 46.
AUGUREINUS: in period 37-41. Coins in Crete, Svoronos Gortyna 193-4, Hierapytna 49, Polyrrhenia 53, etc. *PIR* [2] A1397.
FLAVIUS or FABIUS: in period 37-41. Coins in Crete, Svoronos Hieraptyna 51. *PIR* [2] F182, where it is suggested that he might be the same as F268, C. Flavius Figulus, quaestor in Cyprus.
CELER: 30's or 40's. Xvir Stil. Iud., Quaestor of Cos. 32, Aed. Cerealis, Praetor, Procos. Cret. et Cyr., Leg. Prov. Hisp. Ult. (for his cousin). *ILS* 961.
CAESERNUS VEIENTO: 45/6. *AE* 1951. 207.
Q. CASSIUS GRATUS: 40's. Legate in Africa afterwards. *AE* 1949. 17.
CESTUS PROCULUS: in period 50-56. Acquitted on extortion charge in 56. Tacitus *Annals* XIII.30. *PIR* [2] C193.
PEDIUS BLAESUS: 59. Convicted of extortion, Tacitus *Annals.* XIV.18. *PIR* P151.
L. TURPILIUS DEXTER: 63. Cos. Suff. in 80's. *IC.* I.XXVI.2. *PIR* T293.
RUTILIUS RUFUS: 66/7. Mentioned as governor of Crete in the Prologue to Dictys of Crete.
M. ANTONIUS FLAMMA: 70. Probably a Cyrenaican: convicted for extortion: Tacitus, *Hist.* IV.45. *PIR* [2] A831.
L. MINICIUS RUFUS: 71/2. After Crete Leg. Aug. P. P. Lugdunensis, possibly Cos. Ord. 88 with Domitian.

AE 1951.209. *PIR* M442. A.N. Sherwin-White *Pliny's Letters, a Commentary* (Oxford 1966) p.660.
CATULLUS: 73. Acts against Jewish revolt in Cyrene: Josephus *BJ.* 7.439.
G. ARINIUS MODESTUS: 74 and 75. Acts Ex. Auct. Aug. over land leases in Cyrenaica. *AE* 1967.531.
SILO: Vespasianic. Coins of the provincial council. Svoronos no. 37. *PIR* S518.
G. ANTIUS AULUS IULIUS A f QUADRATUS: 84/5. Adlected as Praetorian by Vespasian in 70, Leg. P. P. Ponti et Bith., Leg. Asiae twice, Leg. Aug. Cappadociae, Procos. Cret. et Cyr., Leg. Aug. P.P. Lycia et Pamphylia, Cos. Suff. 94, Leg. Aug. Syria, Cos. Ord. 105, Procos. Asiae. *PIR* [2] 1507.
G. POMPONIUS GALLUS DIDIUS RUFUS: 88/9 or 89/90. *AE* 1954. 188.
C. MEMMIUS: period 98-100. *AE*1960. 198.
L. LABERIUS or LARCIUS VINDEX: 1st century. *IC.* I.VIII. 24.
P. MUNATIUS PRISCUS DECIANUS: 1st century. *IC.* I.XXIV.5.
LUCIUS ELUFRIUS SEVERUS: 100. Possibly the same man as P. Manlius Vopiscus Vicinillianus Lucius Elufrius Severus Iulius Quadratus Bassus, but since the latter was Quaestor to Trajan it seems impossible for him to be governor in Crete by 100. *IC.* IV.331. *PW* XVI.554.
L. AEMILIUS HONORATUS: Trajanic. IIIvir Capitalis, Quaestor Prov. Ponti et Bith., Aedile Plebs, Praetor, Praef. Frumenti Dandi Esc., Procos. Cret. et Cyr. *ILS* 1048. *PIR* [2] Aem 350.
SALVIUS CARUS: 134/5. *AE* 1951. 122, and *Digest* 48.16.14.
FIDUS GALLUS: Hadrianic. Quaestor Prov. Macedonicae, Aedile/Trib. Pleb., Praetor, Leg. P.P. Prov. Macedonicae, Procos. Crete et Cyr., Curator Tiburtinae Valeriae, Leg. leg., Leg. Aug. P.P. Aquitanicae. *PIR* [2] F153.
POMPONIUS NAEVIANUS: in period 161-169. *AE* 1960. 200.
Q. CAECILIUS MARCELLUS DENTILIANUS: mid 2c. Xvir. Stil. Iud., Trib. Mil. XI. Cl. p.f., Quaestor Prov. Africae, Aed. Curulis Candidatus Div. Hadriani, Praetor Candidatus Div. Hadriani, Leg. Prov. Hisp., Procos. Cret. et Cyr., Leg. leg. XII Fulminata, Leg. Aug. P.P. Prov. Gall. Aquitanicae, Cos. Suff. 167 (or this could be his son) *ILS* 1096. *PIR* [2] C56.
C. CLAUDIUS TITIANUS DEMOSTRATUS: mid 2c. Xvir Stil. Iudic., Quaestor Prov. Achaeae, Trib. Pleb., Praetor, Procos. Cret. et Cyr., Cos. Suff. 161. *PIR* [2] C1044.
Q. SERVILIUS Q. f. PUDENS; mid 2c. Trib. Mil. IV Scythicae, Quaestor Prov. Siciliae, Trib. Pleb., Praetor, Praef. Frumenti Dandi, Iuridicus Aemiliae et Flaminiae, Procos. Cret. et Cyr., Cos. Ord. 166, ? Procos. Africae. Married L. Verus' sister. *ILS* 1084, *PIR* S424.
L. SEMPRONIUS: in period 185-192. *AE* 1963.140.
Q. CAECILIUS RUFINUS: late 2c. ? Same man as Q. Caecilius Rufinus Crepereianus Cos. Suff. (dat. incert.), Leg. Aug. P.P. Pann.Inf. *IC.* IV.301. *PIR* [2] C75 and 76.
CLAUDIUS ATTALUS: late 2c. Either Leg.Aug. P.P. Thraciae under Commodus, *PIR* [2] C795, or *PIR* [2] C800, Cos. Suff. under Septimius, Leg. Aug. Ponti et Bith.
C. IULIUS SEPTIMIUS CASTINUS: late 2c. Trib. Mil. I Ad. and V. Mac., Quaestor, Trib. Pleb., Praetor Tutelarius, Curator Aeclanesium, Curator Viae Saleriae, Iuridicus per Apul. Cal. Luc. Brut., Procos. Cret. et Cyr., Leg.Leg.I.Min., Dux Vexil. adversus defectores et rebelles, Leg. Aug. P.P. Pann. Inf., Cos. 213, Leg. Aug. P.P. Daciae. *ILS* 1153. *PIR* [2] I566.
P. FLAVIUS PUDENS POMPONIANUS: 2c. Quaestor Siciliae, Trib. Pleb., Praetor, Curator Albensium Fucentium, Praef. Frumenti Dandi Esc., Leg. Aug. P.P. Aquitanicae, Procos. Cret. et Cyr., *ILS* 8981. *PIR* [2] F436.
L. GARGILIUS MACER ACIDINUS: 2c. IIIvir Capitalis, Quaestor Urbanus, Trib. Pleb., Praetor, Procos. Cret. et Cyr.. *PIR* [2] G81.
CN. SUELLIUS RUFUS: 2c. *IC.* I.XVIII.49. *PIR* S692.
NUMISIUS MARCELLINUS: 215. *AE* 1934. 255.
CN. PETRONIUS PROBATUS IUNIOR IUSTUS: early 3c. IVvir Viarum Curandum, Curator Reipublicae Ardeatinorum, Quaestor Africae, Trib. Pleb., Praetor Fideii Comisarii, Leg. Prov. Achaeae, Procos. Cretae, Leg. Leg. XIV Gem. VIII Aug., Leg. Aug. P.P. Numidiae. *ILS* 1179.
SEXTUS TADIUS S. f. LUSIUS NEPOS PAULLINUS: mid 3c. Xvir Stil. Iud., Trib. Mil. IV Flaviae, Quaestor Ponti et Bith., Aed. Curulis, Praetor , Leg. P.P. Macedonicae, Leg. P.P. Asiae, Praef. Frumenti Dandi, Leg. P. P. Africae, Procos. Cret. et Cyr.. *PIR* T2. *CIL* IX.4119.
AGLAUS: in period 284 to 297. *PLRE* p.30, A457. IXX. *IC.* IV.281.

The Governors of Crete Alone

M. AURELIUS BYZES: in period 297-305. *PLRE* p.166. *IC.* IV.282-3.
AGRIANUS: 304. *PLRE* p.30. Rather dubious as he is only known from the *Martyrium S. Cyrilli.*
FLAVIUS FURSIDIUS ARISTIDES: in period 372-6. *PLRE* p.105. *IC.* IV.312. Cretan.
OECUMENIUS DOSITHEUS ASCLEPIODOTUS: 382-4. *PLRE* p.115. *IC.* IV.313-20, etc.
AEMILIUS QUINTILIUS PYRRHUS: after 383, late 4c. *PLRE* p.756. *IC.* IV.324. Cretan.
CALLINICUS: ? 5c. *IC.* IV.325.
BASIL: 8c. G.Zacos and A.Veglery *Byzantine Lead Seals* (Basel 1972), I.2, no.1782, p.1017.
JOHN: 8c. *Ibid.* no.2001, p.1122.
? LEON: 8c. *Ibid.* no.2646, p.1423.
CONSTANTINE: 8c. *Ibid.* no.2646, p.1423.
NICOLAOS: 8c. *Ibid.* no.2646, p.1423.
PETRONAS: 8c. *Ibid.* no.2646, p.1423.

STEPHEN: mid 8c. *IC* IV.517. May not have been in Crete.
THEOPHANES LARDOTYROS: Mid 8c. Life of St. Stephen the Younger (Detorakes Οἱ ἅγιοι τῆς πρώτης Βυζαντινῆς περιόδου τῆς Κρήτης [Athens 1970], p.191).

The Quaestors

LEPIDUS: 43 B.C. Commander for Brutus. Appian *BCV*.2.
CAPITO: in period 23-17. *BMC Cyr.* VIII. *PIR*²C405.
M. TITIUS: period 20-12. ? Land Officer in Cyrene. *PW* VIa, 1565, T24.
? FLAVIUS VESPASIANUS: early 30's. The Emperor. Suetonius *Life* 2.3.
Q. PACONIUS AGRIPPINUS: 50's. Quaestor iterum and 'Orothetes', probably special land officer. *IC* III. III.25-9.
A. LARCIUS LEPIDUS SULPICIANUS: 60's. Xvir Stil. Iudic., Quaestor, Trib. Pleb., Leg. Leg. X Fretensis in Judaean War, Leg. Ponti et Bith. *IC* IV.292. *PIR* ² L94.
P. TULLIUS VARRO: mid 1c. Xvir Stil. Iudic., Trib. Mil. VIII Aug., Quaestor Urbanus and Pro Q. Cret. et Cyr., Aed. Plebis, Praetor, Procos. Macedonicae, Leg. Leg. XIII Gem. *ILS* 1002.
SOSPES: 70's or 80's. IIIvir AAAFF, Trib. Mil. XIII Primigenia, Quaestor Cret. et Cyr., Aed. Cerealis, Praetor, Curator Col. et Municip. . . , Leg. Leg. XIII Gem., Leg. Aug. P.P. Galatiae. *PIR* S567. *CIL* III.291.
C. CASSIUS AGRIPPA: late 1c. Trib. Mil., Quaestor Cret. et Cyr. or Ponti et Bith., Trib. Pleb., Praetor, Leg. Cret et Cyr., Leg. Leg. XX Val. Vic., Procos. Hisp. Baet., ? Cos. 130. *AE* 1950. 251.
Q. FULVIUS TUSCUS: ? 1c. Xvir Stil. Iudic. . . *IC* I. XVII.54.
SILIUS PLAUTIUS ATERIANUS: period 161-9. *AE* 1960. 200.
M. ROSCIUS LUPUS MURENA: late 2c. Trib. Mil. VII Claudia, 'Praepositus IV Flavia', Quaestor Cret. et Cyr. and may have died there. *IC* IV.296-7. *PIR* R69.
P. SEPTIMIUS GETA: late 2c. Quaestor Cret. et Cyr., Aed. Cerealis, Curator Rei Publicae Anconitarum, Praetor, Leg. Leg., Proconsul Siciliae, Leg. Aug. P.P. Lusitaniae, Leg. Aug. P.P. Daciae, Cos. Suff. (dat. incert.). Brother of the Emperor. *IC* IV.302. *PIR* S326.
Q. FABIUS CILO SEPTIMINUS CATINIUS ACILIANUS LEPIDUS FULCINIANUS: late 2c. Xvir. Stil. Iudic., Trib. Mil. laticlav. XI Cl. p.f., Quaestor Cret. et Cyr., Trib. Pleb., Leg. P.P. Narbonensis, Praetor Urbanus, Leg. Leg. XVI Flaviae, Procos. Narbonensis, Praef. Aerarii Militaris, Leg. Aug. Galatiae, Cos. Suff. 193, Praepositus res Illyricis Perinthi tendentibus, Leg. Aug. P.P. Ponti et Bith., Comes Septimii Severi, Leg. Aug. P.P. Pann. Sup., Praef. Urbi, Cos. Ord. 204. *ILS* 1141.
C. LUXILIUS SABINUS EGNATIUS PROCULUS: 230's. Trib. Mil. Laticlav. IV Flaviae, Quaestor Cret. et Cyr., Aed. Cerealis, Praetor, Leg. Achaeae, Curator Viarum, Praef. Alimentorum Clodiae et Cohaerentium, Iuridicus Regionis Transpadanae, Leg. Leg. X Gem., Gordianae, Curator Rerum Publicarum Pisaurensum et Fanestrum. *PIR* ² L452. *CIL* XI 6338.
CN. PAPIRIUS AKTIUS: 2 or 3c. *IC* IV.306A.
M. AURELIUS SERANUS: early 3c. Quaestor Crete only, Aed. pleb. designatus. *PIR* ² A1607.
L. CALPURNIUS FIDUS AEMILIANUS CREMENTIUS: 3c. Quaestor Cret. et Cyr., Trib. Pleb., Praetor. *PIR* ² C264.
JOHN: Turmachos in Crete, 1st half of 9c. Zacos and Veglery, *op.cit.,* no.2059, p.1149.

Legati

C. IULIUS CORNUTUS TERTULUS: 80's. Quaestor Urbanus, Aed. Cerealis, Adlectus inter praetorios, Leg. P.P. Cret. et Cyr., Praef. Aerarii Saturnii, Curator Viae Aemiliae, Leg. P.P. Aquitanicae, Leg. P.P. Ponti et Bith., Procos. Narbonensis., Cos. Suff. 100, Procos. Africae. *ILS* 1024.
P. SESTIUS POLLIO: late 1c. Quaestor, Aed. Curulis, Leg. P.P. Cret. et Cyr., Cyrenaican. *JRS* XLIX, 1959, p.96.
C. CASSIUS AGRIPPA: late 1c. See under quaestors.
CN. POMPEIUS HERMIPPUS AELIANUS: mid 2c. Quaestor Asiae, Trib. Pleb., Leg. P.P. Cret. et Cyr., Leg. Aug. Pamphyliae et Lyciae. *AE* 1924.76.
M. ACILIUS GLABRIO CORNELIUS SEVERUS: Hadrianic. IIIvir AAAFF, Trib. Mil. XV Apoll., Leg. P.P. Cret. et Cyr., Leg. P.P. Africae, Quaestor of Antoninus Pius, Praetor, Leg. Asiae, Cos. Ord. 152. *ILS* 1072. *PIR* ² A73.
ULPIUS QUIRINUS QUADRATIANUS: 2c, ? Hadrianic. Adlectus inter tribunicios, Praetor renuntiatus?, Praetorius creatus, Leg. P.P. Cret. et Libyae! *IGRR* 3.392.
TI. CLAUDIUS PRISCUS RUFINUS: early 3c. Trib. Mil. VII Cl., Adlectus inter quaestores, Praetor Urbanus, Leg. P.P. Narbonensis, Leg. P.P. Cretae (not with Cyr.), Praef. Miniciae, Procos. Achaeae, Leg. P.P. Africae. *PIR* ² C935.
TI. URSIDIUS MANILIANUS TITULEIUS AELIANUS: early 3c. Trib. Mil. XIV Gem., Quaestor Achaeae, Aed. Plebis, Leg. P.P. Cret. et Cyr.; W. Eck, Zu den prokonsularen Legationen in der Kaiserzeit, *Epigraphische Studien* IX (Bonn 1972), p.34.

There are also Acilius Strabo and Q. Paconius Agrippinus who were special land officers in Cyrene alone in 59 and 71 respectively. (Tacitus, *Annals* XIV.18 and see for the latter under his entry as a quaestor).

APPENDIX II: Cretans in the Service of Rome

From the early 2c B.C. Rome, like all the other contemporary powers, employed Cretan mercenaries in various of its wars [1] and even its its domestic upheavals, for Cretan archers were amongst the forces that disposed of Gaius Gracchus [2]. This was of course before Crete was conquered, but even after this it is likely that the Cretan archers used by Caesar in Gaul [3] against the Remi should be considered still as mercenaries rather than auxilia. Again the status of the Cretan archers used by Pompey in the Civil War [4] and others summoned by Caesar to aid him in Egypt [5] is not made clear. The half legion raised by Pompey in Crete[6] cannot really be considered Cretan since it was composed of veterans. However, it is possible that the Military Tribune of Leg. XXXI, whose monument was restored at Priansos by the proconsul, could have been a Cretan serving in Octavian's legions [7].

No regular Cretan unit is known before the Flavians, but in the Claudio-Neronian period the fort at Bingen on the Rhine was garrisoned by the Coh.I. Sagittariorum which contained at least one Cretan, Hyperanor, son of Hyperanor, of Lappa, who was aged sixty with eighteen years of service at the time of his death[8]. The Coh.I. Cretum is first known from a Diploma of A.D. 93 from Moesia Superior [9], where it appears to have been permanently stationed at least into the 3c [10], at Egeta. However, it took part in Trajan's Dacian campaigns, for tiles with its stamp have been found associated with his bridge [11] and there is one Diploma of 110 mentioning the unit in Dacia [12]. A veteran of the unit is known from Niš, one Ti. Claudius Valerius, originally from Hierapytna, who died there at the age of 60 [13]. Coh. II Cretum is only known from the Notitia Dignitatum where it is listed [14] as stationed by the Jordan. Other Cretans in the army included a Praetorian guard, L. Tatinius Cnosus, who served under the Flavians [15] and Theander son of Aristomenus, who died at the age of 45, having served 26 years as optio in the Coh. I Noricorum [16]. Finally the *SHA* records in the life of Claudius Gothicus [17] that Cretan archers helped in his campaigns. Once Crete became a frontier province it is extremely likely that its garrison would have included locals, but nothing at all is known of the composition of this force.

Cretan Senators

If Sextus Aurelius Victor [18] could but be believed, the earliest Cretan senator was none other than the Emperor Nerva. However, since this contradicts all the other much better evidence for his Italian origins, it must sadly be rejected. The first definitely Cretan senator was L. Flavius Sulpicianus Dorion Polymnis, who was quaestor in Bithynia, adlected among the tribunes and praetor elect when his father L. Flavius Sulpicianus Dorion put up the dedications giving us his son's *cursus honorum* [19] in their home town of Hierapytna. The date of these inscriptions is not fixed absolutely, but ought to date to the 170's - 180's, when his father's career is considered. He had dedicated statues to the emperors in 163 [20] and at some date after 175 [21], and his father, T. Flavius Sulpicianus Dorion, had been Archiereus when the council had put up a dedication to Hadrian at Gortyna in 129 [22]. Even before Polymnis had started his career the family had not been limited to Crete, for a Flavius Sulpicianus Dorion as Archon of the Panhellenion had put up a dedication in memory of Annia Regilla, wife of Herodes Atticus, shortly after 160/1 [23]. Guarducci considers this man to have been another son of Titus, but there seems no reason why he should not have been the first Lucius. It may well have been this connection with Herodes that helped the third generation of Sulpiciani into the senate, and it is highly likely that the T. Flavius Sulpicianus, father-in-law of Pertinax, his Praefectus Urbi and defeated contestant for the imperial office was another son of L. Flavius Sulpicianus Dorion. The Cretan link is not definite, but there are no other known Flavii Sulpiciani and his career, elected as Arval Frater between 169 and 176, proconsul of Asia under Commodus, would make it likely that he was the elder brother of Polymnis, named after his grandfather. Another slight piece of evidence supporting his Cretan origins is the fact that the family disappears in Crete as well after his failure and eventual execution under Severus.

In the third century the only possible Cretan senator is Cn. Papirius Actius, who as quaestor in the province was honoured by the Archiereus Claudius Charmosynus, his fellow student[24]. This has been taken as possible evidence for Papirius' Cretan origins, [25] but there really seems no reason to assert this from the mere fact that he had studied at an unknown centre with a leading Cretan who might very well have gone to Athens or elsewhere for his higher education. Also, there are no other Papirii or even Actii known from Crete.

In the late 4c there were two governors who do seem to have been Cretans: Flavius Fursidius Aristides, governor in the period 372-6, who ought to be related to Ulpius Fursidius Panhellenius, a contemporary leading Gortynian [26]. This latter had together with Aemilius Quintilius Pyrrhus honoured the then governor Oecumenius and a little later Aemilius himself seems to have become governor [27]. His Cretan origins can be deduced from the identification of an elder Pyrrhus mentioned on the inscription of the younger man when governor as the Pyrrhus who had earlier put up an inscription together with the Boule of Gortyna honouring Marcellinus, probably Praefectus Praetorio Italiae et Illyrici [28].

---

1. References collected by G.T.Griffith *The Mercenaries of the Hellenistic World* (Cambridge 1935), p.234-5.
2. Plutarch *C. Gracchus* 16.
3. Caesar *De Bello Gallico* 2.7.
4. Caesar *De Bello Civili* 3.4.3.
5. Caesar *De Bello Alexandrino* 1.1.
6. Caesar *De Bello Civili* 3.3.4.
7. *IC.* I.XXIV.5.
8. Dr.G.Behrens, *Kataloge west-und süddeutscher Altertums-sammlungen* IV, (1920), Bingen p.127, *ILS* 2570.
9. *CIL* XVI.39.
10. *AE* 1966.336. Also *Starinar* IV (15-16), 1965, p.173. Also *CIL* XVI.46 of A.D.100, 111 of 160, *AE* 1972.657 of 161, all from Moesia Superior.
11. *CIL* III.1703.
12. *CIL* Suppl. XVI.163.
13. *AE* 1964.262.
14. *Not. Dig. Or.* XXXIV.47.
15. *AE* 1933.87.
16. *AE* 1965.251.
17. 16.2.
18. *De Caes.* 12.
19. *IC.* III.III.20-1.
20. *IC.* III.III.16-17.
21. *IC.* III.III.18.
22. *IC.* IV.275.
23. A.E. Raubitschek 'Greek Inscriptions', *Hesperia* XII, 1943, p.73-6 no.22.
24. *IC.* IV.306A.
25. G.Barbieri *L'Albo Senatorio da Settimio Severo a Carino* (Rome 1952), p.333, no.1906.
26. *IC.* IV.312-3, with *PLRE* p.105.
27. *IC.* IV.324 with *PLRE* p.756.
28. *IC.* IV.323 with *PLRE* p.756 and 545.

APPENDIX III: Sea Level Fluctations

The problem of the change in sea and land levels has attracted a good deal of attention since Spratt's survey for the Admiralty. The two most obvious facets of this geological change are the uplift of west Crete at some date and the general rise in sea level in the Mediaeval and Modern period all round the island. These changes can only be dated by their association with datable archaeological sites; generally the uplift of west Crete had been dated to the Late Roman period, but in fact as will be made clear below there is very little evidence for this, and some against.

The relevant sites will be listed from east to west: the bibliography for each site can be found in the Gazetteer.

Samonium Shrine (1/40) Submerged building.

Itanos (1/39) Rise in sea level in relation to the lower part of the site seems likely, since the area between the churches is now very swampy.

Hierapytna (2/8) Roman harbour works below modern sea level.

Inatos (7/31) No direct evidence but general impression of a rise in sea level is given by the number of buildings on the present beach.

Lasea (10/25) Some rise in sea level has eroded buildings on the seashore, but not submerged the breakwater.

Matala (11/8) Tombs of probably early Roman date are submerged here, indicating a rise of about 2m. However, the ship shed seems to be about right in relation to the present sea level, but is likely to be earlier, Classical or Hellenistic in date.

Petras (1/13) The ship shed here ends on the present edge of the sea, probably indicating a slight drop in sea level or rise in land level here since its construction.

Siteia (1/12) Here again the fish tanks indicate a relative drop in sea level by about ½m.

Mochlos (1/1) The houses and fish tanks again indicate a rise in sea level: the former were being eroded by the sea and the latter are totally submerged.

Pseira (2/19) Concrete fragments, perhaps of harbour works, have been found 2m below present sea level.

Olus (3/7) General rise in sea level in relation to the placing of the site on the isthmus.

Kolokythia (3/8) The basilica has been eroded by the sea here.

Mallia (6/20) Walls right by the present shore and the present water levels at the basilica site indicate a rise in sea level.

Chersonisos (6/7) The level of the harbour works and the fish tanks indicate a rise of about 1m in sea level.

Stavromenos (13/1) Most of the site is well above the sea, but there is at least one building exposed by the stream close to the present shore.

Rethimnon (14/4) The ship shed here extends into the sea and indicates that the sea level here is approximately the same as when this was constructed.

Suia (19/17) Roman buildings exist below the level of the notch which marks the sea level before the uplift of the land.

Ayios Yioryios (i) and (ii) (19/4,5) At (i) there are the remains of what was probably a villa close to the present sea level and at (ii) the Roman site extends over the old beach line.

Biennos (19/1) The remains of a basilica, presumably of 5/6c date, are actually in the sea.

Phalasarna (20/2) All the ancient remains are above the sea notch, including the harbour, but there is no evidence for any occupation after the 4c B.C.

Kissamos (20/10) The possible remains of a mole at Mavro Molo are entirely on dry land; this ought to be Roman by its construction.

Diktynnaion (20/29) The only part of the site in direct relation to the sea is the quay on the northern side of the bay, but since this was extensively rebuilt in World War II it is not possible to estimate the relationship between the ancient portions and sea level.

Minoa (18/17) Remains of the probably 2c Roman building are only 0.70m above present sea level and it would seem most likely that there has been a rise in sea level.

Kisamos (17/1) At Kalami below Aptera ancient moles are marked below sea level on the 1843 charts.

From the above survey the evidence for the post-Roman rise in sea levels all round the island is clear; the only exceptions are the fish tanks at Siteia and the Kissamos mole. These two can be explained as being caused by purely local disturbances. Elsewhere the degree of the rise obviously varies, with a maximum of about 2m at Pseira. However, the land rise is more confused: the evidence at Phalasarna is clear, and good evidence for a Hellenistic date exists for the rise here. The basilica at Biennos gives a definite *terminus ante quem* for any rise here although this does not exclude an early Roman date. However, the tombs at Matala are early Roman and have been submerged as opposed to the ship shed which is probably earlier and is now at the right level. If here also the land rise is a late Hellenistic phenomenon then this evidence fits very neatly: the shed would have been above the sea in the Roman period and as the sea rose in the post-Roman period the shed would once again have reached its proper position. If this was the case, here at least the land rise must have been about the same as the sea level change since the Roman period, i.e. about 2m here. A similar situation is possible at Petras, but here the rise of the sea has not equalled the land rise. This suggests that, like the sea level rise in the post-Roman period, the land rise was not limited to west Crete but probably extended all over the island and, also like the sea level change, there was a good deal of local variation [1].

1. This Appendix owes much to the published work of Dr.N.C.Flemming, and also to conversations with him: needless to say all geological howlers are my own.

BIBLIOGRAPHY

This includes only general works: those quoted for parallels or on specific sites can be found in the relevant place in the text.

Alföldy, G., 'Ein *quaestor* der römischen Provinz *Creta et Cyrenae', Epigraphica* XXXV, 1973, p.40.

Allbaugh, L. G., *Crete: A case study of an Underdeveloped Area* (Princeton 1953).

Ashton, R. H. J., Some Cnossian Coins of Tiberius; *NC* 7th series XIII, 1973, p.40.

Bandy, A. C., *The Greek Christian Inscriptions of Crete* (Athens 1970).

Belli, O., See S. Spanake and E. Falkener.

Boardman, J., *The Cretan Collection in Oxford: the Dictaean Cave and Iron Age Crete* (Oxford 1961).

Budde, L., *A Catalogue of Greek and Roman Sculpture in the Fitzwilliam Museum, Cambridge* (Cambridge 1964).

Chapman, A. E., 'Some First Century BC Bronze coins of Knossos', *NC* 7th series VIII, 1968, p.13.

Christern, J., 'Die Datierung von A. Titos in Gortys Kreta', *Acts of the 3rd Cretological Congress* II (Athens 1974) p.37.

Coldstream, J. N., *Knossos: the Sanctuary of Demeter, ABSA* Suppl. Vol.8 (London 1973).

Cornelius, F. L., *Creta Sacra* (Venice 1755).

Davaras, K., ' Ἐπιγραφαί ἐκ Κρήτης I', ', *Kret. Khron.* XIV, 1960, p.457.

Davaras, K., ' Ἐπιγραφαί ἐκ Κρήτης II',', *A. Delt.* XVIII.1, 1963, p.141.

Davaras, K., ' Κεραμεικὴ κάμινος εἰς Ἴστρωνα ἀνατολικῆς Κρήτης', *A. Delt.* XXVIII.1, 1973, p.110.

Davies, O., *Roman Mines in Europe* (Oxford 1935); Crete p.266.

Detorakes, Th. E., *Οἱ ἅγιοι τῆς πρώτης Βυζαντινῆς περιόδου τῆς Κρήτης καὶ ἡ σχετικὴ πρὸς αὐτοὺς φιλολογία* (Athens 1970).

Ducrey, P., 'Trois nouvelles inscriptions crétoises.', *BCH* XCIII, 1969, p.841.

Ducrey, P., and Effenterre, H. van, 'Un règlement d'époque romaine sur les bains d'Arcades'; *Kret. Khron.* XXV, 1973, p.281.

Dunand, F., *Le culte d'Isis dans le bassin oriental de la Méditerranée* (Leiden 1973).

Dunbabin, T., 'Antiquities of the Amari', *ABSA* XLII, 1947, p'190'

Falkener, E., 'A Description of some important Theatres and other Remains in Crete, from a MS History of Candia by Onorio Belli in 1856', *Museum of Classical Antiquities*, supplement (London 1854).

Falkener, E. (ed.), 'Antiquities of Candia I', *Museum of Classical Antiquities* II (London 1860), p.263.

Faure, P., 'Grottes crétoises', *BCH* LXXX, 1956, p.95.

Faure, P., 'Spéléologie et topographie crétoises', *BCH* LXXXII, 1958, p.495.

Faure, P., 'La Crète aux cent villes', *Kret. Khron.* XIII, 1959, p.171.

Faure, P., 'Nouvelles recherches de spéléologie et de topographie crétoises', *BCH* LXXXIV, 1960, p.189.

Faure, P., 'Cavernes et sites aux deux extrémités de la Crète', *BCH* LXXXVI, 1962, p.36.

Faure, P., 'Cultes de sommets et cultes de cavernes en Crete', *BCH* LXXXVII, 1963, p. 504.

Faure, P., 'Nouvelles localisations de villes crétoises', *Kret. Khron.* XVII, 1963, p.16.

Faure, P., *Fonctions des cavernes crétoises* (Paris 1964).

Faure, P., 'Recherches sur le peuplement des montagnes de Crète: sites, cavernes et cultes', *BCH,* LXXXIX, 1965, p.27.

Faure, P., 'Sept nouvelles villes de la Crète antique', *Kret. Khron.* XIX, 1965, p.222.

Faure, P., 'Les minerais de la Crète antique', *Rev. Arch.* 1966, p.45.

Faure, P., 'Nouvelles recherches sur trois sortes de sanctuaires crétois', *BCH* XCI, 1967, p.114.

Faure, P., 'Le problème du cuivre dans la Crète antique', *Acts of the 2nd Cretological Congress* II, (Athens 1968), p.174.

Faure, P., ''Ἐπιγραφαί ἐκ Κρήτης', *Kret. Khron.* XXI, 1969, p.314.

Faure, P., 'Sur trois sortes de sanctuaires crétois II', *BCH* XCIII, 1969, p.174.

Faure, P., 'Cultes populaires dans la Crète antique', *BCH* XCVI, 1972, p.389.

Gerola, G., *I monumenti veneti dell' isola Creta* (Venice 1905).

Giuliano, A., *Il commercio die sarcofagi attici* (Rome 1962).

Glykatzi-Ahrweiler, H., 'L'administration militaire de la Crète byzance', *Byzantion* XXXI, 1961, p.217.

Guarducci, M., *Inscriptiones Creticae* I-IV (Rome 1939-50).

Halbherr, F., 'Some Cretan Sculptures', *AJA* new series I, 1897, p.239.

Hatzfeld, J., *Les trafiquants italiens dans l'orient hellénique* (Paris 1919).

Hayes, J. W., *Late Roman Pottery* (London 1972).

Hazzidakis, J., *Les villas minoennes de Tylissos* (Paris 1934), ch.V, p.66.

Heilmeyer, W. D., *Korinthische Normalkapitelle* (Heidelberg 1970).

Hood, M.S.F., 'Minoan Sites in the Far West of Crete', *ABSA* LX, 1965, p.99.

Hood, M. S. F., 'Some Ancient Sites in S. W. Crete', *ABSA* LXII, 1967, p. 47.
Hood, M. S. F., *An Archaeological Survey of the Knossos area* (London n.d.).
Hood, M. S. F., and Leatham, J., 'Sub-marine Exploration in Crete, 1955', *ABSA* LIII-LIV, 1958-9, p.263.
Hood, M. S. F., and Warren, P., and Cadogan, G., 'Travels in Crete, 1962'; *ABSA* LIX, 1964, p.50.
Hood, M. S. F., and Warren, P., 'Ancient sites in the Province of Ayios Vasilios, Crete', *ABSA* LXI, 1966, p.163.
Jenkins, G. K., 'The Cameron Collection of Cretan Coins', *NC* 6th series IX, 1949, p.36.
Kautzsch, R., *Kapitellstudien* (Berlin 1936).
Konidares, G. I., '*Αἱ ἐπισκοπαὶ τῆς Κρήτης μέχρι καὶ τοῦ ι' αἰῶνος* ', *Kret. Khron.* VII, 1953, p.462.
Krautheimer, R., *Early Christian and Byzantine Architecture* (Harmondsworth 1975).
Lassithiotakes, K., ' *Ὁ ναὸς εἰσοδίων καὶ μιὰ παλαιότερη βασιλικὴ στὸ Φόδελε*', *Kret. Khron.* V, 1951, p.76.
Lassithiotakes, K., ' *Ἐκκλησίες τῆς Δυτικῆς Κρήτης* I', *Kret. Khron.* XXI, 1969, p.177.
Lassithiotakes, K., ' *Ἐκκλησίες τῆς Δυτικῆς Κρήτης* III', *Kret. Khron.* XXII, 1970, p.133.
Lassithiotakes, K., ' *Ἐκκλησίες τῆς Δυτικῆς Πρήτης* IV', *Kret. Khron.* XXIII, 1971, p.95.
Laurent, V., 'Le statut de la Crète byzance avant et après sa libération du joug arabe', *Kret. Khron.* XV-XVI.2 1961-2 (Acts of the 1st Cretological Congress), p. 382.
Le Rider, G., 'Monnaies crétoises du Ve au 1er siècle av. J. C.', (Paris 1966).
Logidios Platon, S., ' *Ἱστορικὴ βυζαντινὴ ἐπιγραφὴ ἐξ Ἡρακλείου*', *Kret. Khron.* XV-XVI, 1961-1962 (Acts of the 1st Cretological Congress), p. 47.
Macdonald, G., 'The Silver Coinage of Crete', *Proc. of the British Academy* IX, 1919-20, p.289.
Mariani, L., 'Antichità Cretesi', *Mon. Ant.* VI, 1895, p.155.
Mariani, L., 'Some Cretan sculptures in the Museum of the Syllogos of Candia', *AJA* new series I, 1897, p.266.
Marinatos, S., ' *Ἐπιγραφὴ εἰς Βριτομάρτιν ἐκ Χερσονήσου*', *A. Delt.* IX, 1924-5, p.79.
Marinatos, S., ' *Οἱ Νιοβίδαι τῆς Ἰνάτου*', *AE* 1934, p.1.
Matz, F. (ed.), *Forschungen auf Kreta* (Berlin 1951).
Mendel, G., *Musées Imperiaux Ottomans, Catalogues des Sculptures* I-III, (Constantinople 1912-14).
Mikrogiannakis, E. I., ' *Ἡ Κρήτη κατὰ τοὺς Ἑλληνιστικους Χρόνους* (Athens 1967).
Miles, G. C., 'Byzantium and the Arabs: relations in Crete and the Aegean area', *DOP* XVIII, 1964, p.1.
Miles, G. C., 'Excavations at Ay. Petros, Heraklion, 1967', *Acts of the 3rd Cretological Congress* III, (Athens 1975), p.225.
Miles, G. C., 'Coins from the excavation at Ayios Petros, Heraklion', *American Numismatic Society Museum Notes* XVII, 1971, p. 163.
Milne, J. G., 'The Evans Collection at Oxford', *NC* 6th series III, 1943, p.77.
Myres, J. C., 'On some bronze coins from Crete', *NC* 3rd series XIV, 1894, p.89.
Orth, W., 'Ein vernachlässigtes Zeugnis zur Geschichte der römischen Provinz Creta et Cyrenae', *Chiron* III, 1973, p.255.
Papastamos, D., and Staehler, K., ' *Ἄγαλμα Ἀφροδίτης ρωμαϊκῶν αὐτοκρατορικῶν χρόνων*', *Kret. Khron.* XIV, 1972, p.93.
Pashley, R., *Travels in Crete* (London 1837).
Pelekanides, S., *Σύνταγμα τῶν παλαιοχριστιανικῶν ψηφιδωτῶν δαπέδων τῆς Ἑλλάδος* I (Thessaloniki 1974).
Pendlebury, J. D. S., 'Journeys in Crete', *ABSA* XXXIII, 1932-3, p.85.
Pendlebury, J. D. S., 'Excavations in the Plain of Lassithi', *ABSA* XXXVI, 1935-6, p.1.
Pendlebury, J. D. S., *The Archaeology of Crete* (London 1939).
Perl, G., 'Die Römischen Provinzbeamten in Cyrenae und Creta zur Zeit der Republik', *Klio* LII, 1970, p.319.
Pernier, L., and Banti, L., *Guida degli scavi italiani in Creta* (Rome 1947).
Petorakes, Th., ' *Αἱ ἀραβικαὶ ἐπιδρομαὶ καὶ ἡ ἐν Κρήτῃ ἀραβοκρατία*', *Kret. Khron.* XXI, 1969, p.119.
Platon, N., ' *Δύο ὀνόματα ἀνυπάρκτων Κρητικῶν πόλεων*', *Kret. Khron.* I, 1947, p.14.
Platon, N., ' *Αἱ ξυλόστεγαι παλαιοχριστιανικαὶ βασιλικαὶ τῆς Κρήτης*', *Acts of the 9th Congress of Byzantine Studies at Thessalonike* I, (Athens 1955), p.415.
Platon, N., *Guide to Heraklion Museum* (Athens 1968).
Ramsden, S. E., *Roman Mosaics in Greece: the mainland and the Ionian islands.* Ph.D. Thesis, London, 1971.
Raven, E. J. P., 'The Hierapytnan Hoard of Greek and Roman Coins', *NC* 5th series XVIII, 1938, p.133.
Rizza, G., and Scrinari, R., *Il santuario sull'acropoli di Gortyna* (Rome 1968).
Robinson, E. S. G., *Catalogue of the Greek coins of Cyrenaica* (in the British Museum), (London 1927).
Ruggiero, E., *Dizionario epigrafico di antichità romane* (Rome 1910). Creta: II.2, p.1257.
Sackett, H., 'Post Minoan Occupation above the Unexplored Mansion', *AR* 1972-3, p.62.
Savignoni, L., and De Sanctis, G., 'Esplorazione archeologica delle provincie occidentali di Creta', *Mon. Ant.* XI, 1901, p.285.
Schachermeyer, F., 'Vorbericht über eine Expedition nach Ostkreta', *Arch. Anz.* 1938, p.467.

Seager, R. B., 'A Cretan Coin Hoard', *Numismatic Notes and Monographs* 1924, p.1.
Spanake, S., ' Τὸ θέατρο στή ρωμαϊκὴ Κρήτη', *Acts of the 2nd Cretological Congress* II, (Athens 1968), p.142.
Spanake, S., *Crete: A Guide* I-II (Iraklion, n.d.).
Spratt, T. A. B., *Travels and Researches in Crete* (London 1865).
Spyridakis, G.K., 'Τὸ *θέμα* Κρήτης *πρὸ τῆς κατακτήσεως τῆς νήσου ὑπὸ τῶν* 'Αράβων', *EEBS* 1951, p.59. 951, p.59.
Spyridakis, G.K., *Ptolemaic Itanos and Hellenistic Crete* (California 1970).
Svoronos, J. N., *Numismatique de la Crète ancienne* , (Paris 1890).
Svoronos, J. N., *Sylloge Numorum Graecorum* (Copenhagen 1944).
Taramelli, A., 'Richerche archeologiche Cretesi', *Mon. Ant.* IX, 1899, p.285..
Taramelli, A., 'Gortyna', *AJA* VI, 1902, p.101.
Van der Mijnsbrugge, M., *The Cretan Koinon,* (New York 1931).
Van Effenterre, H., 'Le Temple d'Aphrodite et d'Arès à sta Lenika', *BCH* LXII, 1938, p.386.
Van Effenterre, H., *La Crète et le monde grec,* (Paris 1948).
Van Effenterre, H., 'Le sarcophage attique à guirlandes de Mallia', *BCH* C, 1976, p. 525.
Vermeule, C. C., *Roman Imperial Art in Greece and Asia Minor* (Harvard 1968).
Vermeule, C. C., 'Hellenistic and Roman Cuirassed Statues', *Berytus* XIII.1, 1959, p.1.
Ward-Perkins, J. B., and Boethius, A., *Etruscan and Roman Architecture* (Harmondsworth 1970).
Watrous, L. V., *An archaeological survey of the Lasithi plain in Crete from the Neolithic to the Late Roman,* Ph.D. Thesis, University of Pennslyvania, 1974.
Zacos, G., and Veglery, A., *Byzantine lead seals,* (Basel 1972).